ECONOMIC INDICATORS FOR SOUTH AND CENTRAL ASIA

INPUT–OUTPUT TABLES

DECEMBER 2020

ASIAN DEVELOPMENT BANK

© 2020 Asian Development Bank
6 ADB Avenue, Mandaluyong City, 1550 Metro Manila, Philippines
Tel +63 2 8632 4444; Fax +63 2 8636 2444
www.adb.org

Some rights reserved. Published in 2020.

ISBN 978-92-9262-536-8 (print); 978-92-9262-537-5 (electronic); 978-92-9262-538-2 (ebook)
Publication Stock No. TCS200240-2
DOI: http://dx.doi.org/10.22617/TCS200240-2

CONTENTS

TABLES AND FIGURES

TABLES

FIGURES

FOREWORD

I n the 1990s and early 2000s, trade was defined by global value chains. Automation and developments in transport, information, and communications technologies enabled firms to fragment their production processes across the globe to gain efficiencies from a broadened economic network. Participation in value chains became a more viable path toward economic and social transformation, especially for developing economies. Trade in tasks and inputs became as important as traditional trade in finished goods, and its measurement was seen as crucial in assessing economic performance and shaping policies.

Following more than a decade of generally unfettered growth, a series of economic crises and downturns created new challenges for the increasingly interconnected and interdependent economies. More recently, international trade tensions have disrupted production in major regional hubs, while the coronavirus disease pandemic continues to adversely impact consumption patterns, production, and supply and distribution chains in every economy. In a short period of time, the question has quickly shifted from "How can we participate in global value chains?" to "How can we ensure a stable and resilient global economy, given increasing global value chain participation?"

Answering the latter question heightens the demand for better and more timely statistics on the interrelationships between economies. Monitoring economic activities is not only essential for keeping track of development objectives, but also for safeguarding the beneficial outcomes from decades of solid economic growth. Managing risks entails compiling relevant statistics that reveal production and trade patterns at the economy, bilateral, regional, and global levels.

Since 2014, the Asian Development Bank (ADB) has been compiling and updating the Multi-Regional Input–Output Tables (MRIOTs) database. The comprehensive summaries of transactions across industries and final users in several economies have enabled the derivation of relevant production, trade, and value chain statistics. In 2018, ADB produced a three-volume compendium of input–output tables and derived indicators for East Asia, South and Central Asia, and Southeast Asia and the Pacific to inform policy and stimulate discourse in development research.

This current three-volume publication is an update and expansion on the 2018 edition. Here, we present economy-specific input–output tables, aggregated into 15 industrial sectors and five final demand categories for 2000 and 2018. Traditional input–output-based indicators, as well as new ones, are calculated from the latest available data to provide more timely and comprehensive insights on the changing trade and production structures of different economies in the Asia and Pacific region.

I would like to thank all those who contributed to these publications—the consultants, the industry experts, ADB staff, and the official statistical agencies and other government organizations of economies participating in ADB's statistical and analytical capacity-building initiatives. I commend them for their dedication, cooperation, and hard work. We hope that these updated reports will be valuable resources for economic research and policy implementation.

Yasuyuki Sawada
Chief Economist and Director General
Economic Research and Regional Cooperation Department
Asian Development Bank

ACKNOWLEDGMENTS

The successful integration of the supply and use framework into the national accounts systems of 19 economies across Asia and the Pacific was made possible by the strong cooperation and significant contributions of the participating governments and national statistics offices. This collaborative undertaking was facilitated under the Regional Capacity Development Technical Assistance 8838: Updating and Constructing Supply and Use Tables for Selected Developing Member Economies. Building on the progress made from this technical assistance, the Asian Development Bank (ADB) further expanded its data development initiative by compiling input–output tables and creating a Multi-Regional Input–Output Tables database based on the supply and use tables from 25 economies. This expansion was financially supported through four programs: (i) Knowledge and Support Technical Assistance (KSTA) 9659: Key Indicators for Asia and the Pacific 2020; (ii) KSTA-9356: Data for Development (Phase I); (iii) KSTA 9646: Data for Development (Phase II); and (iv) KSTA 9624: Supporting Knowledge Solutions in Central and West Asian Countries.

ADB gratefully acknowledges the valuable contributions of the heads, coordinators, and members of the specialist supply and use teams within the participating official statistical agencies; without their expert input, which was provided in a timely manner even during these challenging times, this undertaking would not have been possible. These implementing agencies include the Bureau of Statistics, Bangladesh; the National Statistics Bureau, Bhutan; the Department of Economic Planning and Development, Brunei Darussalam; the National Institute of Statistics, Cambodia; the National Bureau of Statistics, the People's Republic of China; the Bureau of Statistics, Fiji; the Census and Statistics Department, Hong Kong, China; the Central Statistics Office, India; Badan Pusat Statistik, Indonesia; the Committee on Statistics of the Ministry of National Economy, Kazakhstan; the National Statistical Committee, the Kyrgyz Republic; the Statistics Bureau, the Lao People's Democratic Republic; the Department of Statistics, Malaysia; the Department of National Planning, Maldives; the National Statistical Office, Mongolia; the Central Bureau of Statistics, Nepal; the Bureau of Statistics, Pakistan; the Department of Census and Statistics, Sri Lanka; the Directorate-General of Budget, Accounting and Statistics, Taipei,China; the National Economic and Social Development Board, Thailand; and the General Statistics Office, Viet Nam.

This set of three publications covers all 25 economies in Asia and the Pacific. These volumes were developed under the overall supervision of Mahinthan Joseph Mariasingham, and were prepared by John Arvin Bernabe, Marc Alvin Elmino, Patricia Georgina Gonzales, and Kenneth Reyes of the Statistics and Data Innovation Unit within the Economic Research and Regional Cooperation Department of ADB. Michael John Barsabal, Janine De Vera, Clara Delos Santos, Krizia Anne Garay, Angelo Jose Lumba, Julieta Magallanes, Sarah Mae Manuel, Ana Francesca Rosales, and Jonarie Vergara provided technical assistance. Eric Suan coordinated the review and publication process and Rose Ann Dumayas provided additional administrative support. Paul Dent edited the text, while Joe Mark Ganaban led the typesetting process, and Nikko Antonio designed the cover. These volumes were published with the support of ADB's Department of Communications.

Elaine Tan
Advisor, Office of the Chief Economist and Director General,
and Head, Statistics and Data Innovation Unit,
Economic Research and Regional Cooperation Department

ABBREVIATIONS

ADB	Asian Development Bank
APL	average production length
DVA	domestic value-added
FVA	foreign value-added
GDP	gross domestic product
GFC	global financial crisis
GFCF	gross fixed capital formation
GVA	gross value-added
GVC	global value chain
ICT	information and communication technology
IOT	input–output table
MRIOT	Multi-Regional Input–Output Table
NPISH	nonprofit organizations and institutions serving households
NRCA	new revealed comparative advantage
PDC	pure double-counted term
PRC	People's Republic of China
RCA	revealed comparative advantage
RoW	rest of the world
SUT	supply and use tables
TRCA	traditional revealed comparative advantage
WIOD	World Input–Output Database

EXECUTIVE SUMMARY

An input–output table (IOT) is a matrix representation of the exchanges within an economy for any given accounting period. The use of IOTs for economic accounting and analysis dates back to the 1930s and this has since made substantial contributions to the understanding of economic phenomena. Today, IOTs are employed in a wide range of analyses for various purposes including, but not limited to: supply chain, production, and distribution management; investment; and macroeconomic planning and policymaking.

Key to the analytical strength of an IOT is its explicit detailing of economic relationships between any two sectors within an economy. This is particularly useful in determining the potential impacts of internal changes and exogenous shocks and for identifying sectors that have high growth-inducing effects both domestically and internationally. Because of globalization and the fragmentation of production processes, one of the more common applications of input–output analysis is measuring value-added contributions of individual economies in global value chains (GVCs).

IOTs are also relevant as a compilation framework. Supply-use tables (SUTs), on which IOTs are based, are an integral part of the System of National Accounts. Ideally, an SUT serves as the main framework used in the compilation of a single and coherent estimate of gross domestic product, as it fundamentally integrates all components of production, income, and expenditure approaches. SUTs and its transformation, IOTs, describe how products are produced and delivered into the economy and how they are used. These tables also provide the links between industry or sector inputs and outputs, which are important in analyzing the interactions between different productive activities.

The Asian Development Bank's Multi-Regional Input–Output Tables (MRIOTs) are a major contribution to the growing data and analytical needs of today's increasingly globalized economic environment. The MRIOTs combine the input–output systems of 62 economies, plus an aggregate of other economies called "rest of the world." They include data on 35 harmonized and interconnected sectors for each economy. The database is regularly updated to ensure the relevance and timeliness of analyses conducted at domestic, regional, and international levels. A suite of statistical and analytical indicators based on the MRIOTs is compiled and presented in this report.

Part 1 of the report introduces indicators relevant for describing the structure of, and interlinkages within domestic economies in the Asia and Pacific region. The supply-use relationships among different producing industries and final demand sectors are analyzed, along with their respective growth trends and change effects. Domestic input-output tables are also used to identify key sectors in the economy.

Moving from the internal economy to the external sector, a range of analytical indicators concerning international trade openness and dependencies, comparative advantages, and degrees of participation in GVCs for 25 economies in the region are presented in Part 2. These demonstrate multiple approaches for extracting insights on an economy's key position in international trade and how domestic activities ultimately contribute to the global economy.

Part 3 provides individual profiles of economies from the South and Central subregion based on measures of their respective internal and external linkages. Economies included in this volume are Bangladesh, Bhutan, India, Kazakhstan, the Kyrgyz Republic, Maldives, Nepal, Pakistan, and Sri Lanka.

The 15 by 15 sector input–output tables of each economy in the subregion which underlie the 2000 and 2018 ADB MRIOTs and on which the data and analyses throughout the report were based on are compiled in Part 4.

This publication hopes to enrich data-driven policymaking and development discourse by providing quantitatively verified insights on the domestic and international structures and linkages economies in Asia and the Pacific. Research grounded in the interconnectivity of economic elements is especially useful in our current context of a globalizing business environment with increasing trade and fragmentation of production. Recent events— ranging from international trade conflicts, a withdrawal from an economic union, and a sweeping viral pandemic—challenge the strength of our global economic network and its ability to deliver the same level of growth and development it did in earlier times. In this regard, it is hoped the data provided in these volumes inform future efforts to build more resilient and stable economies.

Please note that the data presented in this publication are not official statistics and are intended for research purposes only.

INTRODUCTION

Any discussion of input–output analysis will almost invariably make a reference to the Nobel laureate Wassily Leontief who developed the pioneering framework in the 1930s. Unlike traditional tools in economics, which generalize systems or handpick details in favor of theoretical elegance, the input–output approach starts by capturing masses of observed economic data on outputs, activities, transactions, or other flows, and then organizes them in matrices representative of the economic system. It places equal weight on observations of actual economic flows as much as it does theory. Actual and observed data in input–output tables (IOTs)—e.g., tons of steel, millions of dollars, hours of work, volumes of emissions—enabled users to concretely understand how the economy works. In an address during the 1985 United States Census Bureau Conference, Leontief explained rationale behind the input–output framework:

> A major problem in economics is to be able to describe an entire forest in terms of individual trees and their interrelationships—to perceive the totality, while preserving all the minutiae in clear detail. The macroeconomist deals with broad concepts and aggregated data, far removed from real behavior. The microeconomist may work with fine detail but lose sight of the larger world. Now, of course, modern mathematics and modern techniques of data processing have broken down the barriers in research. We now have the means to preserve the tiny details while seeing at the same time the total picture. For me, the study of the interdependence between different sectors and the relation of the parts to the whole picture is really the most interesting part of economics. Input–output analysis gives you a method to describe that forest in terms of individual trees.

More than 80 years after Leontief's seminal work was published, the literature utilizing the input–output approach continues to expand extensively, both in number and scope, with applications in technology, industrial ecology, sustainable development, labor productivity, growth, energy, and, more recently, international trade. Innovations in data and advances in computing capacity made Leontief's framework increasingly practicable and even largely scalable. Aside from its analytical applications, it is gaining ground as an economic accounting framework used by official statistics compilers to calculate and reconcile economic accounts from production, income, and expenditure approaches accurately and consistently.

The Basic Framework

IOTs are systematic numerical representations of the mutual interrelationships among producers and consumers in an economy. At the very least, an IOT describes the sales and purchase transactions between different industries and sectors. They are matrices containing observed economic data on how the produced outputs (both goods and services) of an industry are used as inputs in the production processes of other industries or consumed as final products by nonproducing economic sectors. Data on interindustry flows, i.e., the sales and purchases of industry goods and services for further use in other production processes (z), are contained in the first quadrant of the IOT (shaded yellow in Table 1), usually called the intermediate transactions matrix. The rows represent the "selling" sectors i to n, whose outputs are purchased by "buying" sectors represented in columns j to n (where n = total number of sectors). Thus, each row indicates the distribution of a particular industry's outputs to all industries, while each column shows a particular industry's required inputs from all industries.

Table 1:   Basic Input-Output Framework

		Buying sectors		Final demand				Total output (x)
		s_1	s_2					
Selling sectors	s_1	z_{11}	z_{12}	c_1	i_1	g_1	e_1	x_1
	s_2	z_{21}	z_{22}	c_2	i_2	g_2	e_2	x_2
Primary inputs	Value-added	l_1	l_2					L
		n_1	n_2					N
	Imports	m_1	m_2	m_c	m_i	m_g	m_e	M
Total inputs (x')		x_1	x_2	C	I	G	E	X

☐ = intermediate transactions matrix,   ☐ = final demand matrix,   ☐ = primary inputs matrix.

Source: Adopted from R.E. Miller and P.D. Blair. 2009. Input–Output Analysis: Foundations and Extensions (2nd Edition). Cambridge, United Kingdom: Cambridge University Press.

However, not all outputs are used as inputs to production processes. The additional columns to the right of the intermediate transactions matrix (shaded green in Table 1) report the flow of outputs to nonproducing sectors or activities. These flows are considered as final demand or consumption, as the products involved are used as they are, without any further transformation through subsequent processing. Final demand is categorized as: private consumption of households and nonprofit institutions serving households (NPISHs) (c), government consumption (g), gross capital formation (i), and exports (e). Though gross capital formation includes fixed assets and inventories, which are products employed in production, they are regarded as final consumption because their use is gradual and spread over more than one accounting period. Exports are treated as final sales by the source economy, but are accounted as either intermediate or final consumption by the destination economy. Summing all the row elements—across intermediate transactions and final demands, but excluding imports—yields the total output per sector (x) for the use or demand perspective.

The additional rows below the intermediate transactions matrix show the primary inputs used in each industry's production (shaded blue in Table 1). Primary inputs mostly capture the gross value-added of an industry or the income of the factors of production employed in productive activities. Gross value-added includes compensation to employees, consumption of fixed capital, other taxes less subsidies on production, and net operating surplus. In Table 1, gross value-added is equivalent to the sum of an industry's labor costs (l), as paid in wages and salaries, and its other primary input costs (n), such as capital. However, in some cases, primary inputs also include imported intermediate inputs (m_1 and m_2). This is true for non-competitive IOTs, where domestically sourced and imported goods and services are distinguished. In either case, column sums (from intermediate inputs to primary inputs) are equal to the total inputs used to produce the same level of output (x') from the use or demand perspective. These vertical summations reflect the supply perspective.

Input–Output Tables and National Accounts

The flows described in the previous section constitute a full set of income, product, and expenditure accounts for an economy. The input–output framework links and integrates these accounts into a single, comprehensive, and internally consistent system, increasingly used as a basis for compiling known aggregate statistics such as gross domestic product (GDP). Given the granularity of data in IOTs, they are also used to analyze industries or sectors and their interactions within the economy.

The basic accounting identity in the input–output system is that the total amount produced by a sector of the economy (total supply) should be equal to the amount of its usage in the economy (total demand). In the IOTs, this identity is established by equating row totals to their corresponding column totals, which implies that economies are modeled in a state of general equilibrium. Moreover, since this basic identity balances production (row) and expenditure (column) accounts, the input–output system becomes an ideal framework for estimating an economy's GDP, wherein all uses and resources must be fully accounted for. This minimizes statistical errors[1] as various data sources are reconciled within a single coherent framework.

From a supply perspective, the total output of the economy (X), calculated by summing the column totals, is equal to the cost of intermediate inputs ($x_1 + x_2$) plus the cost of primary inputs ($L + N$), and the cost of imports (M), i.e., $X = x_1 + x_2 + L + N + M$. Meanwhile, from a demand perspective, output (X) is equal to the sum of the row totals, i.e., the value of output used by industries for production ($x_1 + x_2$) plus the values of output used in final private consumption (C) and final government consumption (G), investment through capital formation (I) and exports (E) or simply, $X = x_1 + x_2 + C + I + G + E$. Given the basic accounting identity, the calculated outputs from both perspectives are necessarily equal: $x_1 + x_2 + L + N + M = X = x_1 + x_2 + C + I + G + E$. Rearranging these components, $L + N + M = C + I + G + E$ or $L + N = C + I + G + (E-M)$. The left side ($L + N$) corresponds to the gross income from the production approach, while the right side ($C + I + G + (E-M)$) corresponds to the GDP from the expenditure approach.

---

[1]   In practice, national accounts do publish an item for statistical discrepancy as a matter of transparency. Some proponents argue that this reminds users that national accounts are far from being 100% reliable, given the expanse of sources used to compile GDP. Others add that these discrepancies can be a source of information and are the subject of numerous business studies (Lequiller and Blades 2014).

IOTs describe the economy from both supply and demand perspectives and thus allows for a holistic understanding of how an economy is structured and how it evolves through time. For example, the level of inventory recorded in the IOT can indicate where an economy is in the general business cycle. Similarly, the level of fixed asset investment can signal how positive the outlook is for the economy. IOTs can also reveal which sectors or economies are most dependent on foreign inputs for their output and, conversely, which contribute most to foreign demand.

THE DOMESTIC ECONOMY

This part explores some basic applications of input–output tables, which comprehensively detail the structure of a given economy and link both supply and demand components in a coherent and consistent framework. By combining input–output observations with standard economic theories, a picture of the domestic economy in terms of its structural composition, diversification, and linkages can be observed.

The data and analyses cover 25 economies in Asia and the Pacific across various sectors. A regional subgrouping and a sectoral aggregation are applied in most parts to streamline and enrich the discussions. Details on the sectors, including their differing levels of aggregation, as well as the economies and subgroupings thereof are provided in Appendixes 1 and 2 of this publication, respectively.

1.1 Economic Composition

Figure 1.1 shows the composition of the economy from the demand perspective, represented by the shares of private consumption, government consumption, gross capital formation, and exports in the total final demand for each economy for 2000 and 2018.

In 2000, private consumption accounted for an average of 47.6% of the total final demand of the 25 economies; gross capital formation, 22.9%; exports, 17.6%; and government consumption, 12.8%. Private consumption had the largest share in the total final demand of most economies, ranging from 35.6% to 66.5%. Pakistan, Bangladesh, the Lao People's Democratic Republic (Lao PDR), Cambodia, and Nepal had the highest shares, with at least 60% of total final demand accounted for by private consumption. On the other hand, the final demand of Maldives, Singapore, and Malaysia were dominated by exports rather than domestic consumption.

Compared to 2000, the composition of final demand in 2018 was less concentrated in private consumption. In addition to Maldives, Singapore, and Malaysia, the total final demands of other economies such as Viet Nam, Brunei Darussalam, and Taipei,China were more export-dominated than others. The total final demand of the rest of the economies remained largely driven by private consumption, with shares ranging from 32.9% to 68.3%.

Figure 1.1: Composition of Final Demand by Economy, 2000 and 2018 (% of GDP)

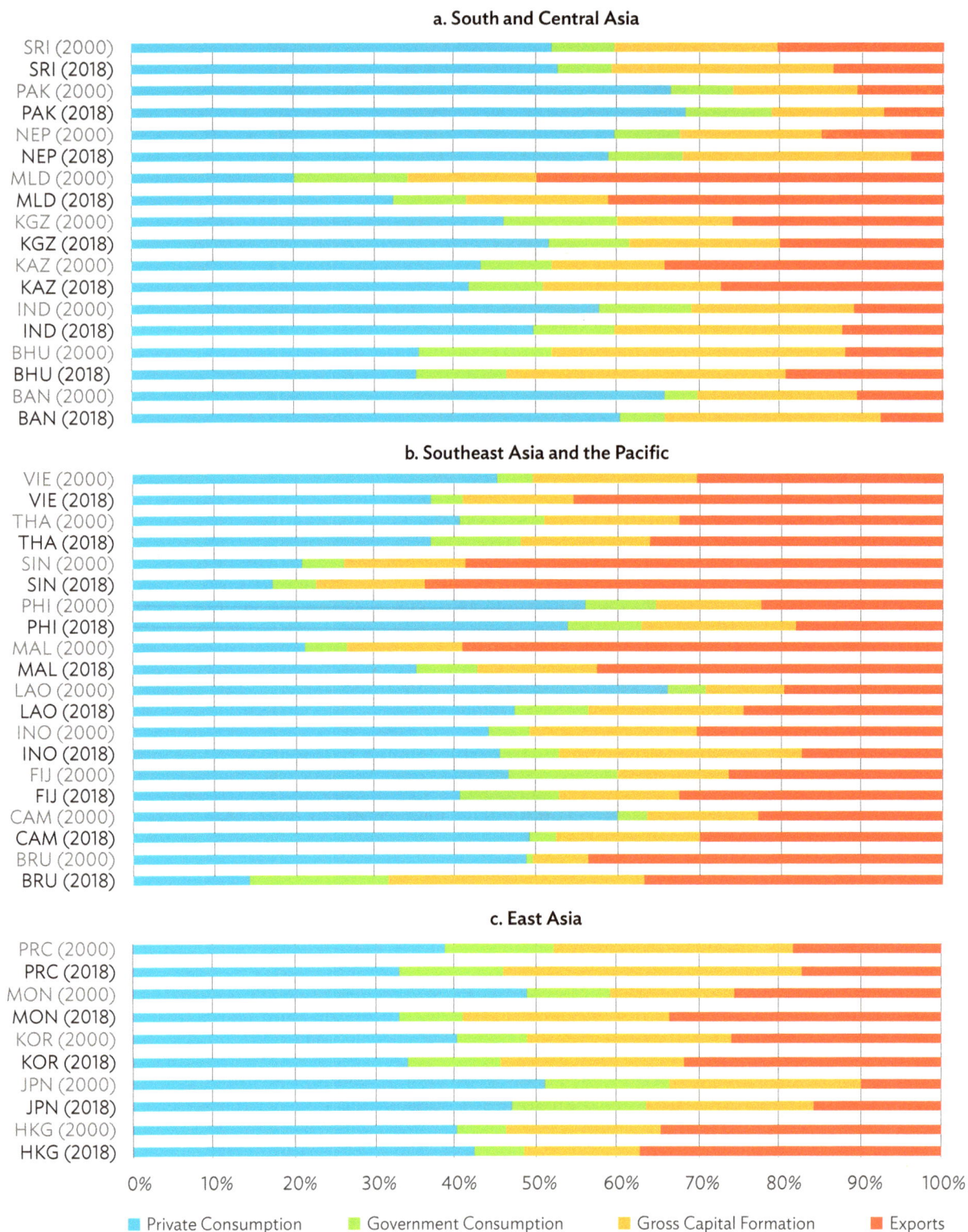

a. South and Central Asia

b. Southeast Asia and the Pacific

c. East Asia

■ Private Consumption ■ Government Consumption ■ Gross Capital Formation ■ Exports

GDP = gross domestic product; BAN = Bangladesh; BHU = Bhutan; BRU = Brunei Darussalam; CAM = Cambodia; FIJ = Fiji; HKG = Hong Kong, China; IND = India; INO = Indonesia; JPN = Japan; KAZ = Kazakhstan; KGZ = Kyrgyz Republic; KOR = Republic of Korea; LAO = Lao People's Democratic Republic; MAL = Malaysia; MLD = Maldives; MON = Mongolia; NEP = Nepal; PAK = Pakistan; PHI = Philippines; PRC = People's Republic of China; SIN = Singapore; SRI = Sri Lanka; TAP = Taipei,China; THA = Thailand; VIE = Viet Nam.

Source: Asian Development Bank. Multi-Regional Input–Output Tables (accessed July 2020).

On the production side, sectoral composition is described using the shares of each sector's value-added in the total gross value-added (GVA) of the economy. This shows which activities the economy generates most of its income from. Across all subregions, the business services sector had the highest share in GVA: 37.6% in 2000 and 45.8% in 2018. In absolute terms, business services in East Asia had the highest value-added among all the subregional groups for both years, even though the sector's share within the subregion decreased from 43.9% in 2000 to 39.7% in 2018 (Figure 1.2).

Meanwhile, the shares of business services sectors in the respective GVAs of South and Central Asia, Southeast Asia and the Pacific, and East Asia increased significantly from 2000 to at least a 40.0% share in 2018. On average, while the shares of the primary, low tech manufacturing, and public and personal services sectors decreased slightly, the share of the high and medium tech manufacturing sector decreased substantially (from 15.5% in 2000 to 9.7% in 2018). This decline was most pronounced in South and Central Asia, where the share of high and medium tech manufacturing dipped to 9.5% in 2018 from 36.1% in 2000. The decline in this subregion was, however, offset by an increase in the share of business services, which surged from 28.0% in 2000 to 48.1% in 2018.

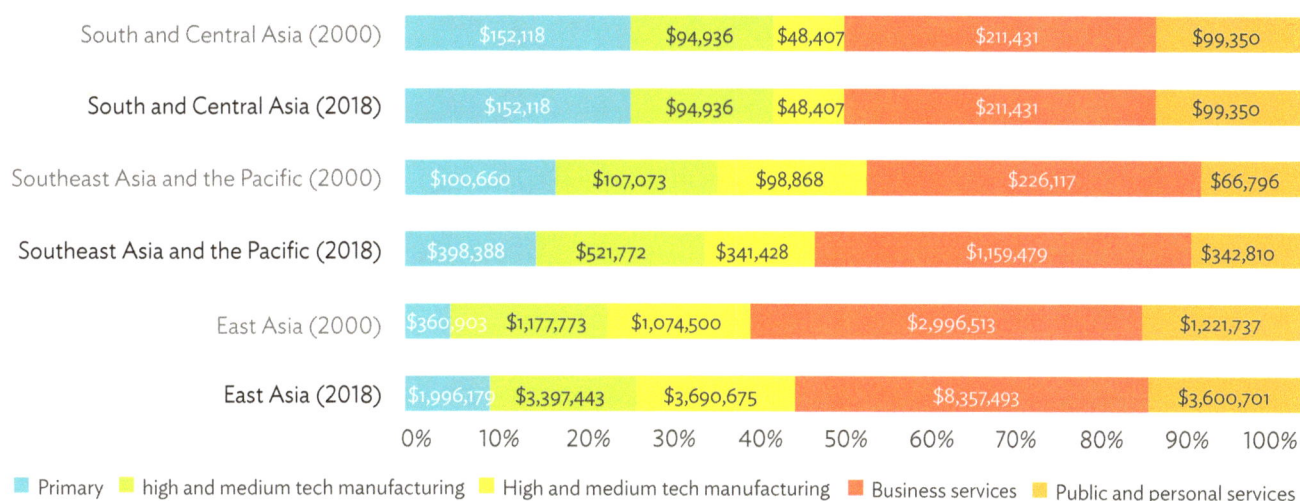

Region (Year)	Primary	high and medium tech manufacturing	High and medium tech manufacturing	Business services	Public and personal services
South and Central Asia (2000)	$152,118	$94,936	$48,407	$211,431	$99,350
South and Central Asia (2018)	$152,118	$94,936	$48,407	$211,431	$99,350
Southeast Asia and the Pacific (2000)	$100,660	$107,073	$98,868	$226,117	$66,796
Southeast Asia and the Pacific (2018)	$398,388	$521,772	$341,428	$1,159,479	$342,810
East Asia (2000)	$360,903	$1,177,773	$1,074,500	$2,996,513	$1,221,737
East Asia (2018)	$1,996,179	$3,397,443	$3,690,675	$8,357,493	$3,600,701

0% 10% 20% 30% 40% 50% 60% 70% 80% 90% 100%

■ Primary   ■ high and medium tech manufacturing   ■ High and medium tech manufacturing   ■ Business services   ■ Public and personal services

GVA = gross value added.

Note: South and Central Asia includes Bangladesh, Bhutan, India, Kazakhstan, Kyrgyz Republic, Maldives, Nepal, Pakistan, and Sri Lanka. Southeast Asia and the Pacific includes Brunei Darussalam, Cambodia, Fiji, Indonesia, the Lao People's Democratic Republic, Maldives, the Philippines, Singapore, Thailand, and Viet Nam. East Asia includes the People's Republic of China; Hong Kong, China; Japan; Mongolia; the Republic of Korea; and Taipei,China.

Source: Asian Development Bank. Multi-Regional Input–Output Tables (accessed July 2020).

Figure 1.3 shows the nominal values of each subregion's GVA in 2000 and 2018, as well as their corresponding compounded annual growth rates between the two years. In terms of nominal GVC, East Asia had the largest economies. Within the subregion, the primary sector had the highest compounded growth rate (9.4%) between 2000 and 2018, as other sectors only grew at rates between 5.5% and 6.7% between the two years. In Southeast Asia and the Pacific, the services and low tech manufacturing sectors grew at impressive rates of 9.0% and 8.7%, respectively, compounded each year. Meanwhile, the growth of the high and medium tech manufacturing sector in Southeast Asia and the Pacific lagged by a couple of percentage points behind the low tech manufacturing sector, possibly due to maturing regional value chains for electronics and transport equipment. The same service- and manufacturing-led growth was observed in South and Central Asia as business services grew at 11.0% each year, followed by public and personal services at 9.4%, high and medium tech manufacturing at 9.1%, and low tech at 9.0%.

Figure 1.3: Sector Value-Added by Subregion, 2000 and 2018 (in $ millions and % CAGR)

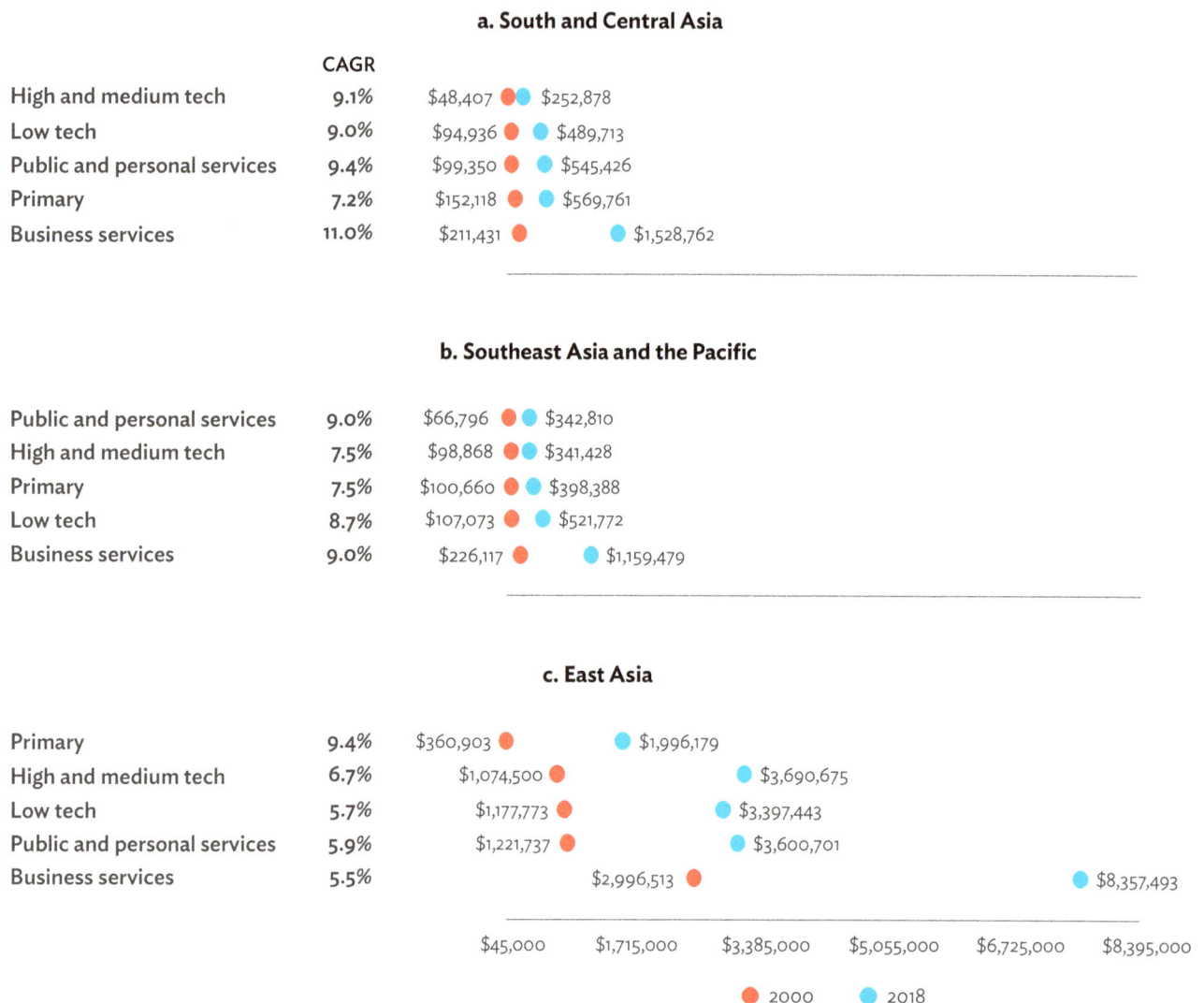

a. South and Central Asia

	CAGR	2000	2018
High and medium tech	9.1%	$48,407	$252,878
Low tech	9.0%	$94,936	$489,713
Public and personal services	9.4%	$99,350	$545,426
Primary	7.2%	$152,118	$569,761
Business services	11.0%	$211,431	$1,528,762

b. Southeast Asia and the Pacific

	CAGR	2000	2018
Public and personal services	9.0%	$66,796	$342,810
High and medium tech	7.5%	$98,868	$341,428
Primary	7.5%	$100,660	$398,388
Low tech	8.7%	$107,073	$521,772
Business services	9.0%	$226,117	$1,159,479

c. East Asia

	CAGR	2000	2018
Primary	9.4%	$360,903	$1,996,179
High and medium tech	6.7%	$1,074,500	$3,690,675
Low tech	5.7%	$1,177,773	$3,397,443
Public and personal services	5.9%	$1,221,737	$3,600,701
Business services	5.5%	$2,996,513	$8,357,493

$45,000 $1,715,000 $3,385,000 $5,055,000 $6,725,000 $8,395,000

● 2000   ● 2018

CAGR = compounded annual growth rate.

Source: Asian Development Bank. Multi-Regional Input–Output Tables (accessed July 2020).

Figure 1.4 presents the shares of each sector within an economy to the total GVA of the said economy for 2000 and 2018. Points above the 45-degree line represent sectors which increased their shares in GVA between the two years (i.e., the sector value-added share in 2018 is greater than the share in 2000), whereas points below the line represent those which had declining shares between the period. Points on the diagonal line represent sectors with shares in GVA in 2000 not significantly different from their corresponding shares in 2018.

The relatively larger number of blue points above the 45-degree line implies a general increase in the share of business services in GVA over time. Meanwhile, significant declines in the share of agriculture value-added were observed for most economies in the Asia and the Pacific region (green points below the line). Brunei Darussalam and Thailand were exceptions, as they retained their respective agriculture value-added shares close to their 2000 values. Some manufacturing activities had declining shares of value-added in the economy as well, most notably light manufacturing activities (yellow points below the line). This decline was more pronounced among economies that shifted toward other manufacturing activities increasingly supported by services. Driving the growth in the share of services value-added is the rapid expansion of the construction, travel, and tourism sectors, consistent with the demand-side observation of consumption-driven, export-oriented, and investment-led (mainly construction) growth in the region.

Figure 1.4: Shares of Total Economy Value-Added by Economy-Sector, 2000 and 2018
(% of GVA)

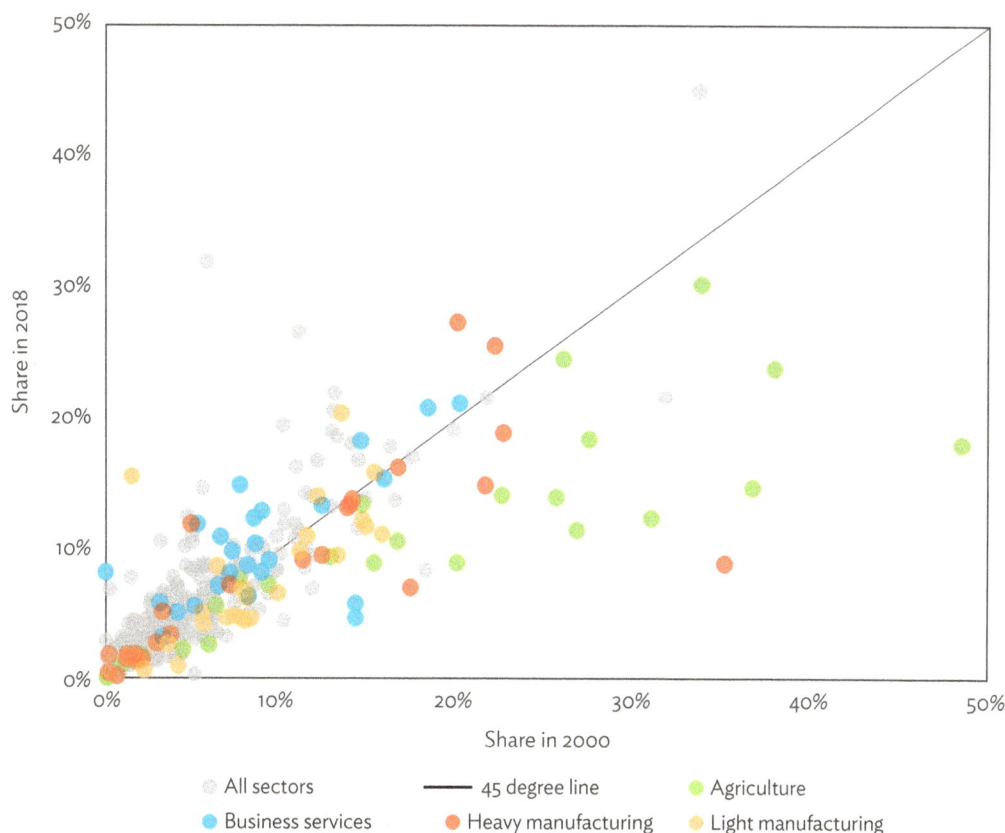

GVA = gross value added.

Source: Asian Development Bank. Multi-Regional Input–Output Tables (accessed July 2020).

This pattern of structural transformation observed in the region – whereby agriculture's share of output and employment first declines as the manufacturing industry's share grows, followed by a decline in the share of manufacturing as services become more dominant due to "deindustrialization" – is similar to the experience of developed economies (ADB 2020).

1.2 Economic Diversification

The shifts in productive activities determine, to some extent, the level of diversification in a given economy. This analysis is particularly important for mineral- and commodity-based economies, which traditionally produce and export a very limited range of products. As the external environment becomes more volatile, the focus on extractive activities exacerbates risks from commodity cycles. Thus, over the years, diversification strategies for broader-based and more sustainable growth have attracted policy attention. Three diversification measures are presented in Figure 1.5; their definitions and calculation methods can be found in Appendix 3. In 2000, the economic activities of Brunei Darussalam, the Lao PDR, and the Kyrgyz Republic were more concentrated (less diversified) than other economies, regardless of the concentration index referred to. By 2018, the Lao PDR and the Kyrgyz Republic have significantly diversified their activities, whereas Brunei Darussalam further increased its concentration (except when using the Theil index). The trend for most developing economies in the region has been toward diversification, while that for the most developed economies such as Singapore; Taipei,China; Hong Kong, China; the Republic of Korea; and Japan has been toward more concentration.

1.3 Structural Decomposition

Within nearly two decades, many economies in Asia and the Pacific made notable changes in their respective economic structures, as undoubtedly influenced by numerous policies and market factors. From an input–output perspective, the structure of demand can be used to explain the drivers of these changes in production. Input–output tables (IOTs) and thus, analyses based on them, rest on the basic identity that demand is equal to supply. Hence, observing how demand has changed can provide insights into how production has been altered as well. The granular and comprehensive information in IOTs enables changes in output to be decomposed[1] into individual components contributing to the change.

Figure 1.6 describes the contributions of consumption, investment, inventories (stock), trade (import substitution and exports), and technology to the growth of output or production for various sectors. For many sectors in the Asia and Pacific region, domestic consumption contributed the most to production. From 2010 to 2018 or the period after the 2008 global financial crisis (post-crisis), private consumption increased output by as much 6.8% annually. Private consumption contributed the least in the construction industry, where demand is normally accounted for as investment. Aside from private consumption, exports also had a generally positive contribution to output growth in the region, especially in the mining and light manufacturing sectors. However, the role of exports from 2010 to 2018 weakened compared to 2000 to 2007, the period before the 2008 global financial crisis (pre-crisis).

---

[1]   This method is formally known as structural decomposition analysis (Appendix 3).

Figure 1.5: Aggregate Measures of Value-Added Economic Diversification by Economy, 2000 and 2018

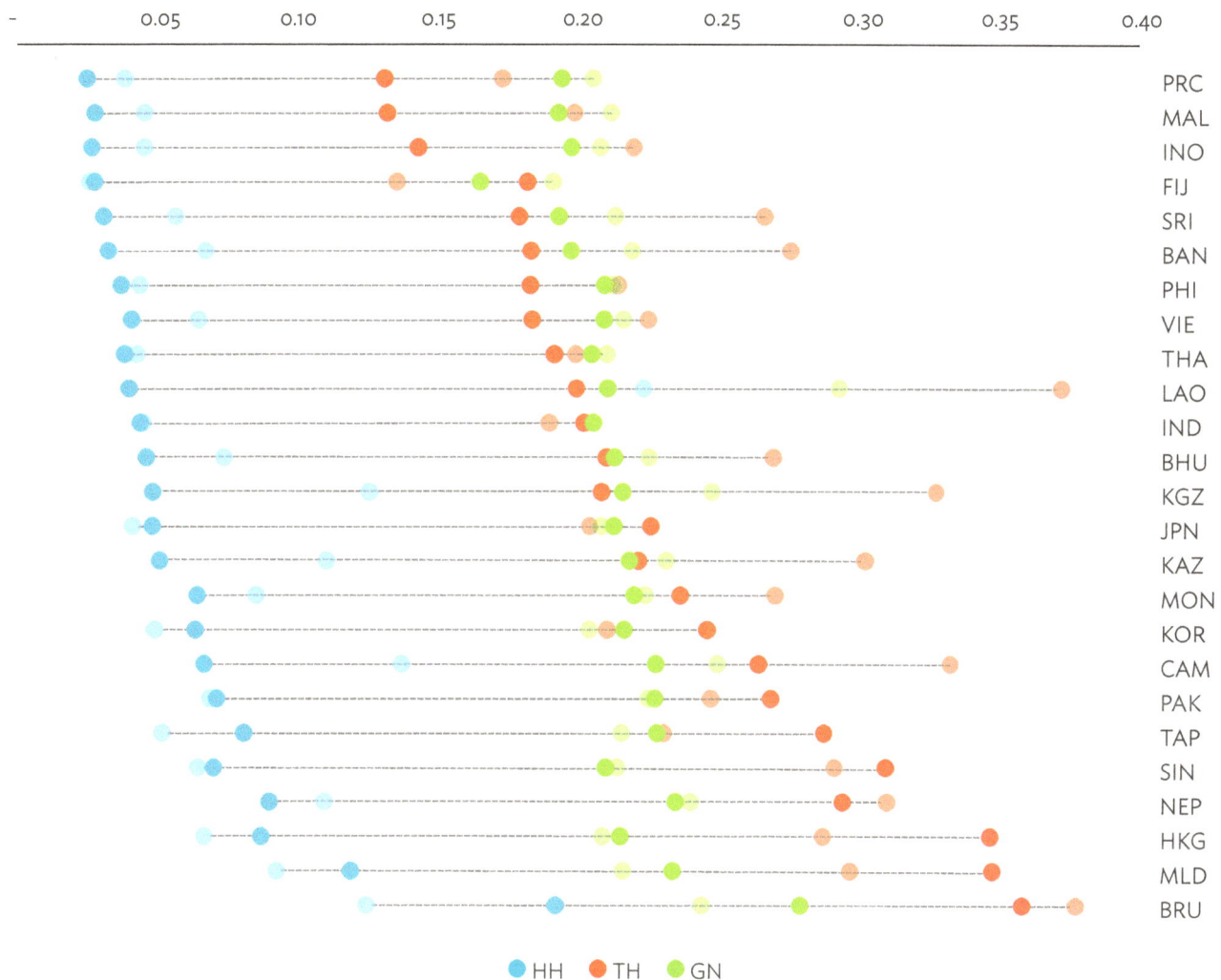

HH = Hirschman-Herfindahl concentration index; TH = Theil concentration index; GN = Gini concentration index; BAN = Bangladesh; BHU = Bhutan; BRU = Brunei Darussalam; CAM = Cambodia; FIJ = Fiji; HKG = Hong Kong, China; IND = India; INO = Indonesia; JPN = Japan; KAZ = Kazakhstan; KGZ = Kyrgyz Republic; KOR = Republic of Korea; LAO = Lao People's Democratic Republic; MAL = Malaysia; MLD = Maldives; MON = Mongolia; NEP = Nepal; PAK = Pakistan; PHI = Philippines; PRC = People's Republic of China; SIN = Singapore; SRI = Sri Lanka; TAP = Taipei,China; THA = Thailand; VIE = Viet Nam.

Note: Lighter shaded markers = 2000, darker shaded markers = 2019. Higher values indicate greater concentration.

Source: Asian Development Bank. Multi-Regional Input–Output Tables (accessed July 2020).

Post-crisis, the roles that consumption, exports, and investments played in facilitating output growth in the region seemed to have been muted. Pre-crisis, these traditional demand components had higher (if not equal) impacts on growth across all sectors. Technology changes negatively impacted energy sectors (i.e., mining and utilities), light manufacturing, and agriculture post-crisis, but they sustained their positive contribution to heavy manufacturing and business services. This pattern is indicative of the higher use of services and heavy manufacturing inputs in production processes relative to traditional resource- and light-manufacturing-based products. The position that these industries take along the domestic value chain may have also influenced the pattern—often, energy

Figure 1.6:   Drivers of Output Changes by Sector, 2000–2007 and 2010–2018 (% Output Growth)

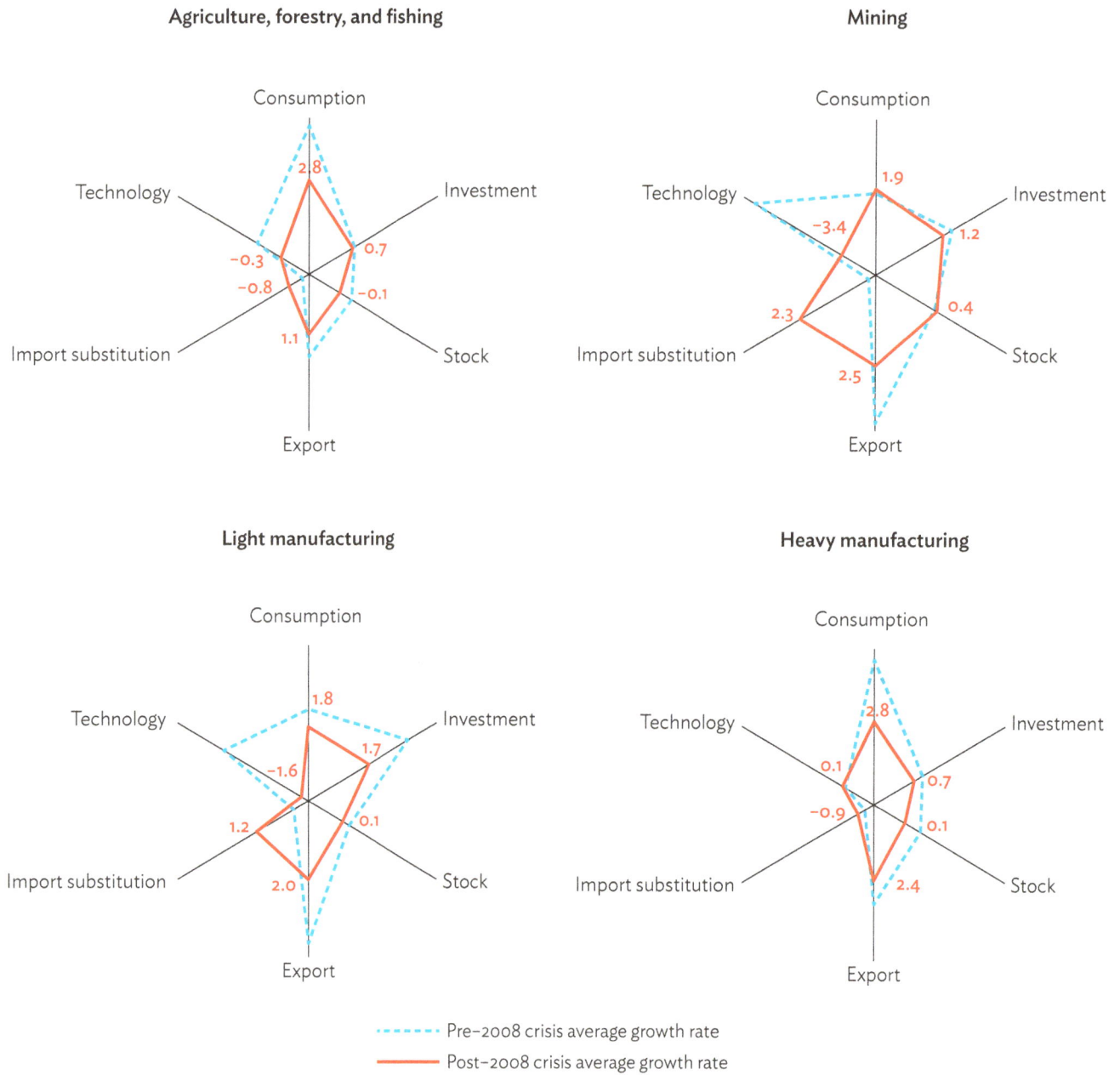

Agriculture, forestry, and fishing

Mining

Light manufacturing

Heavy manufacturing

- - - - Pre–2008 crisis average growth rate
——— Post–2008 crisis average growth rate

continued on next page

Figure 1.6 *continued*

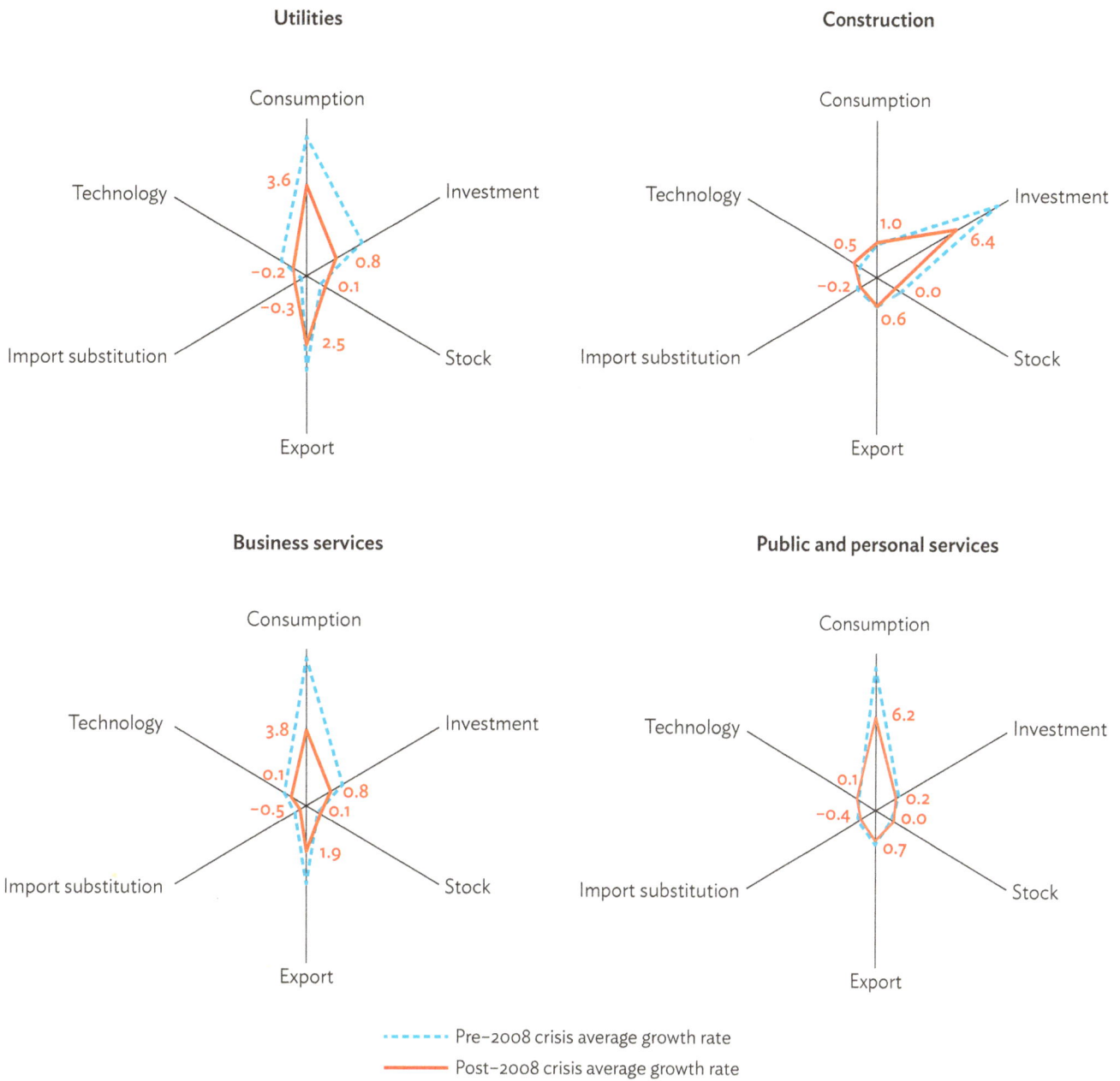

Utilities

Construction

Business services

Public and personal services

- - - - - - Pre–2008 crisis average growth rate
———— Post–2008 crisis average growth rate

Pre-2008 crisis = 2000 to 2007; post-crisis = 2010 to 2018.

Source: Asian Development Bank. Multi-Regional Input–Output Tables (accessed July 2020).

sectors, agriculture, and light manufacturing are upstream[2] suppliers to other productive activities in the economy. The consumption of inputs from more downstream sectors could also indicate that the region is gradually moving toward higher value-added activities in downstream segments of value chains.

The conventional use of the term "technology" may be understood from the context of a sector's use of productive inputs. Historically, IOTs contain values in physical terms, such that the production of a car is described by the amount of steel used, the type of engine, the amount of rubber, etc. Aside from describing a sector's production "recipe," IOTs also show the interindustrial demand for inputs. Therefore, the present technology or production techniques applied by an industry partly determine the output needed from other sectors. Today, the technology originally described by Leontief is more aptly termed as accounting coefficients since IOTs are often compiled in monetary terms for practical reasons.

A closer look at the impacts of each sector's production technologies are shown in Figure 1.7. Red markers (●) show how much a sector's output is affected by changes in the technologies of other sectors, whereas blue markers (●) show how much a change in a sector's technology affects the output of other sectors. In the decade following the 2008 global financial crisis, outputs in sectors such as construction, wholesale and retail trade, and hotels and restaurants were most negatively impacted by the changes in other sectors' technologies. This implies that the outputs of these sectors were less demanded as inputs to the production of other sectors in the economy. Meanwhile, the demand for resource-based sectors (i.e., mining and light manufacturing) remained relatively substantial post-crisis. Technological changes in the construction sector appear to have benefitted other sectors the most in the post-crisis period. Before and after the crisis, technological demand from hotels and restaurants stimulated the production of other sectors the most (i.e. post and telecommunications pre-crisis and construction post-crisis)—a likely result of Asia's tourism boom early in the 21st century. The shift from agriculture to manufacturing can also be gleaned from Figure 1.7. Post-crisis, agriculture's output declined due to changes in the technologies of other sectors, most notably due to falling demand from hotels and restaurants, light manufacturing, and from within the agriculture sector itself. Mining's output was also constrained by weaker demand from its traditional buyers in the manufacturing and construction sectors.

1.4 Economic Complexity

The discussion on technology lays the foundation for measuring economic complexity. From an input–output perspective, the complexity of a sector's production may be understood from the combination of inputs it uses. To produce the same output, two sectors may each use a different combination of inputs. If sector a produces the same output using a narrower range of inputs, while sector b uses a more diverse set of inputs, the production complexity of sector b is higher than that of sector a. Production complexity is a way of gauging a sector's relative importance in the economy, beyond simple measures of value-added shares.

---

[2]   Upstream segments of the value chain pertain to producers further away from final demand, whereas downstream segments consist of producers closer to the final stage of production and thus, final consumption. Upstream producers typically include suppliers and processors of raw materials and commodities, while downstream producers usually include firms involved in assembly, distribution, and other consumer-facing services. The relative position of a firm in the value chain is referred to as its upstreamness or downstreamness (Antràs and Chor, 2017).

Figure 1.7:   Impacts of Technological Changes on Output by Sector, 2000–2007 and 2010–2018
(% Output Growth)

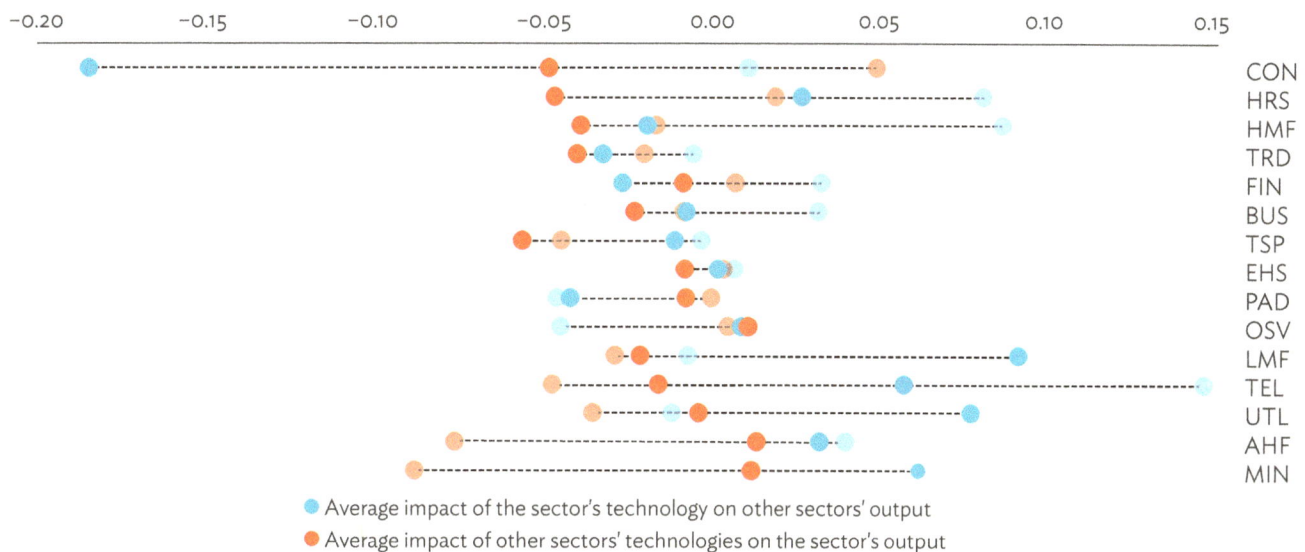

● Average impact of the sector's technology on other sectors' output
● Average impact of other sectors' technologies on the sector's output

AHF = agriculture, hunting, forestry, and fishing; BUS = business services including real estate; CON = construction; EHS = education and health services; FIN = finance and insurance; HMF = heavy manufacturing; HRS = hotel and restaurant services; LMF = light manufacturing; MIN = mining and quarrying; OSV = other services; PAD = public administration; TEL = post and telecommunications; TRD = wholesale and retail trade; TSP = transport services; UTL = utilities.

Note: Lighter shaded markers = 2000–2007 (pre-2008 crisis); darker shaded markers = 2010–2018 (post-2008 crisis).

Source: Asian Development Bank. Multi-Regional Input–Output Tables (accessed July 2020).

Production complexity also describes the number and magnitude of intersectoral connections in the economy—a sector acquires its inputs from within the same sector or from other sectors, creating direct links or connections between itself (as a purchasing sector) and the producing sectors. As such, economic complexity can also be interpreted as the level of interdependence between the different sectors of an economy. The use of a larger amount and a wider variety of inputs from other sectors creates more linkages and thus makes for a higher level of economic complexity.

Several measures of complexity are underscored in the existing literature. Each of these measures attempts to capture and summarize in a single statistic the interdependencies of sectors. Though their values differ, many among these measures use the Leontief inverse model and the matrix of intermediate transactions in their respective calculations. Expectedly, most tests of correlation between different measures of aggregate complexity in Figure 1.8 show strong positive relationships. However, two measures—the index of indirect interrelatedness and the percentage of above-average technical coefficients, both designed to place bias toward relatively high intermediate flows—are weakly correlated with other aggregate measures.[3]

---

[3]   Sources, definitions, and specific formulas for the measures are detailed in Appendix 3. The index of indirect interrelatedness measures the additional amount of intersectoral connections necessary to bring output to an equilibrium (Yan and Ames 1963), while the percentage of above-average coefficients counts the number of sectoral linkages that have higher-than-normal coefficients. The latter measure tends to be biased toward qualitatively high coefficients, rather than on linkages that have quantitatively more sectors participating. The index of indirect interrelatedness, on the other hand, is a subcomponent of the "overall sensitivity of the economy." In this measure, the direct connections tend to correlate more with other complexity measures than the indirect element.

Figure 1.8:   Correlation between Aggregate Measures of Economic Complexity, 2000–2018

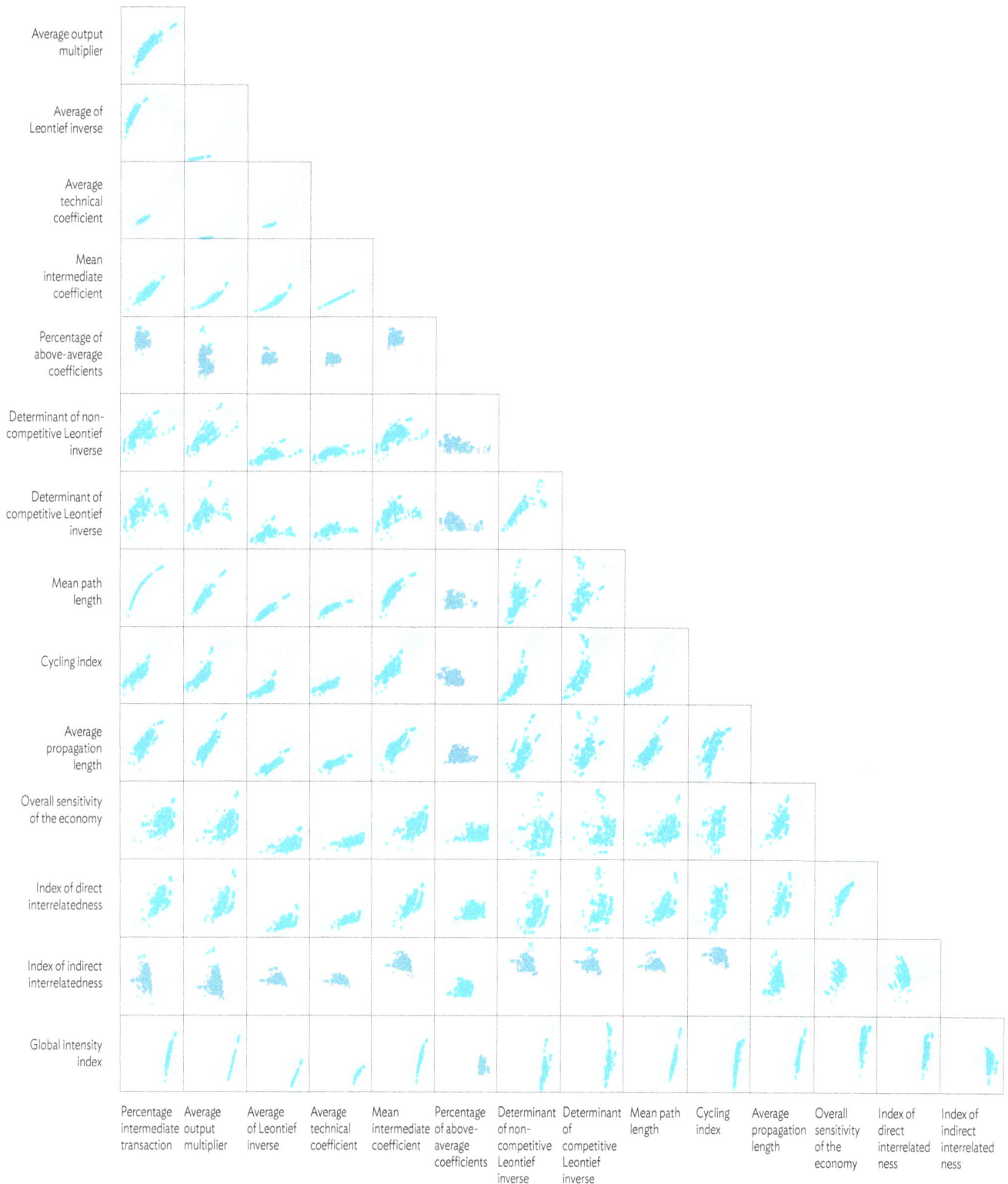

Note: The graph shows the visual correlations of several aggregate measures of complexity as suggested in the relevant literature.

Source: Asian Development Bank. Multi-Regional Input–Output Tables (accessed July 2020).

The rank correlations in Figure 1.9 show that economic complexity measures considering all intersectoral flows irrespective of their relative magnitudes are more highly correlated with economic size i.e., gross domestic product. The People's Republic of China (PRC) and the Republic of Korea generally scored high on these measures, while countries like the Lao PDR and Bhutan had lower complexity indexes.

Figure 1.9: Rank Correlation between Gross Domestic Product and Select Measures of Interrelatedness, 2007–2018

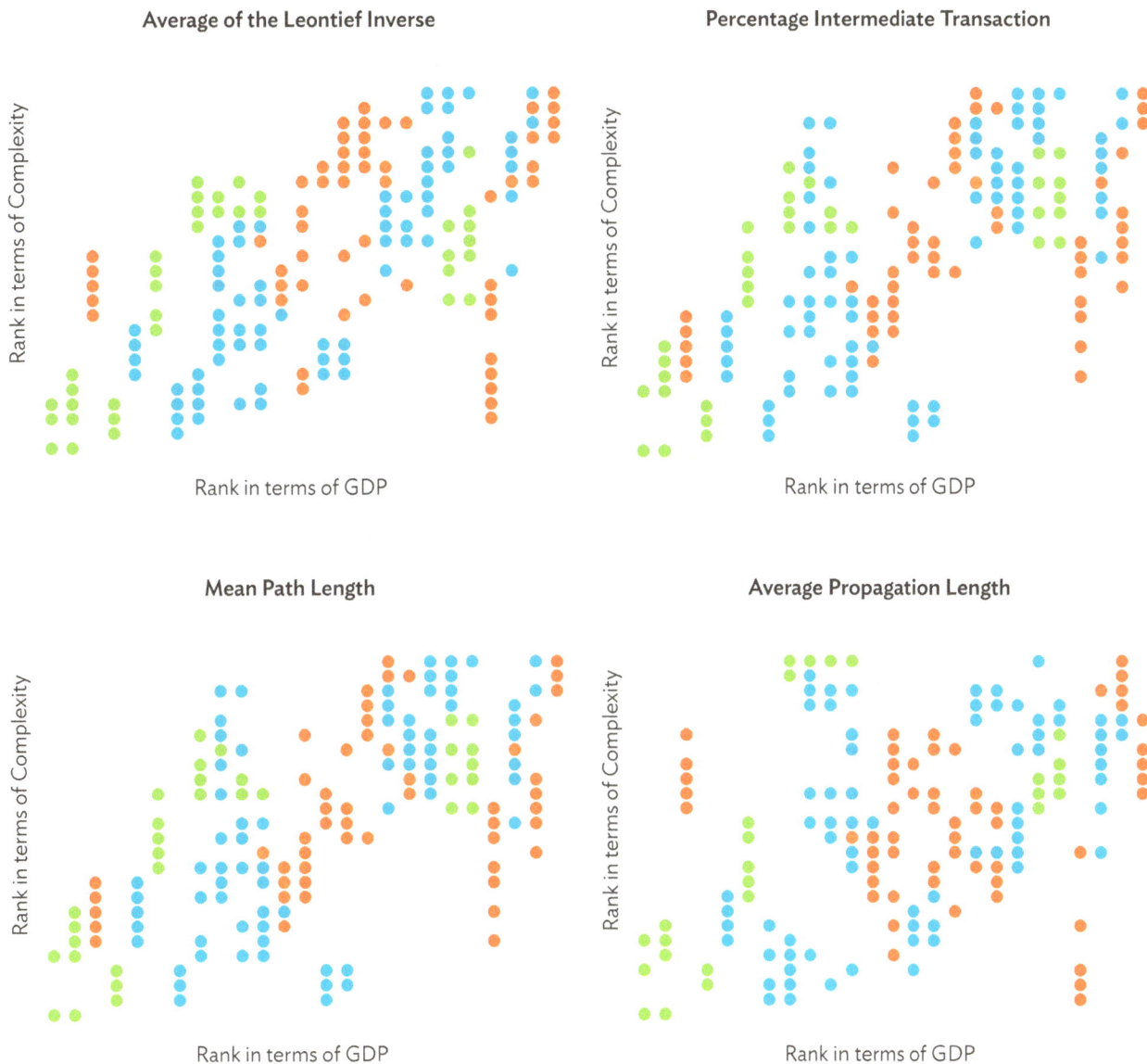

Average of the Leontief Inverse

Percentage Intermediate Transaction

Mean Path Length

Average Propagation Length

GDP = gross domestic product.

Note: The graph shows the Spearman rank correlations of complexity and GDP size of economies in Asia and the Pacific from 2007 to 2018. Spearman rank correlations of GDP against the average of the Leontief inverse, percentage intermediate transactions, mean path lengths, and average propagation lengths are 0.7123, 0.7045, 0.7045, and 0.4776, respectively. Data for each subregion are distinguished by color: economies in East Asia are represented by green dots; Southeast Asia and the Pacific by blue dots; and South and Central Asia by orange dots.

Source: Asian Development Bank. Multi-Regional Input–Output Tables (accessed July 2020).

Patterns of economic complexity are further investigated by studying intermediate flows in the input–output transactions matrix Z, re-expressed as important coefficients in Table 1.2 (a). A color gradient is applied to the table: cells with values above the row-wise average are shaded and their darkness increases with distance from the average. This distinguishes the highest intermediate flows from each row sector to all the column sectors or, succinctly, which purchasing sectors (columns) are most dependent on inputs from the producing sector (row). Meanwhile, Table 1.2 (b) presents the upper threshold or the tolerable limit of each cell in the transactions matrix Z, interpreted as the percentage change in the corresponding intermediate transaction required to induce a one percentage point change in the economy's gross output. Lower thresholds imply that output is more sensitive to the changes in the particular cell.

Considered together, Tables 1.2 (a) and 1.2 (b) suggest that higher magnitudes of intermediate flows tend to be associated with higher thresholds, while lower magnitudes likely correspond to lower thresholds. This implies that, while some intersectoral flows are quantitatively important because of their larger size, output levels will ultimately be determined by the overall dynamics of intersectoral demand and not just the relative magnitude of flows. Changes in more complex sectors with small yet diversified intermediate transactions can potentially impact the production levels of a given sector more than concentrated sectors with large but narrowly diversified input flows. In other words, a producing sector using a relatively narrow range of inputs is more likely to be associated with lower levels of economic activity than a complex producing sector using a wide range of inputs from several sectors.

Observed across time, most measures of complexity move in the opposite direction of economic growth. In Figure 1.10 economic complexity in the region for 2009 and 2018 across measures are compared. Complexity was higher in 2009 (blue bars), which was a period of economic contraction following the 2008 global financial crisis. When consumption and investment are low, producers probably increase intersectoral transactions to compensate for the slump or to manage the risks of the economic downturn and weak external environment. Even when intersectoral flows during contractions are low and reactionary, output can still be sensitive to these linkages, as previous findings show. Thus, domestic production chains can serve as mechanisms through which equilibrium is restored in the economy—diversifying during a slowdown and relaxing during economic recovery. This highlights the role of domestic value chains in stimulating growth during periods of negative to low growth.

Table 1.2: Important Coefficients and Their Respective Upper Thresholds, 2018
(%)

a. Important Coefficients

	AHF	MIN	LMF	HMF	UTL	CON	TRD	HRS	TSP	TEL	FIN	BUS	PAD	EHS	OSV
AHF	3.6	0.1	2.1	1.5	0.3	0.3	2.0	0.1	0.6	0.3	0.7	0.5	0.0	0.0	0.1
MIN	0.1	1.2	0.6	2.2	1.2	0.6	1.1	0.1	0.9	0.2	0.5	1.6	0.0	0.1	0.2
LMF	6.6	0.6	6.4	1.5	1.1	0.4	3.6	0.2	1.1	0.2	0.7	0.7	0.1	0.0	0.2
HMF	0.2	3.3	1.1	7.4	1.2	0.2	2.8	0.1	1.1	0.2	0.6	0.8	0.1	0.0	0.2
UTL	0.2	1.9	0.6	2.4	5.2	1.0	1.8	0.1	0.9	0.3	0.9	1.1	0.1	0.0	0.3
CON	0.3	1.1	4.2	4.0	0.3	4.5	2.6	0.2	1.2	0.3	0.9	1.2	0.1	0.0	0.1
TRD	0.1	0.1	0.9	0.8	0.6	0.9	1.3	0.4	1.8	0.8	1.6	2.3	0.2	0.1	0.3
HRS	3.9	0.1	6.5	0.6	1.4	0.6	2.8	0.5	0.8	0.4	0.8	1.6	0.1	0.0	0.4
TSP	0.2	0.2	0.7	3.6	0.3	0.5	1.9	0.4	3.0	0.7	1.2	1.5	0.1	0.0	0.3
TEL	0.4	0.1	0.9	1.4	0.9	0.5	1.2	0.4	0.9	3.6	1.0	2.8	0.4	0.1	0.6
FIN	0.0	0.0	0.6	0.3	0.4	0.3	0.4	0.4	0.6	0.9	5.0	2.3	0.1	0.1	0.4
BUS	0.0	0.1	0.8	0.8	0.6	1.5	0.7	0.5	0.7	0.7	1.5	2.8	0.1	0.1	0.5
PAD	0.5	0.1	0.9	0.9	0.8	1.5	1.0	0.6	1.1	0.7	1.1	1.9	0.4	0.9	0.4
EHS	0.5	0.1	1.1	1.9	0.8	0.7	1.2	0.5	0.6	0.4	0.8	1.2	0.2	0.5	0.3
OSV	0.2	0.1	1.2	1.0	1.0	0.5	0.9	0.6	0.7	0.8	0.8	2.5	0.2	0.1	2.4

b. Upper Threshold

	AHF	MIN	LMF	HMF	UTL	CON	TRD	HRS	TSP	TEL	FIN	BUS	PAD	EHS	OSV
AHF	11	0	35	1	0	1	0	6	0	0	0	0	2	1	0
MIN	0	3	8	30	8	9	0	0	1	0	0	0	0	0	0
LMF	3	0	19	4	1	9	3	6	1	1	1	2	1	1	1
HMF	3	2	5	26	2	10	2	1	4	1	0	1	1	2	1
UTL	2	4	11	12	16	3	5	5	2	2	2	4	4	4	2
CON	0	1	1	1	1	13	1	1	1	0	0	2	1	1	0
TRD	3	1	11	8	1	6	3	2	3	0	0	1	1	1	1
HRS	1	1	2	2	0	2	3	1	2	1	2	3	2	2	1
TSP	1	2	6	6	1	5	7	2	8	1	1	2	2	1	1
TEL	1	1	3	4	1	3	8	2	4	9	5	5	4	2	2
FIN	2	3	6	5	1	5	10	3	5	1	25	7	3	2	1
BUS	1	2	3	4	1	3	8	2	3	2	3	7	3	2	2
PAD	0	0	0	0	0	1	0	0	0	0	0	0	1	0	0
EHS	0	0	0	0	0	0	0	0	0	0	0	0	2	1	0
OSV	1	1	2	3	1	1	3	3	1	1	1	4	2	2	7

AHF = agriculture, hunting, forestry, and fishing; BUS = business services including real estate; CON = construction; EHS = education and health services; FIN = finance and insurance; HMF = heavy manufacturing; HRS = hotel and restaurant services; LMF = light manufacturing; MIN = mining and quarrying; OSV = other services; PAD = public administration; TEL = post and telecommunications; TRD = wholesale and retail trade; TSP = transport services; UTL = utilities.

Note:　*Important coefficients* are defined as the percentage share of an intersectoral transaction to the total sum of intermediate use. These coefficients are averaged across all 25 economies in Asia and the Pacific. Higher values indicate higher shares in relative to other cells. On the other hand, *upper thresholds* indicate the amount of change required in a specific intersectoral transaction (or "cell") to induce a one percentage change in the economy's gross output. Smaller values indicate more sensitive and/or important (i.e., impactful) cells.

Source:　Asian Development Bank. Multi-Regional Input–Output Tables (accessed July 2020).

Figure 1.10: Aggregate Measures of Complexity, 2009 and 2018 Indexed Values
(%)

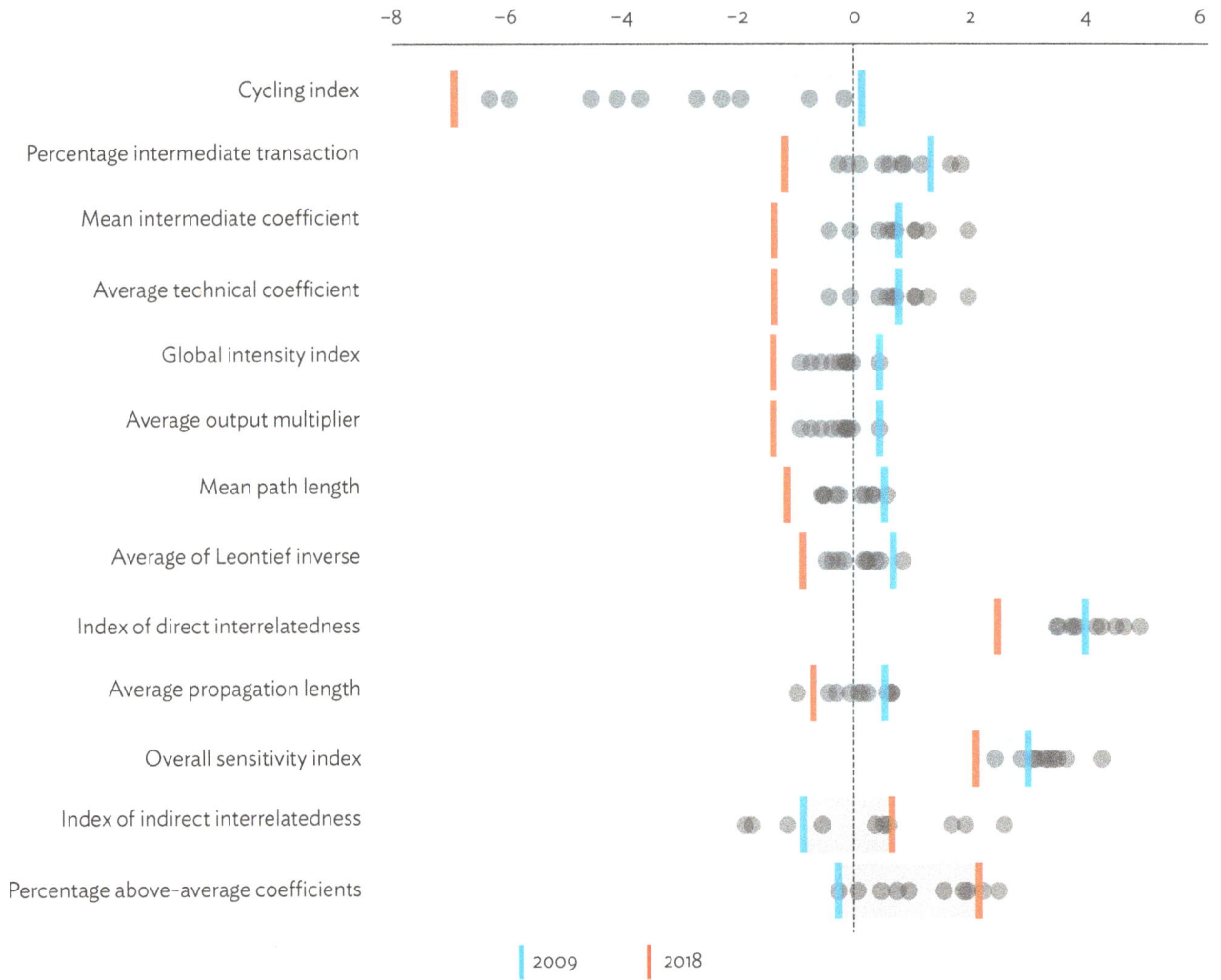

2009   2018

Note: Dots represent the arithmetic averages across economies of the complexity measures from 2000 to 2018. Red-orange bars
          represent the average complexity in 2018 relative to 2000 values, while blue bars represent the average complexity in 2009
          relative to the same benchmark year 2000.

Source: Asian Development Bank. Multi-Regional Input–Output Tables (accessed July 2020).

1.5 Multipliers and Intersectoral Linkage Analysis

Among its many analytical contributions, input–output analysis can also be used to evaluate the impact of critical changes in the macroeconomy, such as demand shocks or rising labor costs, on the overall production levels of the economy. In particular, within an input–output system, an economy is modeled such that the demand in one of its sectors could impact demands (and therefore outputs) in other sectors, through existing connections between them at one or more levels. For example, if a car manufacturer anticipates a decline in sales, it might adjust its production level downwards, in accordance with the reduced demand. This lower production will not only impact the automotive factory or the industry it belongs to, but also other sectors in its supply chain as well. The first degree of impact is felt by the manufacturer's immediate suppliers who, because of lower demand, might have to reduce their own output. These suppliers in turn will also likely cut back on purchases of inputs from their respective suppliers, and so on through more and more upstream suppliers in the supply chain. This chain reaction will have knock-on effects on sectors that indirectly transact with the originally impacted sector. The summary of these reactions is uniquely captured in the Leontief model.

The model starts with the assumption that interindustry flows from sector i to sector j depend entirely on the production level of sector i. For example, a manufacturer producing an aircraft worth \$1,000,000 in a specific year uses steel inputs worth \$200,000 in the process. This intermediate flow z_{ij} from sector i to sector j serves two purposes: (i) directly linking two sectors in the economy, and (ii) explicitly establishing the relationship between input and output. This linkage is operationalized in the input-output model by taking the ratio of the value of steel (input) used to yield the value of the aircraft (output)—i.e., $a_{ij} = \frac{\$200,000}{\$1,000,000} = 0.2$. In the example, \$0.20 worth of steel is required to produce \$1 worth of aircraft. This input to output ratio is called a technical coefficient (a_{ij}) and, given its underlying calculation, it can be used to determine how much a reduction or an expansion in the output of the purchasing sector can affect the demand for input or, accordingly, the output of the supplying sector. If it takes \$0.20 of steel to produce \$1 of aircraft, then doubling the aircraft production would entail increasing the steel requirement to \$400,000 (\$2,000,000 of aircraft × \$0.2 steel per \$ of aircraft). The ratio between input and output remains fixed in the Leontief model, regardless of the level of production, consistent with the assumption of constant returns to scale. Thus, the technical coefficients that describe the production structure (or "recipe") of a given economic activity are assumed to be stable in an input–output system.

Apart from their economic meaning, the intermediate flows serve an important accounting purpose as well. By properly accounting for these inputs, total production (or gross domestic product) can be compiled without double-counting the output that was used as inputs to other production processes. To illustrate using the same steel-aircraft example, double-counting occurs when the aircraft industry's \$1,000,000 worth of output is taken at face value and aggregated with the steel industry's \$200,000 worth of output, even though the latter is already reflected in the aircraft industry's output value. Since steel is not exactly produced by the aircraft manufacturer, the national accountant only wishes to consider the *value* that was *added* by the manufacturer to produce its output. By deducting the intermediate inputs from the gross output, the sector's gross value-added can be derived without double-counting.

Returning to the model, output x_i of any sector i is simply the sum of all its sales to industries $\sum_{j=1}^{n} z_{ij}$, and final consumers $\sum_{1}^{k} f_{ik}$ with k categories (broadly, consumption, government, investment, inventories or stocks, and exports). By aggregating final demand across k categories, a column vector f can be derived with $n \times 1$ dimensions. In matrix format, the output of any sector becomes $x = Z + f$, where x is a $n \times 1$ column vector of output, Z is the $n \times n$ matrix of intermediate transactions, and f is an $n \times 1$ column vector of final demand. Re-expressing elements in Z as technical coefficients (or input to output ratios) yields $x = Ax + f$, where A is the $n \times n$ technical coefficients matrix with elements a_{ij}. Rearranging the terms yields the Leontief inverse matrix L:

$$x = Ax + f$$
$$x - Ax = f$$
$$(I-A)x = f$$
$$(I-A)^{-1}(I-A)x = (I-A)^{-1}f$$
$$Ix = (I-A)^{-1}f$$
$$x = (I-A)^{-1}f$$
$$where\ (I-A)^{-1} = L = [l_{ij}]\ and\ thus,\ x = Lf$$

The well-known equation Lf establishes a clear relationship between output and final demand values for each sector. If the household sector has a predictable demand for $100 million worth of food products, then the food manufacturing sector automatically accounts this as a "direct impact" from the household sector and adjusts its production levels accordingly to accommodate the demand. The food manufacturing sector, to meet the final demand for its products, will in turn require raw supplies from the agriculture sector. This creates additional production of agricultural products on top of the initial production of food products directly motivated by household demand. The second-order effect (on agriculture) is considered an indirect impact of household demand. Aggregating direct and indirect impacts generates the "total" impact of final demand.

The total impacts (direct and indirect) are quantified in the Leontief inverse just described, i.e., $[l_{ij}]$. Expressing the Leontief model $x = Lf$ as a linear equation: $x_i = l_{i1}f_1 + l_{ij}f_j + \ldots + l_{in}f_n$, distinguishes the term $l_{ij}f_j$, which represents the impact of final demand f_j on the output of sector i. The total output of sector i is thus the sum of the impacts across all sectors' final demand. The process of multiplying l_{ij} to final demand f_j to derive total impacts characterizes the elements of Leontief inverse as "multipliers." A summation of the ith row of the Leontief inverse matrix yields the total impacts of all sectors' final demand on the output of sector i, which also represents the sensitivity of sector i's production to the demands of every sector in the economy. Meanwhile, the sum of the jth column of the Leontief inverse matrix equates to the total impacts of sector j's final demand to the overall output of the economy, also indicating the strength of sector j's demand-pull effect on the economy. A column sum of the Leontief inverse is known as the *simple output multiplier*.[4]

In Asia and the Pacific, output multipliers are particularly strong in industries that contemporary economies consider as "critical infrastructure" industries (Table 1.3). These sectors include the light and heavy manufacturing, utilities sectors and, to a lesser but still significant extent, sectors involved in travel and connectivity, such as

---

[4]   Extensions and other variants of multipliers are explained in Appendix 3.

hotels and restaurants, transport services, and telecommunications. The multipliers in Table 1.3 indicate that, on average, a $1 demand in any of these sectors could generate up to $1.55 worth of production. The extra $0.55 is attributable to the indirect production required throughout the economy, since supplying sectors themselves demand inputs as well. In this sense, the intersectoral demand generated within production chains "multiplies" the direct production required to satisfy a dollar worth of demand.

Table 1.3:   Simple Output Multipliers in Asia and the Pacific, 2018

							Sectors								
	AHF	MIN	LMF	HMF	UTL	CON	TRD	HRS	TSP	TEL	FIN	BUS	PAD	EHS	OSV
BAN	1.4	1.1	1.9	1.6	1.5	1.9	1.2	1.9	1.4	1.4	1.4	1.2	1.4	1.2	1.2
BHU	1.1	1.3	1.6	1.7	1.3	1.5	1.2	1.2	1.3	1.4	1.1	1.2	1.5	1.2	1.4
BRU	1.3	1.2	1.1	1.6	1.6	1.6	1.4	1.3	1.8	1.3	1.2	1.2	1.4	1.3	1.1
CAM	1.2	1.3	1.7	1.4	1.8	1.4	1.5	1.8	1.4	1.6	1.2	1.7	1.6	1.3	1.4
FIJ	1.3	1.4	1.5	1.4	1.3	1.6	1.3	1.5	1.1	1.2	1.2	1.4	1.2	1.3	1.1
HKG	1.3	1.0	1.4	1.4	1.3	2.1	1.5	1.4	1.6	1.6	1.5	1.3	1.2	1.2	1.5
IND	1.4	1.6	2.2	2.1	1.7	2.0	1.2	1.8	1.3	1.2	1.2	1.3	1.0	1.3	1.3
INO	1.2	1.4	1.8	1.7	2.2	2.0	1.4	1.7	1.7	1.4	1.4	1.4	1.6	1.5	1.8
JPN	1.8	1.6	2.0	2.0	1.7	1.8	1.5	1.9	1.6	1.6	1.6	1.4	1.5	1.5	1.6
KAZ	1.5	1.6	1.6	1.8	1.7	1.7	1.4	1.5	1.5	1.5	1.3	1.3	1.7	1.6	1.4
KGZ	2.3	1.6	1.8	1.8	1.5	1.7	1.3	1.7	1.4	1.2	4.8	1.4	1.4	1.3	1.5
KOR	1.8	1.7	2.2	2.1	1.7	1.9	1.7	1.8	1.9	2.0	1.7	1.5	1.5	1.7	1.9
LAO	1.1	1.2	1.6	1.4	1.2	1.6	1.3	1.6	1.2	1.3	1.3	1.1	1.4	1.3	1.3
MAL	1.6	1.2	2.3	1.7	1.6	2.0	1.6	2.0	1.9	2.1	1.9	1.7	1.7	1.4	1.8
MLD	1.4	1.0	1.8	1.3	1.5	1.4	1.8	1.6	1.4	1.6	1.3	1.3	1.4	1.3	1.4
MON	1.3	1.4	1.7	1.5	1.7	1.6	1.3	1.7	1.2	1.2	1.2	1.3	1.3	1.2	1.3
NEP	1.3	1.2	1.8	1.5	1.7	1.5	1.3	1.9	1.1	1.8	1.3	1.5	1.5	1.4	1.6
PAK	1.4	1.2	1.9	1.7	2.4	1.8	1.2	2.0	1.6	1.5	1.2	1.1	1.6	1.3	1.3
PHI	1.5	1.3	2.0	1.7	1.4	1.5	1.4	2.1	1.6	1.4	1.4	1.5	1.5	1.4	1.6
PRC	1.9	2.2	2.9	3.1	3.0	3.0	1.8	2.5	2.3	1.8	1.6	2.0	2.0	2.2	2.1
SIN	1.5	1.0	1.7	1.5	1.4	2.1	1.4	1.6	1.4	1.5	1.4	1.5	1.8	1.4	1.4
SRI	1.3	1.2	1.6	1.4	1.5	1.5	1.3	1.6	1.5	1.6	1.4	1.3	1.1	1.1	1.6
TAP	1.6	1.4	1.8	1.6	1.2	1.7	1.3	1.6	1.6	1.5	1.4	1.3	1.3	1.3	1.4
THA	1.5	2.1	2.1	2.0	1.7	2.0	1.6	1.9	1.9	1.8	1.4	1.7	1.5	1.7	1.5
VIE	1.8	1.5	2.1	1.8	1.3	1.8	1.4	1.8	1.6	1.8	1.5	1.5	1.3	1.5	1.5

AHF = agriculture, hunting, forestry, and fishing; BAN = Bangladesh; BHU = Bhutan; BRU = Brunei Darussalam; BUS = business services including real estate; CAM = Cambodia; CON = construction; EHS = education and health services; FIJ = Fiji; FIN = finance and insurance; HKG = Hong Kong, China; HMF = heavy manufacturing; HRS = hotel and restaurant services; IND = India; INO = Indonesia; JPN = Japan; KAZ = Kazakhstan; KGZ = Kyrgyz Republic; KOR = Republic of Korea; LAO = Lao People's Democratic Republic; LMF = light manufacturing; MAL = Malaysia; MIN = mining and quarrying; MLD = Maldives; MON = Mongolia; NEP = Nepal; OSV = other services; PAD = public administration; PAK = Pakistan; PHI = Philippines; PRC = People's Republic of China; SIN = Singapore; SRI = Sri Lanka; TAP = Taipei,China; TEL = post and telecommunications; THA = Thailand; TRD = wholesale and retail trade; TSP = transport services; UTL = utilities; VIE = Viet Nam.

Note: Cells with figures in bold indicate that the values are above their respective row averages. Meanwhile, a color gradient is applied to distinguish the highest row values from the lowest, with the lowest having the lightest shades and the highest, the darkest shades.

Source: Asian Development Bank. Multi-Regional Input–Output Tables (accessed July 2020).

Using input–output multipliers, the structure of production can be characterized based on the direct and indirect linkages existing within the economic system. Figure 1.11 visualizes the direct and indirect impacts of demand on the production of each sector in the regional economy. In 2018, mining and quarrying and utilities had the highest proportion of indirect production impacts compared to other sectors. Education and health and other services were straightforwardly demand-oriented, with a relatively small portion of production attributed to indirect production linkages. The output of both the heavy and light manufacturing sectors are notable while their respective shares of indirect production to output were nearly equal in 2018, the indirect impact from exports was larger in heavy manufacturing than in light manufacturing as export activities in the region generally involved more machinery and electronic products. While the share of agriculture in total output diminished over the years, its potential for inducing indirect production ($2.2 trillion in 2018) was still higher than services sectors such as finance and insurance ($1.8 trillion), construction ($675 billion), and post and telecommunications ($568 billion).

Figure 1.11: Direct and Indirect Production by Sectors in Asia and the Pacific, 2018

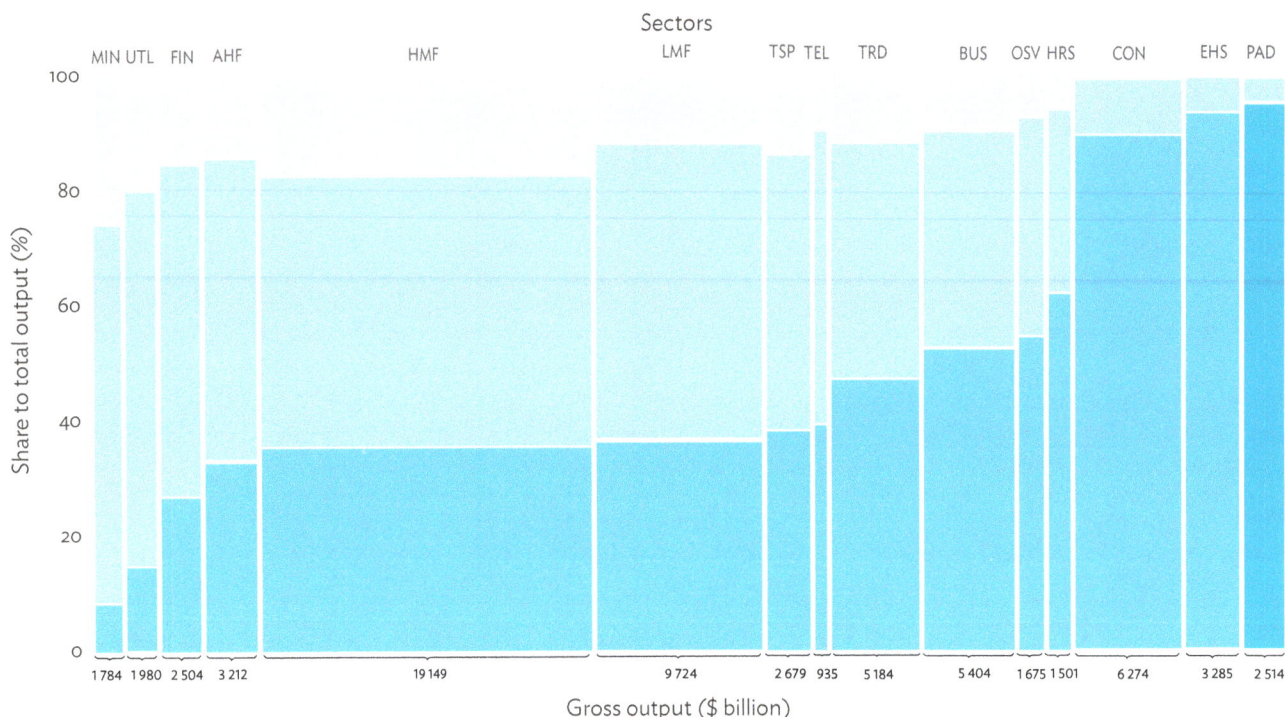

AHF = agriculture, hunting, forestry, and fishing; BUS = business services including real estate; CON = construction; EHS = education and health services; FIN = finance and insurance; HMF = heavy manufacturing; HRS = hotel and restaurant services; LMF = light manufacturing; MIN = mining and quarrying; OSV = other services; PAD = public administration; TEL = post and telecommunications; TRD = wholesale and retail trade; TSP = transport services; UTL = utilities.

Note: Bars in dark blue shades (■) indicate the direct impacts of final demand. Bars in lighter shades of blue indicate the indirect impacts: (■) indicate the indirect impacts attributable to domestic final demand (e.g., sum of household consumption, government consumption, gross fixed capital formation, and changes in inventories); and ( ) indicate the indirect impacts attributable to exports.

Source: Asian Development Bank. Multi-Regional Input–Output Tables (accessed July 2020).

1.6 Forward and Backward Linkages

In the input–output framework, the effect of a particular sector's production on other industries in the economy can be measured from two perspectives: supply and use. The backward linkage of economy-sector j is a measure of its interconnectedness to the other economy-sectors from which its inputs to production are purchased, characterizing the use perspective. On the other hand, the forward linkage of economy-sector j quantifies its interconnectedness to other economy-sectors that purchase its outputs to serve as inputs to their respective production, representing the supply perspective.

Combined measures of backward and forward linkages help determine key sectors in an economy. *Key sectors* in this context refer to sectors with the highest influence in the system—i.e., sectors that are most capable of stimulating production in both upstream and downstream segments of their respective supply chains.[5] For instance, if the backward linkage of economy-sector i is greater than that of economy-sector j, then increasing production in economy-sector i could induce higher economic activity from more sectors in its upstream chain than could increasing production in economy-sector j. Thus, a policy favoring sector i could potentially be more beneficial to the whole economy. Meanwhile, if the forward linkage of economy-sector j is greater than that of economy-sector k, then an increase in output of economy-sector j is more beneficial or stimulating because it induces an increase in production among sectors in its downstream supply chain.

In its simplest form, the direct backward linkage of economy-sector j can be measured by summing all the elements of the jth column of the input coefficient matrix A, $\sum_{i=1}^{n} a_{ij}$—i.e., the direct backward linkage is equivalent to the total value of all inputs required to produce \$1 worth of sector j's output. For comparability, the direct backward linkage of economy-sector j can be normalized. The normalized value is equal to the ratio of economy-sector j's direct backward linkage (as defined earlier) to the arithmetic mean of all the direct backward linkages in the economy—i.e.,

$$\overline{BL}(d)_j = \frac{\sum_{i=1}^{n} a_{ij}}{(1/n) \sum_{i=1}^{n} a_{ij} \sum_{j=1}^{n} a_{ij}}.$$

To measure both direct and indirect backward linkages, the Leontif inverse matrix L is used. Specifically, the total (direct and indirect) backward linkage of economy-sector j is equal to the sum of the elements in the jth column of the total requirements or Leontief inverse matrix—i.e., $\sum_{i=1}^{n} l_{ij}$.

---

[5] Several linkage measures for identifying key sectors have been proposed such as in Rasmussen (1957), Hirschmann (1958), McGilvray (1977), Hewings (1982), and Miller and Blair (2009).

Meanwhile, the direct forward linkage of economy-sector i is defined as the sum of all the elements in the ith row of the direct output coefficient matrix B—i.e., $\sum_{i=1}^{n} b_{ij}$. The output coefficient matrix B is derived by dividing each element of the intermediate transactions matrix to its corresponding row total or output. The normalized form of the direct forward linkage of economy-sector i, defined as the ratio of its forward linkage to the arithmetic mean of all the forward linkages in the economy, is given by:

$$\overline{FL}(d)_i = \frac{\sum_{j=1}^{n} b_{ij}}{(1/n) \sum_{i=1}^{n} b_{ij} \sum_{j=1}^{n} b_{ij}}.$$

For measuring both direct and indirect forward linkages, the Ghosh inverse matrix G is used. The total (direct and indirect) forward linkage of economy-sector i is equal to the sum of the elements in the ith row of the Ghosh inverse matrix G—i.e., $\sum_{j=1}^{n} g_{ij}$. The Ghosh inverse is the supply-side model analog of the Leontief inverse, defined as $G = (I-B)^{-1}$ in matrix form.

The combined measures of normalized backward and forward linkages of sectors in the economy can be used as a metric to identify key sectors. Numerically, a sector is considered *key* if both its normalized backward and forward linkage measures have values greater than 1. Economy-sectors are classified according to their dependence on other sectors as given by their respective normalized linkage measures: as (I) generally independent of other sectors when both measures are less than 1; (II) generally dependent on other sectors when both measures are greater than 1; (III) dependent on interindustry supply when the backward measure is greater than 1 but the forward measure is less than 1; and (IV) dependent on interindustry demand when the forward measure is greater than 1 but the backward measure is less than 1. This four-way classification is summarized in Table 1.4.

Table 1.4:   Classification of Key Sectors Using Forward and Backward Linkages

		Forward Linkage	
		Low (<1)	High (>1)
Backward Linkage	Low (<1)	(I) Generally independent	(II) Dependent on interindustry demand
	High (>1)	(IV) Dependent on interindustry supply	(III) Generally dependent

Source: R. Miller and P. Blair. 2009. *Input–Output Analysis: Foundations and Extensions.* Cambridge: Cambridge University Press.

Figures 1.12 (a) and 1.12 (b) show the normalized forward and backward linkages of sectors of the Asia and Pacific regional economy for 2000 and 2018, respectively. For simplicity, the linkage measures are averaged over all 25 economies covered in this report. Two intersecting lines corresponding to the mean value of 1 for both the normalized forward and backward linkages are placed for ease of classification. In 2000, public administration, education, health, and other services sectors were generally independent of other sectors. Meanwhile, use-oriented light and heavy manufacturing sectors, transport services, utilities, and financial intermediation sectors were generally dependent on other sectors for their inputs. From 2000 to 2018, transport and finance sectors became less dependent on interindustry supply but remained highly dependent on interindustry demand. This is expected as transport services and financial intermediation

Figure 1.12: Forward and Backward Linkages in Asia and the Pacific, 2000 and 2018

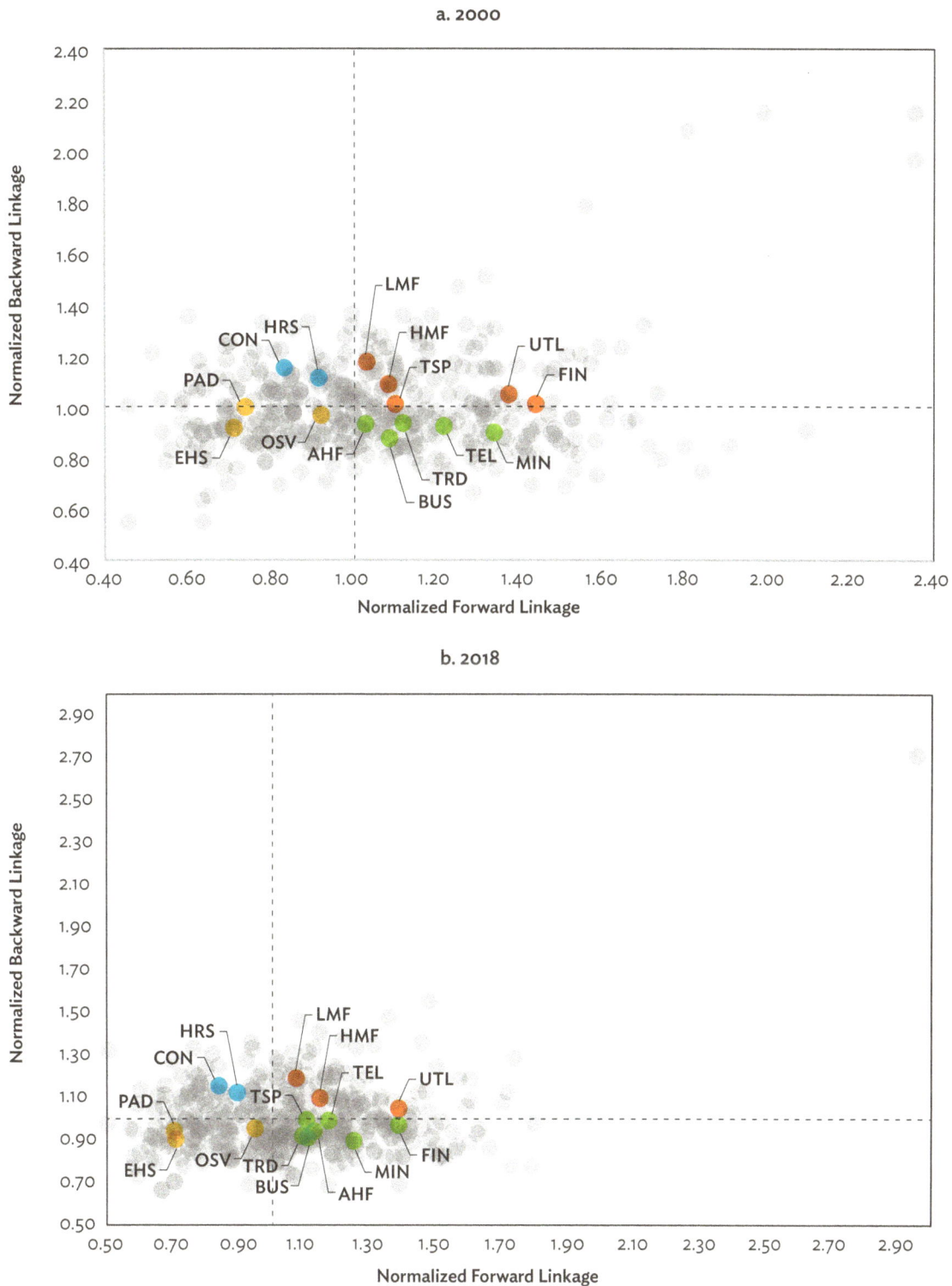

a. 2000

b. 2018

AHF = agriculture, hunting, forestry, and fishing; BUS = business services including real estate; CON = construction; EHS = education and health services; FIN = finance and insurance; HMF = heavy manufacturing; HRS = hotel and restaurant services; LMF = light manufacturing; MIN = mining and quarrying; OSV = other services; PAD = public administration; TEL = post and telecommunications; TRD = wholesale and retail trade; TSP = transport services; UTL = utilities.

Source: Asian Development Bank. Multi-Regional Input–Output Tables (accessed July 2020).

became more crucial in businesses (higher interindustrial supply), while requiring relatively fewer inputs than industrial counterparts (lower interindustrial demand). In both 2000 and 2018, the construction and hotel and restaurants sectors remained dependent on interindustry supply, while agriculture, hunting, forestry, and fishing; real estate, renting, and business activities; trade services, telecommunications; and mining and quarrying consistently depended on interindustry demand.

However, the strength of these linkages does not provide a full picture of an economy-sector's impact on an economy—whether the impact spreads to several sectors or to a select few also needs to be considered. The spread of these impacts is represented by the distribution of an economy-sector's interindustry flows across all sectors. If an economy-sector purchases (or sells) its inputs (or outputs) from (or to) several sectors, then its direct backward (or forward) linkages are considered diversified. However, if the economy-sector engages only with a narrow set of suppliers and buyers, then its linkages are concentrated. The degree of a linkage's concentration can describe the potential spread, dispersion, or spillover of a given impact.

The dispersion of these impacts is calculated using backward and forward concentration ratios (Figure 1. 13). These values range from 0 (totally concentrated) to 1 (totally diversified). Results for Asia and the Pacific indicate a high dispersion of backward linkages. From 2000 to 2018, direct linkages were increasingly spread across other sectors, heightening the likelihood of spillovers across the economy. On the other hand, the results show a low dispersion of forward linkages: sales patterns to other sectors were generally less diversified, especially for business services where average ratios declined from their

Figure 1.13: Dispersion of Impacts from Direct Linkages in Asia and the Pacific, 2000–2018

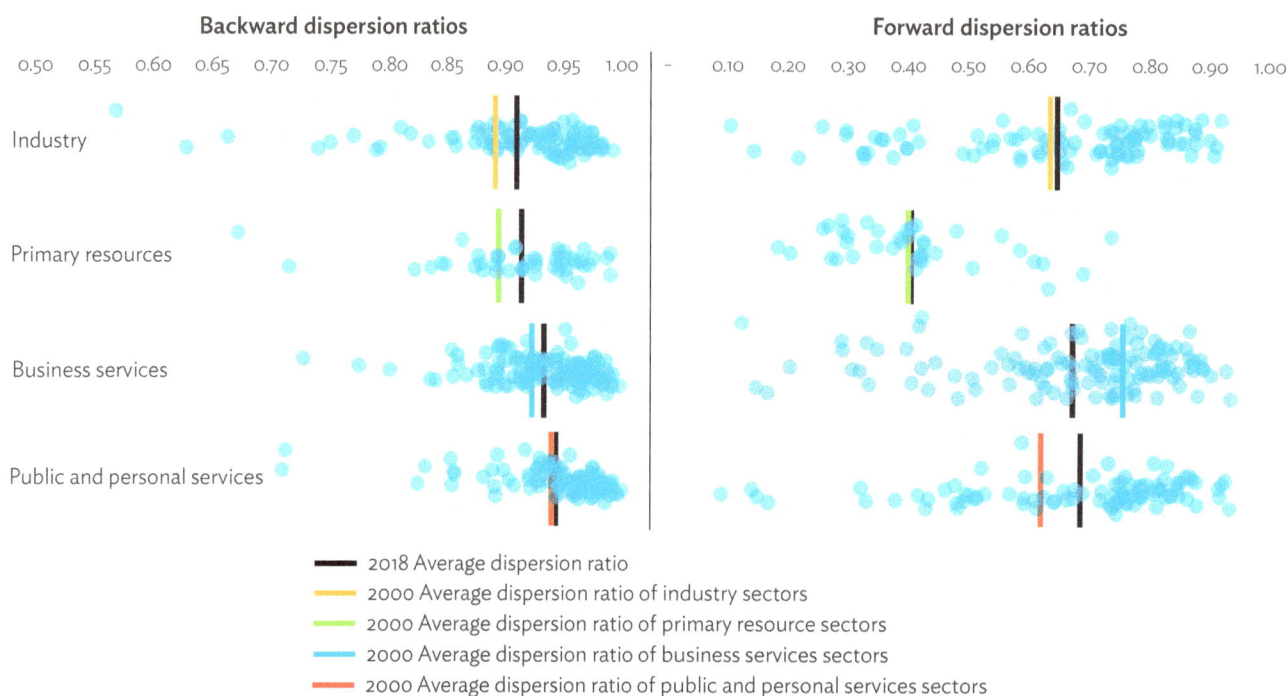

Source: Asian Development Bank. Multi-Regional Input–Output Tables (accessed July 2020).

2000 levels. While the business services sector requires inputs from various suppliers, demand for its output is consolidated among only a few buyers (e.g., manufacturing). Direct forward linkages in sectors other than business services spread across more sectors from 2000 to 2018. The dispersion of forward ratios for each observation (represented as dots) was more erratic than for backward ratios, implying that production patterns were more stable than sales patterns in the economies examined.

To analyze the impact of an economy-sector, both in terms of the strength and the spread of its linkages, a hypothetical extraction or insertion of the said sector can be modeled. These models estimate the total amount of production attributable to a specific sector— i.e., by measuring the change in the economy, all other things constant, when the sector is removed (hypothetical extraction) or when it is added (hypothetical insertion). This way, what is captured is not only the amount of value-added or output of the "extracted" or "inserted" sector but also the value-added or output it induces from other sectors that supply its inputs or use its outputs. For example, if an exporting sector is extracted from the economy, the extraction will not only affect the economy's total exports but also the sector's upstream suppliers in the production chain. Moreover, if the extracted sector happens to produce inputs for other sectors, then these downstream buyers would also be confronted with disrupted supplies. Thus, the use of hypothetical scenarios considers both direct and indirect linkages from forward and backward perspectives.

The counterfactuals created for measuring the impacts of a sector should, however, be treated as an accounting exercise rather than an actual scenario. If a critical sector, such as energy, is eliminated from the economy, the real-life impact would extend beyond what is simulated in the model, as it would most likely handicap the operability of many sectors. This could also happen to sectors whose production structures are rigid (i.e., without crucial inputs, production would halt). Nonetheless, the impacts imputed from the model provide notions of the importance of a sector by accounting for its production linkages.

Applying the hypothetical extraction model to each sector in the Asia and Pacific regional economy yields the results presented in Figure 1.14. Rows represent extracted sectors, while columns represent affected sectors from the scenario. Given the economic structure in 2018, the manufacturing and construction sectors were the most influential in the economy—i.e., their hypothetical extractions had the largest impacts on other sectors. The utilities and mining and quarrying sectors, as well as wholesale and retail trade sector, were particularly affected by the changes. Interestingly, agriculture was among the sectors least likely to induce negative impacts in the economy but was among the most-affected sectors if other industries were extracted from the economy. Specifically, agriculture was most sensitive to output changes in manufacturing, construction, and hotel and restaurant services. Services, meanwhile, had the least impact on other sectors' production in the event of its extraction. Generally, the extraction impacts widened from 2000 to 2018, pointing to an increase in interdependence among sectors.

Reversing the analysis, the impact of inserting a new sector into the economy can be examined. Should new sectors appear in the economy, intersectoral demand for inputs would rise and new value chains would likely be created. Any new sector is assumed to have the same technology and production structure as existing industries.

Figure 1.14: Impacts of the Hypothetical Extraction of Key Sectors in Asia and the Pacific, 2018
(%)

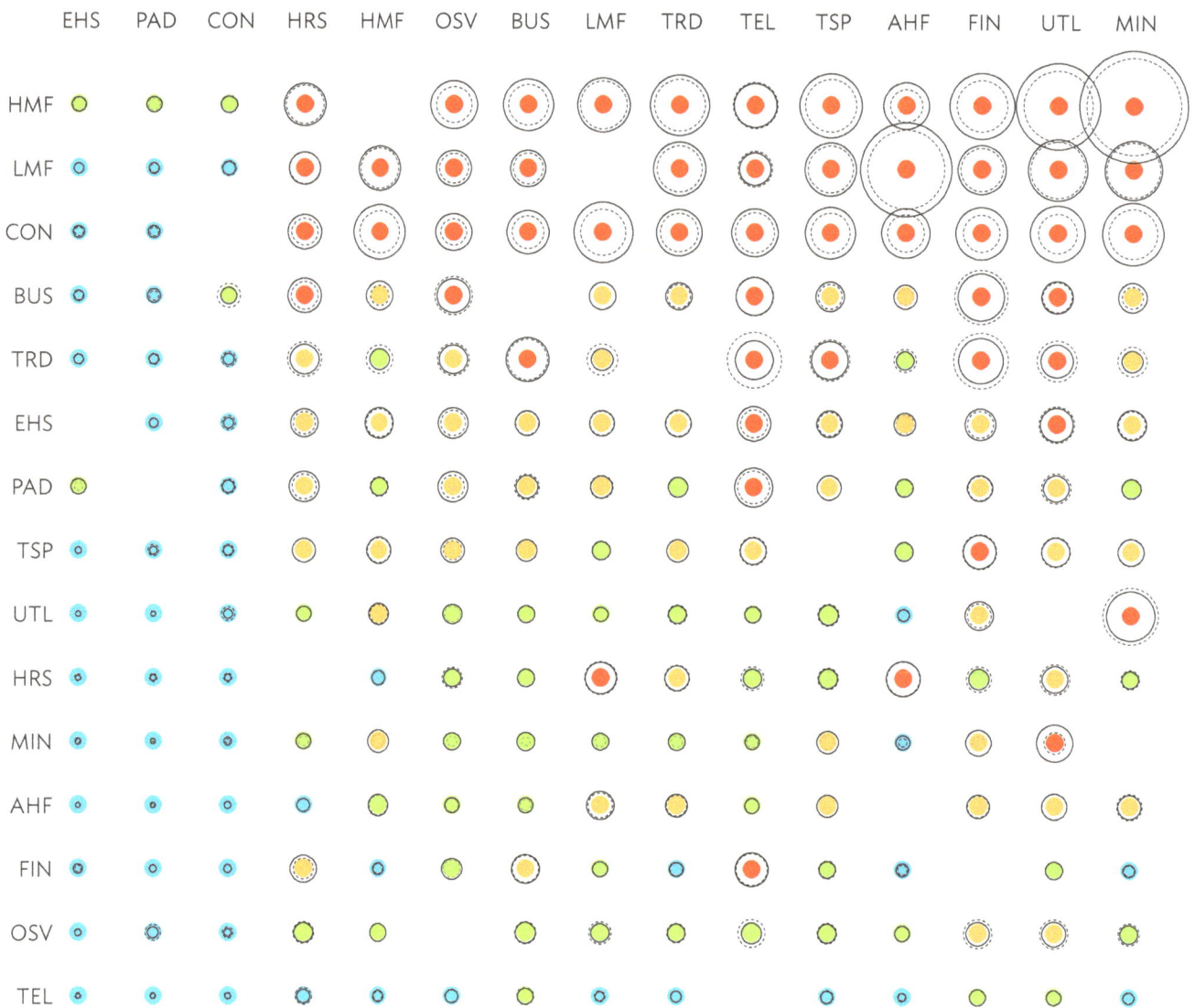

AHF = agriculture, hunting, forestry, and fishing; BUS = business services including real estate; CON = construction; EHS = education and health services; FIN = finance and insurance; HMF = heavy manufacturing; HRS = hotel and restaurant services; LMF = light manufacturing; MIN = mining and quarrying; OSV = other services; PAD = public administration; TEL = post and telecommunications; TRD = wholesale and retail trade; TSP = transport services; UTL = utilities.

Note: Rows represent "extracted" sectors, while columns represent affected sectors from this scenario. Orange dots represent percentage change in output in the first quartile; yellow in the second quartile; green in the third quartile; and blue in the fourth quartile. Rows indicate the sector that was extracted. while columns indicate the affected sectors from extraction exercise. Area of circles describe the magnitude of the impact in 2000 and 2018.

Source: Asian Development Bank. Multi-Regional Input–Output Tables (accessed July 2020).

This impacts of hypothetically inserting each sector in the regional economy is summarized in Figure 1.15. As in Figure 1.14, the column sectors represent affected (existing) sectors, while the row sectors in the rows represent the newly inserted sectors. Similar to the extraction process, the light and heavy manufacturing sectors induced the most intersectoral demand when added to the subregional economy. Particularly, the introduction of a heavy manufacturing sector would greatly affect mining, utilities, finance, and transport services. Light manufacturing industries, meanwhile, would mostly impact agriculture, mining, and utilities. New entrants in the telecommunications sector, albeit critical to the functioning of economies, were less likely to induce significant impacts than other sectors. If any, financial and business services sectors were most likely to benefit.

Figure 1.15: Impacts of the Hypothetical Insertion of New Sectors in Asia and the Pacific, 2018
(%)

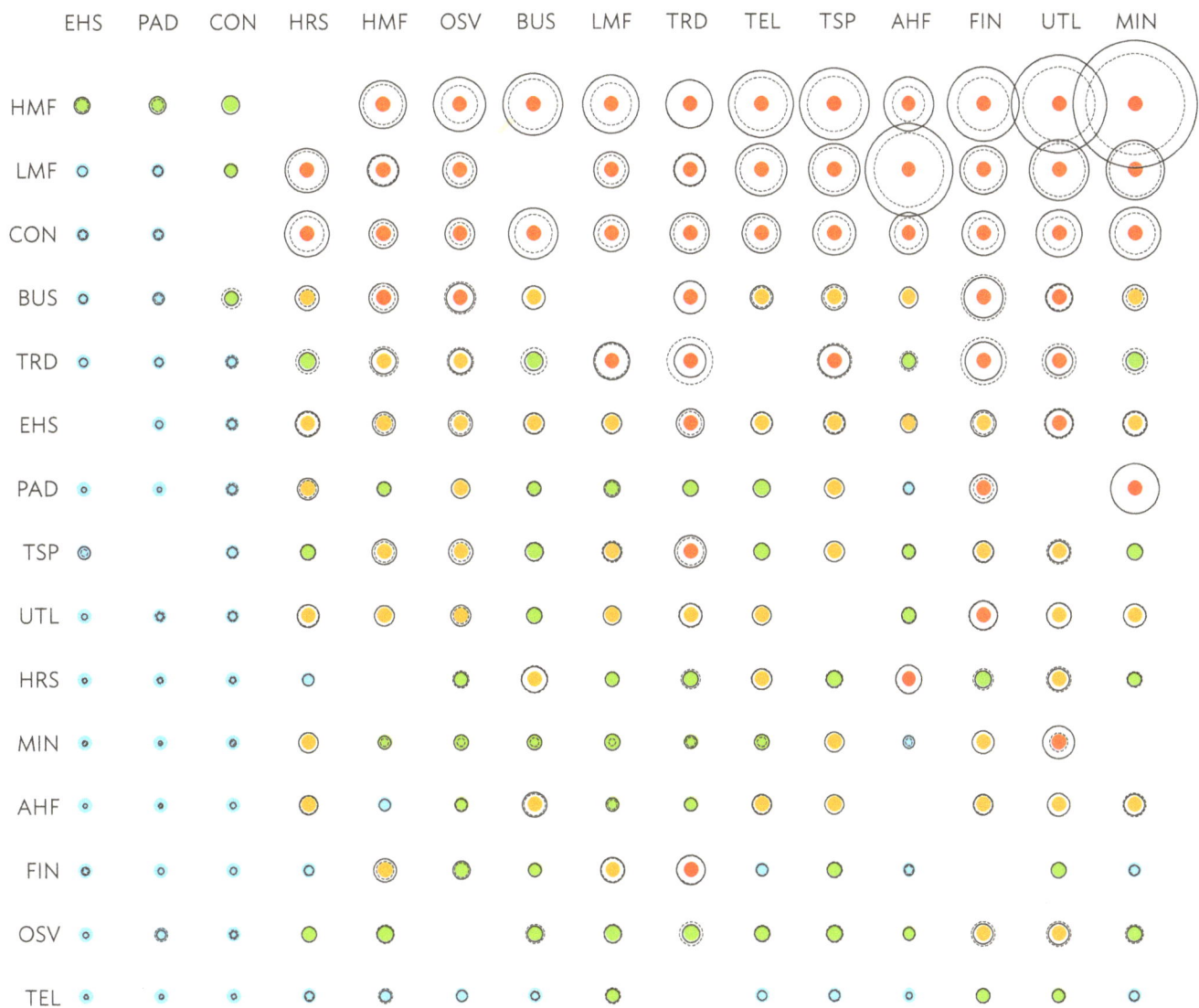

AHF = agriculture, hunting, forestry, and fishing; BUS = business services including real estate; CON = construction; EHS = education and health services; FIN = finance and insurance; HMF = heavy manufacturing; HRS = hotel and restaurant services; LMF = light manufacturing; MIN = mining and quarrying; OSV = other services; PAD = public administration; TEL = post and telecommunications; TRD = wholesale and retail trade; TSP = transport services; UTL = utilities.

Note: Rows represent "inserted" sectors, while columns represent affected sectors from this scenario. Orange dots represent percentage change in output in the first quartile; yellow in the second quartile; green in the third quartile; and blue in the fourth quartile. Rows indicate the sector that was inserted, while columns indicate the affected sectors from insertion exercise. Area of circles describe the magnitude of the impact in 2000 and 2018.

Source: Asian Development Bank. Multi-Regional Input–Output Tables (accessed July 2020).

1.7 Conclusion

The indicators and analyses in this part demonstrate the various applications of input–output data. They are intended to describe the characteristics of domestic economies across Asia and the Pacific and determine the underlying relationships among their various sectors. Since 2000, dynamic changes in the structure of economies have been observed—there has been a shift from commodity-based production to more industrial and service-oriented activities and a rise in demand led by private consumption and exports. There have also been changes in the complexities of production technologies within economies. In a closed input–output system, shifts in demand induce changes in the supply-side components of the economy and vice versa. The range of indicators present the different channels through which changes in one sector may reverberate throughout the economy. The key linkage analysis illustrated that, as much as sectors can have growth-inducing effects on other sectors, negative changes can have potentially damaging impacts on other sectors as well. Other results indicate that a manufacturing decision to connect with the services supply chain could be as stimulating to the system as a direct investment.[6]

The input–output analyses applied to the domestic economy in this part may be extended to the external economy. With globalization and the fragmentation of production processes across the world, domestic input–output linkages can no longer fully explain economic trends. Domestic sectors are now connected with foreign producers and purchasers, forming value chains that cross international borders. Evidently, the Asia and Pacific region is increasingly becoming export-oriented. Within this increasingly globalized context, examining the international linkages of an economy is as important as a localized consideration of the input–output relations within its domestic borders. This international perspective is the subject of the next part of this publication.

---

[6]   This type of analysis is accomplished through a structural decomposition of the economy as presented in Figure 1.6. For some economies in the region, intersectoral connections showed higher impacts than investment. Details can be found in Part 2.

Key Messages

- Input–output tables (IOTs) provide a comprehensive picture of an economy by detailing how different components interact with each other to generate economic output. Contemporary applications of IOTs cover both statistical and analytical uses.

- IOTs are used to describe the historical structures of economies, the interrelatedness of sectors, and the impacts of changes in production technologies. Data on economies of Asia and the Pacific underscore the importance of key manufacturing sectors, construction, and trade.

- Measures of economic complexity point to economies diversifying or increasing their range of inputs for production from 2000 to 2018. However, economies relying heavily on primary extractive sectors struggled to transform their economic structure.

- Aside from the composition of final demand, an economy's structure can also be described in terms of the complexity of production. The mix of inputs, and therefore the dependency on other sectors, shows that larger economies tend to have more complex production structures.

- A producer's dependence on other sectors' inputs characterizes the strength of interindustrial linkages in an economic system. These linkages are the channels through which changes ripple across sectors belonging to the same or a related production chain. Within the Asia and Pacific region, the light and heavy manufacturing sectors, as well as the utilities sector, have significant linkages to other sectors.

INTERNATIONAL LINKAGES

This part discusses the growing need for input–output analyses across economies and geographic regions of the world. It presents a series of indicators relevant for measuring cross-border production linkages using international input–output tables. The discussion on domestic linkages is extended to a multi-economy context, to examine the interconnections that give rise to spillovers. This includes analyzing the trade structure of an economy, exploring its dependency on imports and exports in contrast to domestic production. The degree to which economies participate in global value chains (GVCs) will be explored, along with novel approaches to decompose exports based on value-added contributions.

Input–output analyses have traditionally been applied on independent economy-specific input-output tables. While such analyses are important, globalization and the fragmentation of production processes across international borders necessitates the use of more comprehensive and internationally linked input–output tables. The heightened exchange of inputs from one economy for use in the production of another creates broader and increasingly complex trade and production patterns affected by both local and international changes in business operations and public policy. The expansion in intermediate flows is influenced by a myriad of factors, from technology, cost, and market access to trade policy.

While the exchange of inputs is as old as trade itself, statistical systems have long fallen short in properly accounting for intermediate trade. What is often captured is traditional trade that is entirely attributed to the final seller. These common measures do not say much about the extent to which the traded goods and services were actually created in the exporting economy, nor about what industries in which parts of the world contributed to their final value. Furthermore, they do not indicate whether imports were fully used in domestic consumption or employed as inputs by local industries for exports. As the exchange of goods and services becomes more incremental, the risk of double-counting increases, justifying the need for modern trade accounting practices.

Several statistical initiatives capture global interrelationships and value-added trade—most using combined information from economy-specific input–output tables and standard trade databases to construct international input–output tables. Examples of these include: the World Input–Output Database (WIOD) created by the University of Groningen, the Trade in Value-Added Database compiled by the Organization for Economic Cooperation and Development, and the Eora global supply chain database maintained by the University of Sydney. One of the most common applications of these databases is to trace the value-added contributions of each economy, sector, or economy-sector to the production of a particular final product, or to the overall global production.

In a globally integrated economy, each trade flow can be composed of both domestic value-added and foreign value-added. For example, the value of a car with imported steel from the PRC and electronic components from Germany, which is finally assembled in Viet Nam for export to Australia, cannot be solely attributed to the exporting economy (Viet Nam) since multiple economies contributed to the final value of the product. As economies' value-added accumulates in subsequent trade flows, bilateral trade becomes a multilateral activity, creating implications for measuring the balance of trade.

International input–output tables detail the domestic and foreign inputs necessary for production, and trace the respective sources and destinations of their value-added.

2.1 Multi-Regional Input–Output Tables

A multi-economy or multi-regional input–output framework and the resulting multi-regional input–output tables (MRIOTs) are extensions of the economy-specific input-output framework and tables described in Part 1. In an MRIOT, each product is produced either by a domestic or foreign sector (Table 2.1). In a simplified schematic, economy *1*'s intermediate and final uses of products are split into domestically produced or imported commodities or services from economies *2* to *G*. The product's origin is further traced back to its producing industry, so that both the domestic and international flows of goods and services are combined in a comprehensive and integrated view of the global economy. The result is a rich database explicitly documenting links between economy-sectors.

Table 2.1: Simplified Multi-Regional Input-Output Table

		Intermediate Uses				Final Uses				Gross Outputs
		Economy 1	Economy 2	...	Economy G	1	2	...	G	
Intermediate Inputs	1	Z_{11}	Z_{12}	...	Z_{1G}	f_{11}	f_{12}	...	f_{1G}	x_1
	2	Z_{21}	Z_{22}	...	Z_{2G}	f_{21}	f_{22}	...	f_{2G}	x_2
	...	...	...	...	...	...	...	...	...	...
	G	Z_{G1}	Z_{G2}	...	Z_{GG}	f_{G1}	f_{G2}	...	f_{GG}	x_G
Value-Added		v_1'	v_2'	...	v_G'					
Total Inputs		x_1	x_2	...	x_G					

Note: Z_{ij} is the intermediate inputs used by economy *j* from economy *i*; f_{ij} is the final goods consumed by economy *j* from economy *i*; v_j is the value-added of economy *j*; and x_j is the output of economy *j*.

Source: R. Miller and P. Blair. 2009. *Input Output Analysis: Foundations and Extensions*. Cambridge: Cambridge University Press.

The granularity and range of detail in these tables is a result of merging, harmonizing, and balancing data from several sources, such as national accounts, economy-specific supply-use and input–output tables, and international trade statistics. Often, national accounts are limited and additional work is required in compiling the national statistics needed for MRIOTs.

Since 2008, ADB has been maintaining MRIOTs and providing technical assistance to its member economies, promoting various statistical initiatives related to input–output accounting. An initial project resulted in the completion of 19 benchmark supply-use tables. These, together with the extant WIOD, served as the building blocks for the first set of ADB MRIOTs. Specifically, the WIOD, which then contained data on input–output transactions for 42 economies, was augmented using the 19 supply-use tables to cover the Asia and the Pacific region more broadly. ADB continues to build on the multi-regional input–output database, adding more economies and updating for recent years. Currently, the database has tables covering 63 economies for 13 years (i.e., 2000 and 2007–2018). The values in the MRIOTs may differ from official statistics, as some harmonization and transformation procedures were implemented on source data.[7]

The uses of MRIOTs, while diverse, are frequently applied in the analysis of international trade flows. General trends in international trade activity among economies in the region are summarized in Figure 2.1. Total trade in the Asia and Pacific region has grown significantly from 2000 levels, despite some temporary dips during periods of economic slowdown, such as the global financial crisis (GFC) in 2008 and other localized contractions in 2015 and 2016. From 2000 to 2018, the region's exports grew at an annual average rate of 6.3%, while imports increased at an annual average rate of 6.9%. Accordingly, growth rates of trade fluctuated with production. In the last 2 years observed, 2017 and 2018, the level of trade rose, but its growth remained below the rates recorded prior to the 2008 crisis.

Using input–output analysis, imports and exports are disaggregated into domestic and foreign components or factor content (Figure 2.1). For Asia and the Pacific, foreign intermediates represented more than two-thirds (or 72%) of the total imports into the

Figure 2.1:   Total Imports and Exports in Asia and the Pacific, 2000–2018 ($ billion)

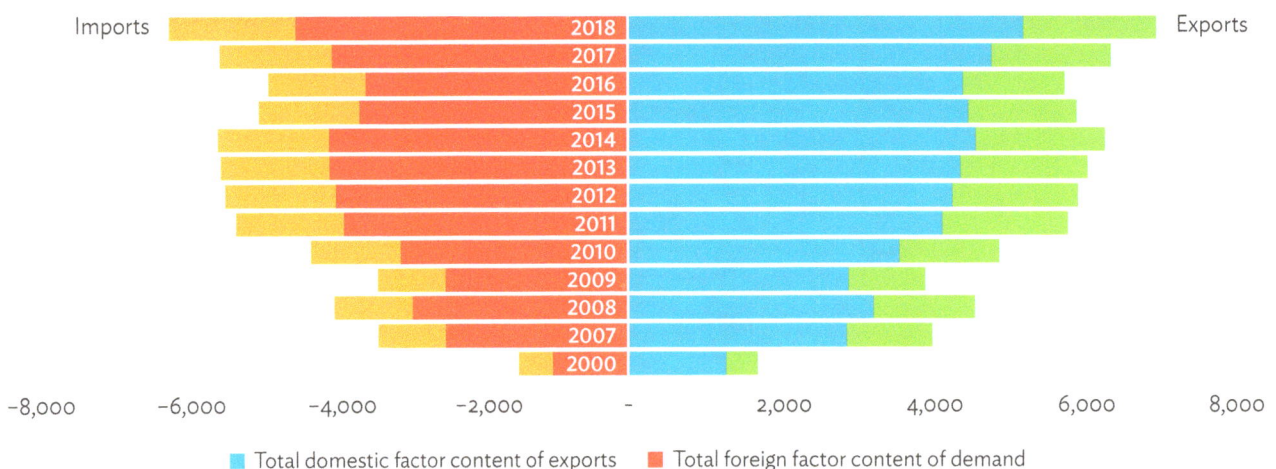

Note: "Total domestic factor content of exports" is the amount of domestic gross value-added in the economy that is attributable to foreign demand, while "total foreign factor content of demand" is the amount of foreign intermediates attributable to local demand.

Source: Asian Development Bank. Multi-Regional Input–Output Tables (accessed July 2020).

---

[7]   These procedures generally follow the construction of the World Input–output Database (Timmer et al. 2012). Details on the compilation of the 19 supply-use tables for Asia and the Pacific can be found in ADB (2017).

region from 2000 to 2018.[8] This proportion has been growing since the 1990s, peaking in the early 2000s. The region's exports, on the other hand, were primarily composed of domestic factor content or economic contributions from domestic sectors, accounting for an average of 73% of total exports from 2000 to 2018. These ratios highlight the consistently strong involvement of domestic sectors in export production, as well as the increasing role of imports in production.

The region's dependence on imports for production, as well as the contributions of its exports to value chains, places its economies in a unique and influential position within the global production and trading network. On average, international trade activity in 2018 was 85% of gross domestic product in the region. This openness to trade, however, differed widely across individual economies, depending on their respective degrees of specialization. Figure 2.2 summarizes these varying degrees of trade openness from 2000 to 2018, with

	2000	2007	2008	2009	2010	2011	2012	2013	2014	2015	2016	2017	2018
SIN	2.19	2.32	2.46	2.02	2.15	2.42	2.29	2.23	2.23	2.08	1.98	2.18	2.24
MLD	1.50	1.61	1.48	1.76	1.38	1.74	1.49	1.50	1.59	1.49	1.50	1.44	1.44
MAL	2.17	1.90	1.74	1.61	1.57	1.53	1.46	1.41	1.42	1.32	1.27	1.34	1.29
VIE	1.00	1.02	1.05	1.07	1.19	1.25	1.21	1.27	1.31	1.37	1.41	1.53	1.51
TAP	0.98	1.28	1.31	1.09	1.30	1.34	1.30	1.26	1.27	1.13	1.11	1.17	1.23
KGZ	0.81	1.07	1.35	1.03	1.30	1.15	1.32	1.35	1.23	1.07	1.11	1.03	1.05
HKG	0.93	1.11	1.17	1.11	1.23	1.31	1.29	1.25	1.22	1.12	1.12	1.15	1.15
CAM	0.80	0.96	0.87	0.77	0.81	0.77	0.83	0.89	0.95	0.94	0.94	0.94	0.94
MON	0.94	0.99	1.00	0.99	0.93	1.15	0.96	0.87	0.95	0.80	0.83	1.02	1.07
THA	0.90	0.97	1.05	0.93	0.94	1.03	1.00	0.97	0.95	0.90	0.84	0.91	0.91
FIJ	1.02	0.88	0.91	1.27	0.91	0.94	0.95	0.94	0.94	0.85	0.81	0.95	1.05
BRU	0.74	0.87	0.85	0.94	0.89	0.89	0.92	0.94	0.92	0.85	0.87	0.85	0.94
KOR	0.63	0.69	0.91	0.88	0.88	1.02	1.02	0.96	0.90	0.88	0.82	0.82	0.83
BHU	0.53	0.87	0.94	0.92	0.95	0.94	0.86	1.00	0.80	0.94	0.89	0.79	0.79
LAO	0.70	0.45	0.45	0.44	0.48	0.68	0.67	0.75	0.73	0.78	0.72	0.76	0.72
KAZ	0.95	0.92	0.91	0.76	0.74	0.78	0.78	0.67	0.62	0.53	0.59	0.59	0.59
INO	0.68	0.53	0.57	0.45	0.46	0.50	0.49	0.48	0.48	0.42	0.38	0.40	0.43
PHI	0.57	0.87	0.76	0.53	0.54	0.50	0.49	0.47	0.48	0.49	0.51	0.56	0.59
BAN	0.29	0.40	0.43	0.40	0.38	0.47	0.48	0.46	0.45	0.42	0.38	0.35	0.37
SRI	0.69	0.49	0.46	0.54	0.44	0.44	0.44	0.42	0.43	0.43	0.43	0.41	0.42
NEP	0.45	0.37	0.39	0.45	0.40	0.34	0.36	0.40	0.42	0.43	0.39	0.46	0.51
PRC	0.40	0.64	0.58	0.46	0.52	0.51	0.47	0.44	0.42	0.36	0.34	0.35	0.35
JPN	0.20	0.33	0.34	0.25	0.29	0.30	0.31	0.34	0.39	0.36	0.31	0.35	0.37
IND	0.26	0.42	0.41	0.36	0.39	0.40	0.40	0.38	0.35	0.30	0.29	0.29	0.29
PAK	0.26	0.30	0.33	0.37	0.30	0.32	0.30	0.31	0.31	0.31	0.28	0.26	0.29

BAN = Bangladesh; BHU = Bhutan; BRU = Brunei Darussalam; CAM = Cambodia; FIJ = Fiji; HKG = Hong Kong, China; IND = India; INO = Indonesia; JPN = Japan; KAZ = Kazakhstan; KGZ = Kyrgyz Republic; KOR = Republic of Korea; LAO = Lao People's Democratic Republic; MAL = Malaysia; MLD = Maldives; MON = Mongolia; NEP = Nepal; PAK = Pakistan; PHI = Philippines; PRC = People's Republic of China; SIN = Singapore; SRI = Sri Lanka; TAP = Taipei,China; THA = Thailand; VIE = Viet Nam.

Note: Darker shades of blue indicate higher degrees of trade openness, while darker shades of red-orange indicate lower degrees of trade openness.

Source: Asian Development Bank. Multi-Regional Input–Output Tables (accessed July 2020).

---

8   A refinement of this measure is presented in relation to vertical specialization.

cells in darker shades of blue implying higher degrees of trade openness, while cells in darker shades of red-orange imply lower degrees. Small island states, such as Singapore and Maldives, were more open to trade than their peers in the region. Conversely, large economies with sizable domestic markets and productive capacities, such as Japan and the PRC, were less open to trade. Among the subregions, economies in Southeast Asia and the Pacific had higher-than-average degrees of trade openness.

Trade openness also appears to be affected by global shocks, as evidenced by the decline in values during the initial years following the GFC and the trade collapse in 2015–2016. After these periods of contraction, the Asia and Pacific region rebounded, but not to the overall degree of openness that was evident prior to the GFC. While openness to trade increases exposure to external volatilities, integration into the global economy also improves access to markets, which can be leveraged to manage internal or economy-specific risks and capabilities. In the case of Maldives—where there is a limited domestic market for goods and services, scarcity in arable land, and a relatively weak manufacturing base—tourism and fish exports have been the two most significant sources of growth.

Openness to international trade is important from both demand and supply perspectives. While some economy-sectors rely crucially on imported goods as inputs, others depend on exports to international markets to sustain demand. Figure 2.3 presents the average export and import orientation of economies, through the export–gross output and import–total input ratios, respectively, for 2000 and 2018. Singapore had the highest export concentration in 2018, while Nepal ranked lowest in the region. Singapore likewise had the highest dependency on imports for inputs, while the PRC had the lowest dependence. Viet Nam and Malaysia notably had higher import and export ratios, implying a greater dependence on the external economy in general. Accordingly, Brunei Darussalam and Kazakhstan, both being major suppliers of energy commodities to the world market, had relatively high export–output ratios but rather low import–input ratios.

An economy's degree of dependence on external linkages can be conversely viewed as its degree of self-sufficiency. Self-sufficiency can be measured as the proportion of domestic output to domestic demand, which includes both intermediate consumption by industries and final demand by households, government, and investment. The resulting ratios are used to evaluate the capacities of economies to supply their own needs. The ratios for economies of Asia and the Pacific are displayed in Figure 2.4. Several economies from East and Southeast Asia had values greater than 1 (blue bars), implying that their production levels are more than enough to cover their respective domestic demand levels—i.e., they are highly self-sufficient. Upstream energy suppliers, such as Brunei Darussalam and Kazakhstan, had particularly high self-sufficiency ratios likely stemming from their very wide resource bases, especially relative to their small domestic markets. Economies with self-sufficiency ratios less than 1 (red bars) are often those with large consumer markets but highly specialized domestic production and, to address these supply gaps, they turn to imports of final goods and services.

Though informative, the domestic output–domestic demand ratio does not provide a complete picture of an economy's self-sufficiency. Though a high ratio value implies that a particular economy's production is enough to cover the value of its demand, so that its income is sufficient for its needs, the ratio value says nothing of an economy's product-level self-sufficiency. As economies specialize in certain types of production,

Figure 2.3: Export–Output Ratios and Import–input Ratios in Asia and the Pacific, 2000 and 2018 (%)

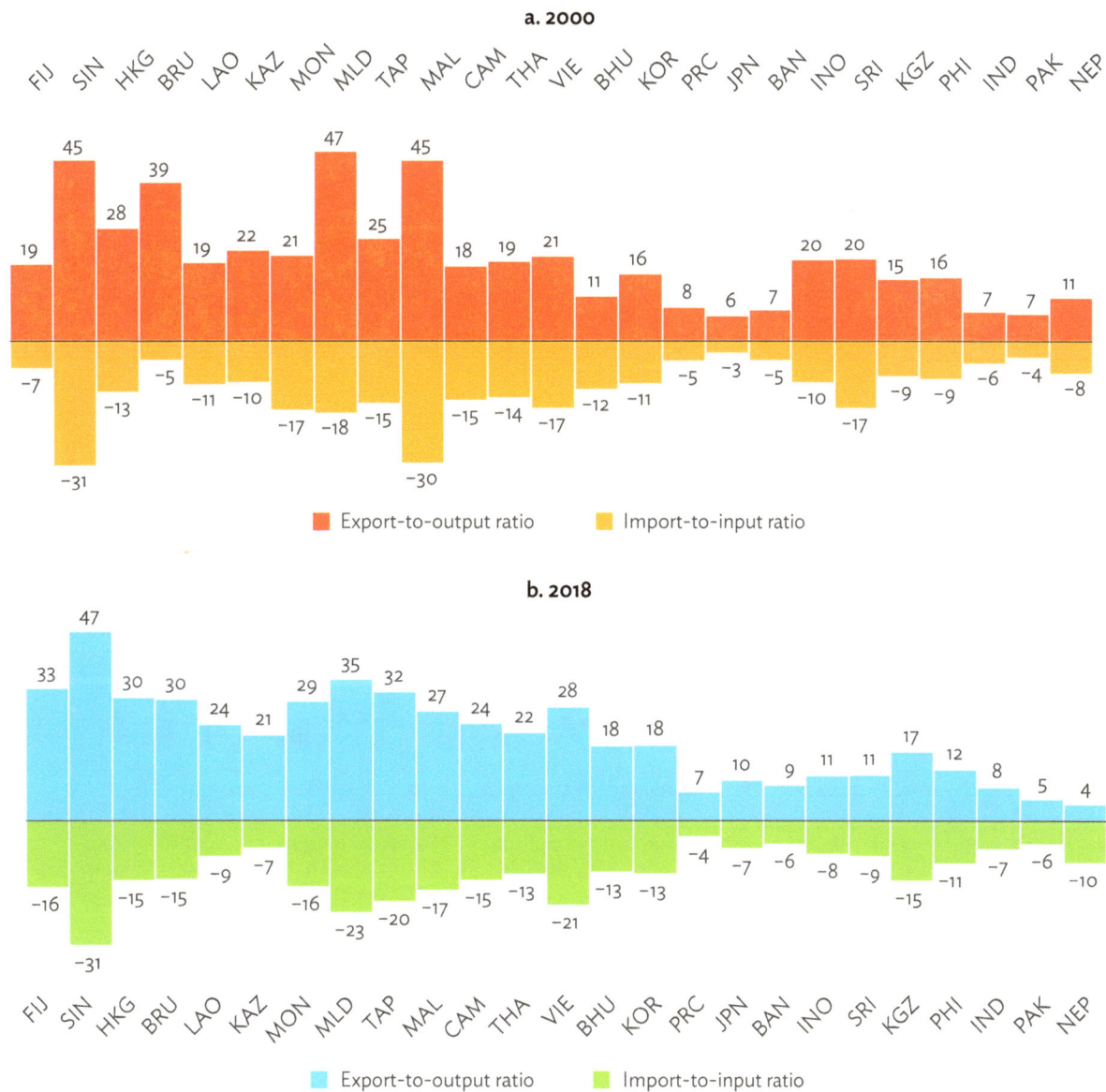

a. 2000

Export-to-output ratio   Import-to-input ratio

b. 2018

Export-to-output ratio   Import-to-input ratio

BAN = Bangladesh; BHU = Bhutan; BRU = Brunei Darussalam; CAM = Cambodia; FIJ = Fiji; HKG = Hong Kong, China; IND = India; INO = Indonesia; JPN = Japan; KAZ = Kazakhstan; KGZ = Kyrgyz Republic; KOR = Republic of Korea; LAO = Lao People's Democratic Republic; MAL = Malaysia; MLD = Maldives; MON = Mongolia; NEP = Nepal; PAK = Pakistan; PHI = Philippines; PRC = People's Republic of China; SIN = Singapore; SRI = Sri Lanka; TAP = Taipei,China; THA = Thailand; VIE = Viet Nam.

Source: Asian Development Bank. Multi-Regional Input–Output Tables (accessed July 2020).

Figure 2.4: Self-Sufficiency Ratios in Asia and the Pacific, 2018

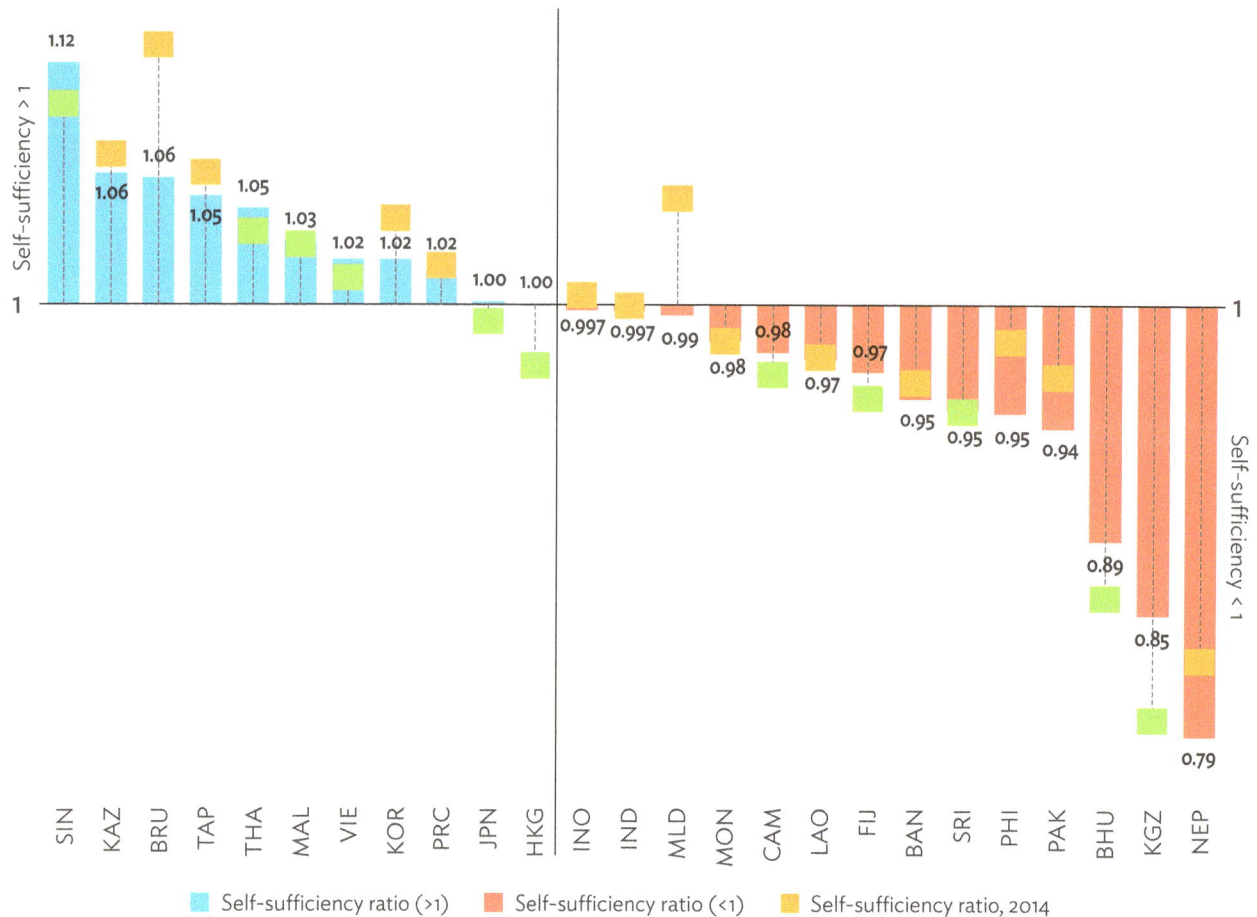

BAN = Bangladesh; BHU = Bhutan; BRU = Brunei Darussalam; CAM = Cambodia; FIJ = Fiji; HKG = Hong Kong, China; IND = India; INO = Indonesia; JPN = Japan; KAZ = Kazakhstan; KGZ = Kyrgyz Republic; KOR = Republic of Korea; LAO = Lao People's Democratic Republic; MAL = Malaysia; MLD = Maldives; MON = Mongolia; NEP = Nepal; PAK = Pakistan; PHI = Philippines; PRC = People's Republic of China; SIN = Singapore; SRI = Sri Lanka; TAP = Taipei,China; THA = Thailand; VIE = Viet Nam.

Source: Asian Development Bank. Multi-Regional Input–Output Tables (accessed July 2020).

the variety of products demanded in the local economy may not be satisfied by what is available locally. However, the increased income from specialization and extensive exports enables economies to import products that are demanded but otherwise unavailable in their domestic markets. Resource-rich but highly specialized economies—Singapore, Brunei Darussalam, and Kazakhstan, for example—use their foreign exchange earnings from oil commodities to purchase imported products and satisfy domestic demand. The indicator is therefore useful in determining whether supply and demand gaps exist in an economy and, by extension, how imports could be crucial in meeting those demands, but it does not capture exactly where the gaps exist and what imports are most necessary to bridge them.

As GVCs developed, international trade increasingly involved intermediate rather than final products. The amount of intermediate trade reflected not only sourcing decisions, but also the production technologies related to specific types of output. With improvements in information and communication technologies, transport and logistics services, and automation, the cost of importing commodities fell relative to the costs of producing them domestically. Many firms were therefore incentivized to source components from foreign counterparts, leading to increased trade flows among economies. These international flows of intermediate goods and services represent direct links between the production of two economies in a multi-regional input–output model.

Before looking into the role of imports, a first-order assessment of the relative levels of input dependence by industry is given in Figure 2.5. The fabrication effect is an indicator often used in regional science to measure the intensity of the input use of a sector in a specific region relative to the input use of the same sector in the entire economy. In the context of this report, the measure is applied to the intensity of input use in a particular sector of each economy relative to the intensity of input use in the same sectors across all economies in the world. A measure of 1 indicates equality in intensity of input use

Figure 2.5: Fabrication Effects in Asia and the Pacific, 2000 versus 2018

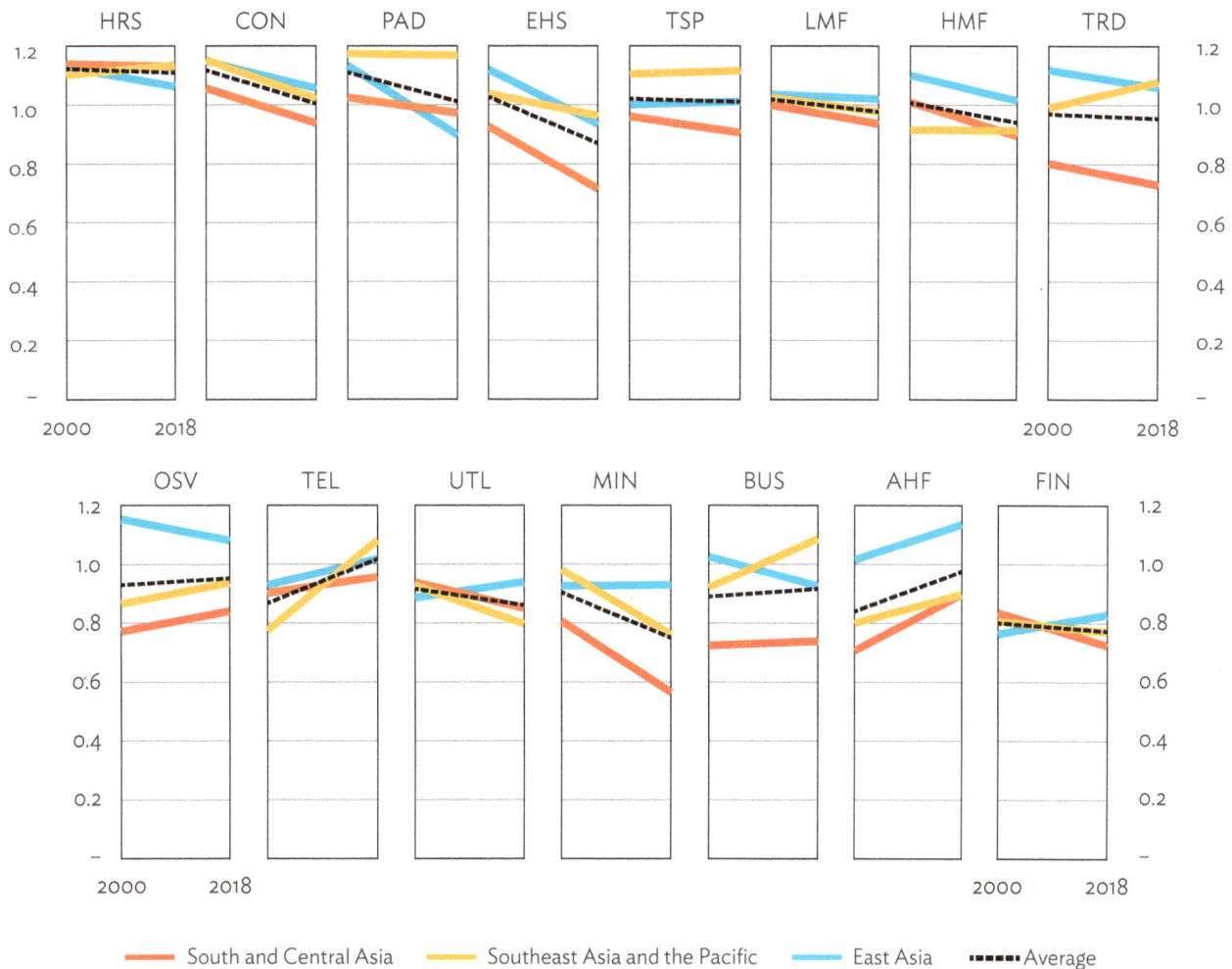

AHF = agriculture, hunting, forestry, and fishing; BUS = business services including real estate; CON = construction; EHS = education and health services; FIN = finance and insurance; HMF = heavy manufacturing; HRS = hotel and restaurant services; LMF = light manufacturing; MIN = mining and quarrying; OSV = other services; PAD = public administration; TEL = post and telecommunications; TRD = wholesale and retail trade; TSP = transport services; UTL = utilities.

Source: Asian Development Bank. Multi-Regional Input–Output Tables (accessed July 2020).

between the economy and the world, i.e., the degree of input use of the economy-sector is the same as the world-sector. A measure exceeding 1 indicates that, for a given sector, the economy uses more inputs per unit of output than the average for other economies of the world. A measure below 1 implies that, for a particular sector, the economy is, on average, less input-dependent than other economies.

Sectors in Asia and the Pacific exhibited nearly the same level of input dependence as the rest of the world in 2018. Relative input dependence was generally higher for hotels and restaurants and construction, but lower for several other sectors, most notably finance. There was also a general decline in input dependence across multiple sectors from 2000 to 2018, probably brought about by efficiencies in production processes and innovations in technology—simply, economies are able to produce more with less. This is consistent with the increasing share of value-added in the overall revenue structure of these sectors. The telecommunications and agriculture sectors were an exception, as the share of their interindustry inputs rose relative to their outputs over the review period.

Using data from MRIOTs, interindustrial inputs are broken down according to their source in Figure 2.6. Economies of the Asia and Pacific region generally leaned toward domestic producers as primary sources of intermediates—this was especially true for larger and more mature economies with relatively high domestic input shares. Meanwhile, small open economies and those that rely heavily on natural resources had shares of foreign inputs that were higher than the regional average.

The decision to source inputs from foreign counterparts depends on several factors, such as minimizing costs, securing supplies tailored to specific production technologies, and improving quality. Within the input–output framework, the flows of foreign inputs are framed as "leakage effects" caused by evolving domestic production requirements. Leakage effects, sometimes called "import multipliers", suggest that, since economies use foreign inputs in their production processes, the gains from production do not accrue entirely to the domestic economy and, in reality, partially "leak" into other economies. By involving foreign counterparts in the production process (specifically through imports of their goods and services), demand and income are split between the domestic economy and foreign economies.

The degree to which a foreign supplier benefits from another economy's domestic demand depends on its involvement in the value chain. Given the disaggregated presentation of intermediate flows in the MRIOTs, a sector's exposure to foreign inputs can easily be quantified. Then, the Leontief insight can further be applied to capture second-degree linkages and so forth.

Figure 2.6: Share of Foreign and Domestic Inputs by Economy, 2018

(% of gross output)

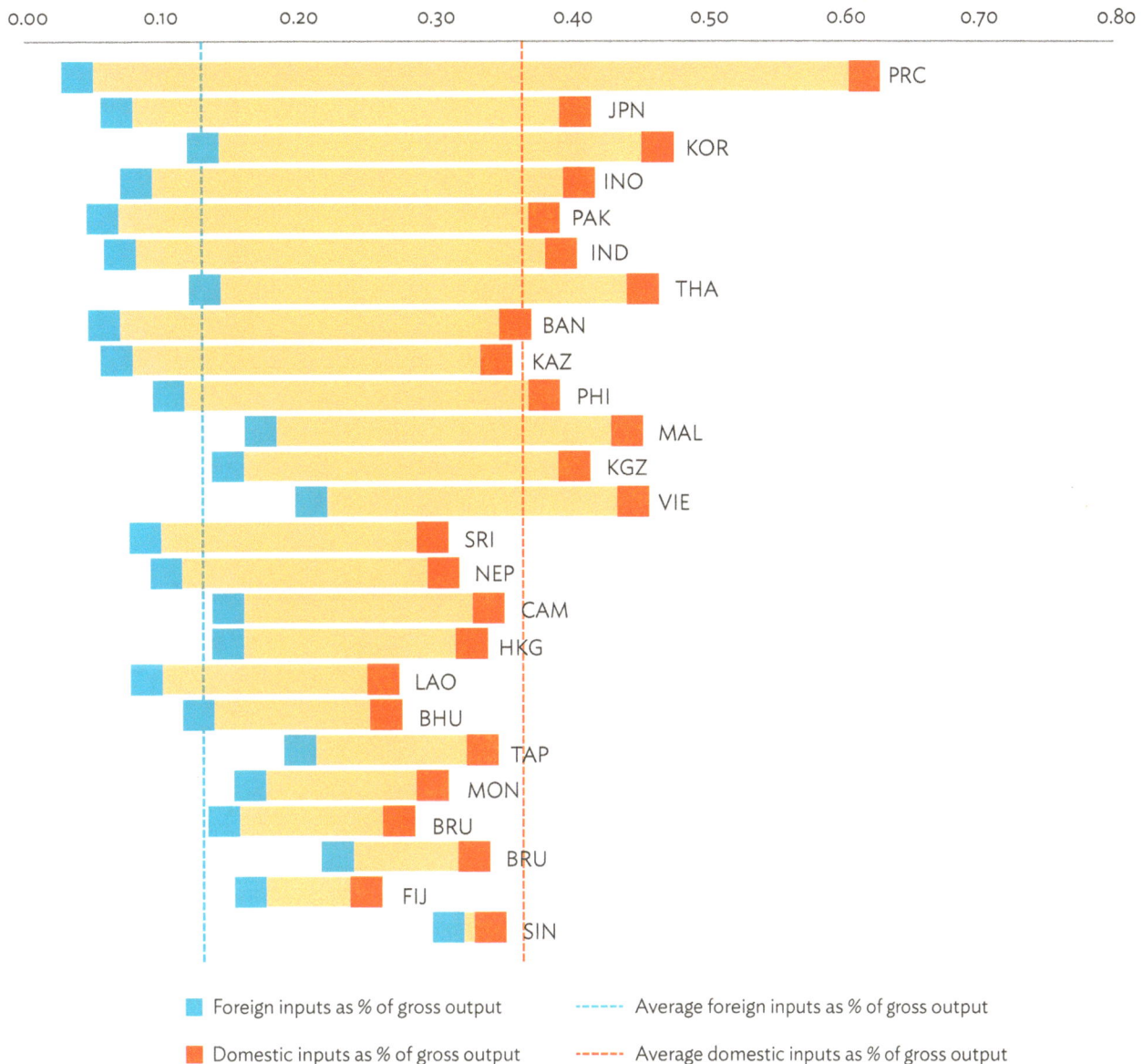

BAN = Bangladesh; BHU = Bhutan; BRU = Brunei Darussalam; CAM = Cambodia; FIJ = Fiji; HKG = Hong Kong, China; IND = India;
INO = Indonesia; JPN = Japan; KAZ = Kazakhstan; KGZ = Kyrgyz Republic; KOR = Republic of Korea; LAO = Lao People's Democratic Republic;
MAL = Malaysia; MLD = Maldives; MON = Mongolia; NEP = Nepal; PAK = Pakistan; PHI = Philippines; PRC = People's Republic of China;
SIN = Singapore; SRI = Sri Lanka; TAP = Taipei,China; THA = Thailand; VIE = Viet Nam.

Source: Asian Development Bank. Multi-Regional Input–Output Tables (accessed July 2020).

The distribution of import leakage effects in the Asia and Pacific region are shown by sector for 2000 and 2018 in Figure 2.7. Industrial sectors in the region, including services sectors related to travel and mobility, generally exhibited high import leakage effects. This is especially true for economies such as Viet Nam and Malaysia, which have manufacturing activities requiring complex and diverse inputs that can only be satisfied by economies entrenched and specialized in the production of those inputs. Primary or resource-based sectors were in the median range, which is expected of upstream industries. Meanwhile, the public and private services sector remained at the low end of the distribution, alongside supporting or intermediary services. Overall, from 2000 to 2018, average import leakages increased as imports became a more important and reliable source of productive inputs.

While leakage effects describe the impacts that local economy-sectors can have on foreign counterparts, the impact of foreign demand to local production can likewise be measured. A decomposition of multipliers in the multi-regional input–output model distinguishes three major components of an output effect: the impact of domestic demand on domestic sectors (M1), the impact of foreign demand on domestic sectors (M2), and the interaction of domestic and foreign demand on domestic sectors (M3). The sum of final demand and these three components is equal to the output produced by an economy-sector.

M2 and M3 capture the "spillover effects" of the rest of the world to the domestic economy, as they quantify the pull of foreign demand on domestic production. Figure 2.8 plots the share of international spillover effects against domestic transfer effects for all sectors in the regional economy. The clustering of observations in the lower part of the graph implies that the output of most economy-sectors in the region was more heavily influenced by domestic linkages rather than external spillover effects. This pattern remained consistent from 2000 to 2018. Despite the general observation, spillover effects varied at the economy-sector level as external linkages depended on their respective productive structures, capabilities, and comparative advantages. In more open economies, such as Singapore and Maldives, as exports comprised a greater proportion of domestic output, domestic demand was driven more by spillover effects. Notably, economy-sectors that exhibited higher spillover effects belonged to open economies specializing in the export of manufactured goods, including mining and energy-related products.

Overall, the results suggest that many economies are turning inwards over time, with domestic consumption becoming the most consequential for output. This is more pronounced in larger and more mature economies, such as the PRC—a potential explanation for stagnating trade since 2015. The slowdown in Asia's major trading economies, and their increasingly domestic-oriented or inward-looking approach to sourcing and production, affected their trading partners and, in addition, third-party economies linked to the value chain. Structural changes in the PRC as it moves upstream and the United States' expansion of its energy sector have both impacted individual economies and the overall growth of GVCs (World Bank 2020). The degree of these impacts depends on the positions of each economy-sector and their respective trading partners within GVCs.

Figure 2.7: Import Leakage Effects as a Share of Final Demand in Asia and the Pacific, 2000 and 2018 ($ million)

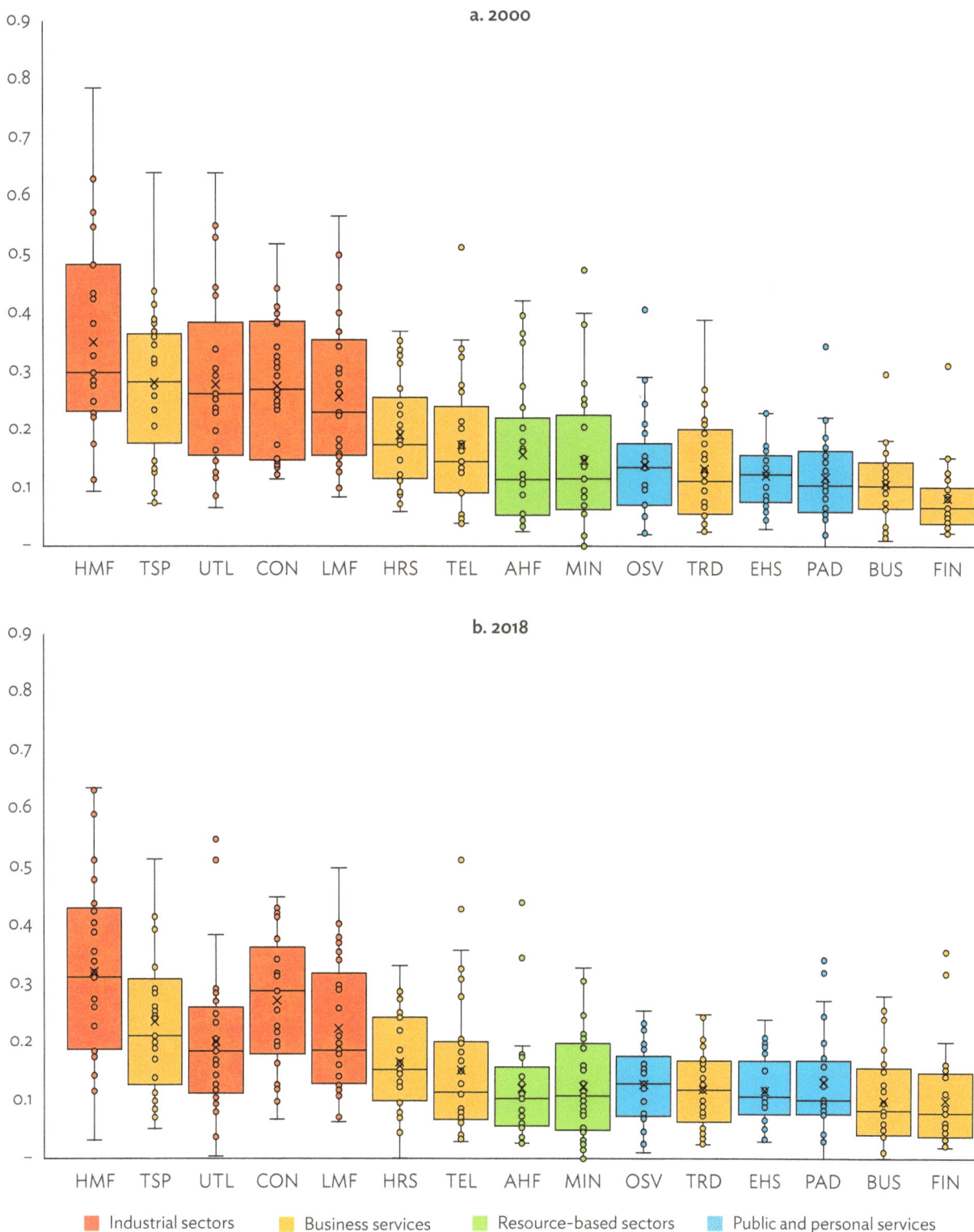

AHF = agriculture, hunting, forestry, and fishing; BUS = business services including real estate; CON = construction; EHS = education and health services; FIN = finance and insurance; HMF = heavy manufacturing; HRS = hotel and restaurant services; LMF = light manufacturing; MIN = mining and quarrying; OSV = other services; PAD = public administration; TEL = post and telecommunications; TRD = wholesale and retail trade; TSP = transport services; UTL = utilities.

Source: Asian Development Bank. Multi-Regional Input–Output Tables (accessed July 2020).

Figure 2.8: Domestic Transfer Effects and International Spillover Effects in Asia and the Pacific, 2000 and 2018 (% of sectoral output)

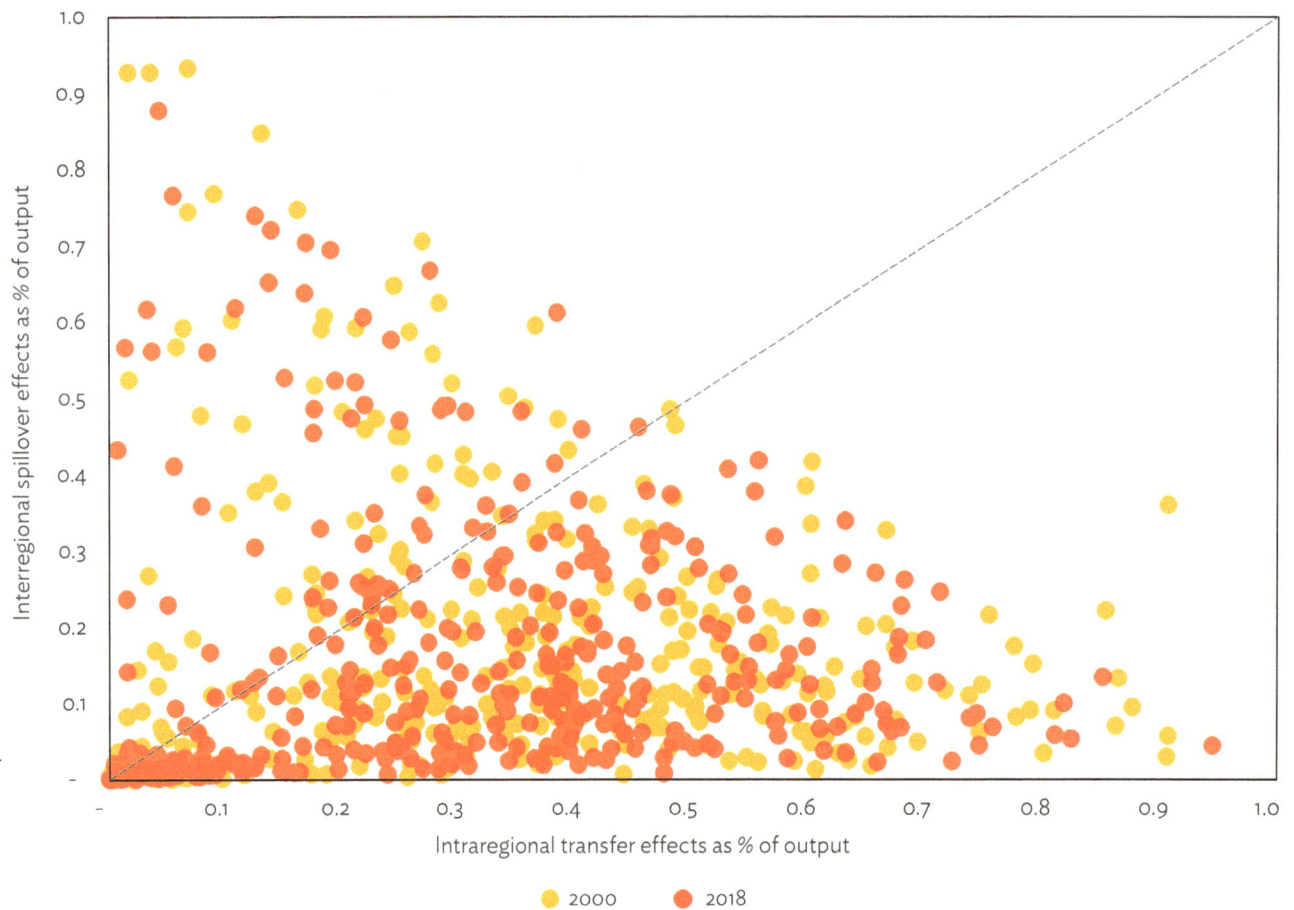

Note: Each dot represents an economy-sector value of transfer and spillover effects expressed as a percentage share of its corresponding total gross output.

Source: Asian Development Bank. Multi-Regional Input–Output Tables (accessed July 2020).

2.2 Measuring Global Value Chains

Since the 1990s, the fragmentation of production processes across domestic borders has pervaded the global economy. When the English economist David Ricardo was formulating his theory of comparative advantage in the nineteenth century, he had in mind Portuguese wine being exchanged for English cloth. This, however, has given way to more complex arrangements where Japanese electronics may be assembled in Chinese factories using American blueprints, before ultimately being purchased by consumers across the globe. The value chain connecting primary inputs to final consumption has become globalized, with far-reaching consequences for consumers, producers, and policymakers (Timmer et al. 2014).

Input–output tables are uniquely capable of analyzing this phenomenon. This section presents input–output indicators that summarize information on the extent and nature of GVCs.

To what extent does a sector participate in GVCs? Wang et al. (2017b) devised a measure that expresses GVC activity as a fraction of a given sector's total economic activity. Because value chains can be approached from either a downstream or an upstream perspective (i.e., from primary inputs to final consumption or vice versa), GVC participation can also be measured in two ways.

Under the first approach, one can start from the beginning of the chain and decompose where its value-added is ultimately absorbed. Take, for example, the sector "textiles and textile products" in Bangladesh. Some of its value-added is consumed either as final goods by Bangladeshi consumers or as intermediate goods by Bangladeshi firms, who use them to produce final goods that are then consumed by Bangladeshi consumers. This portion of value-added is, in short, absorbed domestically, and we label it V_D. Some value-added is also exported abroad as final goods that are consumed by foreigners. This portion is what we call "traditional" trade, and we label it V_F. Finally, some value-added is exported as intermediate goods that are used by foreign firms to produce either final goods or more intermediate goods, which then in turn travel further along the value chain. This last portion is what we call GVC activity, and we label it V_{GVC}. In summary, we have the identity

$$\text{VA} = V_D + V_F + V_{GVC}$$

The ratio V_{GVC}/VA is the forward-based GVC participation index (GVC_F). It is the fraction of a sector's value-added that passes through GVC activities, before arriving at the terminus of the final consumer.

The second approach to measuring GVC participation starts from the end of the chain and decomposes where its final product originated from. There are again three portions, each analogous to that in the first approach: a portion of final product comes from domestic value-added (Y_D), a portion comes from imports of final goods (Y_F), and a portion comes from processes involved in GVCs (Y_{GVC}). From the identity

$$Y = Y_D + Y_F + Y_{GVC}$$

we get the ratio Y_{GVC}/Y. This is the backward-based GVC participation index (GVC_B), which measures the fraction of a sector's final consumption that passed through GVC activities.

These two measures, GVC_F and GVC_B, are similar but not equivalent. As seen in Figure 2.9, some sectors, such as electricals, scored high on both counts for 2018, while others, such as real estate, scored low on both. Other sectors, however, scored high in one but not the other. For example, mining and quarrying, which includes in its products the supremely important intermediate good of crude oil, had a far higher forward-based GVC participation index, reflecting its upstream position in GVCs. Others, such as construction, had a higher backward-based index, suggesting their more downstream position in value chains.

Figure 2.9: Global Value Chain Participation by Sector, 2000 and 2018
(World Average, %)

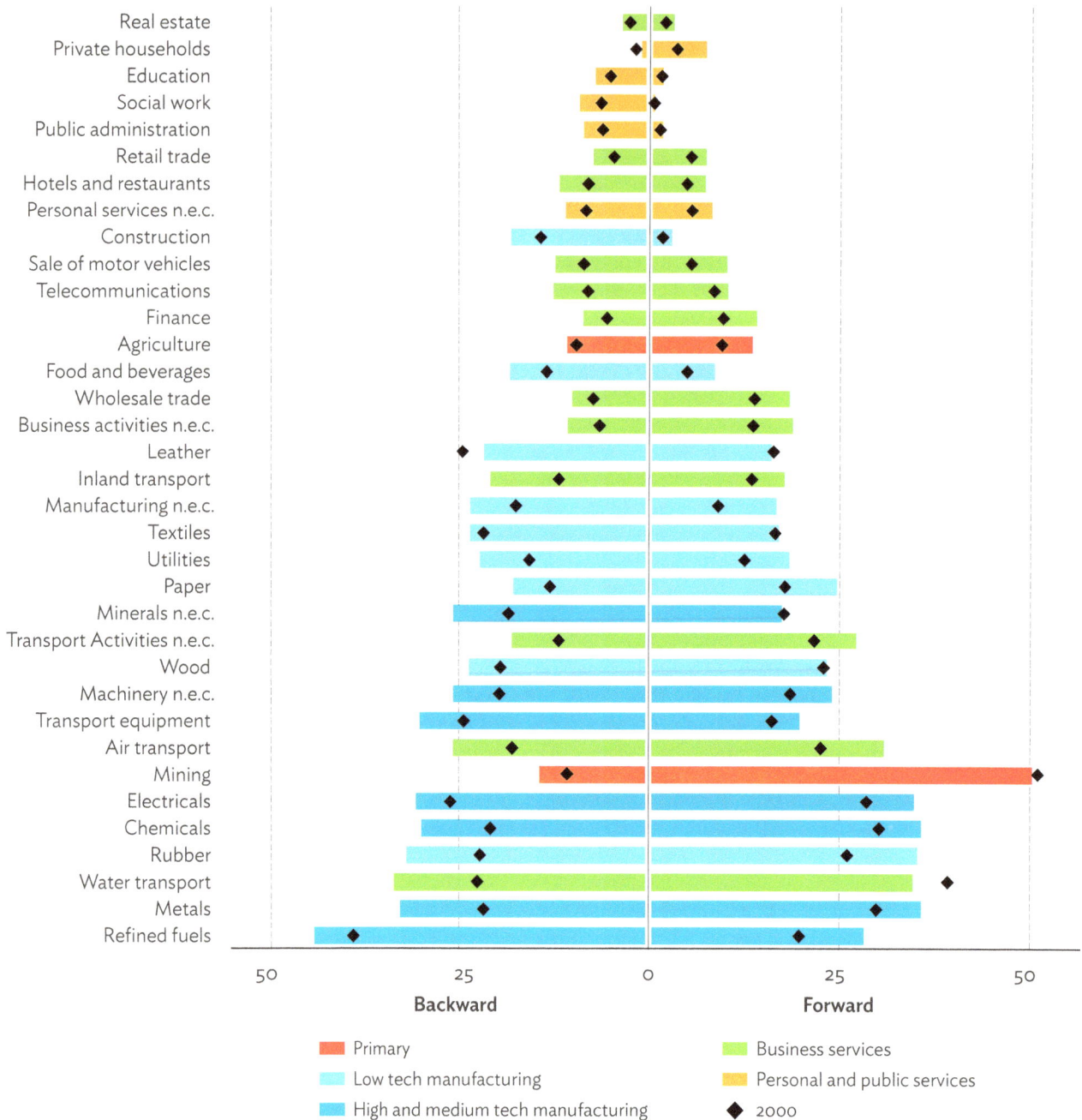

n.e.c. = not elsewhere classified.

Note: Asian Development Bank estimates are based on the methodology of Wang et al. (2017b).

Source: Asian Development Bank. Multi-Regional Input–Output Tables (accessed July 2020).

Figure 2.10 shows the GVC participation in 2000 and 2018 of the 25 economies covered in this report, with a colored dot indicating each economy by subregion and the size of the dot representing the relative size of the economy. It is immediately noticeable that the largest economies generally had the lowest GVC participation rates in both years, though it is important to note that the measure is a ratio—because of their large domestic economies, the share of GVC activities in output may be low, even as the level remains high. Care must then be given to the interpretation of this measure: the United States, the PRC, and Japan scored relatively low in the GVC participation index, yet they are clearly dominant players in numerous GVCs.

The figure shows the growth in importance of GVCs across the world from 2000 to 2018. Whereas many dots are clustered below the 20%–20% mark in 2000, more have made their way closer to the 40%–40% mark by 2018. This trend applied across the subregions, though variations for economies within subregions are high. For example, in Southeast Asia and the Pacific (yellow dots), economies may be found both below 20% and above 40%.

Figure 2.10: Global Value Chain Participation of Economies by Subregion, 2000 and 2018
(%)

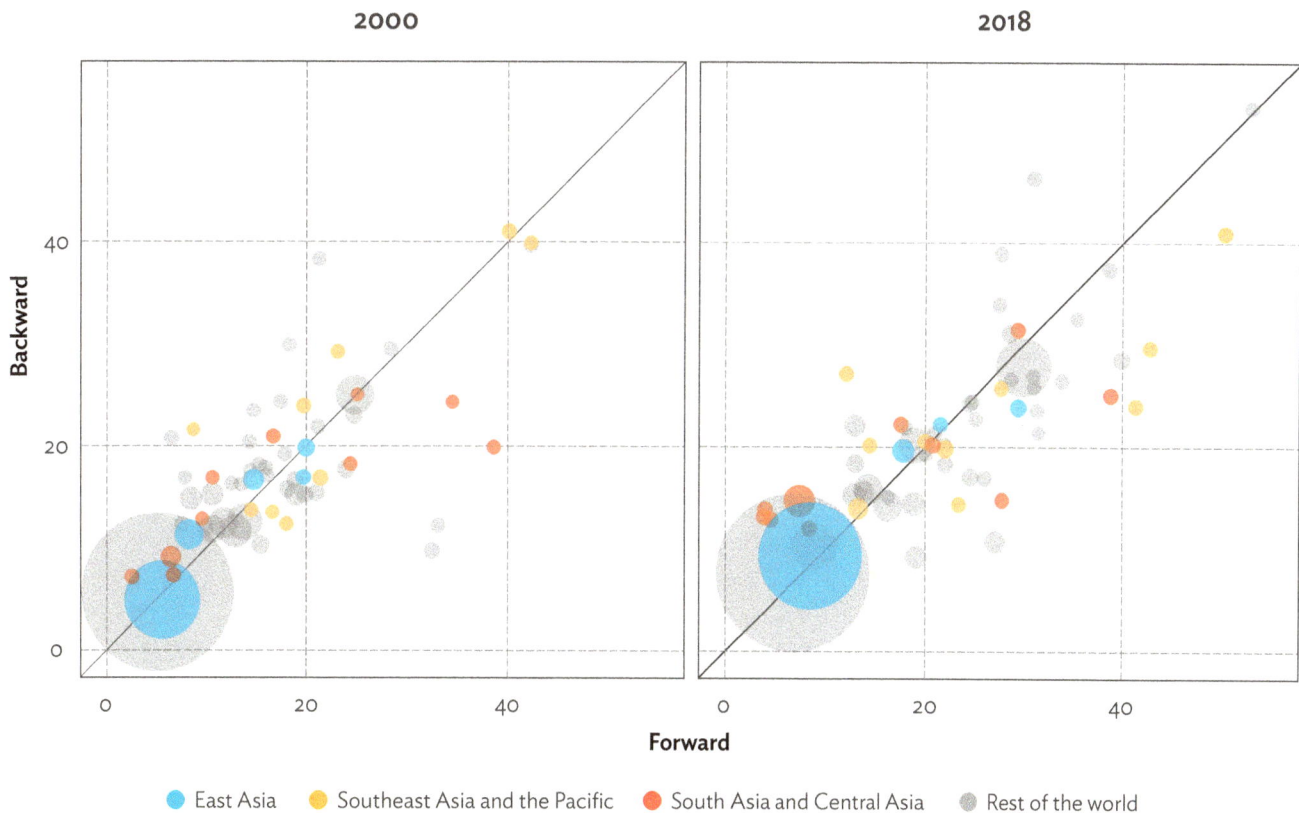

Note: Asian Development Bank estimates are based on the methodology of Wang et al. (2017b). Point sizes reflect gross domestic product at current prices.

Source: Asian Development Bank. Multi-Regional Input–Output Tables (accessed July 2020).

Another way to measure GVC participation is through the concept of "vertical specialization", as first proposed by Hummels et al. (2001). Rather than specializing only in products, as in David Ricardo's day, economies may now also specialize in a particular stage of the production chain, so that, alongside exports of purely homegrown final goods (e.g., tea and wine), they may also import half-finished goods, endow them with added value (through, for example, assembly), then pass them on to the next link in the production chain.

Widely available exports statistics aggregate the two very distinct activities of exporting final and nonfinal goods. To properly measure the extent of vertical specialization, Wang, Wei, and Zhu (2013) used data in input–output tables to decompose gross exports into three broad categories (otherwise known as WWZ decomposition). First are exports of domestic value-added, be they in the form of final goods or intermediate goods: we label these DVA. Second are exports of foreign value-added, labeled FVA. If Viet Nam, for example, exports apparel made using sewing machines imported from the Republic of Korea, then the value of exports will contain both Vietnamese and Korean value-added, with Vietnamese value-added counted in DVA and Korean value-added counted in FVA. The third and final category are pure double-counted terms, labeled PDC. With increasingly complex cross-border production-sharing arrangements, it can often happen that DVA is exported, imported back, then exported again. These two export events leave separate footprints in trade statistics, though conceptually they are equivalent. Such occurrences count under PDC. In summary, the WWZ decomposition of exports results in the identity

$$\text{Exports} = DVA + FVA + PDC.$$

The ratio of FVA + PDC to exports then measures the extent of vertical specialization in an economy's (or sector's) gross exports.

Figure 2.11 charts the change in the vertical specialization ratio for the 25 reviewed economies from 2000 to 2018. Apart from a few notable cases, the general trend is that of an increasing share of vertical specialization in gross exports. Brunei Darussalam posted the largest increase—from having the second-lowest vertical specialization ratio in 2000 to being above the regional average in 2018. Conversely, Malaysia registered the largest decline, though its 2018 ratio is still among the highest in the group, behind only Singapore, Viet Nam, and Maldives.

In his classic treatise on political economy, David Ricardo argued that, by the principle of comparative advantage, free trade can improve the welfare of all participants, be they big or small, advanced or developing. Balassa (1965) operationalized this idea through his index of "revealed" comparative advantage (RCA), which uses existing patterns of trade to identify which sectors a given economy has a comparative advantage in. The idea is fairly simple: take sector i and calculate the share of that sector in economy r's exports. Call this E_{ri}. Now, take the share of that sector in total world exports. Call this E_i. The ratio E_{ri}/E_i is the RCA index. If it is greater than 1, then economy r has a comparative advantage in i, as revealed by that sector's relative dominance in r's exports. If, however, the index is less than 1, then economy r has a comparative disadvantage in i.

This index can be refined by incorporating the rise of GVCs. As Wang, Wei, and Zhu (2013) showed, gross exports are not necessarily equivalent to exports of DVA: due to vertical specialization, some portions of it may either be exports of FVA or else are the result of

Figure 2.11: Vertical Specialization in Economies of Asia and the Pacific, 2000 and 2018

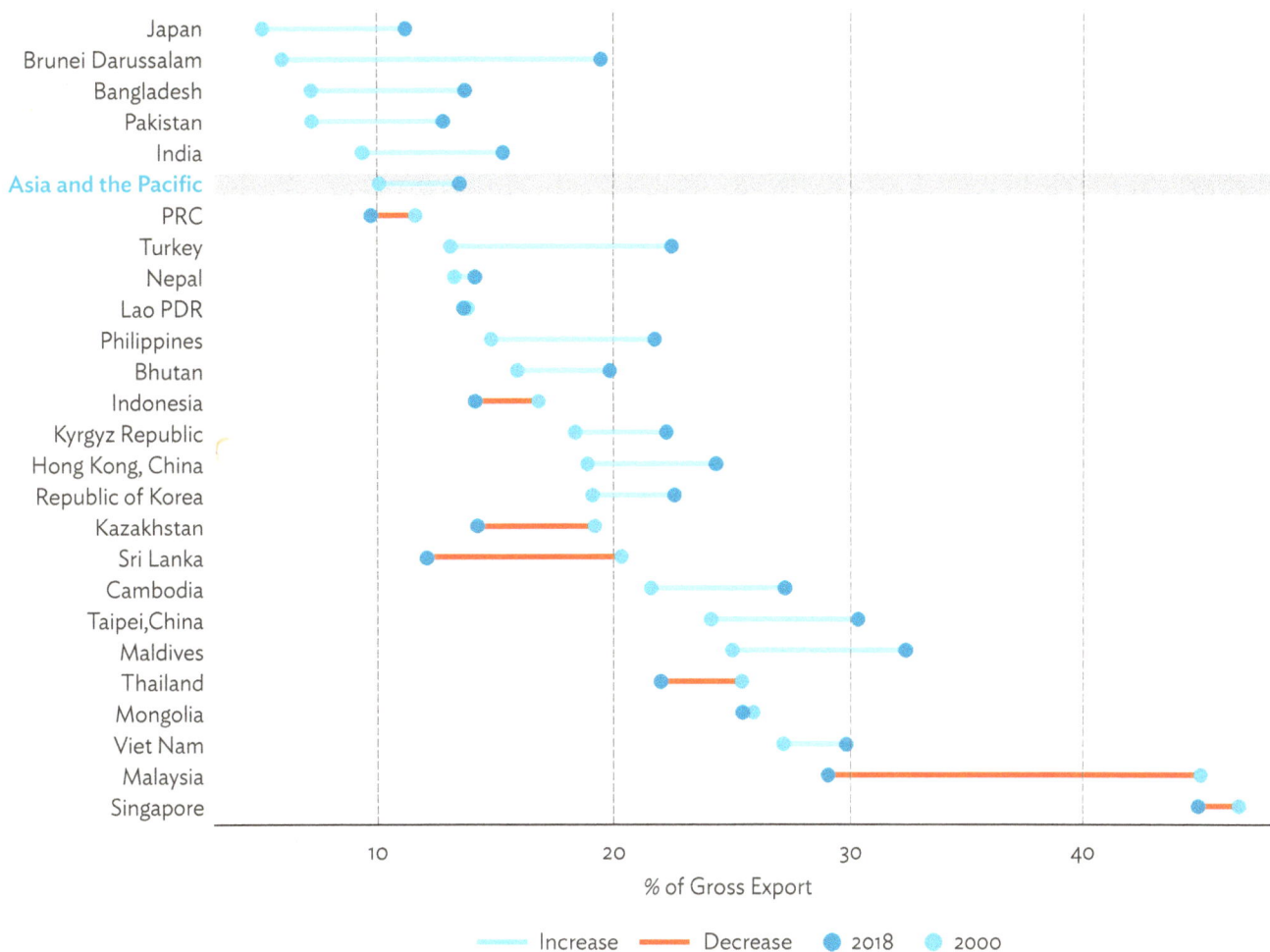

PRC = People's Republic of China, Lao PDR = Lao People's Democratic Republic

Note: Asian Development Bank estimates are based on the methodology of Wang, Wei, and Zhu (2013).

Source: Asian Development Bank. Multi-Regional Input–Output Tables (accessed July 2020).

double-counting. Using the WWZ decomposition formula, we can adjust gross exports for these terms to arrive at DVA exports. Using this in lieu of gross exports in the RCA formula gives the new revealed comparative advantage (NRCA) index—to be differentiated from the traditional RCA (TRCA) index, which does not take into account cross-border production-sharing arrangements.

Figure 2.12 charts the TRCA and NRCA of four manufacturing sectors with the highest exposures to GVCs. Though the two measures are strongly correlated, there are instances where the conclusion on comparative advantage flips. For example, Malaysia's rubber and plastics sector had a TRCA of 1.84 and an NRCA of 0.87 in 2018, so it is said to have a comparative advantage in one, but a comparative disadvantage in the other. This suggests that Malaysia's exports from that sector had significant FVA—netting these out revealed that the sector was not as dominant in that economy as first appeared.

Figure 2.12: Traditional and New Revealed Comparative Advantage of Economies by Subregion, 2018

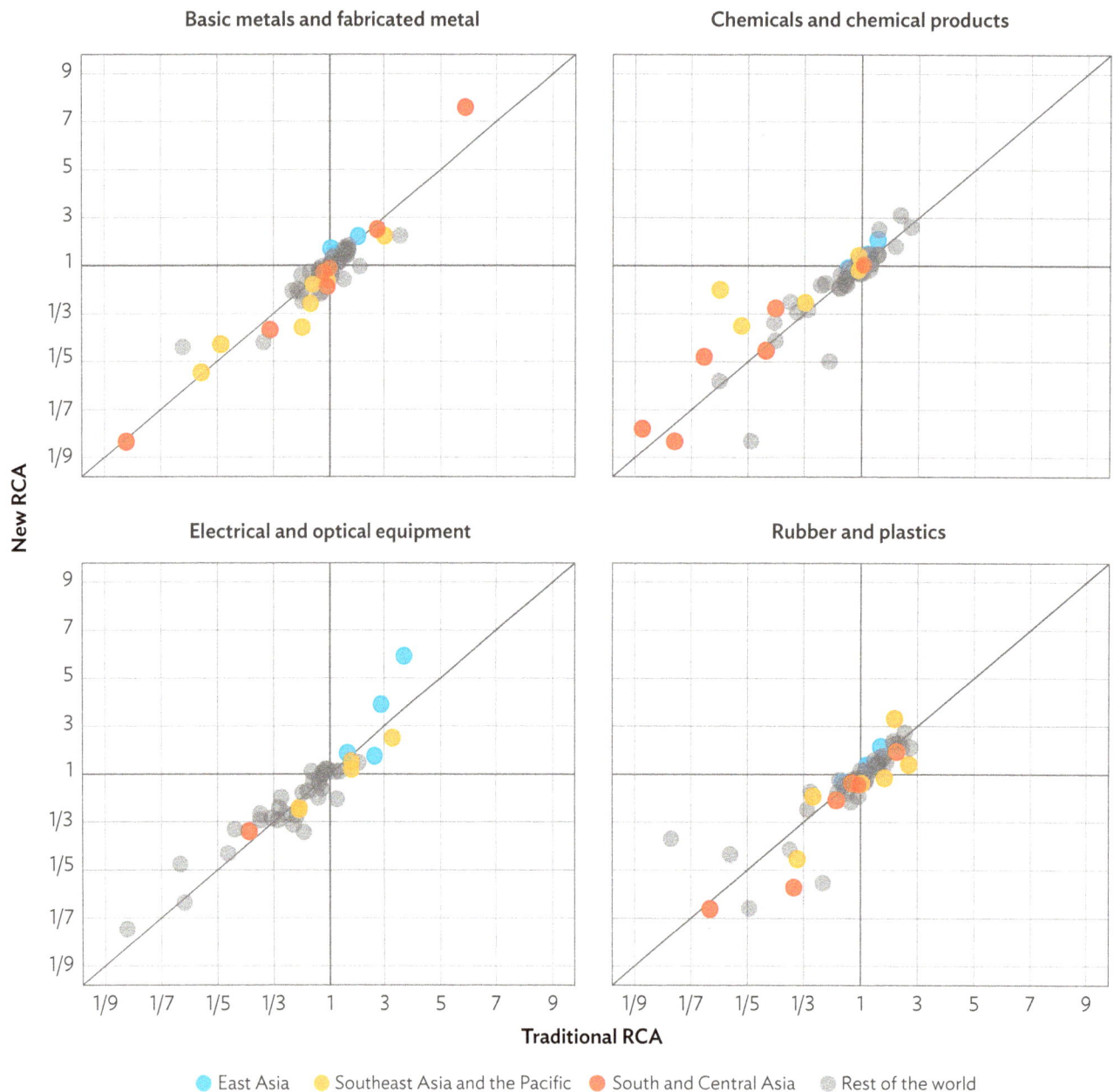

RCA = revealed comparative advantagee.

Notes: Asian Development Bank estimates are based on the methodology of Balassa (1965) and Wang, Wei, and Zhu (2013). Outliers are excluded to improve figure readability.

Source: Asian Development Bank. Multi-Regional Input–Output Tables (accessed July 2020).

Related to the issue of specialization and comparative advantages is the positioning of firms, sectors, or economies within GVCs. This question of which stages of global production economies specialize in became more relevant with the view that high value-adding activities are not equally distributed along the chain. Determining positions in value chains also provides a wider perspective on the entire structure of the production sequence. It therefore becomes important not only to understand the magnitude of participation in GVCs, but also the position and length of these linkages.

Fally (2012) and Antràs and Chor (2013) proposed a measure of position in GVCs of an economy-sector through the upstreamness index. The index is the average distance from a sector to its final use. Miller and Temurshoev (2017) described an upstream sector to be that whose outputs go through multiple stages before being absorbed as final use in the economy. A simpler measure of upstreamness relates the share of gross output of an economy-sector that is sold to final consumers. In this case, an economy-sector that sells a large amount of its output for intermediate use, i.e., it has a lower ratio between final use and total output, is said to be relatively upstream. On the other hand, a sector that sells a higher proportion of output to final consumers would be relatively downstream.

Figure 2.13 shows the evolution of economy-level upstreamness indexes of the 25 reviewed economies in 2000 and 2018. On average, indexes for 2000 indicate that outputs of economies in Asia and the Pacific underwent at least two production stages before being converted into final use. Kazakhstan, the Kyrgyz Republic, the PRC, Singapore, and Malaysia had strong intermediate supply links with other economies in terms of relevant GVCs, thereby exhibiting the highest upstreamness in the same period. Meanwhile, low upstreamness in 2000 was observed in Bhutan, Sri Lanka, Bangladesh, the Lao PDR, and Cambodia, whose significant portion of gross outputs were used to satisfy final demand levels.

Figure 2.13: Upstreamness Index of Economies of Asia and the Pacific, 2000 and 2018

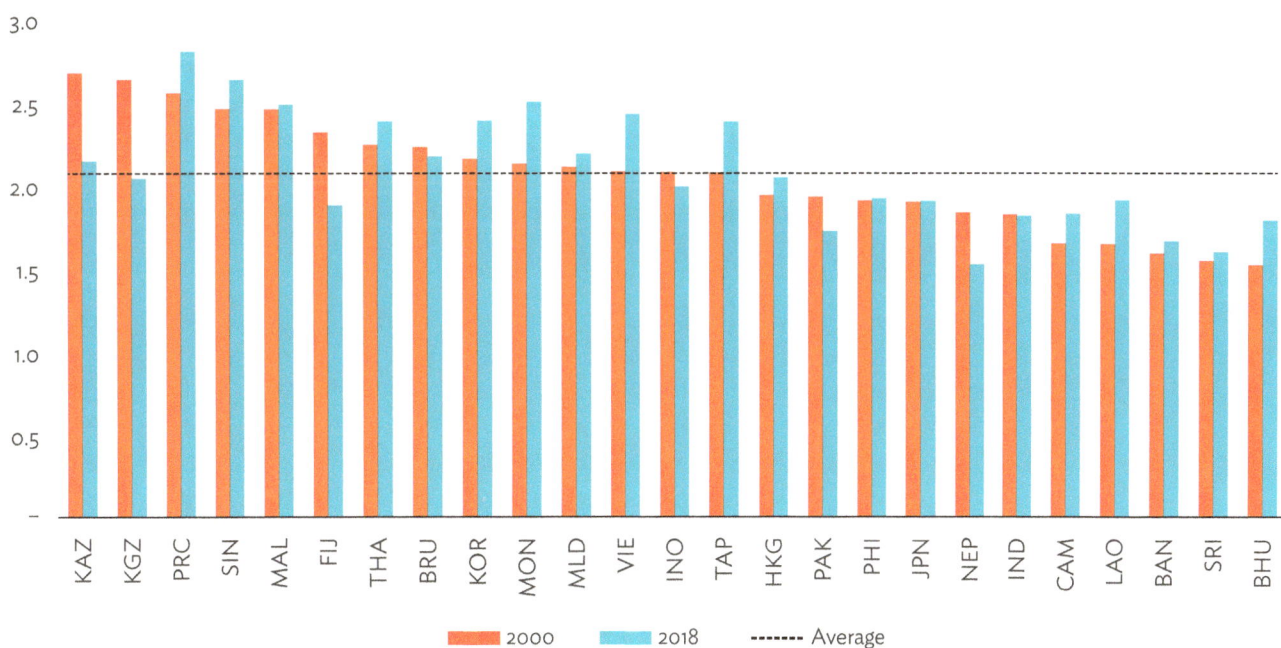

BAN = Bangladesh; BHU = Bhutan; BRU = Brunei Darussalam; CAM = Cambodia; FIJ = Fiji; HKG = Hong Kong, China; IND = India; INO = Indonesia; JPN = Japan; KAZ = Kazakhstan; KGZ = Kyrgyz Republic; KOR = Republic of Korea; LAO = Lao People's Democratic Republic; MAL = Malaysia; MLD = Maldives; MON = Mongolia; NEP = Nepal; PAK = Pakistan; PHI = Philippines; PRC = People's Republic of China; SIN = Singapore; SRI = Sri Lanka; TAP = Taipei,China; THA = Thailand; VIE = Viet Nam.

Source: Asian Development Bank. Multi-Regional Input–Output Tables (accessed July 2020).

By 2018, a majority of these economies exhibited marginal to modest (positive) changes in their upstreamness indexes. This indicates that economies became more involved in the intermediates supply chain. By rule of cardinality, outputs of most economies in 2018 still went through at least two production stages before being converted to final use. However, Kazakhstan, the Kyrgyz Republic, Fiji, Pakistan, Nepal, Brunei Darussalam, Indonesia, and India saw declines in their upstreamness index from 2000 to 2018. This indicates that their gross outputs moved closer to final use.

Positions within GVCs are closely related to measures of production length, in so far as both share the same philosophy of economic distances in internationally fragmented chains. The production length of an economy-sector is defined as the average distance between its value-added and the final products of another economy-sector. The average production length gives the proportion of gross output that is attributable to the value-added that induced it. Wang et al. (2017a) proposed two measures of average production length based on forward and backward industrial linkages. As a ratio of total output to the total valued-added from an economy-sector that induced it, "production length based on forward industrial linkage" measures the number of downstream processes that the value-added of an economy-sector counted as gross output. Hence, this measure also gives the relative upstreamness of an economy or economy-sector. On the other hand, "production length based on backward industrial linkage" is a ratio of total intermediate inputs to the total units of final product that induce it. In other words, this measure gives the number of upstream processes before the final product is realized in the economy, i.e., the relative downstreamness of an economy or economy-sector.

Figure 2.14 shows the trends in economy-level average production length (APL) based on forward industrial linkage across economies, with the subregions of Asia and the Pacific highlighted in colored lines. Except for a slight leveling off after 2015, economies in East Asia had a steadily increasing trend in APL based on forward industrial linkage. From 2007 to 2018, value-added originating from East Asia underwent about 2.5 downstream processes before reaching final consumption. On the other hand, South and Central Asia recorded a much shorter APL of about 2 stages in 2007 before undergoing a steady decline; by 2018 its APL was about 1.75. Southeast Asia's APL maintained a stable trend during the review period, with an APL index of about 2.25 stages.

The trends in economy-level APL based on backward industrial linkage across economies from 2007 to 2018 are shown according to the subregions (in colored lines) in Figure 2.15. Similar to the observed trend in APL based on forward linkage, East Asia's APL based on backward linkage has been steadily increasing from 2007 to 2018, with a slight decline after 2015. The average APL of East Asia shows that a unit of final product of the region induced about 2.5 intermediate inputs from 2007 to 2018. Meanwhile, a stable trend in backward APL in Southeast Asia meant that its final products underwent an average of about 2.25 upstream processes before being consumed in the economy. The APL based on backward linkage of South and Central Asia followed a slightly declining trend, starting in 2007 at around 2 and finishing by 2018 at a little below that.

Figure 2.14: Trends in Average Production Length Based on Forward Linkage across Economies, 2007–2018

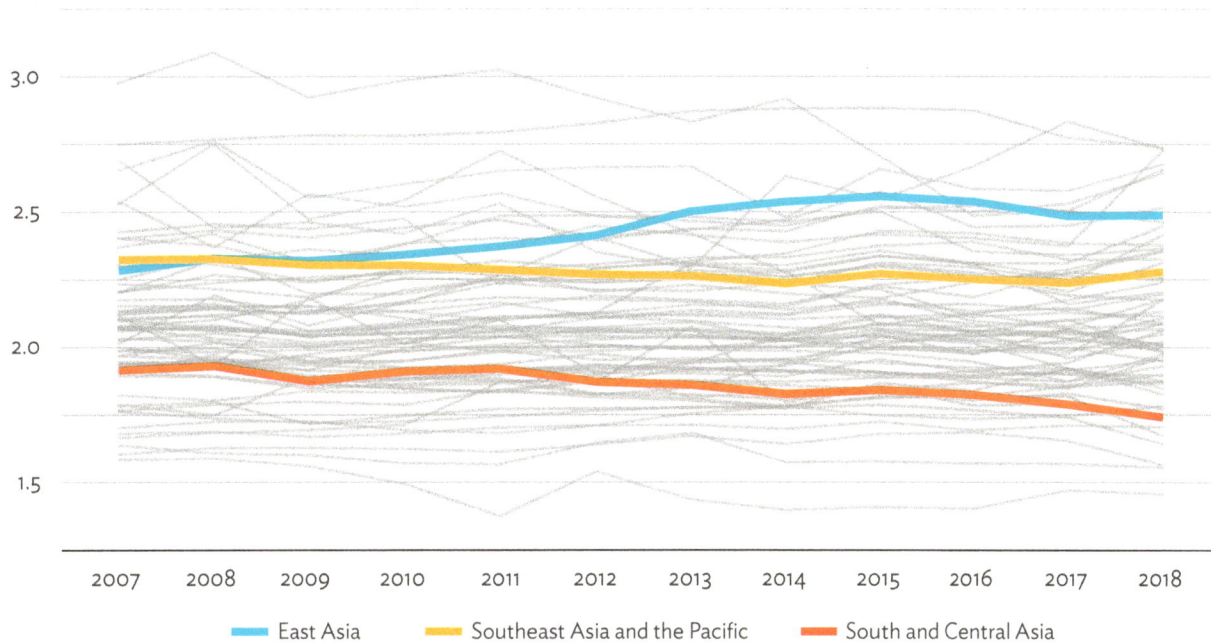

— East Asia   — Southeast Asia and the Pacific   — South and Central Asia

Note: Asian Development Bank estimates are based on the methodology of Wang et al. (2017b).
Source: Asian Development Bank. Multi-Regional Input–Output Tables (accessed July 2020).

Figure 2.15: Trends in Average Production Length Based on Backward Linkage across Economies, 2007–2018

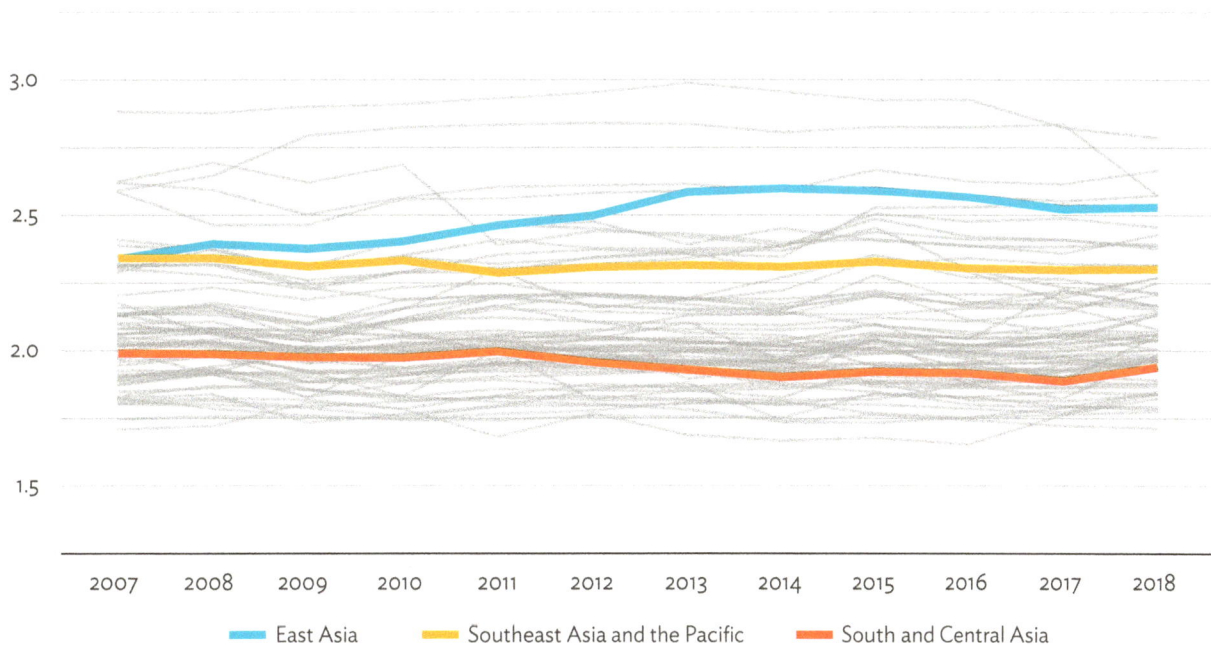

— East Asia   — Southeast Asia and the Pacific   — South and Central Asia

Note: Asian Development Bank estimates are based on the methodology of Wang et al. (2017b).
Source: Asian Development Bank. Multi-Regional Input–Output Tables (accessed July 2020).

2.3 Conclusion

This chapter presents some of the analytical tools and indicators used in characterizing GVCs. Illustrations of these indicators were drawn from the construction of MRIOTs. This allows users to explore the supply-use relationships of two sectors from different economic territories, and to gain a macro perspective of GVC trade—a phenomenon that has driven international economic activity since the 1990s. The impact of involvement in a production network can differ substantially, depending on the degree of specialization, capacity for value addition, and position in the value chain of any given producer. Understanding these aspects at the sectoral level reveals nuances that could be useful for shaping economic policies related to trade. The mix of indicators and methodologies outlined here is presented as a crucial first step in building a knowledge base for understanding production linkages at a global and regional level.

Key Messages

- Individual economy-specific input–output tables can be consolidated and linked to form MRIOTs. These "international" tables facilitate important analyses of economic structures and interrelationships at bilateral and multilateral levels.

- The relative importance of trade for each economy or sector is quantified using a range of indicators derived from MRIOTs. Economies of Asia and the Pacific have varying degrees of trade openness. For many of these economies, however, this measure has weakened since the 2008 global financial crisis.

- Import leakages measure an economy's dependence on foreign inputs for production. On average, manufacturing and tourism-related sectors have the largest leakage effects in the Asia and Pacific region.

- Participation in GVCs is highest for economies with significant manufacturing of electronics, metals, rubber, and chemicals. Other service-oriented economies, such as Singapore, have similarly high participation in GVCs, particularly through contributions in transport services.

- Measures of revealed comparative advantage could change to a comparative disadvantage when significant foreign value-added is discounted from an economy's exports. The reverse could also happen when accounting for value-added from domestic sectors indirectly exporting.

- The position and length of economy-sectors in GVCs are both rooted in the concept of economic distance. This is an important complementary indicator to participation, since it provides an indication of the type of value-adding activities and enables a wider perspective on the structure of production sequences involved. Data show that economies in East and Southeast Asia and the Pacific are relatively more downstream, while economies in South and Central Asia are more upstream.

ECONOMY PROFILES

This part compiles and tabulates indicators and model-based results to form comprehensive profiles for each economy, based on the strengths and characteristics of the economy's respective input–output linkages. Specifically, the internal and external linkages of the 9 economies in the South and Central Asia subregion are quantified and compared using various metrics derived from the ADB Multi-Regional Input–Output Tables.

Each economy profile is organized into two sections. Section A characterizes an economy's internal linkages, or the input–output flows that happen within its domestic boundaries. Section B describes the economy's external linkages, or the input–output flows that occur in exchange with other economies. Related indicators under each section are grouped together and considered within the context of shared themes.

The shared themes in Section A are as follows:

i.   *Structure of the Economy*, which covers measures of macroeconomic variables describing the level and diversification of output in the economy and characterizing the structural changes that took place between 2000 and 2018;

ii. *Strength of Linkages*, which contains well-established input–output multipliers derived from both supply- and demand-side models;

iii. *Spread of Economic Linkages*, which consists of analytical indicators quantifying the dispersion of economic impacts based on both forward and backward linkage perspectives; and

iv. *Sensitivity of Economic Linkages*, which presents aggregate measures of economic complexity based on production technologies.

Section B indicators are organized under the following four themes:

i.   *Participation in Global Value Chains* (GVCs), which contains indicators representing an economy's degree of dependency on foreign trade and its participation in GVCs;

ii. *Specialization in GVCs*, which consolidates indicators describing the intensities or degrees of concentration and comparative advantages of each sector of economic activity;

iii. *Position in GVCs*, which presents the upstreamness index measuring the distance of each economic activity from final use; and

iv. *Production Length of GVCs*, which shows backward and forward measures of average production lengths attributable to global production arrangements.

Each indicator is presented in terms of a value, score, rank, variance from the subregional average, 10-year average growth rate, and 10-year mean value.

- *Value* refers to the actual observed measure or index derived from the corresponding model or framework.
- *Score* is the normalized value of a measure, based on the minimum and maximum values observed for the measure across the 25 economies of Asia and the Pacific covered in this report. The highest value is 1, while the lowest is 0.
- *Rank* shows an economy's relative position or place for a measure when the values for the 25 economies are ordered from largest to smallest: 1 represents the highest rank for the respective indicator, while 25 represents the lowest.
- *Variance from the subregional average* is depicted using colored icons: a green icon denotes that the value corresponding to an economy is above the subregional average; a red icon signifies that the value is below the average; and a yellow icon represents equality with the average. The subregional groupings are described in detail in Appendix 2.
- *10-year average growth rate* is the arithmetic average of annual growth rates from 2009 to 2018.
- *10-year mean value* is the arithmetic average of the indicator's values from 2009 to 2018.

Details of each indicator's description and derivation method are provided in Appendix 3.

3.1 Bangladesh

3.1A Internal Linkages

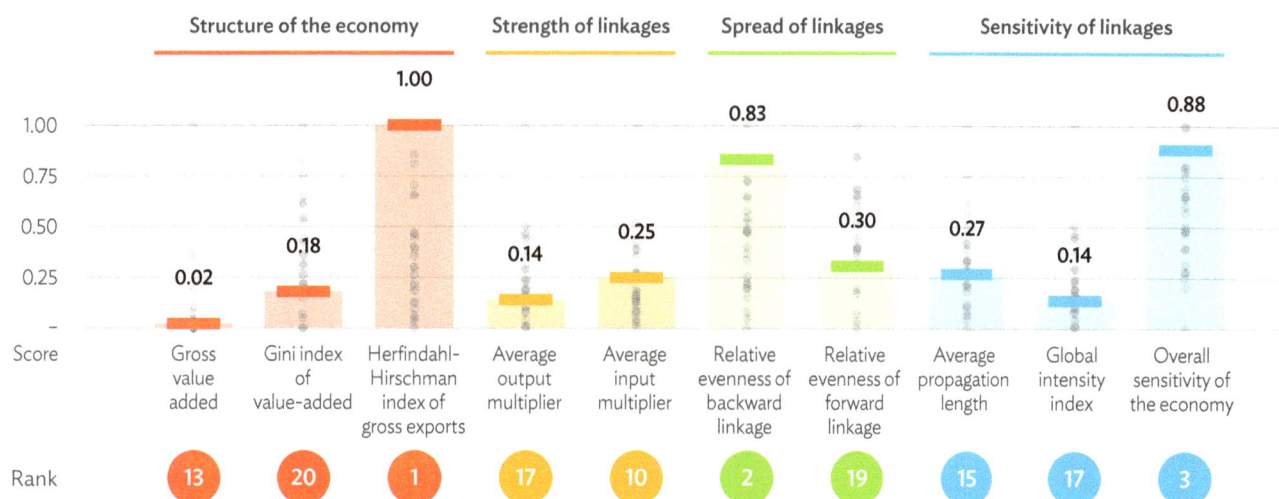

Note: The scores of the economy in focus are shown in the horizontal bars with labels. The colored dots represent the indicator performance of the economy in focus compared to other economies in the region. The highest rank among economies is 1 while the lowest rank is 25. The indicators shown in the chart are selected from a broader set of indicators (see the technical appendix for more details).

Source: Asian Development Bank Multi-Regional Input–Output Database. https://mrio.adbx.online/ (accessed 4 August 2020).

		Value (2018)	Score (0–1)	Rank (out of 25)	Distance to subregional average	10–year average growth rate (%)	10–year mean value
STRUCTURE OF THE ECONOMY							
Economic Indicators							
Gross output	($)	447,593	0.01	14	▼	11.6	275,095
Gross value-added	($)	254,992	0.02	13	▼	11.4	156,990
Value-added content of domestic final demand		222,795	0.02	10		11.8	133,360
Value-added content of exports		32,197	0.01	14		9.3	23,630
Intermediate inputs	($)	186,584	0.01	14	▼	11.8	114,727
Domestic inputs		160,702	0.01	14		12.3	97,317
Foreign inputs		25,882	0.02	14		10.4	17,410
Direct production	($)	286,891	0.02	14	▼	11.2	177,778
Domestic final demand		248,368	0.02	12		11.6	149,493
Exports		38,523	0.01	14		9.4	28,285
Indirect production	($)	160,702	0.01	14	▼	12.3	97,317
Indirect production embedded in domestic final demand		127,563	0.01	12		13.1	73,207
Indirect production embedded in exports		33,138	0.01	13		10.0	24,110
Economic Diversification							
Gross output		0.27	0.36	12	▲	-0.4	0.28
Gini concentration index of gross output		0.45	0.42	11		-0.4	0.46
Herfindahl-Hirschman concentration index of gross output		0.06	0.26	13		0.0	0.06
Theil concentration index of gross output		0.29	0.34	12		-0.4	0.30

continued on next page

Bangladesh 3.1A *continued*

	Value (2018)	Score (0–1)	Rank (out of 25)	Distance to subregional average	10–year average growth rate (%)	10–year mean value
Gross value-added	**0.21**	**0.14**	**20**	▼	**−1.8**	**0.23**
Gini concentration index of gross value added	0.38	0.18	20		−1.4	0.41
Herfindahl-Hirschman concentration index of gross value added	0.03	0.05	20		−3.3	0.04
Theil concentration index of gross value added	0.21	0.15	20		−2.2	0.24
Gross exports	**0.84**	**1.00**	**1**	▲	**0.4**	**0.83**
Gini concentration index of gross exports	0.89	1.00	1		0.1	0.89
Herfindahl-Hirschman concentration index of gross exports	0.74	1.00	1		1.0	0.72
Theil concentration index of gross exports	0.88	1.00	1		0.2	0.87

Structural Changes

	Value (2018)	Score (0–1)	Rank (out of 25)	Distance to subregional average	10–year average growth rate (%)	10–year mean value
Changes in output due to technological changes	**−0.1%**	**0.75**	**12**	▼	**–**	**–**
Agriculture, hunting, forestry, and fishing	−0.5%	0.52	15			
Mining and quarrying	0.0%	0.74	10			
Light manufacturing	0.4%	0.40	7			
Heavy manufacturing	−1.0%	0.66	15			
Utilities	−0.4%	0.48	12			
Construction	0.6%	0.20	9			
Trade services	0.0%	0.44	13			
Hotels and restaurants	0.2%	0.07	15			
Transport services	−0.3%	0.59	13			
Telecommunications	−1.0%	0.13	18			
Financial intermediation	1.3%	0.59	6			
Real estate, renting, and business activities	0.2%	0.68	13			
Public administration and defense	0.6%	0.52	2			
Education, health, and social work	0.3%	0.86	5			
Other personal services	−1.2%	0.18	24			
Changes in output due to structural changes in consumption (%)	**7.3%**	**0.71**	**2**	▲	**–**	**–**
Agriculture, hunting, forestry, and fishing	6.4%	1.00	1			
Mining and quarrying	4.9%	0.30	2			
Light manufacturing	5.3%	0.65	3			
Heavy manufacturing	2.8%	0.47	8			
Utilities	8.7%	0.86	2			
Construction	1.1%	0.26	8			
Trade services	7.1%	1.00	1			
Hotels and restaurants	9.7%	0.32	3			
Transport services	7.9%	1.00	1			
Telecommunications	5.3%	0.72	4			
Financial intermediation	7.0%	0.75	3			
Real estate, renting, and business activities	9.8%	0.43	2			
Public administration and defense	12.1%	0.78	3			
Education, health, and social work	12.2%	0.39	4			
Other personal services	9.8%	0.67	2			
Changes in output due to structural changes in investment (%)	**3.2%**	**0.94**	**2**	▲	**–**	**–**
Agriculture, hunting, forestry, and fishing	0.9%	0.23	4			
Mining and quarrying	5.2%	1.00	1			
Light manufacturing	2.2%	0.64	2			

continued on next page

Bangladesh 3.1A *continued*

	Value (2018)	Score (0–1)	Rank (out of 25)	Distance to subregional average	10-year average growth rate (%)	10-year mean value
Heavy manufacturing	8.8%	1.00	1			
Utilities	3.6%	0.99	2			
Construction	12.1%	0.75	2			
Trade services	2.7%	0.62	4			
Hotels and restaurants	1.9%	1.00	1			
Transport services	1.8%	0.49	4			
Telecommunications	1.5%	0.36	4			
Financial intermediation	4.2%	1.00	1			
Real estate, renting, and business activities	1.1%	0.32	7			
Public administration and defense	0.7%	1.00	1			
Education, health, and social work	0.1%	0.08	6			
Other personal services	0.6%	0.35	6			
Changes in output due to structural changes in stock (%)	**0.0%**	**0.29**	**14**	▼	–	–
Agriculture, hunting, forestry, and fishing	0.0%	0.53	12			
Mining and quarrying	0.0%	0.38	13			
Light manufacturing	0.0%	0.17	12			
Heavy manufacturing	0.0%	0.30	16			
Utilities	0.0%	0.12	13			
Construction	0.0%	0.75	12			
Trade services	0.0%	0.29	14			
Hotels and restaurants	0.0%	0.45	13			
Transport services	0.0%	0.06	17			
Telecommunications	0.0%	0.46	12			
Financial intermediation	0.0%	0.90	12			
Real estate, renting, and business activities	0.0%	0.15	13			
Public administration and defense	0.0%	0.64	13			
Education, health, and social work	0.0%	0.23	15			
Other personal services	0.0%	0.42	12			
Changes in output due to structural changes in export	**1.2%**	**0.30**	**12**	▲	–	–
Agriculture, hunting, forestry, and fishing	1.0%	0.51	10			
Mining and quarrying	1.5%	0.17	11			
Light manufacturing	4.4%	0.44	5			
Heavy manufacturing	0.6%	0.25	19			
Utilities	1.5%	0.08	9			
Construction	0.3%	0.09	8			
Trade services	0.6%	0.10	18			
Hotels and restaurants	1.0%	0.11	14			
Transport services	0.7%	0.44	18			
Telecommunications	1.6%	0.20	11			
Financial intermediation	2.1%	0.39	9			
Real estate, renting, and business activities	0.8%	0.32	16			
Public administration and defense	1.9%	0.49	3			
Education, health, and social work	0.3%	0.13	8			
Other personal services	0.3%	0.06	23			

continued on next page

Bangladesh 3.1A *continued*

	Value (2018)	Score (0–1)	Rank (out of 25)	Distance to subregional average	10–year average growth rate (%)	10–year mean value
Changes in output due to import substitution on intermediate demand	**0.1%**	**0.39**	**11**	▼	**–**	**–**
Agriculture, hunting, forestry, and fishing	0.0%	0.68	9			
Mining and quarrying	0.7%	0.32	8			
Light manufacturing	−0.1%	0.80	14			
Heavy manufacturing	0.4%	0.27	13			
Utilities	0.1%	0.69	8			
Construction	0.0%	0.86	8			
Trade services	0.0%	0.76	13			
Hotels and restaurants	0.0%	0.97	6			
Transport services	0.1%	0.46	13			
Telecommunications	−0.1%	0.94	10			
Financial intermediation	−0.1%	0.59	15			
Real estate, renting, and business activities	0.0%	0.72	10			
Public administration and defense	0.0%	0.65	12			
Education, health, and social work	0.0%	0.59	7			
Other personal services	0.0%	0.53	7			
Changes in output due to import substitution on domestic final demand	**0.0%**	**0.83**	**6**	▼	**–**	**–**
Agriculture, hunting, forestry, and fishing	0.0%	0.56	8			
Mining and quarrying	0.1%	0.52	11			
Light manufacturing	−0.1%	0.78	11			
Heavy manufacturing	0.4%	0.61	6			
Utilities	0.0%	0.78	9			
Construction	0.0%	0.67	8			
Trade services	0.0%	0.91	7			
Hotels and restaurants	0.0%	0.67	9			
Transport services	0.1%	0.91	5			
Telecommunications	−0.1%	0.72	12			
Financial intermediation	0.0%	0.82	10			
Real estate, renting, and business activities	0.0%	0.55	7			
Public administration and defense	0.2%	0.38	4			
Education, health, and social work	0.0%	0.87	4			
Other personal services	0.0%	0.93	7			

STRENGTH OF LINKAGES

Demand-side Linkages

	Value (2018)	Score (0–1)	Rank (out of 25)	Distance to subregional average	10–year average growth rate (%)	10–year mean value
Direct backward linkage	**0.29**	**0.21**	**17**	▼	**0.2**	**0.29**
Agriculture, hunting, forestry, and fishing	0.23	0.30	15		1.1	0.22
Mining and quarrying	0.08	0.14	22		−1.4	0.09
Light manufacturing	0.58	0.75	9		−0.2	0.59
Heavy manufacturing	0.40	0.35	15		−1.2	0.45
Utilities	0.39	0.43	11		−1.0	0.39
Construction	0.56	0.61	4		0.6	0.54
Trade services	0.15	0.01	23		0.5	0.14
Hotels and restaurants	0.63	1.00	1		0.4	0.62
Transport services	0.27	0.42	16		0.0	0.26
Telecommunications	0.25	0.28	19		−1.2	0.26

continued on next page

Bangladesh 3.1A *continued*

	Value (2018)	Score (0–1)	Rank (out of 25)	Distance to subregional average	10-year average growth rate (%)	10-year mean value
Financial intermediation	0.25	0.25	13		2.6	0.24
Real estate, renting, and business activities	0.10	0.01	23		1.6	0.10
Public administration and defense	0.28	0.50	13		3.0	0.25
Education, health, and social work	0.14	0.14	23		1.2	0.14
Other personal services	0.10	0.03	23		0.2	0.10
Total backward linkage	**1.45**	**0.14**	**17**	▼	**0.1**	**1.44**
Agriculture, hunting, forestry, and fishing	1.35	0.22	15		0.3	1.31
Mining and quarrying	1.13	0.10	22		–0.1	1.13
Light manufacturing	1.93	0.46	10		0.2	1.92
Heavy manufacturing	1.60	0.16	16		–0.6	1.67
Utilities	1.53	0.20	14		–0.4	1.53
Construction	1.93	0.32	9		0.4	1.87
Trade services	1.23	0.07	23		0.2	1.21
Hotels and restaurants	1.93	0.57	5		0.4	1.89
Transport services	1.41	0.28	16		0.1	1.39
Telecommunications	1.39	0.22	18		–0.3	1.39
Financial intermediation	1.38	0.08	12		0.7	1.36
Real estate, renting, and business activities	1.16	0.03	23		0.3	1.15
Public administration and defense	1.37	0.38	16		0.7	1.33
Education, health, and social work	1.22	0.10	21		0.2	1.21
Other personal services	1.16	0.05	23		0.1	1.16
Normalized backward linkage	–	–	–	▬	–	–
Agriculture, hunting, forestry, and fishing	0.93	0.33	11		0.2	0.92
Mining and quarrying	0.78	0.22	21		–0.3	0.79
Light manufacturing	1.33	0.79	2		0.0	1.34
Heavy manufacturing	1.10	0.40	9		–0.7	1.16
Utilities	1.06	0.33	11		–0.5	1.06
Construction	1.33	0.72	3		0.2	1.30
Trade services	0.85	0.21	21		0.1	0.85
Hotels and restaurants	1.34	1.00	1		0.2	1.32
Transport services	0.97	0.37	15		–0.1	0.97
Telecommunications	0.96	0.52	15		–0.4	0.96
Financial intermediation	0.95	0.13	7		0.6	0.95
Real estate, renting, and business activities	0.80	0.18	24		0.1	0.80
Public administration and defense	0.95	0.52	12		0.6	0.93
Education, health, and social work	0.84	0.34	21		0.1	0.84
Other personal services	0.80	0.00	25		0.0	0.81
Net backward linkage	**0.84**	**0.18**	**24**	▼	**0.1**	**0.83**
Agriculture, hunting, forestry, and fishing	0.77	0.63	11		–0.6	0.77
Mining and quarrying	0.01	0.01	22		–9.8	0.05
Light manufacturing	1.16	0.62	10		–0.9	1.24
Heavy manufacturing	0.93	0.56	13		1.1	0.89
Utilities	0.54	0.36	10		4.9	0.49
Construction	1.46	0.35	13		0.3	1.45
Trade services	0.82	0.38	12		0.0	0.82

continued on next page

Bangladesh 3.1A *continued*

	Value (2018)	Score (0–1)	Rank (out of 25)	Distance to subregional average	10–year average growth rate (%)	10–year mean value
Hotels and restaurants	0.96	0.25	23		0.9	0.91
Transport services	0.97	0.50	8		–0.2	0.96
Telecommunications	0.80	0.46	11		–0.4	0.81
Financial intermediation	0.19	0.05	23		2.2	0.19
Real estate, renting, and business activities	0.83	0.76	13		–0.1	0.83
Public administration and defense	1.16	0.19	21		–0.4	1.16
Education, health, and social work	1.01	0.00	25		–0.6	1.04
Other personal services	0.97	0.62	17		2.3	0.85
Growth equalized output multipliers	**0.10**	**0.18**	**12**	▲	**0.3**	**0.10**
Agriculture, hunting, forestry, and fishing	0.17	0.49	6		–2.6	0.20
Mining and quarrying	0.02	0.04	15		1.8	0.02
Light manufacturing	0.40	0.68	3		0.8	0.39
Heavy manufacturing	0.09	0.11	16		0.4	0.08
Utilities	0.02	0.05	21		0.7	0.02
Construction	0.20	0.34	7		2.3	0.18
Trade services	0.14	0.28	16		–0.7	0.15
Hotels and restaurants	0.03	0.05	19		2.3	0.03
Transport services	0.11	0.57	9		–0.2	0.12
Telecommunications	0.01	0.08	24		–2.9	0.02
Financial intermediation	0.05	0.14	17		3.2	0.04
Real estate, renting, and business activities	0.09	0.28	16		0.4	0.09
Public administration and defense	0.06	0.25	17		3.7	0.05
Education, health, and social work	0.06	0.21	18		1.6	0.05
Other personal services	0.10	0.56	2		–0.6	0.11

Supply-Side Linkages

	Value (2018)	Score (0–1)	Rank (out of 25)	Distance to subregional average	10–year average growth rate (%)	10–year mean value
Direct forward linkage	**0.42**	**0.46**	**8**	▲	**0.1**	**0.42**
Agriculture, hunting, forestry, and fishing	0.43	0.37	16		1.4	0.41
Mining and quarrying	0.99	1.00	1		0.6	0.95
Light manufacturing	0.40	0.36	13		2.2	0.36
Heavy manufacturing	0.42	0.53	18		–1.8	0.46
Utilities	0.65	0.68	17		–1.5	0.68
Construction	0.24	0.50	7		0.8	0.23
Trade services	0.33	0.35	18		0.5	0.32
Hotels and restaurants	0.51	0.96	2		–0.3	0.52
Transport services	0.31	0.30	20		0.8	0.31
Telecommunications	0.42	0.37	18		0.3	0.41
Financial intermediation	0.86	0.97	2		0.0	0.86
Real estate, renting, and business activities	0.28	0.13	22		1.4	0.27
Public administration and defense	0.15	0.70	2		12.2	0.13
Education, health, and social work	0.17	0.65	2		5.4	0.14
Other personal services	0.17	0.16	19		–3.0	0.26
Total forward linkage	**1.67**	**0.25**	**10**	▲	**0.2**	**1.66**
Agriculture, hunting, forestry, and fishing	1.70	0.27	14		0.9	1.65
Mining and quarrying	2.58	0.51	6		0.4	2.50
Light manufacturing	1.63	0.23	11		1.0	1.54

continued on next page

Bangladesh 3.1A *continued*

	Value (2018)	Score (0–1)	Rank (out of 25)	Distance to subregional average	10–year average growth rate (%)	10–year mean value
Heavy manufacturing	1.65	0.30	17		−0.7	1.71
Utilities	2.05	0.33	16		−0.6	2.07
Construction	1.36	0.39	7		0.2	1.33
Trade services	1.51	0.23	17		0.2	1.49
Hotels and restaurants	1.81	0.67	2		−0.1	1.82
Transport services	1.50	0.18	16		0.3	1.48
Telecommunications	1.71	0.36	17		0.3	1.68
Financial intermediation	2.35	0.28	5		0.1	2.32
Real estate, renting, and business activities	1.46	0.12	20		0.4	1.44
Public administration and defense	1.24	0.70	2		1.4	1.20
Education, health, and social work	1.22	0.71	2		0.8	1.18
Other personal services	1.27	0.19	19		−1.2	1.41
Normalized forward linkage	–	–	–	▬	–	–
Agriculture, hunting, forestry, and fishing	1.02	0.29	17		0.7	1.00
Mining and quarrying	1.78	1.00	2		0.2	1.74
Light manufacturing	1.13	0.64	9		0.8	1.07
Heavy manufacturing	1.14	0.53	14		−0.9	1.19
Utilities	1.42	0.65	14		−0.7	1.44
Construction	0.94	0.51	5		0.0	0.93
Trade services	1.04	0.33	16		0.1	1.04
Hotels and restaurants	1.25	1.00	1		−0.2	1.27
Transport services	1.04	0.32	18		0.2	1.03
Telecommunications	1.18	0.47	12		0.1	1.17
Financial intermediation	1.62	0.38	2		0.0	1.62
Real estate, renting, and business activities	1.01	0.22	19		0.3	1.00
Public administration and defense	0.86	0.80	2		1.2	0.84
Education, health, and social work	0.84	0.93	3		0.7	0.82
Other personal services	0.88	0.22	17		−1.3	0.98
Net forward linkage	**1.08**	**0.84**	**2**	▲	**0.4**	**1.06**
Agriculture, hunting, forestry, and fishing	1.21	0.51	10		0.7	1.18
Mining and quarrying	2.27	1.00	1		0.6	2.18
Light manufacturing	0.51	0.42	9		1.1	0.47
Heavy manufacturing	0.83	0.90	3		1.8	0.73
Utilities	1.09	0.57	5		1.5	1.06
Construction	0.47	0.56	11		0.2	0.46
Trade services	1.24	0.62	5		0.1	1.22
Hotels and restaurants	0.53	0.28	15		0.4	0.53
Transport services	1.00	0.58	5		0.7	0.98
Telecommunications	1.20	0.56	5		0.9	1.16
Financial intermediation	1.67	0.63	5		−0.5	1.66
Real estate, renting, and business activities	1.28	0.68	5		0.2	1.26
Public administration and defense	0.84	0.77	5		0.5	0.84
Education, health, and social work	0.96	0.95	2		0.8	0.92
Other personal services	1.10	0.79	3		−1.2	1.22

continued on next page

Bangladesh 3.1A *continued*

	Value (2018)	Score (0–1)	Rank (out of 25)	Distance to subregional average	10–year average growth rate (%)	10–year mean value
Growth equalized input multipliers	**0.10**	**0.19**	**12**	▲	**0.3**	**0.10**
Agriculture, hunting, forestry, and fishing	0.24	0.49	9		–2.0	0.27
Mining and quarrying	0.05	0.07	11		2.3	0.04
Light manufacturing	0.23	0.65	3		1.8	0.21
Heavy manufacturing	0.08	0.16	15		2.0	0.07
Utilities	0.03	0.10	18		2.0	0.03
Construction	0.11	0.17	7		2.4	0.09
Trade services	0.20	0.38	17		–0.7	0.20
Hotels and restaurants	0.02	0.04	22		2.5	0.02
Transport services	0.13	0.72	5		0.4	0.13
Telecommunications	0.02	0.04	22		–2.1	0.02
Financial intermediation	0.09	0.19	14		2.5	0.08
Real estate, renting, and business activities	0.13	0.24	16		0.6	0.12
Public administration and defense	0.05	0.25	17		4.1	0.04
Education, health, and social work	0.06	0.36	13		2.3	0.06
Other personal services	0.13	0.88	2		–1.9	0.15

Impacts from Hypothetical Extraction

	Value (2018)	Score (0–1)	Rank (out of 25)	Distance to subregional average	10–year average growth rate (%)	10–year mean value
Changes in gross output due to hypothetical extraction	**–9.1%**	**0.79**	**15**	▲	**0.1**	**–0.09**
Agriculture, hunting, forestry, and fishing	–13.3%	0.55	19		–2.7	–15.4
Mining and quarrying	–1.3%	0.97	9		1.4	–1.2
Light manufacturing	–36.4%	0.23	24		0.0	–37.0
Heavy manufacturing	–8.2%	0.85	9		0.1	–7.6
Utilities	–2.2%	0.95	5		0.0	–2.2
Construction	–21.7%	0.49	21		2.1	–19.3
Trade services	–11.1%	0.83	8		–0.8	–11.4
Hotels and restaurants	–3.9%	0.94	10		2.4	–3.6
Transport services	–10.0%	0.46	17		–0.4	–10.5
Telecommunications	–1.3%	0.89	2		–3.3	–1.6
Financial intermediation	–4.2%	0.84	11		3.5	–3.7
Real estate, renting, and business activities	–6.7%	0.76	9		0.4	–6.4
Public administration and defense	–4.8%	0.76	9		4.1	–3.9
Education, health, and social work	–4.5%	0.85	8		1.5	–4.1
Other personal services	–7.6%	0.59	24		–0.7	–8.1

Impacts from Hypothetical Insertion

	Value (2018)	Score (0–1)	Rank (out of 25)	Distance to subregional average	10–year average growth rate (%)	10–year mean value
Changes in gross output due to hypothetical insertion	**3.8%**	**0.18**	**12**	▲	**1.0**	**0.04**
Agriculture, hunting, forestry, and fishing	3.8%	0.15	7		–1.4	4.1
Mining and quarrying	0.2%	0.01	19		0.5	0.1
Light manufacturing	23.6%	0.66	3		0.9	23.3
Heavy manufacturing	3.4%	0.05	17		–0.8	3.5
Utilities	0.8%	0.06	20		–0.6	0.8
Construction	12.1%	0.52	4		3.0	10.2
Trade services	2.1%	0.07	23		0.1	2.0
Hotels and restaurants	1.9%	0.10	14		2.9	1.7
Transport services	3.0%	0.41	11		–0.1	3.0
Telecommunications	0.4%	0.07	23		–4.0	0.5
Financial intermediation	1.2%	0.09	13		6.2	1.0

continued on next page

Bangladesh 3.1A *continued*

	Value (2018)	Score (0–1)	Rank (out of 25)	Distance to subregional average	10–year average growth rate (%)	10–year mean value
Real estate, renting, and business activities	0.9%	0.07	22		2.4	0.8
Public administration and defense	1.3%	0.31	16		6.8	1.0
Education, health, and social work	0.8%	0.10	21		2.7	0.7
Other personal services	1.1%	0.14	12		–0.1	1.1

SPREAD OF ECONOMIC LINKAGES

Demand-side
Relative evenness of direct backward linkage	**0.62**	**0.83**	**2**	▲	**–0.4**	**0.63**
Relative evenness of total backward linkage	**0.20**	**0.25**	**5**	▼	**0.0**	**0.19**
		0.00				
Backward measure of concentration based on input coefficients	**0.94**	**1.00**	**1**	▲	**0.0**	**0.94**
Agriculture, hunting, forestry, and fishing	0.91	0.79	13		0.0	0.89
Mining and quarrying	0.97	0.71	4		0.0	0.98
Light manufacturing	0.91	0.68	9		–0.2	0.92
Heavy manufacturing	0.97	1.00	1		0.2	0.96
Utilities	0.96	0.95	4		–0.1	0.96
Construction	0.95	0.96	6		–0.1	0.96
Trade services	0.97	1.00	1		0.2	0.96
Hotels and restaurants	0.90	0.76	15		0.1	0.90
Transport services	0.97	1.00	1		–0.1	0.98
Telecommunications	0.97	1.00	1		0.0	0.97
Financial intermediation	0.98	1.00	1		0.0	0.98
Real estate, renting, and business activities	0.96	0.96	6		0.0	0.96
Public administration and defense	0.81	0.00	25		–0.4	0.82
Education, health, and social work	0.94	0.59	19		–0.1	0.94
Other personal services	0.95	0.88	18		–0.1	0.95
Relative evenness of direct forward linkage	**0.58**	**0.30**	**19**	▼	**–0.6**	**0.58**
Relative evenness of total forward linkage	**0.24**	**0.16**	**15**	▼	**–0.4**	**0.23**
Forward measure of concentration based on output coefficients	**0.66**	**0.59**	**12**	▲	**0.0**	**0.66**
Agriculture, hunting, forestry, and fishing	0.42	0.54	7		0.8	0.41
Mining and quarrying	0.63	0.87	3		–0.2	0.63
Light manufacturing	0.52	0.39	22		–0.2	0.52
Heavy manufacturing	0.72	0.73	8		1.0	0.69
Utilities	0.68	0.46	20		0.6	0.67
Construction	0.63	0.73	10		–0.6	0.65
Trade services	0.66	0.29	19		0.0	0.66
Hotels and restaurants	0.80	0.71	11		–0.3	0.80
Transport services	0.76	0.69	16		–0.1	0.76
Telecommunications	0.77	0.40	19		0.1	0.76
Financial intermediation	0.72	0.78	15		–0.1	0.72
Real estate, renting, and business activities	0.87	0.81	6		0.3	0.86
Public administration and defense	0.80	0.87	5		–0.2	0.79
Education, health, and social work	0.14	0.00	25		–3.3	0.17
Other personal services	0.83	0.82	7		0.0	0.83

continued on next page

Bangladesh 3.1A *continued*

	Value (2018)	Score (0–1)	Rank (out of 25)	Distance to subregional average	10-year average growth rate (%)	10-year mean value
SENSITIVITY OF ECONOMIC LINKAGES						
Economic Complexity						
Percentage intermediate transaction	0.36	0.30	12	▲	0.5	0.35
Average output multiplier	1.45	0.14	17	▼	0.1	1.44
Average of Leontief inverse	0.19	0.12	17	▼	0.1	0.18
Average technical coefficient	0.02	0.21	17	▼	0.2	0.02
Mean intermediate coefficient	0.29	0.21	17	▼	0.2	0.29
Percentage of above-average coefficients (%)	0.27	0.44	10	▼	−0.9	0.28
Determinant of non-competitive Leontief inverse	2.16	0.03	19	▼	0.5	2.12
Determinant of competitive Leontief inverse	2.65	0.01	24	▼	0.1	2.67
Mean path length	1.56	0.18	12	▲	0.3	1.54
Cycling index	0.11	0.32	14	▲	1.7	0.10
Average propagation length	1.73	0.27	15	▼	0.3	1.70
Overall sensitivity of the economy	0.83	0.88	3	▲	0.9	0.82
Index of direct interrelatedness	0.67	0.74	4	▲	0.0	0.68
Index of indirect interrelatedness	0.16	0.59	8	▼	7.2	0.14
Global intensity index	21.72	0.14	17	▼	0.1	21.55

Note: The scores of the economy in focus are shown in the horizontal bars with labels. The colored dots represent the indicator performance of the economy in focus compared to other economies in the region. The highest rank among economies is 1 while the lowest rank is 25. The indicators shown in the chart are selected from a broader set of indicators (see the technical appendix for more details).

Source: Asian Development Bank Multi-Regional Input–Output Database. https://mrio.adbx.online/ (accessed 4 August 2020).

3.1B External Linkages

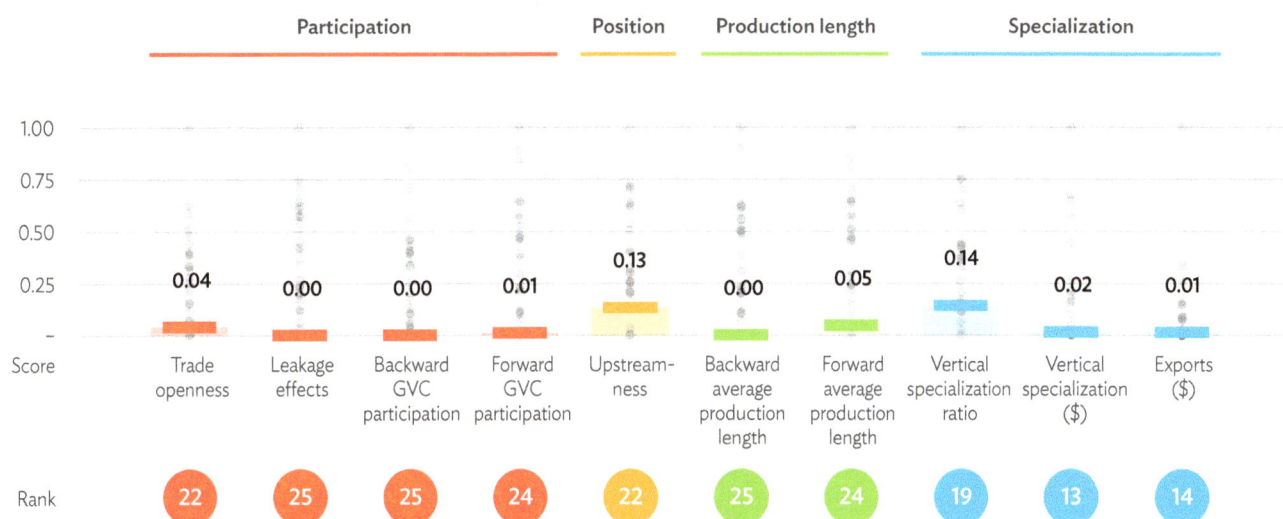

$ = United States dollars, GVC = global value chain.

Note: The scores of the economy in focus are shown in the horizontal bars with labels. The colored dots represent the indicator performance of the economy in focus compared to other economies in the region. The highest rank among economies is 1, while the lowest rank is 25. The indicators shown in the chart are selected from a broader set of indicators (see the technical appendix for more details).

Source: Asian Development Bank Multi-Regional Input–Output Database. https://mrio.adbx.online/ (accessed 4 August 2020).

		Value (2018)	Score (0–1)	Rank (out of 25)	Distance to subregional average	10–year average growth rate (%)	10–year mean value
PARTICIPATION IN GLOBAL VALUE CHAINS							
International Trade Coefficients							
Trade openness		0.37	0.04	22	▼	–1.1	0.42
Self-sufficiency ratio		0.95	0.50	19	▲	0.0	0.96
Regional supply percentage		0.87	0.79	6	▲	0.2	0.86
Regional purchase coefficient		0.92	0.91	2	▲	0.1	0.91
Sectoral purchase coefficient		0.95	0.98	2	▲	0.2	0.94
Simple location quotient of gross output		1.12	0.42	15	▼	–0.5	1.15
Fabrication effect		0.69	0.00	25	▼	0.0	0.69
Exports	($)	38,523	0.01	14	▼	9.4	28,285
Export-to-output ratio		0.04	0.04	23	▼	–3.4	0.06
Agriculture, hunting, forestry, and fishing		0.01	0.00	25		–6.0	0.01
Mining and quarrying		0.00	0.00	22		–15.1	0.01
Light manufacturing		0.29	0.53	8		–1.8	0.36
Heavy manufacturing		0.02	0.00	25		–3.8	0.05
Utilities		0.00	0.00	25		–20.0	0.00
Construction		0.00	0.05	15		37.9	0.00
Trade services		0.00	0.00	25		–7.9	0.00
Hotels and restaurants		0.00	0.00	25		–0.3	0.00
Transport services		0.00	0.00	25		33.8	0.00
Telecommunications		0.13	0.41	8		6.9	0.15

continued on next page

Bangladesh 3.1B *continued*

		Value (2018)	Score (0–1)	Rank (out of 25)	Distance to subregional average	10-year average growth rate (%)	10-year mean value
Financial intermediation		0.01	0.02	21		−2.5	0.01
Real estate, renting, and business activities		0.03	0.09	14		0.5	0.03
Public administration and defense		0.16	0.39	3		−7.0	0.22
Education, health, and social work		0.00	0.00	24		69.9	0.00
Other personal services		0.00	0.00	24		−9.5	0.00
Imports	($)	59,920	0.03	13	▼	10.5	39,246
Import-to-input ratio		0.04	0.09	24	▼	−2.5	0.05
Agriculture, hunting, forestry, and fishing		0.04	0.09	18		−2.2	0.05
Mining and quarrying		0.01	0.03	21		−3.8	0.02
Light manufacturing		0.10	0.15	18		1.3	0.10
Heavy manufacturing		0.09	0.06	22		−3.5	0.12
Utilities		0.06	0.04	23		−5.9	0.08
Construction		0.08	0.14	21		−2.5	0.10
Trade services		0.01	0.05	23		0.1	0.02
Hotels and restaurants		0.07	0.20	16		1.4	0.08
Transport services		0.05	0.07	23		−2.5	0.06
Telecommunications		0.03	0.06	21		−1.6	0.04
Financial intermediation		0.02	0.08	19		−1.1	0.03
Real estate, renting, and business activities		0.01	0.01	23		0.4	0.01
Public administration and defense		0.03	0.16	18		−0.4	0.03
Education, health, and social work		0.05	0.25	15		−2.2	0.07
Other personal services		0.02	0.03	23		−0.8	0.02
Total foreign factor content of consumption	($)	11,548	0.02	14	▼	9.9	7,751
Total foreign factor content of investment	($)	8,783	0.01	13	▼	11.1	5,520
Total foreign factor content of exports	($)	5,551	0.02	13	▼	10.9	4,138

Interregional Multipliers

	Value (2018)	Score (0–1)	Rank (out of 25)	Distance to subregional average	10-year average growth rate (%)	10-year mean value
Import Leakage Effects	0.07	0.00	25	▼	−2.1	0.08
Agriculture, hunting, forestry, and fishing	0.05	0.08	19		−1.7	0.07
Mining and quarrying	0.02	0.04	21		−3.9	0.03
Light manufacturing	0.16	0.15	18		0.6	0.16
Heavy manufacturing	0.12	0.04	23		−4.0	0.16
Utilities	0.09	0.04	24		−5.3	0.11
Construction	0.14	0.06	21		−2.1	0.16
Trade services	0.03	0.00	24		−0.1	0.03
Hotels and restaurants	0.12	0.19	19		−0.7	0.13
Transport services	0.07	0.00	24		−2.2	0.08
Telecommunications	0.05	0.03	21		−2.0	0.06
Financial intermediation	0.04	0.06	19		0.2	0.05
Real estate, renting, and business activities	0.02	0.02	24		0.5	0.02
Public administration and defense	0.05	0.13	23		0.1	0.05
Education, health, and social work	0.07	0.20	22		−2.0	0.08
Other personal services	0.02	0.01	23		−0.7	0.03
Intraregional transfer multiplier	1.45	0.14	17	▼	0.1	1.44
Agriculture, hunting, forestry, and fishing	1.35	0.22	15		0.3	1.31
Mining and quarrying	1.13	0.10	22		−0.1	1.13

continued on next page

Bangladesh 3.1B *continued*

	Value (2018)	Score (0–1)	Rank (out of 25)	Distance to subregional average	10–year average growth rate (%)	10–year mean value
Light manufacturing	1.93	0.46	10		0.2	1.92
Heavy manufacturing	1.60	0.16	16		–0.6	1.67
Utilities	1.53	0.20	14		–0.4	1.53
Construction	1.93	0.32	9		0.4	1.87
Trade services	1.23	0.07	23		0.2	1.21
Hotels and restaurants	1.93	0.57	5		0.4	1.89
Transport services	1.41	0.28	16		0.1	1.39
Telecommunications	1.39	0.22	18		–0.3	1.39
Financial intermediation	1.38	0.08	12		0.7	1.36
Real estate, renting, and business activities	1.16	0.03	23		0.3	1.15
Public administration and defense	1.37	0.38	16		0.7	1.33
Education, health, and social work	1.22	0.10	21		0.2	1.21
Other personal services	1.16	0.05	23		0.1	1.16
Interregional spillover multiplier	**1.11**	**0.12**	**24**	▼	**–0.3**	**1.14**
Agriculture, hunting, forestry, and fishing	1.09	0.12	18		–0.3	1.13
Mining and quarrying	1.04	0.04	21		–0.2	1.05
Light manufacturing	1.25	0.18	19		0.2	1.24
Heavy manufacturing	1.24	0.10	22		–0.9	1.31
Utilities	1.16	0.05	23		–0.9	1.21
Construction	1.21	0.17	21		–0.6	1.26
Trade services	1.03	0.06	23		0.0	1.04
Hotels and restaurants	1.16	0.19	16		–0.6	1.19
Transport services	1.13	0.08	23		–0.4	1.15
Telecommunications	1.08	0.07	21		–0.2	1.09
Financial intermediation	1.05	0.11	16		–0.1	1.07
Real estate, renting, and business activities	1.02	0.01	22		0.0	1.02
Public administration and defense	1.06	0.14	18		–0.1	1.08
Education, health, and social work	1.15	0.34	14		–0.3	1.19
Other personal services	1.04	0.03	22		–0.1	1.04
Interregional feedback multiplier	**1.000**	**0.01**	**16**	▼	**0.0**	**1.00**
Agriculture, hunting, forestry, and fishing	1.000	0.01	16		0.0	1.00
Mining and quarrying	1.000	0.00	17		0.0	1.00
Light manufacturing	1.000	0.03	14		0.0	1.00
Heavy manufacturing	1.000	0.00	18		0.0	1.00
Utilities	1.000	0.01	18		0.0	1.00
Construction	1.000	0.01	16		0.0	1.00
Trade services	1.000	0.00	18		0.0	1.00
Hotels and restaurants	1.000	0.02	15		0.0	1.00
Transport services	1.000	0.00	19		0.0	1.00
Telecommunications	1.000	0.01	18		0.0	1.00
Financial intermediation	1.000	0.01	14		0.0	1.00
Real estate, renting, and business activities	1.000	0.00	19		0.0	1.00
Public administration and defense	1.000	0.01	17		0.0	1.00
Education, health, and social work	1.000	0.01	16		0.0	1.00
Other personal services	1.000	0.00	17		0.0	1.00

continued on next page

Bangladesh 3.1B *continued*

	Value (2018)	Score (0–1)	Rank (out of 25)	Distance to subregional average	10–year average growth rate (%)	10–year mean value
Global Value Chain (GVC) Participation Index						
Backward GVC Participation	**8.9%**	**0.00**	**25**	▼	**−0.8**	**0.10**
Simple GVCs	**5.3%**	**0.00**	**25**	▼	**−0.9**	**0.06**
Agriculture, hunting, forestry, and fishing	0.4	0.16	10		−5.0	0.65
Mining and quarrying	0.0	0.10	20		−6.9	0.00
Light manufacturing	1.5	0.31	8		1.3	1.39
Heavy manufacturing	0.4	0.08	15		−2.2	0.45
Utilities	0.0	0.02	23		1.0	0.06
Construction	1.6	0.10	20		−0.4	1.72
Trade services	0.2	0.04	23		−1.4	0.21
Hotels and restaurants	0.1	0.07	22		2.2	0.16
Transport services	0.4	0.23	18		−3.1	0.53
Telecommunications	0.0	0.02	24		−6.1	0.04
Financial intermediation	0.0	0.01	23		6.1	0.02
Real estate, renting, and business activities	0.1	0.01	24		0.3	0.08
Public administration and defense	0.1	0.03	23		5.0	0.11
Education, health, and social work	0.2	0.09	22		−1.6	0.27
Other personal services	0.2	0.12	16		0.5	0.17
Complex GVCs	**3.5%**	**0.03**	**22**	▼	**−0.3**	**0.04**
Agriculture, hunting, forestry, and fishing	0.2	0.14	9		−4.7	0.23
Mining and quarrying	0.0	0.01	21		−0.3	0.00
Light manufacturing	1.9	0.18	5		0.3	2.12
Heavy manufacturing	0.2	0.01	19		−0.8	0.24
Utilities	0.0	0.02	24		4.1	0.02
Construction	0.6	0.09	19		1.4	0.64
Trade services	0.1	0.00	23		0.1	0.08
Hotels and restaurants	0.0	0.00	23		2.2	0.05
Transport services	0.2	0.07	23		−1.7	0.21
Telecommunications	0.0	0.02	23		−1.7	0.02
Financial intermediation	0.0	0.00	23		6.5	0.01
Real estate, renting, and business activities	0.0	0.02	24		2.3	0.03
Public administration and defense	0.1	0.04	23		7.1	0.06
Education, health, and social work	0.1	0.09	22		−0.3	0.12
Other personal services	0.1	0.13	16		0.1	0.06
Forward GVC Participation	**4.1%**	**0.01**	**24**	▼	**−2.4**	**0.05**
Simple GVCs	**2.6%**	**0.00**	**25**	▼	**−2.8**	**0.03**
Agriculture, hunting, forestry, and fishing	0.3	0.15	17		−4.8	0.54
Mining and quarrying	0.0	0.00	18		1.2	0.06
Light manufacturing	0.9	0.24	9		0.2	1.21
Heavy manufacturing	0.1	0.00	23		−4.9	0.10
Utilities	0.0	0.00	23		−1.7	0.04
Construction	0.0	0.01	19		−1.2	0.04
Trade services	0.1	0.00	25		−3.3	0.21
Hotels and restaurants	0.0	0.00	24		0.3	0.02
Transport services	0.1	0.00	25		−1.0	0.15
Telecommunications	0.1	0.04	20		−2.3	0.14

continued on next page

Bangladesh 3.1B *continued*

	Value (2018)	Score (0–1)	Rank (out of 25)	Distance to subregional average	10–year average growth rate (%)	10–year mean value
Financial intermediation	0.1	0.02	21		−0.6	0.18
Real estate, renting, and business activities	0.1	0.00	25		−8.0	0.12
Public administration and defense	0.4	0.41	3		6.2	0.44
Education, health, and social work	0.1	0.43	6		14.2	0.08
Other personal services	0.1	0.03	21		0.1	0.13
Complex GVCs	**1.5%**	**0.04**	**24**	▼	**−1.1**	**0.02**
Agriculture, hunting, forestry, and fishing	0.2	0.10	17		−2.5	0.27
Mining and quarrying	0.0	0.00	18		3.9	0.03
Light manufacturing	0.6	0.28	8		2.9	0.67
Heavy manufacturing	0.0	0.00	23		−1.9	0.05
Utilities	0.0	0.00	22		1.1	0.02
Construction	0.0	0.01	18		0.6	0.02
Trade services	0.1	0.00	25		−1.1	0.11
Hotels and restaurants	0.0	0.00	22		2.9	0.01
Transport services	0.1	0.00	25		1.5	0.08
Telecommunications	0.0	0.05	20		−0.2	0.06
Financial intermediation	0.1	0.04	22		1.7	0.10
Real estate, renting, and business activities	0.0	0.00	25		−5.0	0.07
Public administration and defense	0.3	0.46	3		5.2	0.25
Education, health, and social work	0.1	0.51	2		13.0	0.04
Other personal services	0.0	0.07	19		0.9	0.07

SPECIALIZATION IN GLOBAL VALUE CHAINS

Vertical Specialization

	Value (2018)	Score (0–1)	Rank (out of 25)	Distance to subregional average	10–year average growth rate (%)	10–year mean value
Vertical Specialization Ratio	**14.4%**	**0.14**	**19**	▼	**0.7**	**0.15**
Agriculture, hunting, forestry, and fishing	5.4%	0.07	19		−1.7	0.07
Mining and quarrying	2.1%	0.04	21		−3.8	0.03
Light manufacturing	15.8%	0.16	18		0.6	0.16
Heavy manufacturing	11.8%	0.04	23		−4.0	0.16
Utilities	0.0%	0.00	25		−40.0	0.04
Construction	13.9%	0.06	21		−2.1	0.16
Trade services	2.5%	0.00	24		−11.4	0.02
Hotels and restaurants	11.7%	0.19	19		−0.7	0.13
Transport services	7.4%	0.00	25		−2.2	0.08
Telecommunications	5.3%	0.03	21		−2.0	0.06
Financial intermediation	4.1%	0.06	19		0.3	0.05
Real estate, renting, and business activities	1.6%	0.02	24		0.4	0.02
Public administration and defense	4.6%	0.13	23		0.1	0.05
Education, health, and social work	6.8%	0.20	22		−2.0	0.08
Other personal services	2.5%	0.02	23		−0.6	0.03

Revealed Comparative Advantages

Traditional RCA Index

	Value (2018)	Score (0–1)	Rank (out of 25)	Distance to subregional average	10–year average growth rate (%)	10–year mean value
Agriculture, hunting, forestry, and fishing	0.34	0.06	18	▼	−7.4	0.67
Mining and quarrying	0.00	0.00	21	▼	−6.6	0.01
Light manufacturing	5.62	1.00	1	▲	0.4	5.52

continued on next page

Bangladesh 3.1B *continued*

	Value (2018)	Score (0–1)	Rank (out of 25)	Distance to subregional average	10–year average growth rate (%)	10–year mean value
Heavy manufacturing	0.03	0.01	22	▼	–3.2	0.05
Utilities	0.00	0.00	25	▼	–40.0	0.00
Construction	1.03	0.13	10	▼	35.4	0.40
Trade services	0.00	0.00	25	▼	0.9	0.00
Hotels and restaurants	0.00	0.00	24	▼	2.2	0.01
Transport services	0.03	0.00	25	▼	37.1	0.03
Telecommunications	1.97	0.32	10	▼	4.6	2.44
Financial intermediation	0.09	0.02	19	▼	1.5	0.10
Real estate, renting, and business activities	0.25	0.08	9	▼	1.2	0.23
Public administration and defense	16.31	0.59	3	▲	–3.1	16.96
Education, health, and social work	0.01	0.00	24	▼	–9.4	0.02
Other personal services	0.06	0.00	22	▼	36.4	0.12

New RCA Index (Based on Domestic Value Added)

	Value (2018)	Score (0–1)	Rank (out of 25)	Distance to subregional average	10–year average growth rate (%)	10–year mean value
Agriculture, hunting, forestry, and fishing	2.75	0.39	6	▲	–3.4	3.24
Mining and quarrying	0.24	0.03	12	▼	5.2	0.19
Light manufacturing	4.39	1.00	1	▲	1.1	4.21
Heavy manufacturing	0.11	0.05	18	▼	0.0	0.11
Utilities	0.57	0.03	15	▼	0.8	0.56
Construction	1.50	0.08	7	▼	2.3	1.20
Trade services	0.52	0.12	23	▼	–2.3	0.56
Hotels and restaurants	0.58	0.01	16	▼	1.6	0.59
Transport services	0.67	0.18	17	▼	1.5	0.69
Telecommunications	1.30	0.31	9	▼	2.3	1.61
Financial intermediation	0.96	0.24	7	▲	0.9	0.91
Real estate, renting, and business activities	0.34	0.17	13	▼	0.2	0.33
Public administration and defense	6.98	0.63	3	▲	–2.6	6.98
Education, health, and social work	1.77	0.40	3	▲	1.4	1.55
Other personal services	1.01	0.12	7	▼	–2.0	1.76

POSITION IN GLOBAL VALUE CHAINS

	Value (2018)	Score (0–1)	Rank (out of 25)	Distance to subregional average	10–year average growth rate (%)	10–year mean value
Upstreamness Index	**1.8**	**0.13**	**22**	▼	**–0.1**	**1.8**
Agriculture, hunting, forestry, and fishing	1.8	0.21	18		0.7	1.8
Mining and quarrying	2.7	0.61	15		0.3	2.6
Light manufacturing	1.9	0.25	14		0.8	1.8
Heavy manufacturing	1.7	0.00	25		–1.3	1.8
Utilities	2.1	0.13	22		–0.7	2.2
Construction	1.4	0.32	9		0.1	1.3
Trade services	1.6	0.05	24		0.2	1.5
Hotels and restaurants	1.9	0.58	9		–0.1	1.9
Transport services	1.5	0.07	24		0.3	1.5
Telecommunications	1.9	0.23	17		0.1	2.0
Financial intermediation	2.5	0.28	11		0.0	2.5
Real estate, renting, and business activities	1.5	0.04	24		–0.1	1.5
Public administration and defense	1.6	1.00	1		–0.4	1.7
Education, health, and social work	1.3	0.68	2		0.8	1.2
Other personal services	1.3	0.11	22		–1.2	1.5

continued on next page

Bangladesh 3.1B *continued*

	Value (2018)	Score (0–1)	Rank (out of 25)	Distance to subregional average	10–year average growth rate (%)	10–year mean value
PRODUCTION LENGTH OF GLOBAL VALUE CHAINS						
Backward Measures of Average Production Length						
Production Length of Global Value Chain Activity (B)	**0.3**	**0.00**	**25**	▼	**−1.7**	**0.3**
Agriculture, hunting, forestry, and fishing	0.2	0.07	20		−1.4	0.3
Mining and quarrying	0.1	0.05	21		−3.2	0.1
Light manufacturing	0.7	0.20	18		0.6	0.6
Heavy manufacturing	0.5	0.05	23		−3.6	0.7
Utilities	0.3	0.03	24		−4.2	0.4
Construction	0.6	0.03	21		−1.6	0.7
Trade services	0.1	0.00	25		0.0	0.1
Hotels and restaurants	0.5	0.18	20		−1.0	0.5
Transport services	0.3	0.00	25		−1.8	0.3
Telecommunications	0.2	0.03	22		−2.0	0.2
Financial intermediation	0.2	0.09	19		0.6	0.2
Real estate, renting, and business activities	0.1	0.02	24		0.7	0.1
Public administration and defense	0.2	0.13	23		0.5	0.2
Education, health, and social work	0.3	0.16	22		−1.6	0.3
Other personal services	0.1	0.01	23		−0.6	0.1
Forward Measures of Average Production Length						
Production Length of Global Value Chain Activity (F)	**0.2**	**0.05**	**24**	▼	**−2.8**	**0.2**
Agriculture, hunting, forestry, and fishing	0.2	0.07	23		−0.4	0.2
Mining and quarrying	0.2	0.06	20		−0.4	0.3
Light manufacturing	0.4	0.18	20		0.5	0.5
Heavy manufacturing	0.1	0.00	25		−6.0	0.2
Utilities	0.2	0.02	24		−3.6	0.3
Construction	0.0	0.03	21		−2.5	0.0
Trade services	0.1	0.00	25		−1.5	0.1
Hotels and restaurants	0.1	0.06	20		−1.4	0.2
Transport services	0.1	0.00	25		−0.5	0.1
Telecommunications	0.4	0.15	19		0.4	0.5
Financial intermediation	0.3	0.09	23		−2.0	0.4
Real estate, renting, and business activities	0.1	0.00	25		−6.2	0.1
Public administration and defense	0.6	0.72	2		4.4	0.7
Education, health, and social work	0.1	0.63	2		12.3	0.1
Other personal services	0.0	0.00	25		−0.2	0.1

Note: The scores of the economy in focus are shown in the horizontal bars with labels. The colored dots represent the indicator performance of the economy in focus compared to other economies in the region. The highest rank among economies is 1 while the lowest rank is 25. The indicators shown in the chart are selected from a broader set of indicators (see the technical appendix for more details).

Source: Asian Development Bank Multi-Regional Input–Output Database. https://mrio.adbx.online/ (accessed 4 August 2020).

3.2 Bhutan

3.2A Internal Linkages

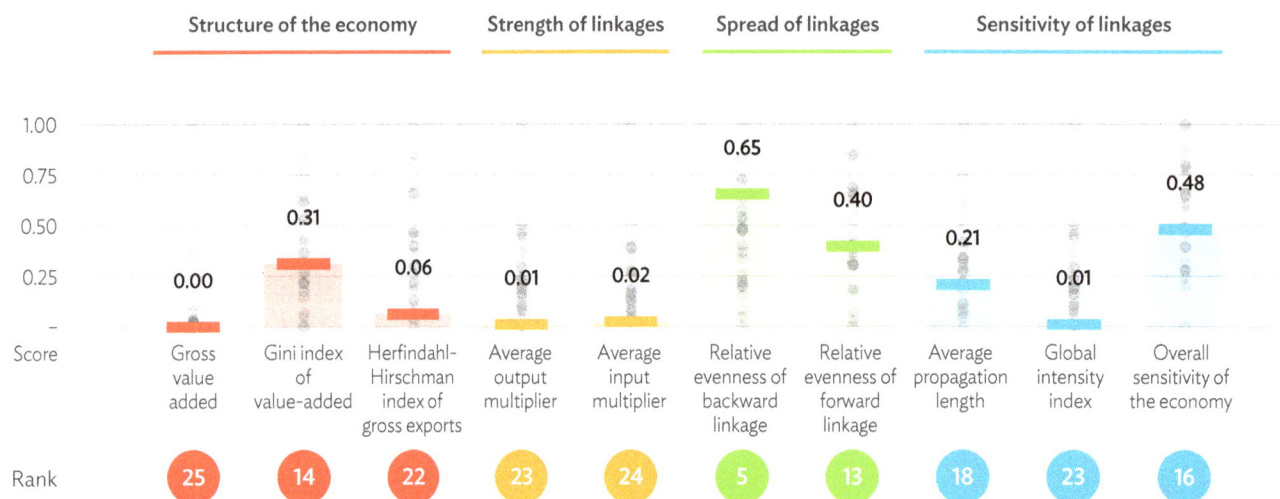

Note: The scores of the economy in focus are shown in the horizontal bars with labels. The colored dots represent the indicator performance of the economy in focus compared to other economies in the region. The highest rank among economies is 1 while the lowest rank is 25. The indicators shown in the chart are selected from a broader set of indicators (see the technical appendix for more details).

Source: Asian Development Bank Multi-Regional Input–Output Database. https://mrio.adbx.online/ (accessed 4 August 2020).

		Value (2018)	Score (0–1)	Rank (out of 25)	Distance to subregional average	10-year average growth rate (%)	10-year mean value
STRUCTURE OF THE ECONOMY							
Economic Indicators							
Gross output	($)	4,117	0.01	25	▼	7.7	3,072
Gross value-added	($)	2,448	0.02	25	▼	7.5	1,796
Value-added content of domestic final demand		1,822	0.02	25		9.6	1,283
Value-added content of exports		626	0.01	25		5.3	512
Intermediate inputs	($)	1,608	0.01	25	▼	8.3	1,241
Domestic inputs		1,087	0.01	25		8.9	822
Foreign inputs		522	0.02	25		7.7	419
Direct production	($)	3,031	0.02	25	▼	7.6	2,250
Domestic final demand		2,276	0.02	25		9.8	1,637
Exports		754	0.01	25		5.9	613
Indirect production	($)	1,087	0.01	25	▼	8.9	822
Indirect production embedded in domestic final demand		845	0.01	25		11.7	637
Indirect production embedded in exports		242	0.01	25		9.5	185
Economic Diversification							
Gross output		0.25	0.36	17	▼	0.7	0.26
Gini concentration index of gross output		0.44	0.42	16		0.4	0.44
Herfindahl-Hirschman concentration index of gross output		0.05	0.26	16		3.5	0.06
Theil concentration index of gross output		0.27	0.34	17		1.0	0.28

continued on next page

Bhutan 3.2A *continued*

	Value (2018)	Score (0–1)	Rank (out of 25)	Distance to subregional average	10-year average growth rate (%)	10-year mean value
Gross value-added	**0.24**	**0.14**	**14**	▼	**−1.2**	**0.25**
Gini concentration index of gross value added	0.42	0.18	14		−0.8	0.43
Herfindahl-Hirschman concentration index of gross value added	0.05	0.05	14		−2.4	0.05
Theil concentration index of gross value added	0.25	0.15	14		−1.6	0.27
Gross exports	**0.38**	**1.00**	**24**	▼	**−1.6**	**0.40**
Gini concentration index of gross exports	0.56	1.00	25		−1.7	0.60
Herfindahl-Hirschman concentration index of gross exports	0.12	1.00	22		1.2	0.12
Theil concentration index of gross exports	0.45	1.00	24		−1.8	0.49
Structural Changes						
Changes in output due to technological changes	**−0.5%**	**0.75**	**20**	▲	**–**	**–**
Agriculture, hunting, forestry, and fishing	−0.2%	0.52	11			
Mining and quarrying	3.7%	0.74	3			
Light manufacturing	−5.1%	0.40	25			
Heavy manufacturing	−1.2%	0.66	17			
Utilities	−1.0%	0.48	19			
Construction	0.8%	0.20	5			
Trade services	0.6%	0.44	5			
Hotels and restaurants	1.4%	0.07	4			
Transport services	0.7%	0.59	5			
Telecommunications	−2.2%	0.13	25			
Financial intermediation	−2.0%	0.59	23			
Real estate, renting, and business activities	−0.6%	0.68	21			
Public administration and defense	−0.8%	0.52	23			
Education, health, and social work	−0.3%	0.86	23			
Other personal services	−2.0%	0.18	25			
Changes in output due to structural changes in consumption (%)	**3.2%**	**0.71**	**14**	▼	**–**	**–**
Agriculture, hunting, forestry, and fishing	5.0%	1.00	4			
Mining and quarrying	2.9%	0.30	6			
Light manufacturing	2.2%	0.65	14			
Heavy manufacturing	1.5%	0.47	12			
Utilities	1.1%	0.86	21			
Construction	1.6%	0.26	7			
Trade services	4.6%	1.00	7			
Hotels and restaurants	1.9%	0.32	21			
Transport services	3.5%	1.00	9			
Telecommunications	4.1%	0.72	9			
Financial intermediation	5.4%	0.75	6			
Real estate, renting, and business activities	2.4%	0.43	14			
Public administration and defense	5.7%	0.78	14			
Education, health, and social work	0.3%	0.39	24			
Other personal services	6.0%	0.67	9			
Changes in output due to structural changes in investment (%)	**1.0%**	**0.94**	**15**	▼	**–**	**–**
Agriculture, hunting, forestry, and fishing	0.5%	0.23	9			
Mining and quarrying	0.9%	1.00	12			
Light manufacturing	0.9%	0.64	7			

continued on next page

Bhutan 3.2A *continued*

	Value (2018)	Score (0–1)	Rank (out of 25)	Distance to subregional average	10-year average growth rate (%)	10-year mean value
Heavy manufacturing	−1.1%	1.00	25			
Utilities	1.6%	0.99	5			
Construction	4.8%	0.75	16			
Trade services	1.7%	0.62	7			
Hotels and restaurants	0.4%	1.00	7			
Transport services	1.9%	0.49	3			
Telecommunications	0.5%	0.36	14			
Financial intermediation	0.9%	1.00	10			
Real estate, renting, and business activities	1.6%	0.32	5			
Public administration and defense	0.0%	1.00	12			
Education, health, and social work	0.0%	0.08	24			
Other personal services	0.1%	0.35	16			
Changes in output due to structural changes in stock (%)	**−0.1%**	**0.29**	**18**	▼	–	–
Agriculture, hunting, forestry, and fishing	−0.4%	0.53	20			
Mining and quarrying	−0.1%	0.38	20			
Light manufacturing	−0.1%	0.17	17			
Heavy manufacturing	0.0%	0.30	18			
Utilities	0.0%	0.12	17			
Construction	0.0%	0.75	17			
Trade services	0.0%	0.29	17			
Hotels and restaurants	0.0%	0.45	17			
Transport services	0.0%	0.06	21			
Telecommunications	0.0%	0.46	15			
Financial intermediation	0.0%	0.90	19			
Real estate, renting, and business activities	0.0%	0.15	17			
Public administration and defense	0.0%	0.64	19			
Education, health, and social work	0.0%	0.23	17			
Other personal services	0.0%	0.42	14			
Changes in output due to structural changes in export	**2.3%**	**0.30**	**9**	▲	–	–
Agriculture, hunting, forestry, and fishing	0.2%	0.51	19			
Mining and quarrying	5.6%	0.17	4			
Light manufacturing	−0.9%	0.44	24			
Heavy manufacturing	1.1%	0.25	17			
Utilities	2.7%	0.08	5			
Construction	0.4%	0.09	7			
Trade services	1.3%	0.10	13			
Hotels and restaurants	12.1%	0.11	1			
Transport services	1.5%	0.44	12			
Telecommunications	3.8%	0.20	6			
Financial intermediation	0.3%	0.39	19			
Real estate, renting, and business activities	1.3%	0.32	11			
Public administration and defense	0.4%	0.49	7			
Education, health, and social work	0.5%	0.13	4			
Other personal services	3.9%	0.06	2			

continued on next page

Bhutan 3.2A *continued*

	Value (2018)	Score (0–1)	Rank (out of 25)	Distance to subregional average	10–year average growth rate (%)	10–year mean value
Changes in output due to import substitution on intermediate demand	**0.2%**	**0.39**	**10**	▼	–	–
Agriculture, hunting, forestry, and fishing	0.2%	0.68	3			
Mining and quarrying	1.8%	0.32	5			
Light manufacturing	3.1%	0.80	1			
Heavy manufacturing	1.4%	0.27	6			
Utilities	0.4%	0.69	4			
Construction	−0.5%	0.86	23			
Trade services	0.1%	0.76	7			
Hotels and restaurants	−0.2%	0.97	18			
Transport services	−0.4%	0.46	22			
Telecommunications	−0.4%	0.94	19			
Financial intermediation	0.0%	0.59	11			
Real estate, renting, and business activities	−1.1%	0.72	22			
Public administration and defense	0.0%	0.65	5			
Education, health, and social work	−0.2%	0.59	25			
Other personal services	−1.0%	0.53	24			
Changes in output due to import substitution on domestic final demand	**−0.1%**	**0.83**	**15**	▼	–	–
Agriculture, hunting, forestry, and fishing	1.3%	0.56	1			
Mining and quarrying	0.9%	0.52	2			
Light manufacturing	−0.1%	0.78	8			
Heavy manufacturing	3.1%	0.61	1			
Utilities	0.2%	0.78	4			
Construction	−0.7%	0.67	23			
Trade services	0.1%	0.91	5			
Hotels and restaurants	−0.6%	0.67	25			
Transport services	−0.1%	0.91	14			
Telecommunications	−1.1%	0.72	24			
Financial intermediation	0.0%	0.82	7			
Real estate, renting, and business activities	−1.3%	0.55	23			
Public administration and defense	0.0%	0.38	11			
Education, health, and social work	−2.8%	0.87	25			
Other personal services	−1.3%	0.93	23			

STRENGTH OF LINKAGES

Demand-side Linkages

	Value (2018)	Score (0–1)	Rank (out of 25)	Distance to subregional average	10–year average growth rate (%)	10–year mean value
Direct backward linkage	**0.25**	**0.21**	**23**	▼	**−0.5**	**0.25**
Agriculture, hunting, forestry, and fishing	0.07	0.30	25		3.2	0.06
Mining and quarrying	0.24	0.14	12		2.8	0.23
Light manufacturing	0.46	0.75	18		−2.1	0.49
Heavy manufacturing	0.52	0.35	6		0.9	0.49
Utilities	0.19	0.43	23		28.6	0.09
Construction	0.34	0.61	21		1.1	0.35
Trade services	0.15	0.01	24		−0.1	0.22
Hotels and restaurants	0.20	1.00	25		−3.0	0.26
Transport services	0.26	0.42	18		1.4	0.24
Telecommunications	0.26	0.28	18		−2.9	0.29

continued on next page

Bhutan 3.2A *continued*

	Value (2018)	Score (0–1)	Rank (out of 25)	Distance to subregional average	10–year average growth rate (%)	10–year mean value
Financial intermediation	0.07	0.25	25		5.1	0.08
Real estate, renting, and business activities	0.15	0.01	22		−1.6	0.18
Public administration and defense	0.37	0.50	6		1.3	0.34
Education, health, and social work	0.15	0.14	21		−5.9	0.20
Other personal services	0.28	0.03	17		1.4	0.26
Total backward linkage	**1.33**	**0.14**	**23**	▼	**−0.2**	**1.33**
Agriculture, hunting, forestry, and fishing	1.09	0.22	25		0.1	1.08
Mining and quarrying	1.33	0.10	14		0.5	1.31
Light manufacturing	1.59	0.46	21		−0.8	1.61
Heavy manufacturing	1.68	0.16	10		0.4	1.64
Utilities	1.27	0.20	23		1.2	1.12
Construction	1.47	0.32	23		0.1	1.49
Trade services	1.19	0.07	25		−0.3	1.29
Hotels and restaurants	1.23	0.57	25		−0.8	1.30
Transport services	1.33	0.28	21		0.2	1.30
Telecommunications	1.35	0.22	19		−1.0	1.40
Financial intermediation	1.09	0.08	25		0.1	1.11
Real estate, renting, and business activities	1.21	0.03	22		−0.7	1.24
Public administration and defense	1.52	0.38	8		0.2	1.47
Education, health, and social work	1.20	0.10	22		−1.8	1.28
Other personal services	1.36	0.05	17		0.2	1.34
Normalized backward linkage	**–**	**–**	**–**	▬	**–**	**–**
Agriculture, hunting, forestry, and fishing	0.82	0.33	24		0.3	0.81
Mining and quarrying	1.00	0.22	6		0.7	0.98
Light manufacturing	1.20	0.79	14		−0.6	1.21
Heavy manufacturing	1.27	0.40	3		0.6	1.23
Utilities	0.96	0.33	15		1.4	0.84
Construction	1.11	0.72	17		0.2	1.12
Trade services	0.89	0.21	16		−0.1	0.97
Hotels and restaurants	0.93	1.00	25		−0.6	0.98
Transport services	1.00	0.37	12		0.4	0.98
Telecommunications	1.02	0.52	10		−0.8	1.05
Financial intermediation	0.82	0.13	22		0.4	0.83
Real estate, renting, and business activities	0.91	0.18	12		−0.5	0.93
Public administration and defense	1.14	0.52	2		0.4	1.10
Education, health, and social work	0.91	0.34	14		−1.6	0.96
Other personal services	1.02	0.00	7		0.5	1.01
Net backward linkage	**0.94**	**0.18**	**10**	▲	**0.0**	**0.91**
Agriculture, hunting, forestry, and fishing	0.90	0.63	5		0.1	0.85
Mining and quarrying	0.62	0.01	10		0.9	0.65
Light manufacturing	0.88	0.62	19		−2.4	0.89
Heavy manufacturing	1.24	0.56	3		−0.3	1.26
Utilities	0.92	0.36	3		2.3	0.79
Construction	1.25	0.35	18		0.3	1.30
Trade services	0.80	0.38	13		1.1	0.85

continued on next page

Bhutan 3.2A *continued*

	Value (2018)	Score (0–1)	Rank (out of 25)	Distance to subregional average	10-year average growth rate (%)	10-year mean value
Hotels and restaurants	0.90	0.25	24		1.5	0.91
Transport services	0.75	0.50	17		–0.6	0.73
Telecommunications	0.95	0.46	5		1.7	0.83
Financial intermediation	0.49	0.05	16		3.5	0.45
Real estate, renting, and business activities	0.50	0.76	23		–3.4	0.52
Public administration and defense	1.49	0.19	7		0.6	1.39
Education, health, and social work	1.19	0.00	18		–1.6	1.26
Other personal services	1.16	0.62	9		3.9	0.98
Growth equalized output multipliers	**0.09**	**0.18**	**23**	▼	**0.0**	**0.09**
Agriculture, hunting, forestry, and fishing	0.16	0.49	8		–0.2	0.16
Mining and quarrying	0.05	0.04	9		7.7	0.03
Light manufacturing	0.10	0.68	20		–4.4	0.12
Heavy manufacturing	0.08	0.11	17		–1.0	0.09
Utilities	0.17	0.05	1		–1.9	0.15
Construction	0.32	0.34	2		4.9	0.33
Trade services	0.08	0.28	23		5.3	0.07
Hotels and restaurants	0.02	0.05	23		5.4	0.02
Transport services	0.13	0.57	6		0.4	0.12
Telecommunications	0.03	0.08	15		–1.5	0.03
Financial intermediation	0.05	0.14	19		–1.2	0.05
Real estate, renting, and business activities	0.03	0.28	25		–2.5	0.04
Public administration and defense	0.10	0.25	5		0.4	0.10
Education, health, and social work	0.04	0.21	25		–3.5	0.05
Other personal services	0.01	0.56	25		–1.2	0.01

Supply-Side Linkages

	Value (2018)	Score (0–1)	Rank (out of 25)	Distance to subregional average	10-year average growth rate (%)	10-year mean value
Direct forward linkage	**0.30**	**0.46**	**24**	▼	**0.0**	**0.32**
Agriculture, hunting, forestry, and fishing	0.18	0.37	25		4.1	0.21
Mining and quarrying	0.53	1.00	13		2.2	0.50
Light manufacturing	0.45	0.36	10		3.5	0.45
Heavy manufacturing	0.26	0.53	23		3.1	0.23
Utilities	0.28	0.68	24		0.0	0.30
Construction	0.15	0.50	13		0.0	0.13
Trade services	0.32	0.35	19		–1.6	0.34
Hotels and restaurants	0.26	0.96	11		5.3	0.29
Transport services	0.44	0.30	13		1.8	0.44
Telecommunications	0.30	0.37	23		–2.8	0.40
Financial intermediation	0.55	0.97	16		–0.6	0.59
Real estate, renting, and business activities	0.58	0.13	3		4.7	0.58
Public administration and defense	0.02	0.70	16		0.0	0.05
Education, health, and social work	0.01	0.65	22		1.5	0.02
Other personal services	0.14	0.16	20		–7.9	0.27
Total forward linkage	**1.41**	**0.25**	**24**	▼	**–0.1**	**1.44**
Agriculture, hunting, forestry, and fishing	1.23	0.27	25		0.4	1.28
Mining and quarrying	1.74	0.51	15		0.6	1.70
Light manufacturing	1.57	0.23	13		1.0	1.57

continued on next page

Bhutan 3.2A *continued*

	Value (2018)	Score (0–1)	Rank (out of 25)	Distance to subregional average	10–year average growth rate (%)	10–year mean value
Heavy manufacturing	1.35	0.30	23		0.6	1.30
Utilities	1.40	0.33	24		−0.2	1.44
Construction	1.17	0.39	17		−0.3	1.16
Trade services	1.44	0.23	19		−0.6	1.45
Hotels and restaurants	1.37	0.67	13		0.0	1.40
Transport services	1.58	0.18	14		0.5	1.58
Telecommunications	1.43	0.36	24		−1.1	1.59
Financial intermediation	1.78	0.28	17		−0.3	1.83
Real estate, renting, and business activities	1.80	0.12	7		1.7	1.81
Public administration and defense	1.03	0.70	14		−0.4	1.08
Education, health, and social work	1.01	0.71	23		−0.2	1.03
Other personal services	1.20	0.19	20		−1.9	1.38
Normalized forward linkage	–	–	–	▬	–	–
Agriculture, hunting, forestry, and fishing	0.87	0.29	24		0.4	0.89
Mining and quarrying	1.31	1.00	10		0.7	1.28
Light manufacturing	1.19	0.64	6		1.2	1.18
Heavy manufacturing	1.02	0.53	21		0.8	0.97
Utilities	1.06	0.65	23		−0.1	1.08
Construction	0.89	0.51	7		0.0	0.87
Trade services	1.08	0.33	13		−0.5	1.09
Hotels and restaurants	1.03	1.00	5		0.0	1.05
Transport services	1.19	0.32	8		0.7	1.19
Telecommunications	1.08	0.47	17		−0.9	1.19
Financial intermediation	1.34	0.38	11		−0.1	1.37
Real estate, renting, and business activities	1.36	0.22	2		1.9	1.36
Public administration and defense	0.78	0.80	4		−0.2	0.81
Education, health, and social work	0.76	0.93	8		0.1	0.77
Other personal services	0.91	0.22	14		−1.7	1.03
Net forward linkage	**0.91**	**0.84**	**8**	▲	**0.4**	**0.91**
Agriculture, hunting, forestry, and fishing	1.10	0.51	13		0.4	1.15
Mining and quarrying	1.21	1.00	11		0.3	1.18
Light manufacturing	0.64	0.42	5		6.2	0.58
Heavy manufacturing	0.38	0.90	20		1.8	0.36
Utilities	0.96	0.57	9		−1.6	1.20
Construction	0.50	0.56	9		−0.3	0.46
Trade services	1.18	0.62	8		0.3	1.06
Hotels and restaurants	1.02	0.28	1		2.3	0.89
Transport services	0.75	0.58	12		0.8	0.74
Telecommunications	0.93	0.56	15		1.3	0.95
Financial intermediation	1.61	0.63	7		−0.2	1.64
Real estate, renting, and business activities	1.34	0.68	4		3.5	1.32
Public administration and defense	0.55	0.77	20		−1.2	0.64
Education, health, and social work	0.76	0.95	10		2.7	0.72
Other personal services	0.72	0.79	18		−1.8	0.81

continued on next page

Bhutan 3.2A *continued*

	Value (2018)	Score (0–1)	Rank (out of 25)	Distance to subregional average	10–year average growth rate (%)	10–year mean value
Growth equalized input multipliers	**0.09**	**0.19**	**23**	▼	**0.0**	**0.09**
Agriculture, hunting, forestry, and fishing	0.22	0.49	11		0.0	0.23
Mining and quarrying	0.08	0.07	9		7.6	0.05
Light manufacturing	0.08	0.65	19		0.0	0.09
Heavy manufacturing	0.04	0.16	17		−0.5	0.04
Utilities	0.20	0.10	1		−4.2	0.23
Construction	0.20	0.17	2		3.7	0.18
Trade services	0.12	0.38	23		5.0	0.10
Hotels and restaurants	0.03	0.04	14		7.8	0.02
Transport services	0.12	0.72	6		1.2	0.11
Telecommunications	0.03	0.04	13		−0.3	0.03
Financial intermediation	0.09	0.19	16		−1.8	0.10
Real estate, renting, and business activities	0.06	0.24	25		0.0	0.06
Public administration and defense	0.07	0.25	10		−1.0	0.08
Education, health, and social work	0.03	0.36	24		−1.1	0.05
Other personal services	0.01	0.88	25		−3.2	0.01

Impacts from Hypothetical Extraction

	Value (2018)	Score (0–1)	Rank (out of 25)	Distance to subregional average	10–year average growth rate (%)	10–year mean value
Changes in gross output due to hypothetical extraction	**−8.7%**	**0.79**	**9**	▼	**−0.1**	**−0.09**
Agriculture, hunting, forestry, and fishing	−12.7%	0.55	18		0.1	−12.1
Mining and quarrying	−5.0%	0.97	18		8.5	−3.3
Light manufacturing	−11.2%	0.23	8		−4.8	−13.8
Heavy manufacturing	−9.2%	0.85	10		−0.5	−9.8
Utilities	−15.0%	0.95	25		−0.3	−12.6
Construction	−32.7%	0.49	24		4.8	−34.0
Trade services	−7.3%	0.83	3		5.2	−6.9
Hotels and restaurants	−2.2%	0.94	3		4.7	−1.8
Transport services	−11.6%	0.46	21		0.6	−10.9
Telecommunications	−2.5%	0.89	15		−2.3	−2.6
Financial intermediation	−3.6%	0.84	8		−0.7	−4.1
Real estate, renting, and business activities	−3.0%	0.76	1		−2.9	−3.3
Public administration and defense	−11.0%	0.76	23		0.8	−10.5
Education, health, and social work	−3.2%	0.85	2		−4.9	−5.0
Other personal services	−0.6%	0.59	1		−0.8	−0.6

Impacts from Hypothetical Insertion

	Value (2018)	Score (0–1)	Rank (out of 25)	Distance to subregional average	10–year average growth rate (%)	10–year mean value
Changes in gross output due to hypothetical insertion	**2.4%**	**0.18**	**24**	▼	**0.5**	**0.02**
Agriculture, hunting, forestry, and fishing	1.1%	0.15	20		3.9	0.9
Mining and quarrying	1.2%	0.01	7		12.1	0.8
Light manufacturing	4.3%	0.66	21		−5.4	5.6
Heavy manufacturing	3.8%	0.05	16		0.7	4.0
Utilities	3.3%	0.06	3		36.2	1.5
Construction	11.0%	0.52	5		6.1	11.9
Trade services	1.2%	0.07	25		6.4	1.5
Hotels and restaurants	0.4%	0.10	24		2.2	0.4
Transport services	3.1%	0.41	10		2.1	2.7
Telecommunications	0.7%	0.07	19		−4.3	0.8
Financial intermediation	0.3%	0.09	24		5.1	0.4

continued on next page

Bhutan 3.2A *continued*

	Value (2018)	Score (0–1)	Rank (out of 25)	Distance to subregional average	10–year average growth rate (%)	10–year mean value
Real estate, renting, and business activities	0.5%	0.07	25		–3.2	0.7
Public administration and defense	3.8%	0.31	4		2.2	3.4
Education, health, and social work	0.5%	0.10	24		–9.7	1.1
Other personal services	0.1%	0.14	23		0.1	0.2

SPREAD OF ECONOMIC LINKAGES

Demand-side

	Value (2018)	Score (0–1)	Rank (out of 25)	Distance to subregional average	10–year average growth rate (%)	10–year mean value
Relative evenness of direct backward linkage	0.53	0.83	5	▲	0.0	0.53
Relative evenness of total backward linkage	0.13	0.25	16	▼	–0.2	0.13
		0.00				
Backward measure of concentration based on input coefficients	0.90	1.00	15	▼	0.0	0.91
Agriculture, hunting, forestry, and fishing	0.88	0.79	19		0.2	0.87
Mining and quarrying	0.86	0.71	21		–0.4	0.91
Light manufacturing	0.93	0.68	5		0.3	0.94
Heavy manufacturing	0.89	1.00	10		–0.2	0.92
Utilities	0.96	0.95	3		0.0	0.95
Construction	0.95	0.96	5		0.5	0.94
Trade services	0.82	1.00	24		–0.3	0.85
Hotels and restaurants	0.84	0.76	23		0.3	0.82
Transport services	0.92	1.00	16		0.1	0.91
Telecommunications	0.93	1.00	13		0.0	0.93
Financial intermediation	0.89	1.00	14		–0.2	0.90
Real estate, renting, and business activities	0.96	0.96	5		–0.1	0.96
Public administration and defense	0.82	0.00	24		–0.3	0.83
Education, health, and social work	0.93	0.59	20		–0.3	0.95
Other personal services	0.95	0.88	15		–0.1	0.96
Relative evenness of direct forward linkage	0.61	0.30	13	▼	1.9	0.58
Relative evenness of total forward linkage	0.18	0.16	23	▼	1.4	0.18
Forward measure of concentration based on output coefficients	0.63	0.59	17	▲	0.1	0.62
Agriculture, hunting, forestry, and fishing	0.50	0.54	3		–0.7	0.48
Mining and quarrying	0.39	0.87	14		1.9	0.37
Light manufacturing	0.57	0.39	20		–0.8	0.55
Heavy manufacturing	0.60	0.73	16		–1.3	0.62
Utilities	0.63	0.46	22		3.8	0.53
Construction	0.52	0.73	16		–0.9	0.51
Trade services	0.68	0.29	17		–0.5	0.66
Hotels and restaurants	0.62	0.71	24		2.9	0.54
Transport services	0.72	0.69	21		–1.2	0.72
Telecommunications	0.87	0.40	5		–0.3	0.88
Financial intermediation	0.62	0.78	23		–0.7	0.66
Real estate, renting, and business activities	0.83	0.81	11		–0.4	0.84
Public administration and defense	0.77	0.87	9		1.4	0.74
Education, health, and social work	0.41	0.00	21		–0.3	0.46
Other personal services	0.77	0.82	12		1.6	0.72

continued on next page

Bhutan 3.2A *continued*

	Value (2018)	Score (0–1)	Rank (out of 25)	Distance to subregional average	10–year average growth rate (%)	10–year mean value
SENSITIVITY OF ECONOMIC LINKAGES						
Economic Complexity						
Percentage intermediate transaction	0.26	0.30	23	▼	0.3	0.27
Average output multiplier	1.33	0.14	23	▼	–0.2	1.33
Average of Leontief inverse	0.17	0.12	23	▼	–0.2	0.17
Average technical coefficient	0.02	0.21	23	▼	–0.5	0.02
Mean intermediate coefficient	0.25	0.21	23	▼	–0.5	0.25
Percentage of above-average coefficients (%)	0.29	0.44	6	▲	0.7	0.28
Determinant of non-competitive Leontief inverse	1.29	0.03	25	▼	0.0	1.29
Determinant of competitive Leontief inverse	1.64	0.01	25	▼	–0.3	1.65
Mean path length	1.36	0.18	23	▼	0.0	1.37
Cycling index	0.03	0.32	25	▼	1.9	0.03
Average propagation length	1.65	0.27	18	▼	–0.1	1.66
Overall sensitivity of the economy	0.71	0.88	16	▼	–0.6	0.74
Index of direct interrelatedness	0.50	0.74	22	▼	–0.5	0.52
Index of indirect interrelatedness	0.21	0.59	3	▲	–0.3	0.22
Global intensity index	19.89	0.14	23	▼	–0.2	19.98

Note: The scores of the economy in focus are shown in the horizontal bars with labels. The colored dots represent the indicator performance of the economy in focus compared to other economies in the region. The highest rank among economies is 1 while the lowest rank is 25. The indicators shown in the chart are selected from a broader set of indicators (see the technical appendix for more details).

Source: Asian Development Bank Multi-Regional Input–Output Database. https://mrio.adbx.online/ (accessed 4 August 2020).

3.2B External Linkages

$ = United States dollars, GVC = global value chain.

Note: The scores of the economy in focus are shown in the horizontal bars with labels. The colored dots represent the indicator performance of the economy in focus compared to other economies in the region. The highest rank among economies is 1, while the lowest rank is 25. The indicators shown in the chart are selected from a broader set of indicators (see the technical appendix for more details).

Source: Asian Development Bank Multi-Regional Input–Output Database. https://mrio.adbx.online/ (accessed 4 August 2020).

		Value (2018)	Score (0–1)	Rank (out of 25)	Distance to subregional average	10–year average growth rate (%)	10–year mean value
PARTICIPATION IN GLOBAL VALUE CHAINS							
International Trade Coefficients							
Trade openness		0.79	0.04	14	▲	−1.1	0.89
Self-sufficiency ratio		0.89	0.50	23	▼	−0.6	0.88
Regional supply percentage		0.72	0.79	18	▼	0.3	0.70
Regional purchase coefficient		0.73	0.91	20	▼	−1.1	0.78
Sectoral purchase coefficient		0.86	0.98	13	▲	0.4	0.84
Simple location quotient of gross output		1.30	0.42	7	▲	−0.1	1.26
Fabrication effect		0.71	0.00	23	▼	−1.0	0.74
Exports	($)	754	0.01	25	▼	5.9	613
Export-to-output ratio		**0.22**	**0.04**	**4**	▲	**0.8**	**0.23**
Agriculture, hunting, forestry, and fishing		0.10	0.00	11		−6.3	0.18
Mining and quarrying		0.40	0.00	8		0.1	0.46
Light manufacturing		0.16	0.53	17		−8.3	0.25
Heavy manufacturing		0.23	0.00	15		−1.8	0.27
Utilities		0.55	0.00	2		3.7	0.59
Construction		0.02	0.05	9		−7.7	0.04
Trade services		0.20	0.00	9		8.7	0.22
Hotels and restaurants		0.68	0.00	3		5.3	0.65
Transport services		0.24	0.00	11		6.7	0.26
Telecommunications		0.24	0.41	4		54.7	0.15

continued on next page

Bhutan 3.2B *continued*

		Value (2018)	Score (0–1)	Rank (out of 25)	Distance to subregional average	10–year average growth rate (%)	10–year mean value
Financial intermediation		0.03	0.02	11		3.8	0.04
Real estate, renting, and business activities		0.03	0.09	16		50.5	0.02
Public administration and defense		0.05	0.39	6		27.9	0.05
Education, health, and social work		0.04	0.00	5		−7.8	0.03
Other personal services		0.30	0.00	3		−8.1	0.20
Imports	($)	**1,284**	**0.03**	**25**	▼	**7.8**	**1,043**
Import-to-input ratio		**0.10**	**0.09**	**13**	▲	**−1.8**	**0.11**
Agriculture, hunting, forestry, and fishing		0.03	0.09	20		−1.5	0.03
Mining and quarrying		0.05	0.03	15		−1.5	0.07
Light manufacturing		0.11	0.15	16		−1.9	0.12
Heavy manufacturing		0.18	0.06	16		−2.7	0.21
Utilities		0.13	0.04	17		15.5	0.07
Construction		0.21	0.14	8		−0.1	0.23
Trade services		0.03	0.05	19		−0.1	0.04
Hotels and restaurants		0.05	0.20	19		−8.3	0.10
Transport services		0.24	0.07	10		−1.5	0.28
Telecommunications		0.08	0.06	13		−3.7	0.10
Financial intermediation		0.02	0.08	20		7.1	0.02
Real estate, renting, and business activities		0.09	0.01	4		1.8	0.09
Public administration and defense		0.09	0.16	6		5.4	0.07
Education, health, and social work		0.08	0.25	7		−0.7	0.09
Other personal services		0.11	0.03	6		−2.7	0.14
Total foreign factor content of consumption	($)	**169**	**0.02**	**25**	▼	**5.8**	**123**
Total foreign factor content of investment	($)	**235**	**0.01**	**24**	▼	**16.9**	**203**
Total foreign factor content of exports	($)	**118**	**0.02**	**25**	▼	**10.9**	**94**
Interregional Multipliers							
Import Leakage Effects		**0.14**	**0.00**	**16**	▼	**−1.9**	**0.15**
Agriculture, hunting, forestry, and fishing		0.04	0.08	23		−1.1	0.04
Mining and quarrying		0.10	0.04	14		0.0	0.11
Light manufacturing		0.17	0.15	16		−2.4	0.18
Heavy manufacturing		0.25	0.04	16		−2.1	0.27
Utilities		0.16	0.04	19		17.2	0.09
Construction		0.27	0.06	13		−0.3	0.30
Trade services		0.06	0.00	19		−0.9	0.09
Hotels and restaurants		0.07	0.19	24		−7.7	0.12
Transport services		0.28	0.00	14		−1.5	0.31
Telecommunications		0.13	0.03	16		−3.9	0.16
Financial intermediation		0.03	0.06	21		4.9	0.04
Real estate, renting, and business activities		0.12	0.02	11		0.2	0.12
Public administration and defense		0.17	0.13	6		2.6	0.14
Education, health, and social work		0.10	0.20	15		−3.7	0.13
Other personal services		0.14	0.01	11		−2.4	0.17
Intraregional transfer multiplier		**1.33**	**0.14**	**23**	▼	**−0.2**	**1.33**
Agriculture, hunting, forestry, and fishing		1.09	0.22	25		0.1	1.08
Mining and quarrying		1.33	0.10	14		0.5	1.31

continued on next page

Bhutan 3.2B *continued*

	Value (2018)	Score (0–1)	Rank (out of 25)	Distance to subregional average	10–year average growth rate (%)	10–year mean value
Light manufacturing	1.59	0.46	21		−0.8	1.61
Heavy manufacturing	1.68	0.16	10		0.4	1.64
Utilities	1.27	0.20	23		1.2	1.12
Construction	1.47	0.32	23		0.1	1.49
Trade services	1.19	0.07	25		−0.3	1.29
Hotels and restaurants	1.23	0.57	25		−0.8	1.30
Transport services	1.33	0.28	21		0.2	1.30
Telecommunications	1.35	0.22	19		−1.0	1.40
Financial intermediation	1.09	0.08	25		0.1	1.11
Real estate, renting, and business activities	1.21	0.03	22		−0.7	1.24
Public administration and defense	1.52	0.38	8		0.2	1.47
Education, health, and social work	1.20	0.10	22		−1.8	1.28
Other personal services	1.36	0.05	17		0.2	1.34
Interregional spillover multiplier	**1.24**	**0.12**	**14**	▲	**−0.4**	**1.27**
Agriculture, hunting, forestry, and fishing	1.07	0.12	21		−0.2	1.07
Mining and quarrying	1.13	0.04	16		−0.3	1.16
Light manufacturing	1.27	0.18	17		−0.5	1.30
Heavy manufacturing	1.46	0.10	16		−1.0	1.54
Utilities	1.33	0.05	16		0.7	1.19
Construction	1.51	0.17	8		−0.2	1.59
Trade services	1.06	0.06	20		−0.2	1.09
Hotels and restaurants	1.11	0.19	19		−1.4	1.20
Transport services	1.63	0.08	9		−0.6	1.72
Telecommunications	1.20	0.07	14		−0.9	1.24
Financial intermediation	1.04	0.11	20		0.1	1.05
Real estate, renting, and business activities	1.22	0.01	5		−0.4	1.22
Public administration and defense	1.20	0.14	8		0.7	1.15
Education, health, and social work	1.18	0.34	10		−0.5	1.20
Other personal services	1.25	0.03	6		−0.9	1.33
Interregional feedback multiplier	**1.000**	**0.01**	**25**	▼	**0.0**	**1.00**
Agriculture, hunting, forestry, and fishing	1.000	0.01	25		0.0	1.00
Mining and quarrying	1.000	0.00	22		0.0	1.00
Light manufacturing	1.000	0.03	25		0.0	1.00
Heavy manufacturing	1.000	0.00	25		0.0	1.00
Utilities	1.000	0.01	25		0.0	1.00
Construction	1.000	0.01	25		0.0	1.00
Trade services	1.000	0.00	25		0.0	1.00
Hotels and restaurants	1.000	0.02	25		0.0	1.00
Transport services	1.000	0.00	25		0.0	1.00
Telecommunications	1.000	0.01	25		0.0	1.00
Financial intermediation	1.000	0.01	25		0.0	1.00
Real estate, renting, and business activities	1.000	0.00	23		0.0	1.00
Public administration and defense	1.000	0.01	24		0.0	1.00
Education, health, and social work	1.000	0.01	25		0.0	1.00
Other personal services	1.000	0.00	24		0.0	1.00

continued on next page

Bhutan 3.2B *continued*

	Value (2018)	Score (0–1)	Rank (out of 25)	Distance to subregional average	10–year average growth rate (%)	10–year mean value
Global Value Chain (GVC) Participation Index						
Backward GVC Participation	**17.6%**	**0.00**	**14**	▲	**−0.9**	**0.20**
Simple GVCs	**13.0%**	**0.00**	**8**	▲	**0.1**	**0.14**
Agriculture, hunting, forestry, and fishing	0.4	0.16	9		4.5	0.38
Mining and quarrying	0.0	0.10	7		41.6	0.02
Light manufacturing	0.6	0.31	20		8.2	0.64
Heavy manufacturing	1.0	0.08	11		−2.6	1.14
Utilities	0.4	0.02	7		65.2	0.18
Construction	6.9	0.10	2		5.1	8.03
Trade services	0.2	0.04	22		4.8	0.27
Hotels and restaurants	0.0	0.07	25		69.6	0.01
Transport services	1.2	0.23	5		−0.1	1.17
Telecommunications	0.1	0.02	15		−6.1	0.19
Financial intermediation	0.1	0.01	16		13.3	0.08
Real estate, renting, and business activities	0.2	0.01	22		−3.7	0.19
Public administration and defense	1.4	0.03	4		1.9	1.21
Education, health, and social work	0.3	0.09	20		−7.8	0.63
Other personal services	0.0	0.12	21		−1.5	0.06
Complex GVCs	**4.6%**	**0.03**	**16**	▼	**−2.9**	**0.06**
Agriculture, hunting, forestry, and fishing	0.1	0.14	12		−1.7	0.14
Mining and quarrying	0.0	0.01	11		15.1	0.01
Light manufacturing	0.4	0.18	22		−12.2	0.76
Heavy manufacturing	0.5	0.01	16		−2.3	0.61
Utilities	0.2	0.02	9		48.8	0.03
Construction	1.9	0.09	3		4.1	2.27
Trade services	0.1	0.00	22		46.0	0.11
Hotels and restaurants	0.1	0.00	22		1.7	0.07
Transport services	0.6	0.07	7		−5.0	0.79
Telecommunications	0.1	0.02	12		0.3	0.07
Financial intermediation	0.0	0.00	16		10.5	0.02
Real estate, renting, and business activities	0.0	0.02	22		−1.9	0.06
Public administration and defense	0.5	0.04	5		4.4	0.42
Education, health, and social work	0.1	0.09	20		−5.9	0.21
Other personal services	0.0	0.13	22		1.6	0.02
Forward GVC Participation	**20.2%**	**0.01**	**13**	▲	**−0.1**	**0.22**
Simple GVCs	**13.9%**	**0.00**	**13**	▲	**0.0**	**0.16**
Agriculture, hunting, forestry, and fishing	1.2	0.15	6		−5.6	1.92
Mining and quarrying	1.8	0.00	7		7.0	1.34
Light manufacturing	0.4	0.24	20		3.5	0.53
Heavy manufacturing	0.5	0.00	16		−2.6	0.57
Utilities	5.2	0.00	2		−4.6	6.77
Construction	0.4	0.01	3		456.8	0.67
Trade services	1.2	0.00	14		7.8	1.04
Hotels and restaurants	0.7	0.00	4		13.0	0.46
Transport services	1.3	0.00	6		7.6	1.17
Telecommunications	0.3	0.04	9		9.8	0.22

continued on next page

Bhutan 3.2B *continued*

	Value (2018)	Score (0–1)	Rank (out of 25)	Distance to subregional average	10–year average growth rate (%)	10–year mean value
Financial intermediation	0.4	0.02	12		−1.1	0.52
Real estate, renting, and business activities	0.4	0.00	17		7.7	0.33
Public administration and defense	0.1	0.41	6		24.8	0.16
Education, health, and social work	0.0	0.43	24		20.6	0.01
Other personal services	0.1	0.03	17		42.0	0.05
Complex GVCs	**6.3%**	**0.04**	**13**	▲	**0.0**	**0.07**
Agriculture, hunting, forestry, and fishing	0.3	0.10	13		−8.6	0.47
Mining and quarrying	0.2	0.00	9		7.5	0.18
Light manufacturing	0.2	0.28	21		7.9	0.15
Heavy manufacturing	0.2	0.00	16		0.4	0.15
Utilities	3.0	0.00	2		−3.9	3.56
Construction	0.2	0.01	5		8.0	0.20
Trade services	0.7	0.00	15		9.2	0.56
Hotels and restaurants	0.4	0.00	4		16.4	0.23
Transport services	0.6	0.00	7		11.2	0.46
Telecommunications	0.1	0.05	8		13.0	0.10
Financial intermediation	0.2	0.04	16		0.9	0.22
Real estate, renting, and business activities	0.2	0.00	18		6.7	0.14
Public administration and defense	0.1	0.46	6		40.3	0.07
Education, health, and social work	0.0	0.51	24		20.3	0.00
Other personal services	0.1	0.07	13		53.6	0.03

SPECIALIZATION IN GLOBAL VALUE CHAINS

Vertical Specialization

	Value (2018)	Score (0–1)	Rank (out of 25)	Distance to subregional average	10–year average growth rate (%)	10–year mean value
Vertical Specialization Ratio	**15.6%**	**0.14**	**17**	▼	**1.3**	**0.15**
Agriculture, hunting, forestry, and fishing	3.6%	0.07	23		−1.1	0.04
Mining and quarrying	9.9%	0.04	15		0.0	0.11
Light manufacturing	16.9%	0.16	16		−2.4	0.18
Heavy manufacturing	25.2%	0.04	16		−2.1	0.27
Utilities	16.2%	0.00	19		17.2	0.09
Construction	26.5%	0.06	13		−0.3	0.30
Trade services	5.6%	0.00	19		−0.9	0.09
Hotels and restaurants	7.2%	0.19	24		−7.7	0.12
Transport services	27.6%	0.00	14		−1.5	0.31
Telecommunications	13.3%	0.03	16		−3.9	0.16
Financial intermediation	3.4%	0.06	21		4.9	0.04
Real estate, renting, and business activities	11.8%	0.02	11		0.2	0.12
Public administration and defense	16.8%	0.13	6		2.6	0.14
Education, health, and social work	10.4%	0.20	15		−10.7	0.11
Other personal services	14.4%	0.02	11		−2.4	0.17

Revealed Comparative Advantages

	Value (2018)	Score (0–1)	Rank (out of 25)	Distance to subregional average	10–year average growth rate (%)	10–year mean value
Traditional RCA Index						
Agriculture, hunting, forestry, and fishing	2.90	0.06	5	▲	−3.0	4.29
Mining and quarrying	1.14	0.00	6	▲	16.2	0.72
Light manufacturing	0.43	1.00	17	▼	−6.3	0.72

continued on next page

Bhutan 3.2B *continued*

	Value (2018)	Score (0–1)	Rank (out of 25)	Distance to subregional average	10–year average growth rate (%)	10–year mean value
Heavy manufacturing	0.15	0.01	15	▼	−0.2	0.18
Utilities	65.21	0.00	1	▲	7.1	64.88
Construction	3.17	0.13	5	▲	−11.2	7.89
Trade services	0.83	0.00	15	▼	21.1	0.80
Hotels and restaurants	5.31	0.00	6	▼	15.8	4.22
Transport services	2.19	0.00	6	▲	13.4	2.07
Telecommunications	3.26	0.32	4	▲	45.1	1.86
Financial intermediation	0.17	0.02	9	▼	12.0	0.25
Real estate, renting, and business activities	0.05	0.08	21	▼	43.8	0.04
Public administration and defense	5.32	0.59	4	▼	19.1	4.58
Education, health, and social work	1.48	0.00	6	▲	−13.6	1.29
Other personal services	0.54	0.00	8	▼	−3.3	0.37

New RCA Index (Based on Domestic Value Added)

	Value (2018)	Score (0–1)	Rank (out of 25)	Distance to subregional average	10–year average growth rate (%)	10–year mean value
Agriculture, hunting, forestry, and fishing	1.91	0.39	12	▼	−6.4	2.77
Mining and quarrying	0.92	0.03	7	▲	11.3	0.59
Light manufacturing	0.48	1.00	19	▼	−6.6	0.62
Heavy manufacturing	0.14	0.05	17	▼	0.5	0.14
Utilities	13.53	0.03	1	▲	0.7	14.47
Construction	2.38	0.08	5	▼	7.1	2.77
Trade services	0.73	0.12	20	▼	11.3	0.58
Hotels and restaurants	4.92	0.01	5	▲	17.9	3.32
Transport services	1.52	0.18	5	▲	9.3	1.37
Telecommunications	1.63	0.31	7	▲	13.5	1.13
Financial intermediation	0.53	0.24	17	▼	−1.6	0.67
Real estate, renting, and business activities	0.17	0.17	22	▼	7.1	0.15
Public administration and defense	1.67	0.63	5	▼	12.1	1.90
Education, health, and social work	0.84	0.40	10	▼	−10.3	0.69
Other personal services	0.25	0.12	18	▼	0.2	0.18

POSITION IN GLOBAL VALUE CHAINS

	Value (2018)	Score (0–1)	Rank (out of 25)	Distance to subregional average	10–year average growth rate (%)	10–year mean value
Upstreamness Index	1.9	0.13	17	▲	0.0	1.9
Agriculture, hunting, forestry, and fishing	1.4	0.21	25		−1.7	1.5
Mining and quarrying	2.5	0.61	17		−0.6	2.6
Light manufacturing	1.8	0.25	18		0.3	1.8
Heavy manufacturing	1.8	0.00	24		−0.7	1.8
Utilities	2.8	0.13	9		−0.5	2.9
Construction	1.2	0.32	15		2.0	1.3
Trade services	1.9	0.05	17		−1.0	2.0
Hotels and restaurants	2.4	0.58	1		1.2	2.4
Transport services	2.1	0.07	17		1.4	2.1
Telecommunications	1.9	0.23	18		−0.1	2.0
Financial intermediation	2.0	0.28	19		−0.3	2.1
Real estate, renting, and business activities	2.2	0.04	8		2.3	2.1
Public administration and defense	1.1	1.00	14		0.0	1.1
Education, health, and social work	1.0	0.68	24		−0.2	1.0
Other personal services	1.9	0.11	9		2.3	1.8

continued on next page

Bhutan 3.2B *continued*

	Value (2018)	Score (0–1)	Rank (out of 25)	Distance to subregional average	10–year average growth rate (%)	10–year mean value
PRODUCTION LENGTH OF GLOBAL VALUE CHAINS						
Backward Measures of Average Production Length						
Production Length of Global Value Chain Activity (B)	0.5	0.00	18	▼	−2.1	0.6
Agriculture, hunting, forestry, and fishing	0.1	0.07	24		−0.9	0.1
Mining and quarrying	0.4	0.05	14		0.0	0.4
Light manufacturing	0.7	0.20	17		−2.5	0.7
Heavy manufacturing	1.0	0.05	19		−2.0	1.1
Utilities	0.6	0.03	20		17.2	0.4
Construction	1.0	0.03	17		−0.7	1.1
Trade services	0.2	0.00	20		−1.3	0.4
Hotels and restaurants	0.2	0.18	25		−7.1	0.4
Transport services	1.0	0.00	18		−1.9	1.2
Telecommunications	0.5	0.03	16		−4.2	0.6
Financial intermediation	0.1	0.09	23		3.8	0.2
Real estate, renting, and business activities	0.4	0.02	14		−0.6	0.5
Public administration and defense	0.7	0.13	5		2.2	0.6
Education, health, and social work	0.4	0.16	18		−4.8	0.5
Other personal services	0.5	0.01	12		−2.6	0.6
Forward Measures of Average Production Length						
Production Length of Global Value Chain Activity (F)	0.8	0.05	11	▲	2.6	0.7
Agriculture, hunting, forestry, and fishing	0.3	0.07	19		−5.1	0.4
Mining and quarrying	1.3	0.06	13		−0.7	1.5
Light manufacturing	0.4	0.18	18		9.6	0.4
Heavy manufacturing	0.8	0.00	16		0.0	0.8
Utilities	2.1	0.02	3		0.3	2.2
Construction	0.1	0.03	10		1.1	0.2
Trade services	0.8	0.00	13		1.6	0.9
Hotels and restaurants	1.6	0.06	2		5.0	1.5
Transport services	0.9	0.00	15		8.5	0.8
Telecommunications	0.8	0.15	11		8.3	0.6
Financial intermediation	0.5	0.09	13		2.3	0.6
Real estate, renting, and business activities	0.8	0.00	8		8.9	0.6
Public administration and defense	0.1	0.72	9		−8.3	0.1
Education, health, and social work	0.0	0.63	24		−10.1	0.0
Other personal services	1.0	0.00	3		−8.2	0.6

Note: The scores of the economy in focus are shown in the horizontal bars with labels. The colored dots represent the indicator performance of the economy in focus compared to other economies in the region. The highest rank among economies is 1 while the lowest rank is 25. The indicators shown in the chart are selected from a broader set of indicators (see the technical appendix for more details).

Source: Asian Development Bank Multi-Regional Input–Output Database. https://mrio.adbx.online/ (accessed 4 August 2020).

3.3 India

3.3A Internal Linkages

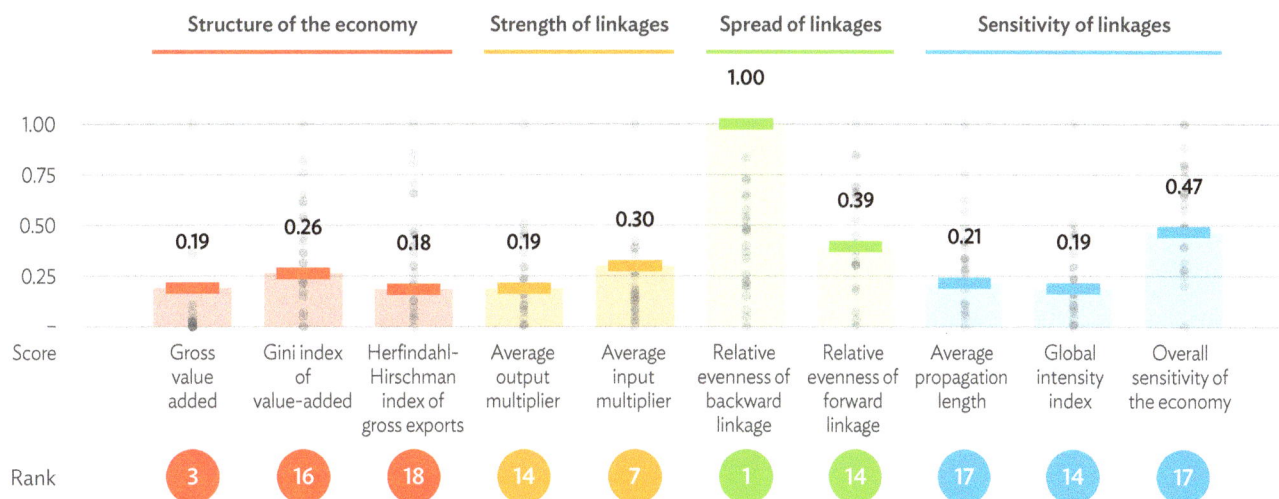

Note: The scores of the economy in focus are shown in the horizontal bars with labels. The colored dots represent the indicator performance of the economy in focus compared to other economies in the region. The highest rank among economies is 1 while the lowest rank is 25. The indicators shown in the chart are selected from a broader set of indicators (see the technical appendix for more details).

Source: Asian Development Bank Multi-Regional Input–Output Database. https://mrio.adbx.online/ (accessed 4 August 2020).

		Value (2018)	Score (0–1)	Rank (out of 25)	Distance to subregional average	10–year average growth rate (%)	10–year mean value
STRUCTURE OF THE ECONOMY							
Economic Indicators							
Gross output	($)	5,112,070	0.13	3	▲	7.3	3,849,642
Gross value-added	($)	2,597,216	0.19	3	▲	7.8	1,910,145
Value-added content of domestic final demand		2,274,807	0.20	3		8.1	1,648,450
Value-added content of exports		322,409	0.14	4		5.9	261,695
Intermediate inputs	($)	2,365,283	0.09	3	▲	6.8	1,832,452
Domestic inputs		2,008,345	0.08	3		7.1	1,542,418
Foreign inputs		356,938	0.23	4		5.6	290,034
Direct production	($)	3,103,725	0.20	3	▲	7.5	2,307,225
Domestic final demand		2,693,219	0.22	3		7.8	1,967,425
Exports		410,506	0.15	5		5.9	339,799
Indirect production	($)	2,008,345	0.08	3	▲	7.1	1,542,418
Indirect production embedded in domestic final demand		1,678,627	0.09	3		7.0	1,291,363
Indirect production embedded in exports		329,719	0.07	4		8.0	251,054
Economic Diversification							
Gross output		0.26	0.33	13	▼	–0.4	0.27
Gini concentration index of gross output		0.45	0.41	13		–0.3	0.46
Herfindahl-Hirschman concentration index of gross output		0.05	0.19	19		–0.9	0.05
Theil concentration index of gross output		0.28	0.31	14		–0.5	0.29

continued on next page

India 3.3A *continued*

	Value (2018)	Score (0–1)	Rank (out of 25)	Distance to subregional average	10–year average growth rate (%)	10–year mean value
Gross value-added	**0.23**	**0.22**	**15**	▼	**1.1**	**0.22**
Gini concentration index of gross value added	0.41	0.26	16		0.7	0.39
Herfindahl-Hirschman concentration index of gross value added	0.04	0.11	15		2.4	0.04
Theil concentration index of gross value added	0.24	0.23	15		1.5	0.23
Gross exports	**0.53**	**0.35**	**17**	▼	**1.6**	**0.50**
Gini concentration index of gross exports	0.73	0.53	17		1.0	0.71
Herfindahl-Hirschman concentration index of gross exports	0.20	0.18	18		4.3	0.18
Theil concentration index of gross exports	0.65	0.48	17		1.5	0.62

Structural Changes

	Value (2018)	Score (0–1)	Rank (out of 25)	Distance to subregional average	10–year average growth rate (%)	10–year mean value
Changes in output due to technological changes	**–0.4%**	**0.70**	**19**	▲	**–**	**–**
Agriculture, hunting, forestry, and fishing	–1.2%	0.48	19			
Mining and quarrying	–5.6%	0.69	22			
Light manufacturing	0.1%	0.38	8			
Heavy manufacturing	–1.2%	0.65	18			
Utilities	1.0%	0.67	5			
Construction	–0.8%	0.00	25			
Trade services	1.6%	1.00	1			
Hotels and restaurants	–1.0%	0.00	25			
Transport services	–0.2%	0.60	12			
Telecommunications	–0.7%	0.16	15			
Financial intermediation	–0.1%	0.47	17			
Real estate, renting, and business activities	1.2%	0.80	4			
Public administration and defense	0.0%	0.36	16			
Education, health, and social work	–0.1%	0.66	21			
Other personal services	0.4%	0.51	8			
Changes in output due to structural changes in consumption (%)	**3.8%**	**0.41**	**10**	▲	**–**	**–**
Agriculture, hunting, forestry, and fishing	3.0%	0.55	12			
Mining and quarrying	1.2%	0.09	10			
Light manufacturing	2.5%	0.36	10			
Heavy manufacturing	1.3%	0.25	13			
Utilities	3.3%	0.37	13			
Construction	0.3%	0.21	11			
Trade services	5.3%	0.78	4			
Hotels and restaurants	5.7%	0.21	9			
Transport services	3.4%	0.50	10			
Telecommunications	2.8%	0.52	15			
Financial intermediation	3.2%	0.42	17			
Real estate, renting, and business activities	6.1%	0.28	6			
Public administration and defense	5.2%	0.39	16			
Education, health, and social work	7.8%	0.26	9			
Other personal services	5.4%	0.44	11			
Changes in output due to structural changes in investment (%)	**1.1%**	**0.33**	**12**	▼	**–**	**–**
Agriculture, hunting, forestry, and fishing	0.4%	0.13	12			
Mining and quarrying	1.4%	0.32	8			
Light manufacturing	1.4%	0.41	4			

continued on next page

India 3.3A *continued*

	Value (2018)	Score (0–1)	Rank (out of 25)	Distance to subregional average	10–year average growth rate (%)	10–year mean value
Heavy manufacturing	1.7%	0.29	11			
Utilities	1.4%	0.56	6			
Construction	3.5%	0.24	20			
Trade services	1.8%	0.46	6			
Hotels and restaurants	0.3%	0.43	11			
Transport services	1.2%	0.30	7			
Telecommunications	0.8%	0.23	8			
Financial intermediation	1.2%	0.27	6			
Real estate, renting, and business activities	0.7%	0.27	10			
Public administration and defense	0.0%	0.01	23			
Education, health, and social work	0.0%	0.02	10			
Other personal services	0.5%	0.31	8			
Changes in output due to structural changes in stock (%)	**0.2%**	**0.43**	**6**	▲	–	–
Agriculture, hunting, forestry, and fishing	0.1%	0.58	5			
Mining and quarrying	0.5%	0.43	7			
Light manufacturing	0.6%	0.40	3			
Heavy manufacturing	0.4%	0.55	5			
Utilities	0.3%	0.27	4			
Construction	0.0%	0.76	7			
Trade services	0.2%	0.59	6			
Hotels and restaurants	0.0%	0.50	5			
Transport services	0.2%	0.08	7			
Telecommunications	0.2%	0.61	4			
Financial intermediation	0.2%	0.94	4			
Real estate, renting, and business activities	0.1%	0.18	6			
Public administration and defense	0.0%	0.64	15			
Education, health, and social work	0.0%	0.23	7			
Other personal services	0.2%	0.55	2			
Changes in output due to structural changes in export	**0.4%**	**0.13**	**18**	▼	–	–
Agriculture, hunting, forestry, and fishing	0.4%	0.46	17			
Mining and quarrying	0.3%	0.12	16			
Light manufacturing	1.1%	0.17	12			
Heavy manufacturing	1.5%	0.35	16			
Utilities	0.8%	0.06	17			
Construction	0.0%	0.04	21			
Trade services	0.6%	0.09	19			
Hotels and restaurants	0.1%	0.04	21			
Transport services	0.1%	0.38	20			
Telecommunications	0.2%	0.09	20			
Financial intermediation	0.6%	0.16	16			
Real estate, renting, and business activities	−0.1%	0.14	21			
Public administration and defense	0.0%	0.12	22			
Education, health, and social work	0.0%	0.01	23			
Other personal services	0.6%	0.13	18			

continued on next page

India 3.3A *continued*

	Value (2018)	Score (0–1)	Rank (out of 25)	Distance to subregional average	10–year average growth rate (%)	10–year mean value
Changes in output due to import substitution on intermediate demand	**0.4%**	**0.44**	**7**	▲	–	–
Agriculture, hunting, forestry, and fishing	−0.1%	0.67	10			
Mining and quarrying	5.1%	0.36	3			
Light manufacturing	−0.2%	0.80	16			
Heavy manufacturing	0.0%	0.25	16			
Utilities	0.2%	0.73	6			
Construction	0.0%	0.89	4			
Trade services	0.0%	0.76	12			
Hotels and restaurants	0.0%	0.97	5			
Transport services	0.1%	0.48	10			
Telecommunications	0.1%	0.99	2			
Financial intermediation	0.0%	0.63	7			
Real estate, renting, and business activities	0.3%	0.79	4			
Public administration and defense	0.0%	0.79	2			
Education, health, and social work	0.1%	1.00	1			
Other personal services	0.1%	0.55	5			
Changes in output due to import substitution on domestic final demand	**0.3%**	**0.97**	**2**	▼	–	–
Agriculture, hunting, forestry, and fishing	0.1%	0.61	4			
Mining and quarrying	0.4%	0.71	6			
Light manufacturing	0.5%	0.90	2			
Heavy manufacturing	0.5%	0.62	5			
Utilities	0.3%	1.00	1			
Construction	0.0%	0.68	5			
Trade services	0.2%	1.00	1			
Hotels and restaurants	0.1%	0.80	4			
Transport services	0.3%	0.98	2			
Telecommunications	0.3%	0.89	3			
Financial intermediation	0.2%	0.94	3			
Real estate, renting, and business activities	0.1%	0.57	6			
Public administration and defense	0.0%	0.33	9			
Education, health, and social work	0.0%	0.87	6			
Other personal services	0.8%	1.00	1			

Demand-side Linkages

	Value (2018)	Score (0–1)	Rank (out of 25)	Distance to subregional average	10–year average growth rate (%)	10–year mean value
Direct backward linkage	**0.30**	**0.23**	**16**	▼	**−0.3**	**0.31**
Agriculture, hunting, forestry, and fishing	0.25	0.32	13		0.4	0.24
Mining and quarrying	0.36	0.59	6		8.4	0.25
Light manufacturing	0.72	0.98	2		0.3	0.71
Heavy manufacturing	0.61	0.73	2		1.8	0.55
Utilities	0.42	0.48	7		−0.5	0.45
Construction	0.55	0.57	6		−0.2	0.55
Trade services	0.14	0.00	25		0.0	0.14
Hotels and restaurants	0.47	0.63	10		−2.8	0.59
Transport services	0.20	0.28	21		−6.1	0.39
Telecommunications	0.13	0.00	25		−3.1	0.15

continued on next page

India 3.3A *continued*

	Value (2018)	Score (0–1)	Rank (out of 25)	Distance to subregional average	10–year average growth rate (%)	10–year mean value
Financial intermediation	0.15	0.11	23		−0.7	0.15
Real estate, renting, and business activities	0.18	0.27	20		2.3	0.15
Public administration and defense	0.00	0.00	25		0.0	0.00
Education, health, and social work	0.17	0.20	20		0.1	0.16
Other personal services	0.17	0.19	22		1.7	0.15
Total backward linkage	**1.50**	**0.19**	**14**	▲	**−0.2**	**1.53**
Agriculture, hunting, forestry, and fishing	1.36	0.24	14		0.0	1.36
Mining and quarrying	1.61	0.49	4		2.0	1.43
Light manufacturing	2.19	0.61	4		0.0	2.20
Heavy manufacturing	2.05	0.42	2		0.9	1.95
Utilities	1.69	0.29	6		−0.4	1.76
Construction	1.96	0.34	6		−0.3	2.01
Trade services	1.21	0.05	24		−0.2	1.23
Hotels and restaurants	1.76	0.43	12		−1.6	1.99
Transport services	1.34	0.22	20		−2.6	1.70
Telecommunications	1.24	0.04	23		−0.8	1.27
Financial intermediation	1.22	0.04	22		−0.3	1.25
Real estate, renting, and business activities	1.28	0.17	19		0.2	1.25
Public administration and defense	1.00	0.00	25		0.0	1.00
Education, health, and social work	1.28	0.16	17		−0.1	1.29
Other personal services	1.26	0.14	20		0.3	1.25
Normalized backward linkage	**–**	**–**	**–**	▬	**–**	**–**
Agriculture, hunting, forestry, and fishing	0.91	0.28	13		0.3	0.89
Mining and quarrying	1.08	0.79	2		2.3	0.94
Light manufacturing	1.46	1.00	1		0.3	1.44
Heavy manufacturing	1.37	1.00	1		1.2	1.27
Utilities	1.13	0.43	7		−0.1	1.15
Construction	1.31	0.67	5		−0.1	1.31
Trade services	0.81	0.14	22		0.1	0.81
Hotels and restaurants	1.18	0.61	8		−1.4	1.30
Transport services	0.89	0.24	21		−2.4	1.11
Telecommunications	0.83	0.26	23		−0.5	0.83
Financial intermediation	0.82	0.06	23		0.0	0.81
Real estate, renting, and business activities	0.85	0.32	20		0.5	0.82
Public administration and defense	0.67	0.00	25		0.3	0.65
Education, health, and social work	0.86	0.39	19		0.1	0.85
Other personal services	0.84	0.12	21		0.5	0.82
Net backward linkage	**0.85**	**0.22**	**23**	▼	**−0.5**	**0.87**
Agriculture, hunting, forestry, and fishing	0.82	0.68	10		0.6	0.79
Mining and quarrying	0.25	0.17	15		−4.0	0.27
Light manufacturing	1.34	0.80	2		0.4	1.32
Heavy manufacturing	1.09	0.76	6		2.3	0.96
Utilities	0.29	0.06	21		−0.6	0.33
Construction	1.65	0.45	6		0.3	1.62
Trade services	0.57	0.09	23		−0.1	0.57

continued on next page

India 3.3A *continued*

	Value (2018)	Score (0–1)	Rank (out of 25)	Distance to subregional average	10–year average growth rate (%)	10–year mean value
Hotels and restaurants	1.11	0.38	20		−0.9	1.18
Transport services	0.70	0.23	19		−3.2	0.92
Telecommunications	0.49	0.06	24		−2.0	0.55
Financial intermediation	0.32	0.19	20		−1.3	0.36
Real estate, renting, and business activities	1.03	1.00	1		−1.2	1.08
Public administration and defense	1.00	0.00	25		0.0	1.00
Education, health, and social work	1.23	0.22	17		−0.2	1.25
Other personal services	0.84	0.53	23		−0.1	0.85
Growth equalized output multipliers	**0.11**	**0.25**	**9**	▲	**−0.2**	**0.11**
Agriculture, hunting, forestry, and fishing	0.15	0.43	9		−2.0	0.18
Mining and quarrying	0.02	0.05	12		−1.1	0.03
Light manufacturing	0.26	0.44	11		0.2	0.27
Heavy manufacturing	0.33	0.40	9		−0.9	0.35
Utilities	0.04	0.13	17		1.1	0.03
Construction	0.15	0.22	9		−2.5	0.17
Trade services	0.20	0.46	8		3.4	0.17
Hotels and restaurants	0.03	0.05	18		−0.6	0.04
Transport services	0.11	0.56	11		−0.7	0.12
Telecommunications	0.01	0.00	25		−3.4	0.01
Financial intermediation	0.05	0.16	13		−0.1	0.05
Real estate, renting, and business activities	0.13	0.45	9		2.2	0.11
Public administration and defense	0.06	0.31	12		0.1	0.06
Education, health, and social work	0.06	0.27	13		2.2	0.06
Other personal services	0.03	0.13	16		2.5	0.03
Supply-Side Linkages						
Direct forward linkage	**0.43**	**0.47**	**7**	▲	**0.4**	**0.42**
Agriculture, hunting, forestry, and fishing	0.40	0.33	17		−0.7	0.42
Mining and quarrying	0.85	0.86	8		1.8	0.81
Light manufacturing	0.39	0.35	14		−0.5	0.40
Heavy manufacturing	0.47	0.60	15		−1.3	0.51
Utilities	0.83	0.89	3		0.2	0.81
Construction	0.16	0.33	11		−2.3	0.19
Trade services	0.53	0.69	5		0.0	0.54
Hotels and restaurants	0.37	0.70	5		−1.0	0.40
Transport services	0.48	0.54	10		0.9	0.46
Telecommunications	0.60	0.77	5		1.2	0.57
Financial intermediation	0.74	0.79	8		0.5	0.71
Real estate, renting, and business activities	0.19	0.00	25		15.5	0.14
Public administration and defense	0.00	0.00	25		0.0	0.00
Education, health, and social work	0.04	0.13	14		3.8	0.03
Other personal services	0.33	0.36	9		1.4	0.31
Total forward linkage	**1.73**	**0.30**	**7**	▲	**0.1**	**1.74**
Agriculture, hunting, forestry, and fishing	1.65	0.23	15		−0.4	1.69
Mining and quarrying	2.54	0.50	8		0.7	2.54
Light manufacturing	1.62	0.22	12		−0.3	1.65

continued on next page

India 3.3A *continued*

	Value (2018)	Score (0–1)	Rank (out of 25)	Distance to subregional average	10–year average growth rate (%)	10–year mean value
Heavy manufacturing	1.81	0.39	11		−0.8	1.91
Utilities	2.56	0.51	2		0.0	2.55
Construction	1.23	0.25	12		−0.5	1.28
Trade services	1.88	0.46	8		−0.2	1.92
Hotels and restaurants	1.60	0.49	5		−0.5	1.68
Transport services	1.81	0.35	8		0.3	1.80
Telecommunications	2.08	0.71	3		0.4	2.04
Financial intermediation	2.27	0.26	7		0.2	2.25
Real estate, renting, and business activities	1.31	0.00	25		1.8	1.22
Public administration and defense	1.00	0.00	25		0.0	1.00
Education, health, and social work	1.06	0.18	13		0.2	1.05
Other personal services	1.57	0.43	7		0.3	1.55
Normalized forward linkage	–	–	–	▬	–	–
Agriculture, hunting, forestry, and fishing	0.95	0.16	22		−0.5	0.97
Mining and quarrying	1.69	0.92	4		0.9	1.66
Light manufacturing	1.08	0.54	11		0.0	1.08
Heavy manufacturing	1.21	0.64	8		−0.6	1.25
Utilities	1.71	0.98	2		0.3	1.67
Construction	0.82	0.37	12		−0.3	0.84
Trade services	1.25	0.64	2		0.1	1.25
Hotels and restaurants	1.07	0.69	3		−0.3	1.10
Transport services	1.21	0.64	6		0.5	1.17
Telecommunications	1.39	0.86	3		0.7	1.34
Financial intermediation	1.52	0.33	6		0.4	1.47
Real estate, renting, and business activities	0.87	0.00	25		2.1	0.80
Public administration and defense	0.67	0.38	16		0.3	0.65
Education, health, and social work	0.71	0.56	13		0.4	0.69
Other personal services	1.05	0.42	6		0.5	1.01
Net forward linkage	**1.04**	**0.77**	**3**	▲	**0.1**	**1.05**
Agriculture, hunting, forestry, and fishing	1.28	0.56	8		−0.2	1.31
Mining and quarrying	1.50	0.66	9		−1.5	1.77
Light manufacturing	0.34	0.11	23		−0.1	0.34
Heavy manufacturing	0.33	0.33	22		−1.1	0.34
Utilities	1.04	0.53	8		−0.3	1.04
Construction	0.43	0.46	13		−0.6	0.44
Trade services	1.59	0.91	2		−0.1	1.62
Hotels and restaurants	0.53	0.27	16		−0.5	0.55
Transport services	0.77	0.38	9		0.3	0.76
Telecommunications	1.75	1.00	1		1.5	1.64
Financial intermediation	1.91	0.79	2		0.4	1.87
Real estate, renting, and business activities	1.05	0.35	18		1.9	0.99
Public administration and defense	1.00	1.00	1		0.0	1.00
Education, health, and social work	0.86	0.75	6		0.3	0.84
Other personal services	1.27	1.00	1		0.4	1.25

continued on next page

India 3.3A *continued*

	Value (2018)	Score (0–1)	Rank (out of 25)	Distance to subregional average	10-year average growth rate (%)	10-year mean value
Growth equalized input multipliers	**0.11**	**0.24**	**9**	▲	**–0.1**	**0.11**
Agriculture, hunting, forestry, and fishing	0.23	0.47	10		–2.5	0.28
Mining and quarrying	0.04	0.06	12		–3.2	0.06
Light manufacturing	0.11	0.29	14		–0.1	0.11
Heavy manufacturing	0.13	0.25	14		–2.3	0.15
Utilities	0.04	0.18	11		0.6	0.04
Construction	0.08	0.11	14		–3.3	0.09
Trade services	0.38	0.92	2		3.0	0.33
Hotels and restaurants	0.02	0.05	17		–1.4	0.02
Transport services	0.10	0.55	9		–0.7	0.11
Telecommunications	0.02	0.06	21		–2.2	0.02
Financial intermediation	0.12	0.29	11		0.0	0.12
Real estate, renting, and business activities	0.16	0.33	13		3.9	0.14
Public administration and defense	0.08	0.40	7		–0.2	0.08
Education, health, and social work	0.07	0.40	12		2.2	0.06
Other personal services	0.04	0.28	11		2.6	0.04

Impacts from Hypothetical Extraction

	Value (2018)	Score (0–1)	Rank (out of 25)	Distance to subregional average	10-year average growth rate (%)	10-year mean value
Changes in gross output due to hypothetical extraction	**–9.3%**	**0.74**	**16**	▲	**–0.2**	**–0.09**
Agriculture, hunting, forestry, and fishing	–10.9%	0.63	16		–1.7	–12.4
Mining and quarrying	–2.3%	0.94	15		1.2	–2.2
Light manufacturing	–27.1%	0.43	19		0.3	–27.3
Heavy manufacturing	–28.7%	0.45	18		0.2	–28.4
Utilities	–3.0%	0.89	11		0.8	–2.9
Construction	–16.2%	0.67	17		–2.2	–18.0
Trade services	–14.6%	0.72	14		3.4	–12.2
Hotels and restaurants	–3.6%	0.95	8		–2.0	–4.1
Transport services	–8.8%	0.54	16		–2.9	–11.5
Telecommunications	–0.7%	1.00	1		–4.1	–0.9
Financial intermediation	–3.8%	0.86	10		–0.2	–3.9
Real estate, renting, and business activities	–9.2%	0.59	13		2.1	–8.2
Public administration and defense	–3.8%	0.83	4		0.3	–3.7
Education, health, and social work	–5.0%	0.80	10		2.2	–4.4
Other personal services	–2.1%	0.91	9		2.8	–1.8

Impacts from Hypothetical Insertion

	Value (2018)	Score (0–1)	Rank (out of 25)	Distance to subregional average	10-year average growth rate (%)	10-year mean value
Changes in gross output due to hypothetical insertion	**4.4%**	**0.26**	**8**	▲	**–0.5**	**0.05**
Agriculture, hunting, forestry, and fishing	3.3%	0.13	9		–1.7	3.7
Mining and quarrying	0.9%	0.08	11		7.9	0.7
Light manufacturing	19.0%	0.53	6		0.5	19.2
Heavy manufacturing	21.1%	0.32	6		1.5	19.8
Utilities	1.5%	0.15	13		0.8	1.5
Construction	8.7%	0.33	9		–3.0	10.2
Trade services	2.6%	0.12	19		2.5	2.3
Hotels and restaurants	1.6%	0.08	16		–3.7	2.1
Transport services	2.3%	0.30	17		–6.9	5.0
Telecommunications	0.1%	0.00	25		–6.3	0.2
Financial intermediation	0.7%	0.04	20		–1.3	0.8

continued on next page

India 3.3A *continued*

	Value (2018)	Score (0–1)	Rank (out of 25)	Distance to subregional average	10-year average growth rate (%)	10-year mean value
Real estate, renting, and business activities	2.2%	0.27	14		3.8	1.7
Public administration and defense	0.0%	0.00	25		0.0	0.0
Education, health, and social work	1.1%	0.16	17		1.8	1.0
Other personal services	0.5%	0.05	19		4.1	0.4

SPREAD OF ECONOMIC LINKAGES

Demand-side

	Value (2018)	Score (0–1)	Rank (out of 25)	Distance to subregional average	10-year average growth rate (%)	10-year mean value
Relative evenness of direct backward linkage	0.69	1.00	1	▲	0.0	0.70
Relative evenness of total backward linkage	0.24	0.35	2	▲	–0.3	0.25
		0.00				
Backward measure of concentration based on input coefficients	0.93	0.91	5	▲	0.1	0.93
Agriculture, hunting, forestry, and fishing	0.87	0.66	21		0.2	0.86
Mining and quarrying	0.95	0.61	6		0.2	0.94
Light manufacturing	0.94	0.82	3		0.0	0.94
Heavy manufacturing	0.89	0.86	9		0.6	0.86
Utilities	0.92	0.80	10		–0.1	0.93
Construction	0.94	0.94	9		0.1	0.94
Trade services	0.94	0.83	16		0.1	0.93
Hotels and restaurants	0.92	0.81	10		0.1	0.91
Transport services	0.94	0.69	9		0.3	0.92
Telecommunications	0.87	0.32	22		0.5	0.86
Financial intermediation	0.96	0.99	3		0.1	0.96
Real estate, renting, and business activities	0.93	0.87	18		–0.3	0.94
Public administration and defense	1.04	1.00	1		0.0	1.04
Education, health, and social work	0.95	0.73	12		0.1	0.95
Other personal services	0.95	0.89	16		–0.1	0.95
Relative evenness of direct forward linkage	0.61	0.39	14	▼	0.1	0.61
Relative evenness of total forward linkage	0.28	0.27	7	▼	0.1	0.28
Forward measure of concentration based on output coefficients	0.55	0.02	24	▼	–0.2	0.56
Agriculture, hunting, forestry, and fishing	0.42	0.55	5		–0.6	0.43
Mining and quarrying	0.12	0.17	22		–2.6	0.19
Light manufacturing	0.56	0.46	21		–0.4	0.57
Heavy manufacturing	0.54	0.39	19		–0.6	0.56
Utilities	0.76	0.64	16		–0.3	0.77
Construction	0.61	0.71	13		0.7	0.60
Trade services	0.63	0.15	23		–0.3	0.64
Hotels and restaurants	0.70	0.45	19		1.6	0.62
Transport services	0.71	0.54	22		–0.3	0.72
Telecommunications	0.73	0.21	20		–0.2	0.74
Financial intermediation	0.76	0.83	13		–0.4	0.78
Real estate, renting, and business activities	0.66	0.23	24		0.2	0.68
Public administration and defense	0.00	0.00	23		0.0	0.00
Education, health, and social work	0.43	0.40	20		0.1	0.46
Other personal services	0.59	0.26	20		–0.1	0.58

continued on next page

India 3.3A *continued*

	Value (2018)	Score (0–1)	Rank (out of 25)	Distance to subregional average	10–year average growth rate (%)	10–year mean value
SENSITIVITY OF ECONOMIC LINKAGES						
Economic Complexity						
Percentage intermediate transaction	0.39	0.39	9	▲	−0.2	0.40
Average output multiplier	1.50	0.19	14	▲	−0.2	1.53
Average of Leontief inverse	0.19	0.18	13	▲	−0.2	0.20
Average technical coefficient	0.02	0.23	16	▼	−0.3	0.02
Mean intermediate coefficient	0.30	0.23	16	▼	−0.3	0.31
Percentage of above-average coefficients (%)	0.25	0.28	15	▼	0.6	0.24
Determinant of non-competitive Leontief inverse	3.39	0.07	12	▼	−0.1	3.44
Determinant of competitive Leontief inverse	4.08	0.03	16	▼	−0.8	4.28
Mean path length	1.65	0.25	9	▲	−0.2	1.67
Cycling index	0.13	0.42	11	▲	−0.7	0.14
Average propagation length	1.66	0.21	17	▼	−0.2	1.69
Overall sensitivity of the economy	0.71	0.47	17	▼	0.1	0.71
Index of direct interrelatedness	0.54	0.24	18	▼	0.0	0.55
Index of indirect interrelatedness	0.16	0.60	7	▼	0.6	0.16
Global intensity index	22.46	0.19	14	▲	−0.2	22.93

Note: The scores of the economy in focus are shown in the horizontal bars with labels. The colored dots represent the indicator performance of the economy in focus compared to other economies in the region. The highest rank among economies is 1 while the lowest rank is 25. The indicators shown in the chart are selected from a broader set of indicators (see the technical appendix for more details).

Source: Asian Development Bank Multi-Regional Input–Output Database. https://mrio.adbx.online/ (accessed 4 August 2020).

3.3B External Linkages

$ = United States dollars, GVC = global value chain.

Note: The scores of the economy in focus are shown in the horizontal bars with labels. The colored dots represent the indicator performance of the economy in focus compared to other economies in the region. The highest rank among economies is 1, while the lowest rank is 25. The indicators shown in the chart are selected from a broader set of indicators (see the technical appendix for more details).

Source: Asian Development Bank Multi-Regional Input–Output Database. https://mrio.adbx.online/ (accessed 4 August 2020).

	Value (2018)	Score (0–1)	Rank (out of 25)	Distance to subregional average	10–year average growth rate (%)	10–year mean value
PARTICIPATION IN GLOBAL VALUE CHAINS						
International Trade Coefficients						
Trade openness	0.29	0.00	24	▼	–3.1	0.35
Self-sufficiency ratio	1.00	0.63	13	▲	0.1	0.99
Regional supply percentage	0.92	0.92	2	▲	0.3	0.90
Regional purchase coefficient	0.83	0.68	14	▲	0.6	0.81
Sectoral purchase coefficient	0.93	0.96	4	▲	0.0	0.94
Simple location quotient of gross output	0.97	0.22	19	▼	–0.4	0.99
Fabrication effect	0.70	0.03	24	▼	0.0	0.69
Exports ($)	410,506	0.15	5	▲	5.9	339,799
Export-to-output ratio	0.06	0.12	20	▼	–4.9	0.08
Agriculture, hunting, forestry, and fishing	0.03	0.11	19		2.2	0.03
Mining and quarrying	0.14	0.15	11		–7.4	0.19
Light manufacturing	0.11	0.15	20		1.6	0.11
Heavy manufacturing	0.16	0.18	17		2.6	0.16
Utilities	0.00	0.00	20		8.2	0.00
Construction	0.00	0.02	22		–6.5	0.00
Trade services	0.03	0.04	23		–7.5	0.05
Hotels and restaurants	0.00	0.00	22		–9.4	0.00
Transport services	0.04	0.05	22		–8.0	0.07
Telecommunications	0.08	0.22	13		–5.1	0.10

continued on next page

India 3.3B *continued*

		Value (2018)	Score (0–1)	Rank (out of 25)	Distance to subregional average	10-year average growth rate (%)	10-year mean value
Financial intermediation		0.01	0.01	23		–8.1	0.01
Real estate, renting, and business activities		0.20	0.65	4		–6.1	0.28
Public administration and defense		0.00	0.00	23		20.4	0.00
Education, health, and social work		0.00	0.01	23		17.6	0.00
Other personal services		0.13	0.16	6		–5.9	0.18
Imports	($)	427,834	0.20	4	▲	4.4	364,265
Import-to-input ratio		0.06	0.19	22	▼	2.5	0.05
Agriculture, hunting, forestry, and fishing		0.01	0.00	25		–6.5	0.01
Mining and quarrying		0.02	0.05	20		–1.2	0.03
Light manufacturing		0.05	0.03	24		–4.1	0.07
Heavy manufacturing		0.15	0.15	20		–3.6	0.21
Utilities		0.15	0.22	13		7.4	0.11
Construction		0.05	0.07	23		–0.8	0.06
Trade services		0.00	0.00	25		–22.6	0.01
Hotels and restaurants		0.20	0.65	4		51.2	0.08
Transport services		0.28	0.54	8		51.2	0.11
Telecommunications		0.01	0.00	25		–3.9	0.03
Financial intermediation		0.00	0.00	25		–8.2	0.01
Real estate, renting, and business activities		0.01	0.01	22		–16.0	0.02
Public administration and defense		0.00	0.00	25		0.0	0.00
Education, health, and social work		0.01	0.00	25		–6.1	0.02
Other personal services		0.00	0.00	25		–16.9	0.02
Total foreign factor content of consumption	($)	162,429	0.32	3	▲	7.6	120,599
Total foreign factor content of investment	($)	112,667	0.17	3	▲	4.4	95,689
Total foreign factor content of exports	($)	61,279	0.17	9	▲	5.0	57,774

Interregional Multipliers

	Value (2018)	Score (0–1)	Rank (out of 25)	Distance to subregional average	10-year average growth rate (%)	10-year mean value
Import Leakage Effects	0.10	0.12	22	▼	0.2	0.10
Agriculture, hunting, forestry, and fishing	0.02	0.00	25		–3.2	0.03
Mining and quarrying	0.08	0.18	18		2.2	0.07
Light manufacturing	0.13	0.09	23		–2.6	0.15
Heavy manufacturing	0.25	0.23	18		–3.1	0.32
Utilities	0.23	0.28	16		3.1	0.19
Construction	0.13	0.04	23		–2.3	0.15
Trade services	0.02	0.00	25		–2.2	0.03
Hotels and restaurants	0.24	0.59	7		17.7	0.13
Transport services	0.31	0.43	11		13.3	0.18
Telecommunications	0.04	0.00	25		–6.5	0.07
Financial intermediation	0.02	0.01	24		–1.5	0.03
Real estate, renting, and business activities	0.02	0.05	22		–8.5	0.04
Public administration and defense	0.00	0.00	25		0.0	0.00
Education, health, and social work	0.04	0.07	24		–2.5	0.05
Other personal services	0.02	0.00	25		–9.5	0.04
Intraregional transfer multiplier	1.50	0.19	14	▲	–0.2	1.53
Agriculture, hunting, forestry, and fishing	1.36	0.24	14		0.0	1.36
Mining and quarrying	1.61	0.49	4		2.0	1.43

continued on next page

India 3.3B *continued*

	Value (2018)	Score (0–1)	Rank (out of 25)	Distance to subregional average	10–year average growth rate (%)	10–year mean value
Light manufacturing	2.19	0.61	4		0.0	2.20
Heavy manufacturing	2.05	0.42	2		0.9	1.95
Utilities	1.69	0.29	6		−0.4	1.76
Construction	1.96	0.34	6		−0.3	2.01
Trade services	1.21	0.05	24		−0.2	1.23
Hotels and restaurants	1.76	0.43	12		−1.6	1.99
Transport services	1.34	0.22	20		−2.6	1.70
Telecommunications	1.24	0.04	23		−0.8	1.27
Financial intermediation	1.22	0.04	22		−0.3	1.25
Real estate, renting, and business activities	1.28	0.17	19		0.2	1.25
Public administration and defense	1.00	0.00	25		0.0	1.00
Education, health, and social work	1.28	0.16	17		−0.1	1.29
Other personal services	1.26	0.14	20		0.3	1.25
Interregional spillover multiplier	**1.16**	**0.21**	**22**	▼	**0.3**	**1.12**
Agriculture, hunting, forestry, and fishing	1.02	0.00	25		−0.2	1.02
Mining and quarrying	1.05	0.06	20		−0.2	1.07
Light manufacturing	1.12	0.05	23		−0.5	1.16
Heavy manufacturing	1.35	0.18	21		−1.1	1.47
Utilities	1.34	0.22	15		1.1	1.24
Construction	1.13	0.08	23		−0.1	1.14
Trade services	1.00	0.00	25		−0.3	1.01
Hotels and restaurants	1.50	0.67	4		4.0	1.19
Transport services	1.72	0.62	8		4.6	1.28
Telecommunications	1.04	0.01	24		−0.5	1.09
Financial intermediation	1.01	0.00	25		−0.2	1.02
Real estate, renting, and business activities	1.02	0.00	23		−0.8	1.05
Public administration and defense	1.00	0.00	25		0.0	1.00
Education, health, and social work	1.04	0.00	24		−0.3	1.06
Other personal services	1.01	0.00	25		−0.7	1.05
Interregional feedback multiplier	**1.000**	**0.22**	**9**	▲	**0.0**	**1.00**
Agriculture, hunting, forestry, and fishing	1.000	0.04	13		0.0	1.00
Mining and quarrying	1.000	0.03	9		0.0	1.00
Light manufacturing	1.000	0.16	11		0.0	1.00
Heavy manufacturing	1.001	0.15	10		0.0	1.00
Utilities	1.001	0.23	7		0.0	1.00
Construction	1.000	0.15	9		0.0	1.00
Trade services	1.000	0.00	23		0.0	1.00
Hotels and restaurants	1.002	1.00	1		0.0	1.00
Transport services	1.002	0.53	2		0.0	1.00
Telecommunications	1.000	0.05	12		0.0	1.00
Financial intermediation	1.000	0.03	12		0.0	1.00
Real estate, renting, and business activities	1.000	0.02	13		0.0	1.00
Public administration and defense	1.000	0.00	25		0.0	1.00
Education, health, and social work	1.000	0.09	12		0.0	1.00
Other personal services	1.000	0.01	14		0.0	1.00

continued on next page

India 3.3B *continued*

	Value (2018)	Score (0–1)	Rank (out of 25)	Distance to subregional average	10-year average growth rate (%)	10-year mean value
Global Value Chain (GVC) Participation Index						
Backward GVC Participation	11.1%	0.07	20	▼	−2.1	0.12
Simple GVCs	7.7%	0.18	21	▼	−2.2	0.09
Agriculture, hunting, forestry, and fishing	0.2	0.07	18		−5.0	0.23
Mining and quarrying	0.0	0.10	18		36.8	0.00
Light manufacturing	1.3	0.28	11		−2.7	1.61
Heavy manufacturing	2.4	0.52	5		−3.3	3.14
Utilities	0.1	0.08	18		4.4	0.10
Construction	1.3	0.07	24		−4.6	1.68
Trade services	0.2	0.03	24		1.7	0.15
Hotels and restaurants	0.4	0.22	11		19.8	0.24
Transport services	1.3	0.82	2		12.0	0.84
Telecommunications	0.0	0.00	25		−9.9	0.02
Financial intermediation	0.0	0.02	22		−2.9	0.03
Real estate, renting, and business activities	0.2	0.07	21		−6.4	0.23
Public administration and defense	0.0	0.00	25		−10.0	0.00
Education, health, and social work	0.2	0.08	23		−0.8	0.22
Other personal services	0.0	0.00	25		−4.7	0.04
Complex GVCs	3.4%	0.03	23	▼	−1.7	0.04
Agriculture, hunting, forestry, and fishing	0.1	0.06	19		−5.1	0.09
Mining and quarrying	0.0	0.03	14		24.2	0.00
Light manufacturing	0.7	0.05	17		−2.2	0.79
Heavy manufacturing	1.3	0.07	10		−2.1	1.52
Utilities	0.0	0.05	22		3.6	0.03
Construction	0.4	0.04	22		−4.0	0.53
Trade services	0.1	0.00	24		2.8	0.05
Hotels and restaurants	0.1	0.01	15		20.6	0.07
Transport services	0.5	0.25	8		12.2	0.33
Telecommunications	0.0	0.00	25		−14.0	0.01
Financial intermediation	0.0	0.00	21		−2.9	0.01
Real estate, renting, and business activities	0.1	0.08	19		−4.5	0.12
Public administration and defense	0.0	0.00	25		−10.0	0.00
Education, health, and social work	0.1	0.06	23		−0.8	0.08
Other personal services	0.0	0.04	21		−9.8	0.03
Forward GVC Participation	7.0%	0.08	22	▼	−3.4	0.08
Simple GVCs	4.2%	0.06	22	▼	−3.6	0.05
Agriculture, hunting, forestry, and fishing	0.3	0.16	15		−1.7	0.45
Mining and quarrying	0.2	0.01	11		−8.3	0.38
Light manufacturing	0.3	0.08	21		1.0	0.35
Heavy manufacturing	0.9	0.08	14		−0.4	0.97
Utilities	0.1	0.01	19		−0.7	0.09
Construction	0.0	0.01	15		−7.9	0.07
Trade services	0.8	0.08	18		−0.8	0.77
Hotels and restaurants	0.0	0.00	21		−6.4	0.03
Transport services	0.3	0.05	19		−4.3	0.35
Telecommunications	0.1	0.03	22		−6.9	0.09

continued on next page

India 3.3B *continued*

	Value (2018)	Score (0–1)	Rank (out of 25)	Distance to subregional average	10–year average growth rate (%)	10–year mean value
Financial intermediation	0.2	0.04	17		−1.3	0.24
Real estate, renting, and business activities	0.9	0.14	9		−6.6	1.29
Public administration and defense	0.0	0.00	25		39.4	0.00
Education, health, and social work	0.0	0.08	16		−1.3	0.02
Other personal services	0.1	0.04	20		0.5	0.05
Complex GVCs	**2.7%**	**0.11**	**22**	▼	**−3.1**	**0.03**
Agriculture, hunting, forestry, and fishing	0.2	0.10	16		−2.0	0.23
Mining and quarrying	0.2	0.01	11		−7.5	0.27
Light manufacturing	0.2	0.07	20		1.0	0.18
Heavy manufacturing	0.7	0.10	14		−1.7	0.73
Utilities	0.1	0.01	19		−0.7	0.06
Construction	0.0	0.01	16		−6.5	0.03
Trade services	0.5	0.13	18		−0.3	0.48
Hotels and restaurants	0.0	0.00	21		−5.9	0.02
Transport services	0.2	0.10	18		−3.8	0.24
Telecommunications	0.1	0.08	16		−1.3	0.06
Financial intermediation	0.1	0.07	17		−1.1	0.15
Real estate, renting, and business activities	0.5	0.15	11		−4.9	0.61
Public administration and defense	0.0	0.00	25		−1.0	0.00
Education, health, and social work	0.0	0.10	13		0.1	0.01
Other personal services	0.0	0.11	18		−0.1	0.03

SPECIALIZATION IN GLOBAL VALUE CHAINS

Vertical Specialization

	Value (2018)	Score (0–1)	Rank (out of 25)	Distance to subregional average	10–year average growth rate (%)	10–year mean value
Vertical Specialization Ratio	**14.9%**	**0.15**	**18**	▼	**−1.3**	**0.17**
Agriculture, hunting, forestry, and fishing	2.5%	0.00	25		−3.2	0.03
Mining and quarrying	8.4%	0.18	18		2.2	0.07
Light manufacturing	12.6%	0.09	23		−2.6	0.15
Heavy manufacturing	24.6%	0.23	18		−3.1	0.32
Utilities	22.6%	0.36	16		3.0	0.19
Construction	12.7%	0.03	23		−2.3	0.15
Trade services	2.4%	0.00	25		−2.2	0.03
Hotels and restaurants	23.7%	0.58	7		7.2	0.12
Transport services	31.2%	0.42	11		13.2	0.18
Telecommunications	3.9%	0.00	25		−6.4	0.07
Financial intermediation	2.5%	0.01	24		−1.5	0.03
Real estate, renting, and business activities	2.5%	0.05	22		−8.5	0.04
Public administration and defense	0.0%	0.00	25		−34.9	0.00
Education, health, and social work	4.4%	0.07	24		−2.5	0.05
Other personal services	1.9%	0.00	25		−9.5	0.04

Revealed Comparative Advantages

Traditional RCA Index						
Agriculture, hunting, forestry, and fishing	1.42	0.24	12	▼	−6.9	1.56
Mining and quarrying	0.35	0.03	11	▼	3.8	0.40
Light manufacturing	1.41	0.25	8	▼	−0.2	1.29

continued on next page

India 3.3B *continued*

	Value (2018)	Score (0–1)	Rank (out of 25)	Distance to subregional average	10–year average growth rate (%)	10–year mean value
Heavy manufacturing	0.90	0.50	9	▲	0.6	0.81
Utilities	0.06	0.00	20	▼	12.0	0.05
Construction	0.26	0.03	18	▼	−6.3	0.55
Trade services	0.63	0.08	19	▼	2.0	0.71
Hotels and restaurants	0.05	0.00	21	▼	−0.4	0.05
Transport services	0.65	0.15	15	▼	−2.4	0.89
Telecommunications	0.77	0.11	16	▼	−3.8	1.11
Financial intermediation	0.09	0.02	20	▼	−3.2	0.12
Real estate, renting, and business activities	2.46	0.78	2	▲	−1.9	3.13
Public administration and defense	0.01	0.00	21	▼	30.4	0.01
Education, health, and social work	0.05	0.01	22	▼	25.1	0.03
Other personal services	2.32	0.13	3	▼	1.4	2.44
New RCA Index (Based on Domestic Value Added)						
Agriculture, hunting, forestry, and fishing	1.61	0.23	15	▼	−5.5	1.86
Mining and quarrying	0.47	0.07	11	▼	−0.5	0.53
Light manufacturing	0.88	0.20	12	▼	−1.1	0.83
Heavy manufacturing	0.76	0.33	11	▲	−0.4	0.71
Utilities	0.78	0.05	9	▼	6.3	0.65
Construction	0.81	0.04	11	▼	−6.6	1.08
Trade services	1.41	0.40	8	▲	3.2	1.25
Hotels and restaurants	0.36	0.01	21	▼	−2.8	0.47
Transport services	0.94	0.28	13	▼	0.9	0.99
Telecommunications	0.93	0.20	15	▼	−1.4	1.07
Financial intermediation	0.86	0.21	10	▲	1.8	0.82
Real estate, renting, and business activities	1.40	0.84	2	▲	−1.3	1.60
Public administration and defense	0.00	0.00	24	▼	26.6	0.01
Education, health, and social work	0.57	0.12	14	▼	11.5	0.51
Other personal services	1.94	0.25	2	▼	2.2	1.90

POSITION IN GLOBAL VALUE CHAINS

	Value (2018)	Score (0–1)	Rank (out of 25)	Distance to subregional average	10–year average growth rate (%)	10–year mean value
Upstreamness Index	**1.9**	**0.26**	**14**	▲	**−0.4**	**2.0**
Agriculture, hunting, forestry, and fishing	1.7	0.18	19		−0.4	1.8
Mining and quarrying	3.2	0.73	12		−1.1	3.4
Light manufacturing	1.8	0.19	19		−0.2	1.8
Heavy manufacturing	2.2	0.32	18		−0.7	2.3
Utilities	2.8	0.39	10		0.0	2.8
Construction	1.2	0.21	14		−0.7	1.3
Trade services	2.0	0.35	15		−0.6	2.1
Hotels and restaurants	1.7	0.43	12		−0.8	1.8
Transport services	2.0	0.29	18		−0.3	2.0
Telecommunications	2.4	0.57	8		0.2	2.4
Financial intermediation	2.4	0.27	12		0.1	2.4
Real estate, renting, and business activities	1.6	0.08	22		−1.2	1.6
Public administration and defense	1.0	0.00	25		0.0	1.0
Education, health, and social work	1.1	0.15	15		0.1	1.1
Other personal services	1.7	0.33	13		0.2	1.6

continued on next page

India **3.3B** *continued*

	Value (2018)	Score (0–1)	Rank (out of 25)	Distance to subregional average	10–year average growth rate (%)	10–year mean value
PRODUCTION LENGTH OF GLOBAL VALUE CHAINS						
Backward Measures of Average Production Length						
Production Length of Global Value Chain Activity (B)	**0.4**	**0.13**	**21**	▼	**0.0**	**0.4**
Agriculture, hunting, forestry, and fishing	0.1	0.00	25		–2.8	0.1
Mining and quarrying	0.4	0.23	16		4.1	0.3
Light manufacturing	0.6	0.16	23		–2.1	0.7
Heavy manufacturing	1.0	0.30	17		–2.6	1.3
Utilities	0.9	0.29	15		2.2	0.8
Construction	0.6	0.02	23		–2.3	0.7
Trade services	0.1	0.01	24		–1.2	0.1
Hotels and restaurants	0.9	0.52	9		11.8	0.6
Transport services	1.2	0.44	11		9.0	0.8
Telecommunications	0.2	0.00	23		–6.2	0.3
Financial intermediation	0.1	0.03	24		–1.2	0.1
Real estate, renting, and business activities	0.1	0.07	22		–6.6	0.2
Public administration and defense	0.0	0.00	25		–10.0	0.0
Education, health, and social work	0.2	0.09	24		–2.0	0.2
Other personal services	0.1	0.01	24		–7.7	0.2
Forward Measures of Average Production Length						
Production Length of Global Value Chain Activity (F)	**0.3**	**0.16**	**21**	▼	**–2.9**	**0.4**
Agriculture, hunting, forestry, and fishing	0.2	0.08	22		0.1	0.2
Mining and quarrying	1.1	0.29	16		–4.4	1.4
Light manufacturing	0.3	0.10	24		0.5	0.3
Heavy manufacturing	0.7	0.22	18		0.1	0.7
Utilities	0.4	0.13	18		–0.6	0.5
Construction	0.0	0.05	16		–4.8	0.1
Trade services	0.3	0.10	22		–3.2	0.3
Hotels and restaurants	0.1	0.06	22		–5.2	0.2
Transport services	0.3	0.09	21		–3.1	0.4
Telecommunications	0.6	0.24	15		–0.7	0.6
Financial intermediation	0.4	0.13	21		–0.9	0.4
Real estate, renting, and business activities	0.4	0.18	17		–7.2	0.6
Public administration and defense	0.0	0.00	25		0.3	0.0
Education, health, and social work	0.0	0.11	15		–2.0	0.0
Other personal services	0.2	0.07	18		–1.2	0.2

Note: The scores of the economy in focus are shown in the horizontal bars with labels. The colored dots represent the indicator performance of the economy in focus compared to other economies in the region. The highest rank among economies is 1 while the lowest rank is 25. The indicators shown in the chart are selected from a broader set of indicators (see the technical appendix for more details).

Source: Asian Development Bank Multi-Regional Input–Output Database. https://mrio.adbx.online/ (accessed 4 August 2020).

3.4 Kazakhstan

3.4A Internal Linkages

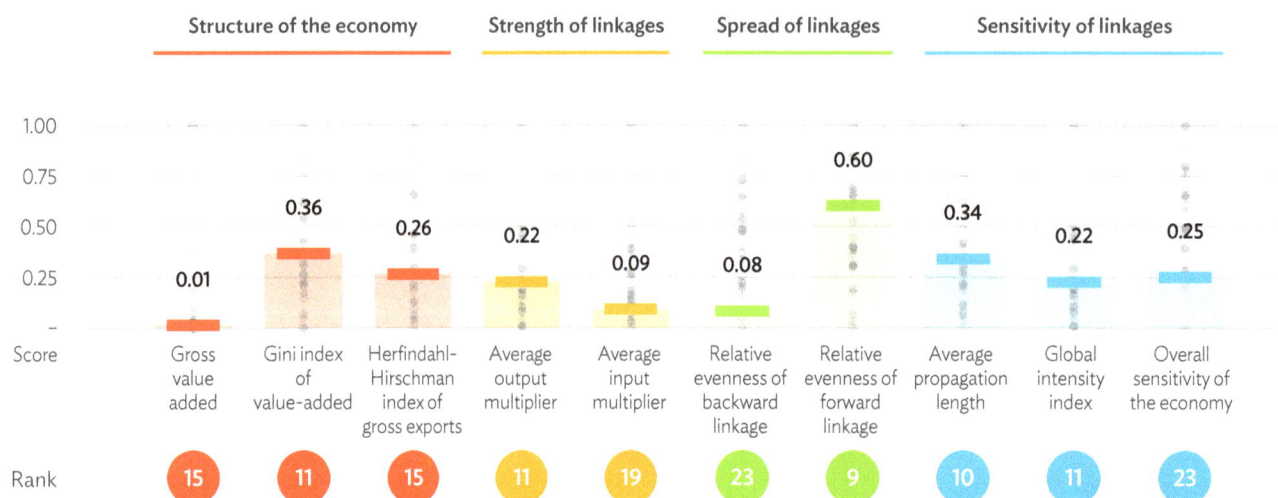

Structure of the economy	Strength of linkages	Spread of linkages	Sensitivity of linkages

Score	Gross value added	Gini index of value-added	Herfindahl-Hirschman index of gross exports	Average output multiplier	Average input multiplier	Relative evenness of backward linkage	Relative evenness of forward linkage	Average propagation length	Global intensity index	Overall sensitivity of the economy
	0.01	0.36	0.26	0.22	0.09	0.08	0.60	0.34	0.22	0.25
Rank	15	11	15	11	19	23	9	10	11	23

Note: The scores of the economy in focus are shown in the horizontal bars with labels. The colored dots represent the indicator performance of the economy in focus compared to other economies in the region. The highest rank among economies is 1 while the lowest rank is 25. The indicators shown in the chart are selected from a broader set of indicators (see the technical appendix for more details).

Source: Asian Development Bank Multi-Regional Input–Output Database. https://mrio.adbx.online/ (accessed 4 August 2020).

		Value (2018)	Score (0–1)	Rank (out of 25)	Distance to subregional average	10–year average growth rate (%)	10–year mean value
STRUCTURE OF THE ECONOMY							
Economic Indicators							
Gross output	($)	**266,165**	**0.01**	**15**	▼	2.0	275,798
Gross value-added	($)	**154,644**	**0.01**	**15**	▼	3.6	157,028
Value-added content of domestic final demand		104,463	0.01	15		5.9	100,049
Value-added content of exports		50,181	0.02	13		1.6	56,979
Intermediate inputs	($)	**109,681**	**0.00**	**15**	▼	0.5	115,166
Domestic inputs		91,866	0.00	15		0.9	94,755
Foreign inputs		17,815	0.01	15		–0.4	20,412
Direct production	($)	**174,299**	**0.01**	**15**	▼	2.8	181,043
Domestic final demand		118,350	0.01	15		5.0	115,460
Exports		55,950	0.02	13		0.9	65,583
Indirect production	($)	**91,866**	**0.00**	**15**	▼	0.9	94,755
Indirect production embedded in domestic final demand		60,693	0.00	15		3.2	58,660
Indirect production embedded in exports		31,173	0.01	14		–0.6	36,095
Economic Diversification							
Gross output		**0.23**	**0.19**	**21**	▼	–1.1	0.24
Gini concentration index of gross output		0.41	0.25	21		–0.8	0.42
Herfindahl-Hirschman concentration index of gross output		0.04	0.11	21		–1.5	0.05
Theil concentration index of gross output		0.23	0.17	21		–1.3	0.25

continued on next page

Kazakhstan 3.4A *continued*

	Value (2018)	Score (0–1)	Rank (out of 25)	Distance to subregional average	10–year average growth rate (%)	10–year mean value
Gross value-added	**0.25**	**0.29**	**11**	▼	**−1.0**	**0.26**
Gini concentration index of gross value added	0.44	0.36	11		−0.8	0.44
Herfindahl-Hirschman concentration index of gross value added	0.05	0.15	11		−0.7	0.05
Theil concentration index of gross value added	0.27	0.29	12		−1.2	0.28
Gross exports	**0.58**	**0.46**	**14**	▲	**0.2**	**0.60**
Gini concentration index of gross exports	0.78	0.67	12		0.1	0.79
Herfindahl-Hirschman concentration index of gross exports	0.25	0.26	15		0.7	0.29
Theil concentration index of gross exports	0.71	0.62	14		0.3	0.73

Structural Changes

	Value (2018)	Score (0–1)	Rank (out of 25)	Distance to subregional average	10–year average growth rate (%)	10–year mean value
Changes in output due to technological changes	**−0.1%**	**0.74**	**13**	▼	**–**	**–**
Agriculture, hunting, forestry, and fishing	−0.9%	0.49	18			
Mining and quarrying	−1.8%	0.72	19			
Light manufacturing	1.6%	0.49	3			
Heavy manufacturing	0.6%	0.73	6			
Utilities	−0.7%	0.43	15			
Construction	0.2%	0.14	13			
Trade services	−1.0%	0.10	24			
Hotels and restaurants	1.3%	0.14	5			
Transport services	1.0%	0.79	3			
Telecommunications	−0.5%	0.19	14			
Financial intermediation	−2.8%	0.23	24			
Real estate, renting, and business activities	1.0%	0.77	5			
Public administration and defense	0.0%	0.38	9			
Education, health, and social work	0.2%	0.80	6			
Other personal services	0.4%	0.50	10			
Changes in output due to structural changes in consumption (%)	**1.5%**	**0.21**	**23**	▼	**–**	**–**
Agriculture, hunting, forestry, and fishing	2.8%	0.53	13			
Mining and quarrying	−0.1%	0.02	24			
Light manufacturing	1.2%	0.24	20			
Heavy manufacturing	0.3%	0.11	23			
Utilities	0.0%	0.07	24			
Construction	0.2%	0.20	15			
Trade services	1.9%	0.38	17			
Hotels and restaurants	0.5%	0.06	22			
Transport services	1.1%	0.24	17			
Telecommunications	−3.4%	0.00	25			
Financial intermediation	2.2%	0.33	20			
Real estate, renting, and business activities	1.6%	0.11	20			
Public administration and defense	3.2%	0.27	20			
Education, health, and social work	1.5%	0.07	23			
Other personal services	9.1%	0.64	4			
Changes in output due to structural changes in investment (%)	**0.0%**	**0.00**	**25**	▼	**–**	**–**
Agriculture, hunting, forestry, and fishing	−0.2%	0.00	25			
Mining and quarrying	0.0%	0.06	24			
Light manufacturing	0.0%	0.00	25			

continued on next page

Kazakhstan 3.4A *continued*

	Value (2018)	Score (0–1)	Rank (out of 25)	Distance to subregional average	10–year average growth rate (%)	10–year mean value
Heavy manufacturing	−0.1%	0.11	23			
Utilities	0.0%	0.29	23			
Construction	−0.4%	0.00	25			
Trade services	1.0%	0.31	10			
Hotels and restaurants	0.0%	0.29	24			
Transport services	0.1%	0.00	24			
Telecommunications	0.6%	0.20	10			
Financial intermediation	0.1%	0.00	25			
Real estate, renting, and business activities	−1.3%	0.00	25			
Public administration and defense	0.0%	0.00	24			
Education, health, and social work	0.0%	0.00	25			
Other personal services	0.1%	0.13	20			
Changes in output due to structural changes in stock (%)	**0.1%**	**0.36**	**7**	▲	–	–
Agriculture, hunting, forestry, and fishing	−0.3%	0.46	18			
Mining and quarrying	1.0%	0.49	4			
Light manufacturing	0.3%	0.30	5			
Heavy manufacturing	0.3%	0.52	6			
Utilities	0.1%	0.16	7			
Construction	0.0%	0.76	6			
Trade services	0.0%	0.32	10			
Hotels and restaurants	0.1%	0.51	3			
Transport services	0.1%	0.07	9			
Telecommunications	−0.3%	0.17	24			
Financial intermediation	0.0%	0.91	7			
Real estate, renting, and business activities	0.1%	0.19	5			
Public administration and defense	0.0%	0.64	9			
Education, health, and social work	0.0%	0.23	6			
Other personal services	0.0%	0.43	7			
Changes in output due to structural changes in export	**−0.2%**	**0.00**	**25**	▼	–	–
Agriculture, hunting, forestry, and fishing	0.2%	0.44	20			
Mining and quarrying	−2.5%	0.01	24			
Light manufacturing	0.2%	0.11	21			
Heavy manufacturing	−0.7%	0.12	24			
Utilities	−0.4%	0.02	24			
Construction	0.1%	0.04	19			
Trade services	1.0%	0.14	14			
Hotels and restaurants	−0.1%	0.02	24			
Transport services	−1.5%	0.21	24			
Telecommunications	0.1%	0.08	23			
Financial intermediation	−0.1%	0.06	23			
Real estate, renting, and business activities	−0.1%	0.14	22			
Public administration and defense	−0.6%	0.00	25			
Education, health, and social work	0.0%	0.00	25			
Other personal services	0.8%	0.16	15			

continued on next page

Kazakhstan 3.4A *continued*

	Value (2018)	Score (0–1)	Rank (out of 25)	Distance to subregional average	10-year average growth rate (%)	10-year mean value
Changes in output due to import substitution on intermediate demand	**0.0%**	**0.38**	**14**	▼	–	–
Agriculture, hunting, forestry, and fishing	−0.2%	0.66	15			
Mining and quarrying	0.6%	0.32	9			
Light manufacturing	−0.3%	0.79	18			
Heavy manufacturing	0.9%	0.29	8			
Utilities	−0.1%	0.66	15			
Construction	−0.5%	0.29	22			
Trade services	0.1%	0.78	9			
Hotels and restaurants	0.0%	0.97	8			
Transport services	0.0%	0.42	16			
Telecommunications	−0.7%	0.82	22			
Financial intermediation	0.2%	0.68	5			
Real estate, renting, and business activities	−0.5%	0.60	20			
Public administration and defense	0.0%	0.65	14			
Education, health, and social work	0.0%	0.59	9			
Other personal services	0.0%	0.50	13			
Changes in output due to import substitution on domestic final demand	**0.3%**	**1.00**	**1**	▼	–	–
Agriculture, hunting, forestry, and fishing	0.1%	0.60	6			
Mining and quarrying	0.1%	0.56	9			
Light manufacturing	0.2%	0.83	5			
Heavy manufacturing	0.5%	0.63	4			
Utilities	0.3%	0.97	2			
Construction	0.7%	1.00	1			
Trade services	0.2%	0.97	3			
Hotels and restaurants	−0.5%	0.12	22			
Transport services	0.2%	0.92	4			
Telecommunications	0.3%	0.89	2			
Financial intermediation	0.4%	0.99	2			
Real estate, renting, and business activities	1.3%	1.00	1			
Public administration and defense	0.6%	0.50	2			
Education, health, and social work	0.0%	0.87	8			
Other personal services	0.1%	0.94	4			

STRENGTH OF LINKAGES

Demand-side Linkages

	Value (2018)	Score (0–1)	Rank (out of 25)	Distance to subregional average	10-year average growth rate (%)	10-year mean value
Direct backward linkage	**0.35**	**0.42**	**9**	▲	**−1.1**	**0.35**
Agriculture, hunting, forestry, and fishing	0.34	0.50	7		2.3	0.33
Mining and quarrying	0.37	0.60	4		−0.9	0.36
Light manufacturing	0.42	0.50	21		−0.2	0.41
Heavy manufacturing	0.50	0.54	8		0.1	0.49
Utilities	0.41	0.46	9		0.2	0.41
Construction	0.45	0.36	13		0.9	0.42
Trade services	0.24	0.24	15		−2.1	0.27
Hotels and restaurants	0.34	0.32	22		−2.0	0.34
Transport services	0.29	0.47	14		1.5	0.29
Telecommunications	0.30	0.39	15		−0.1	0.28

continued on next page

Kazakhstan 3.4A *continued*

	Value (2018)	Score (0–1)	Rank (out of 25)	Distance to subregional average	10–year average growth rate (%)	10–year mean value
Financial intermediation	0.22	0.21	15		–9.6	0.34
Real estate, renting, and business activities	0.22	0.39	15		–3.3	0.25
Public administration and defense	0.49	0.89	2		1.6	0.45
Education, health, and social work	0.41	0.83	2		4.0	0.36
Other personal services	0.28	0.47	15		–2.0	0.29
Total backward linkage	**1.53**	**0.22**	**11**	▲	**–1.1**	**1.55**
Agriculture, hunting, forestry, and fishing	1.51	0.37	8		0.6	1.50
Mining and quarrying	1.57	0.46	5		–0.7	1.55
Light manufacturing	1.63	0.29	19		–0.2	1.62
Heavy manufacturing	1.77	0.26	7		–0.3	1.76
Utilities	1.67	0.28	8		0.0	1.65
Construction	1.71	0.19	14		0.2	1.66
Trade services	1.35	0.28	14		–1.2	1.40
Hotels and restaurants	1.51	0.23	21		–0.8	1.52
Transport services	1.45	0.31	14		0.2	1.44
Telecommunications	1.45	0.30	15		–0.4	1.43
Financial intermediation	1.30	0.06	16		–7.5	1.65
Real estate, renting, and business activities	1.33	0.23	14		–1.7	1.39
Public administration and defense	1.71	0.72	3		0.1	1.65
Education, health, and social work	1.63	0.46	4		1.1	1.54
Other personal services	1.41	0.30	15		–1.2	1.44
Normalized backward linkage	–	–	–	▬	–	–
Agriculture, hunting, forestry, and fishing	0.99	0.44	6		1.8	0.97
Mining and quarrying	1.02	0.69	5		0.5	1.00
Light manufacturing	1.06	0.36	22		1.0	1.05
Heavy manufacturing	1.16	0.52	6		0.8	1.14
Utilities	1.09	0.37	9		1.1	1.07
Construction	1.12	0.31	16		1.3	1.07
Trade services	0.88	0.28	18		0.0	0.90
Hotels and restaurants	0.99	0.15	21		0.3	0.99
Transport services	0.94	0.32	18		1.4	0.94
Telecommunications	0.95	0.49	16		0.8	0.92
Financial intermediation	0.85	0.08	18		–6.8	1.05
Real estate, renting, and business activities	0.87	0.35	18		–0.6	0.90
Public administration and defense	1.11	0.83	3		1.3	1.07
Education, health, and social work	1.06	1.00	1		2.3	1.00
Other personal services	0.92	0.36	16		–0.1	0.93
Net backward linkage	**1.04**	**1.00**	**1**	▲	**0.7**	**1.03**
Agriculture, hunting, forestry, and fishing	0.97	0.87	3		1.7	0.95
Mining and quarrying	1.10	0.76	3		–0.1	1.09
Light manufacturing	1.08	0.53	13		–0.8	1.11
Heavy manufacturing	0.86	0.49	15		–2.9	0.96
Utilities	0.68	0.53	8		1.6	0.68
Construction	1.34	0.29	16		3.2	1.21
Trade services	0.90	0.47	8		0.1	0.86

continued on next page

Kazakhstan 3.4A *continued*

	Value (2018)	Score (0–1)	Rank (out of 25)	Distance to subregional average	10–year average growth rate (%)	10–year mean value
Hotels and restaurants	1.20	0.45	16		8.5	1.16
Transport services	0.72	0.25	18		–0.6	0.79
Telecommunications	1.04	0.78	3		9.2	0.94
Financial intermediation	0.22	0.08	22		0.6	0.26
Real estate, renting, and business activities	0.87	0.81	9		0.2	0.90
Public administration and defense	1.70	0.81	2		0.1	1.65
Education, health, and social work	1.59	0.56	3		1.3	1.51
Other personal services	1.36	0.92	2		0.7	1.33
Growth equalized output multipliers	**0.10**	**0.15**	**13**	▲	**–0.7**	**0.10**
Agriculture, hunting, forestry, and fishing	0.09	0.24	16		2.6	0.08
Mining and quarrying	0.25	0.54	3		–2.7	0.30
Light manufacturing	0.08	0.12	22		–0.3	0.07
Heavy manufacturing	0.18	0.21	13		1.4	0.15
Utilities	0.04	0.16	12		2.0	0.04
Construction	0.11	0.13	18		–4.2	0.13
Trade services	0.24	0.58	3		2.9	0.22
Hotels and restaurants	0.01	0.00	25		–0.1	0.01
Transport services	0.13	0.69	5		0.0	0.13
Telecommunications	0.03	0.27	13		–2.1	0.03
Financial intermediation	0.04	0.10	21		–2.8	0.04
Real estate, renting, and business activities	0.18	0.70	4		–0.6	0.18
Public administration and defense	0.05	0.19	22		3.5	0.04
Education, health, and social work	0.06	0.22	17		3.2	0.06
Other personal services	0.04	0.21	9		8.3	0.03

Supply-Side Linkages

	Value (2018)	Score (0–1)	Rank (out of 25)	Distance to subregional average	10–year average growth rate (%)	10–year mean value
Direct forward linkage	**0.33**	**0.16**	**22**	▼	**–1.7**	**0.33**
Agriculture, hunting, forestry, and fishing	0.36	0.27	18		0.0	0.36
Mining and quarrying	0.30	0.30	20		–0.4	0.30
Light manufacturing	0.34	0.24	16		1.7	0.32
Heavy manufacturing	0.51	0.67	11		4.3	0.45
Utilities	0.59	0.61	19		–0.3	0.59
Construction	0.22	0.45	9		–4.6	0.27
Trade services	0.34	0.36	17		0.5	0.38
Hotels and restaurants	0.21	0.39	15		6.0	0.24
Transport services	0.50	0.58	8		1.5	0.45
Telecommunications	0.28	0.05	24		–4.6	0.34
Financial intermediation	0.83	0.92	5		–0.5	0.83
Real estate, renting, and business activities	0.34	0.22	17		–1.7	0.35
Public administration and defense	0.00	0.01	21		–0.2	0.00
Education, health, and social work	0.02	0.07	18		4.7	0.02
Other personal services	0.04	0.01	24		–4.5	0.07
Total forward linkage	**1.48**	**0.09**	**19**	▼	**–1.5**	**1.51**
Agriculture, hunting, forestry, and fishing	1.52	0.16	17		–0.4	1.52
Mining and quarrying	1.49	0.16	18		–0.1	1.48
Light manufacturing	1.47	0.12	17		0.2	1.45

continued on next page

Kazakhstan 3.4A *continued*

	Value (2018)	Score (0–1)	Rank (out of 25)	Distance to subregional average	10–year average growth rate (%)	10–year mean value
Heavy manufacturing	1.81	0.38	13		1.4	1.70
Utilities	1.85	0.26	20		–1.0	1.88
Construction	1.30	0.33	9		–2.4	1.39
Trade services	1.52	0.23	16		–0.2	1.59
Hotels and restaurants	1.28	0.22	15		–2.3	1.33
Transport services	1.76	0.32	11		0.3	1.69
Telecommunications	1.43	0.10	23		–3.0	1.53
Financial intermediation	2.26	0.26	9		–4.5	2.48
Real estate, renting, and business activities	1.49	0.14	19		–1.8	1.53
Public administration and defense	1.00	0.01	20		0.0	1.00
Education, health, and social work	1.03	0.08	18		–0.6	1.03
Other personal services	1.05	0.02	24		–2.0	1.10
Normalized forward linkage	–	–	–	▬	–	–
Agriculture, hunting, forestry, and fishing	1.02	0.29	16		1.1	1.00
Mining and quarrying	0.97	0.30	20		1.1	0.95
Light manufacturing	0.96	0.27	22		1.4	0.94
Heavy manufacturing	1.18	0.59	11		2.7	1.10
Utilities	1.21	0.42	20		0.1	1.22
Construction	0.85	0.41	9		–1.3	0.90
Trade services	0.99	0.26	21		1.1	1.03
Hotels and restaurants	0.83	0.27	14		–1.4	0.85
Transport services	1.15	0.53	10		1.4	1.09
Telecommunications	0.93	0.01	24		–2.1	0.98
Financial intermediation	1.47	0.31	7		–3.6	1.59
Real estate, renting, and business activities	0.97	0.16	22		–0.7	0.99
Public administration and defense	0.65	0.35	17		1.2	0.65
Education, health, and social work	0.67	0.47	18		0.6	0.67
Other personal services	0.69	0.00	25		–1.0	0.71
Net forward linkage	**0.85**	**0.44**	**13**	▼	**0.6**	**0.84**
Agriculture, hunting, forestry, and fishing	0.88	0.24	19		–1.9	0.91
Mining and quarrying	0.84	0.37	16		1.6	0.82
Light manufacturing	0.71	0.78	4		1.7	0.67
Heavy manufacturing	0.80	0.87	4		2.6	0.73
Utilities	0.93	0.46	10		–0.7	0.93
Construction	0.59	0.80	3		–2.1	0.65
Trade services	1.08	0.48	15		1.2	1.08
Hotels and restaurants	0.74	0.58	5		–1.1	0.75
Transport services	1.05	0.63	3		0.0	1.01
Telecommunications	0.91	0.34	18		–1.8	0.98
Financial intermediation	1.56	0.56	8		31.0	1.36
Real estate, renting, and business activities	1.08	0.39	16		0.8	1.03
Public administration and defense	0.41	0.15	24		–0.1	0.45
Education, health, and social work	0.49	0.00	25		–2.9	0.54
Other personal services	0.70	0.31	20		–0.1	0.71

continued on next page

Kazakhstan 3.4A *continued*

	Value (2018)	Score (0–1)	Rank (out of 25)	Distance to subregional average	10–year average growth rate (%)	10–year mean value
Growth equalized input multipliers	**0.10**	**0.16**	**13**	▲	**−0.6**	**0.10**
Agriculture, hunting, forestry, and fishing	0.08	0.17	18		−0.2	0.09
Mining and quarrying	0.24	0.36	3		−2.3	0.28
Light manufacturing	0.06	0.16	21		0.6	0.06
Heavy manufacturing	0.16	0.31	11		3.3	0.13
Utilities	0.04	0.17	13		0.2	0.04
Construction	0.07	0.10	16		−6.3	0.10
Trade services	0.30	0.66	5		3.4	0.27
Hotels and restaurants	0.01	0.00	25		−2.1	0.01
Transport services	0.15	0.89	2		−0.9	0.15
Telecommunications	0.03	0.12	16		−5.3	0.04
Financial intermediation	0.07	0.12	20		22.7	0.07
Real estate, renting, and business activities	0.22	0.53	6		−0.6	0.21
Public administration and defense	0.02	0.05	24		2.6	0.02
Education, health, and social work	0.03	0.00	25		−0.9	0.04
Other personal services	0.03	0.20	15		7.9	0.03

Impacts from Hypothetical Extraction

	Value (2018)	Score (0–1)	Rank (out of 25)	Distance to subregional average	10–year average growth rate (%)	10–year mean value
Changes in gross output due to hypothetical extraction	**−9.4%**	**0.73**	**17**	▲	**0.0**	**−0.09**
Agriculture, hunting, forestry, and fishing	−7.0%	0.76	10		3.6	−6.6
Mining and quarrying	−22.5%	0.40	23		−1.5	−25.4
Light manufacturing	−8.0%	0.84	4		0.1	−7.2
Heavy manufacturing	−17.5%	0.67	13		1.8	−15.4
Utilities	−4.0%	0.82	16		2.7	−4.0
Construction	−11.9%	0.80	12		−1.8	−12.8
Trade services	−20.9%	0.53	24		2.7	−18.6
Hotels and restaurants	−1.4%	1.00	1		−0.3	−1.3
Transport services	−11.6%	0.33	22		1.0	−11.4
Telecommunications	−2.4%	0.67	12		−2.1	−2.9
Financial intermediation	−3.1%	0.90	7		−3.5	−3.5
Real estate, renting, and business activities	−14.8%	0.23	22		−1.1	−15.0
Public administration and defense	−5.3%	0.72	13		4.3	−4.5
Education, health, and social work	−6.2%	0.66	16		5.4	−6.1
Other personal services	−3.8%	0.81	18		8.0	−3.1

Impacts from Hypothetical Insertion

	Value (2018)	Score (0–1)	Rank (out of 25)	Distance to subregional average	10–year average growth rate (%)	10–year mean value
Changes in gross output due to hypothetical insertion	**3.5%**	**0.15**	**13**	▼	**−2.5**	**0.04**
Agriculture, hunting, forestry, and fishing	2.9%	0.11	10		7.3	2.6
Mining and quarrying	9.4%	0.80	2		−3.7	10.8
Light manufacturing	3.4%	0.09	22		−0.1	2.9
Heavy manufacturing	8.9%	0.14	12		1.5	7.6
Utilities	1.7%	0.19	10		2.8	1.7
Construction	5.1%	0.14	16		−3.0	5.6
Trade services	5.6%	0.35	6		−0.3	5.5
Hotels and restaurants	0.5%	0.01	23		−1.7	0.4
Transport services	3.8%	0.55	7		1.6	3.7
Telecommunications	0.8%	0.19	16		−2.5	0.9
Financial intermediation	0.8%	0.05	17		−14.0	2.1

continued on next page

Kazakhstan 3.4A *continued*

	Value (2018)	Score (0–1)	Rank (out of 25)	Distance to subregional average	10–year average growth rate (%)	10–year mean value
Real estate, renting, and business activities	3.9%	0.56	10		–4.9	4.6
Public administration and defense	2.2%	0.52	10		4.7	1.8
Education, health, and social work	2.4%	0.43	6		8.5	2.2
Other personal services	1.1%	0.15	11		4.8	0.9

SPREAD OF ECONOMIC LINKAGES

Demand-side

	Value (2018)	Score (0–1)	Rank (out of 25)	Distance to subregional average	10–year average growth rate (%)	10–year mean value
Relative evenness of direct backward linkage	**0.26**	**0.08**	**23**	▼	**–0.9**	**0.24**
Relative evenness of total backward linkage	**0.10**	**0.00**	**25**	▼	**–5.7**	**0.11**
		0.00				
Backward measure of concentration based on input coefficients	**0.92**	**0.75**	**10**	▲	**0.1**	**0.91**
Agriculture, hunting, forestry, and fishing	0.88	0.70	17		0.5	0.87
Mining and quarrying	0.93	0.51	12		0.9	0.90
Light manufacturing	0.91	0.67	12		–0.2	0.92
Heavy manufacturing	0.87	0.83	12		–0.1	0.85
Utilities	0.92	0.79	11		–0.3	0.94
Construction	0.92	0.89	12		0.5	0.92
Trade services	0.94	0.82	17		0.0	0.92
Hotels and restaurants	0.89	0.71	16		–0.1	0.91
Transport services	0.93	0.63	12		–0.3	0.94
Telecommunications	0.94	0.83	8		0.1	0.94
Financial intermediation	0.88	0.89	15		3.8	0.83
Real estate, renting, and business activities	0.96	0.96	7		0.0	0.95
Public administration and defense	0.93	0.52	19		–0.2	0.93
Education, health, and social work	0.96	0.83	6		–0.1	0.96
Other personal services	0.90	0.69	23		–0.6	0.92
Relative evenness of direct forward linkage	**0.69**	**0.60**	**9**	▲	**2.5**	**0.68**
Relative evenness of total forward linkage	**0.23**	**0.14**	**18**	▼	**–4.2**	**0.25**
Forward measure of concentration based on output coefficients	**0.68**	**0.67**	**9**	▲	**0.5**	**0.67**
Agriculture, hunting, forestry, and fishing	0.41	0.54	8		–1.7	0.44
Mining and quarrying	0.41	0.57	12		1.6	0.41
Light manufacturing	0.79	0.88	5		–0.5	0.78
Heavy manufacturing	0.80	0.87	4		1.1	0.77
Utilities	0.85	0.86	7		–0.3	0.87
Construction	0.73	0.84	3		1.3	0.70
Trade services	0.83	0.92	3		0.1	0.83
Hotels and restaurants	0.65	0.33	23		–0.7	0.67
Transport services	0.83	0.89	4		0.4	0.80
Telecommunications	0.71	0.09	23		0.9	0.73
Financial intermediation	0.82	0.91	7		9.4	0.75
Real estate, renting, and business activities	0.81	0.64	15		–0.1	0.82
Public administration and defense	0.16	0.18	20		–0.5	0.07
Education, health, and social work	0.63	0.68	11		–0.4	0.66
Other personal services	0.75	0.63	14		–0.7	0.76

continued on next page

Kazakhstan 3.4A *continued*

	Value (2018)	Score (0–1)	Rank (out of 25)	Distance to subregional average	10-year average growth rate (%)	10-year mean value
SENSITIVITY OF ECONOMIC LINKAGES						
Economic Complexity						
Percentage intermediate transaction	0.35	0.26	13	▲	−1.1	0.35
Average output multiplier	1.53	0.22	11	▲	−1.1	1.55
Average of Leontief inverse	0.20	0.22	10	▲	−1.1	0.20
Average technical coefficient	0.02	0.42	9	▲	−1.1	0.02
Mean intermediate coefficient	0.35	0.42	9	▲	−1.1	0.35
Percentage of above-average coefficients (%)	0.30	0.68	4	▲	0.6	0.29
Determinant of non-competitive Leontief inverse	2.45	0.04	16	▼	−10.0	3.75
Determinant of competitive Leontief inverse	3.10	0.02	23	▼	−11.0	5.03
Mean path length	1.53	0.15	13	▲	−0.7	1.53
Cycling index	0.08	0.19	18	▼	−6.0	0.10
Average propagation length	1.82	0.34	10	▲	−0.8	1.77
Overall sensitivity of the economy	0.64	0.25	23	▼	−1.4	0.67
Index of direct interrelatedness	0.53	0.19	20	▼	−1.2	0.56
Index of indirect interrelatedness	0.11	0.20	23	▼	0.4	0.12
Global intensity index	23.00	0.22	11	▲	−1.1	23.20

Note: The scores of the economy in focus are shown in the horizontal bars with labels. The colored dots represent the indicator performance of the economy in focus compared to other economies in the region. The highest rank among economies is 1 while the lowest rank is 25. The indicators shown in the chart are selected from a broader set of indicators (see the technical appendix for more details).

Source: Asian Development Bank Multi-Regional Input–Output Database. https://mrio.adbx.online/ (accessed 4 August 2020).

3.4B External Linkages

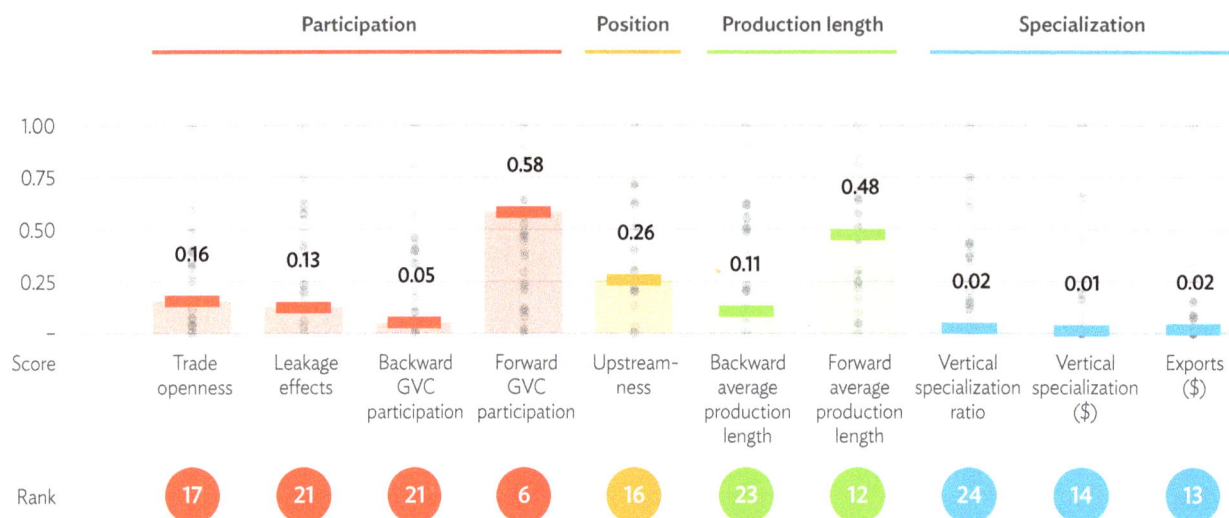

$ = United States dollars, GVC = global value chain.

Note: The scores of the economy in focus are shown in the horizontal bars with labels. The colored dots represent the indicator performance of the economy in focus compared to other economies in the region. The highest rank among economies is 1, while the lowest rank is 25. The indicators shown in the chart are selected from a broader set of indicators (see the technical appendix for more details).

Source: Asian Development Bank Multi-Regional Input–Output Database. https://mrio.adbx.online/ (accessed 4 August 2020).

		Value (2018)	Score (0–1)	Rank (out of 25)	Distance to subregional average	10–year average growth rate (%)	10–year mean value
PARTICIPATION IN GLOBAL VALUE CHAINS							
International Trade Coefficients							
Trade openness		0.59	0.16	17	▼	−3.8	0.69
Self-sufficiency ratio		1.06	0.84	2	▲	−0.3	1.07
Regional supply percentage		0.84	0.70	8	▲	0.7	0.82
Regional purchase coefficient		0.88	0.81	6	▲	0.7	0.85
Sectoral purchase coefficient		0.92	0.94	6	▲	0.4	0.91
Simple location quotient of gross output		1.18	0.50	12	▼	−0.5	1.22
Fabrication effect		0.91	0.48	17	▲	−1.5	0.92
Exports	($)	55,950	0.02	13	▼	0.9	65,583
Export-to-output ratio		0.11	0.32	15	▼	−4.1	0.13
Agriculture, hunting, forestry, and fishing		0.07	0.31	14		−0.9	0.08
Mining and quarrying		0.58	0.64	5		−0.8	0.62
Light manufacturing		0.09	0.11	22		−0.5	0.09
Heavy manufacturing		0.39	0.46	7		0.4	0.43
Utilities		0.03	0.04	9		−0.4	0.03
Construction		0.01	0.12	11		−1.0	0.00
Trade services		0.27	0.37	5		−1.8	0.27
Hotels and restaurants		0.00	0.00	24		4.0	0.05
Transport services		0.13	0.17	17		−0.3	0.19
Telecommunications		0.03	0.08	21		1.4	0.03

continued on next page

Kazakhstan 3.4B *continued*

		Value (2018)	Score (0–1)	Rank (out of 25)	Distance to subregional average	10-year average growth rate (%)	10-year mean value
Financial intermediation		0.01	0.02	20		1.9	0.01
Real estate, renting, and business activities		0.01	0.04	19		10.3	0.02
Public administration and defense		0.00	0.00	25		26.3	0.03
Education, health, and social work		0.00	0.00	25		−16.1	0.00
Other personal services		0.04	0.05	13		−0.7	0.03
Imports	($)	**40,189**	**0.02**	**15**	▼	**−1.0**	**47,042**
Import-to-input ratio		**0.07**	**0.23**	**20**	▼	**−1.7**	**0.08**
Agriculture, hunting, forestry, and fishing		0.07	0.19	13		13.6	0.06
Mining and quarrying		0.06	0.14	13		−2.7	0.07
Light manufacturing		0.11	0.16	17		−1.9	0.12
Heavy manufacturing		0.05	0.00	25		−3.4	0.06
Utilities		0.08	0.07	20		−0.8	0.09
Construction		0.10	0.18	20		−0.5	0.11
Trade services		0.05	0.20	15		4.8	0.04
Hotels and restaurants		0.08	0.25	13		8.8	0.08
Transport services		0.10	0.17	20		1.7	0.10
Telecommunications		0.06	0.15	17		−1.4	0.07
Financial intermediation		0.04	0.19	9		3.8	0.05
Real estate, renting, and business activities		0.05	0.29	12		−3.6	0.06
Public administration and defense		0.08	0.50	9		−0.1	0.09
Education, health, and social work		0.10	0.55	5		1.6	0.10
Other personal services		0.04	0.10	18		−3.6	0.06
Total foreign factor content of consumption	($)	**9,245**	**0.02**	**15**	▼	**2.1**	**9,675**
Total foreign factor content of investment	($)	**2,870**	**0.00**	**15**	▼	**−0.1**	**3,407**
Total foreign factor content of exports	($)	**5,175**	**0.01**	**14**	▼	**−2.2**	**6,950**
Interregional Multipliers							
Import Leakage Effects		**0.11**	**0.13**	**21**	▼	**−3.1**	**0.12**
Agriculture, hunting, forestry, and fishing		0.10	0.20	16		8.9	0.10
Mining and quarrying		0.09	0.20	16		−3.2	0.11
Light manufacturing		0.15	0.14	20		−1.5	0.17
Heavy manufacturing		0.09	0.00	25		−3.6	0.12
Utilities		0.12	0.10	22		−2.0	0.14
Construction		0.14	0.07	20		−1.7	0.16
Trade services		0.07	0.14	17		−0.1	0.07
Hotels and restaurants		0.12	0.21	18		3.6	0.12
Transport services		0.12	0.09	22		0.4	0.13
Telecommunications		0.09	0.11	19		−2.9	0.10
Financial intermediation		0.06	0.13	14		−6.8	0.10
Real estate, renting, and business activities		0.08	0.23	16		−5.1	0.09
Public administration and defense		0.13	0.38	10		−1.3	0.13
Education, health, and social work		0.15	0.59	8		1.3	0.14
Other personal services		0.07	0.13	20		−5.5	0.09
Intraregional transfer multiplier		**1.53**	**0.22**	**11**	▲	**−1.1**	**1.55**
Agriculture, hunting, forestry, and fishing		1.51	0.37	8		0.6	1.50
Mining and quarrying		1.57	0.46	5		−0.7	1.55

continued on next page

Kazakhstan 3.4B *continued*

	Value (2018)	Score (0–1)	Rank (out of 25)	Distance to subregional average	10–year average growth rate (%)	10–year mean value
Light manufacturing	1.63	0.29	19		−0.2	1.62
Heavy manufacturing	1.77	0.26	7		−0.3	1.76
Utilities	1.67	0.28	8		0.0	1.65
Construction	1.71	0.19	14		0.2	1.66
Trade services	1.35	0.28	14		−1.2	1.40
Hotels and restaurants	1.51	0.23	21		−0.8	1.52
Transport services	1.45	0.31	14		0.2	1.44
Telecommunications	1.45	0.30	15		−0.4	1.43
Financial intermediation	1.30	0.06	16		−7.5	1.65
Real estate, renting, and business activities	1.33	0.23	14		−1.7	1.39
Public administration and defense	1.71	0.72	3		0.1	1.65
Education, health, and social work	1.63	0.46	4		1.1	1.54
Other personal services	1.41	0.30	15		−1.2	1.44
Interregional spillover multiplier	**1.17**	**0.25**	**21**	▼	**−0.3**	**1.19**
Agriculture, hunting, forestry, and fishing	1.17	0.23	13		0.9	1.15
Mining and quarrying	1.14	0.17	13		−0.5	1.16
Light manufacturing	1.28	0.20	16		−0.6	1.31
Heavy manufacturing	1.12	0.01	24		−0.6	1.16
Utilities	1.22	0.10	20		−0.1	1.23
Construction	1.23	0.19	20		−0.4	1.28
Trade services	1.11	0.21	15		−0.1	1.09
Hotels and restaurants	1.20	0.25	12		0.7	1.19
Transport services	1.24	0.19	21		0.3	1.25
Telecommunications	1.15	0.16	17		−0.5	1.17
Financial intermediation	1.08	0.18	10		−1.3	1.10
Real estate, renting, and business activities	1.12	0.34	12		−0.7	1.14
Public administration and defense	1.16	0.35	10		−0.7	1.18
Education, health, and social work	1.27	0.68	4		0.2	1.26
Other personal services	1.10	0.10	18		−0.6	1.15
Interregional feedback multiplier	**1.000**	**0.05**	**13**	▲	**0.0**	**1.00**
Agriculture, hunting, forestry, and fishing	1.000	0.09	11		0.0	1.00
Mining and quarrying	1.000	0.02	11		0.0	1.00
Light manufacturing	1.000	0.08	12		0.0	1.00
Heavy manufacturing	1.000	0.01	13		0.0	1.00
Utilities	1.000	0.04	12		0.0	1.00
Construction	1.000	0.05	13		0.0	1.00
Trade services	1.000	0.03	11		0.0	1.00
Hotels and restaurants	1.000	0.06	12		0.0	1.00
Transport services	1.000	0.04	13		0.0	1.00
Telecommunications	1.000	0.04	13		0.0	1.00
Financial intermediation	1.000	0.02	13		0.0	1.00
Real estate, renting, and business activities	1.000	0.03	11		0.0	1.00
Public administration and defense	1.000	0.04	10		0.0	1.00
Education, health, and social work	1.000	0.15	10		0.0	1.00
Other personal services	1.000	0.03	12		0.0	1.00

continued on next page

Kazakhstan 3.4B *continued*

	Value (2018)	Score (0–1)	Rank (out of 25)	Distance to subregional average	10–year average growth rate (%)	10–year mean value
Global Value Chain (GVC) Participation Index						
Backward GVC Participation	10.6%	0.05	21	▼	−2.8	0.12
Simple GVCs	7.8%	0.20	20	▼	−2.8	0.09
Agriculture, hunting, forestry, and fishing	0.6	0.22	8		6.0	0.52
Mining and quarrying	0.3	0.29	3		27.4	0.23
Light manufacturing	0.8	0.14	19		0.6	0.87
Heavy manufacturing	0.2	0.02	22		6.1	0.25
Utilities	0.2	0.15	16		−5.4	0.23
Construction	1.3	0.07	23		−4.7	1.80
Trade services	0.8	0.31	9		16.2	0.64
Hotels and restaurants	0.1	0.07	21		−2.7	0.13
Transport services	0.6	0.37	14		−1.4	0.69
Telecommunications	0.2	0.18	12		−4.6	0.23
Financial intermediation	0.0	0.04	19		16.0	0.09
Real estate, renting, and business activities	0.9	0.58	4		−1.2	1.22
Public administration and defense	0.7	0.17	10		5.0	0.65
Education, health, and social work	0.9	0.48	10		0.3	0.91
Other personal services	0.3	0.22	11		1.0	0.29
Complex GVCs	2.8%	0.00	24	▼	−2.4	0.03
Agriculture, hunting, forestry, and fishing	0.2	0.18	8		6.3	0.17
Mining and quarrying	0.2	0.34	5		4.9	0.24
Light manufacturing	0.3	0.01	23		0.4	0.29
Heavy manufacturing	0.2	0.01	20		10.1	0.21
Utilities	0.1	0.16	15		−3.1	0.08
Construction	0.4	0.03	23		−4.0	0.47
Trade services	0.3	0.04	12		17.6	0.23
Hotels and restaurants	0.0	0.00	24		−1.8	0.04
Transport services	0.3	0.12	19		−2.7	0.35
Telecommunications	0.1	0.09	16		−2.9	0.07
Financial intermediation	0.0	0.00	22		12.4	0.02
Real estate, renting, and business activities	0.3	0.32	5		1.7	0.31
Public administration and defense	0.2	0.13	14		4.0	0.16
Education, health, and social work	0.3	0.37	9		2.5	0.30
Other personal services	0.1	0.22	12		3.5	0.09
Forward GVC Participation	28.3%	0.58	6	▲	−2.9	0.32
Simple GVCs	14.5%	0.42	12	▲	−4.3	0.18
Agriculture, hunting, forestry, and fishing	0.2	0.08	21		5.9	0.24
Mining and quarrying	5.3	0.32	3		−4.2	7.68
Light manufacturing	0.2	0.04	22		2.4	0.22
Heavy manufacturing	1.9	0.17	10		4.2	2.07
Utilities	0.2	0.03	12		0.4	0.23
Construction	0.1	0.03	7		−3.6	0.23
Trade services	4.1	0.50	3		−1.2	4.20
Hotels and restaurants	0.0	0.00	22		7.5	0.05
Transport services	1.3	0.30	7		0.4	1.63
Telecommunications	0.1	0.05	16		−4.1	0.17

continued on next page

Kazakhstan 3.4B *continued*

	Value (2018)	Score (0–1)	Rank (out of 25)	Distance to subregional average	10–year average growth rate (%)	10–year mean value
Financial intermediation	0.3	0.06	16		0.1	0.33
Real estate, renting, and business activities	0.7	0.12	11		2.4	0.83
Public administration and defense	0.0	0.00	24		17.2	0.01
Education, health, and social work	0.0	0.03	22		6.9	0.01
Other personal services	0.0	0.02	22		–1.9	0.04
Complex GVCs	**13.8%**	**0.79**	**3**	▲	**–0.9**	**0.14**
Agriculture, hunting, forestry, and fishing	0.1	0.05	20		7.2	0.12
Mining and quarrying	6.3	0.49	3		2.1	7.36
Light manufacturing	0.2	0.06	22		8.5	0.13
Heavy manufacturing	2.4	0.36	6		11.9	2.03
Utilities	0.2	0.05	9		7.3	0.17
Construction	0.1	0.04	7		3.0	0.17
Trade services	2.6	0.84	2		5.5	2.19
Hotels and restaurants	0.0	0.00	20		14.6	0.03
Transport services	1.0	0.69	3		7.7	1.01
Telecommunications	0.1	0.09	15		1.3	0.10
Financial intermediation	0.2	0.11	11		6.7	0.22
Real estate, renting, and business activities	0.6	0.19	9		8.5	0.58
Public administration and defense	0.0	0.00	24		24.5	0.00
Education, health, and social work	0.0	0.07	16		14.2	0.01
Other personal services	0.0	0.01	24		2.1	0.02

SPECIALIZATION IN GLOBAL VALUE CHAINS

Vertical Specialization

	Value (2018)	Score (0–1)	Rank (out of 25)	Distance to subregional average	10–year average growth rate (%)	10–year mean value
Vertical Specialization Ratio	**9.2%**	**0.02**	**24**	▼	**–3.2**	**0.10**
Agriculture, hunting, forestry, and fishing	10.4%	0.20	16		8.9	0.10
Mining and quarrying	9.4%	0.20	16		–3.2	0.11
Light manufacturing	15.1%	0.14	20		–1.6	0.17
Heavy manufacturing	9.1%	0.00	25		–3.6	0.12
Utilities	12.1%	0.19	22		–2.0	0.14
Construction	14.1%	0.07	20		–1.7	0.16
Trade services	7.5%	0.14	17		–0.1	0.07
Hotels and restaurants	12.1%	0.20	18		–9.6	0.11
Transport services	12.4%	0.09	22		0.4	0.13
Telecommunications	9.2%	0.11	19		–2.9	0.10
Financial intermediation	6.0%	0.13	14		–6.8	0.10
Real estate, renting, and business activities	7.6%	0.23	16		–5.2	0.09
Public administration and defense	12.7%	0.37	10		–9.2	0.11
Education, health, and social work	14.6%	0.59	8		1.3	0.14
Other personal services	6.8%	0.13	20		–5.5	0.09

Revealed Comparative Advantages

Traditional RCA Index

	Value (2018)	Score (0–1)	Rank (out of 25)	Distance to subregional average	10–year average growth rate (%)	10–year mean value
Agriculture, hunting, forestry, and fishing	0.83	0.14	14	▼	11.7	0.79
Mining and quarrying	6.34	0.58	3	▲	1.6	6.15
Light manufacturing	0.14	0.02	22	▼	7.1	0.12

continued on next page

Kazakhstan 3.4B *continued*

	Value (2018)	Score (0–1)	Rank (out of 25)	Distance to subregional average	10-year average growth rate (%)	10-year mean value
Heavy manufacturing	0.47	0.26	13	▲	9.9	0.40
Utilities	0.73	0.01	3	▼	−0.2	0.74
Construction	0.50	0.06	15	▼	−6.5	0.33
Trade services	2.56	0.33	2	▲	−0.4	2.23
Hotels and restaurants	0.00	0.00	25	▼	8.5	0.17
Transport services	0.92	0.21	10	▼	3.4	1.13
Telecommunications	0.35	0.04	20	▼	4.6	0.44
Financial intermediation	0.04	0.01	24	▼	14.1	0.06
Real estate, renting, and business activities	0.10	0.03	17	▼	24.6	0.12
Public administration and defense	0.00	0.00	25	▼	9.7	0.71
Education, health, and social work	0.00	0.00	25	▼	−12.7	0.01
Other personal services	0.43	0.02	12	▼	−1.6	0.26

New RCA Index (Based on Domestic Value Added)

	Value (2018)	Score (0–1)	Rank (out of 25)	Distance to subregional average	10-year average growth rate (%)	10-year mean value
Agriculture, hunting, forestry, and fishing	0.40	0.06	19	▼	11.7	0.41
Mining and quarrying	3.90	0.55	3	▲	−1.3	3.97
Light manufacturing	0.18	0.03	23	▼	5.1	0.15
Heavy manufacturing	0.64	0.28	13	▲	8.0	0.52
Utilities	0.54	0.03	16	▼	3.4	0.49
Construction	0.80	0.04	12	▼	2.6	1.14
Trade services	1.87	0.55	3	▲	2.7	1.68
Hotels and restaurants	0.10	0.00	24	▼	6.7	0.19
Transport services	1.33	0.42	7	▼	5.5	1.38
Telecommunications	0.39	0.03	24	▼	0.3	0.57
Financial intermediation	0.34	0.05	19	▼	5.5	0.31
Real estate, renting, and business activities	0.31	0.15	16	▼	5.8	0.31
Public administration and defense	0.00	0.00	25	▼	22.5	0.16
Education, health, and social work	0.08	0.00	24	▼	9.3	0.09
Other personal services	0.22	0.01	20	▼	0.6	0.15

POSITION IN GLOBAL VALUE CHAINS

	Value (2018)	Score (0–1)	Rank (out of 25)	Distance to subregional average	10-year average growth rate (%)	10-year mean value
Upstreamness Index	**1.9**	**0.26**	**15**	▲	**−2.3**	**2.0**
Agriculture, hunting, forestry, and fishing	1.6	0.13	21		−1.8	1.7
Mining and quarrying	3.3	0.75	8		−1.3	3.5
Light manufacturing	1.7	0.11	23		−0.8	1.7
Heavy manufacturing	3.0	0.81	7		−0.3	3.0
Utilities	2.3	0.19	19		−0.8	2.3
Construction	1.4	0.35	8		−3.1	1.5
Trade services	2.4	0.59	9		−1.4	2.5
Hotels and restaurants	1.4	0.22	20		−3.7	1.5
Transport services	2.4	0.51	12		−1.4	2.4
Telecommunications	1.6	0.00	25		−3.8	1.8
Financial intermediation	2.7	0.32	9		−4.7	3.0
Real estate, renting, and business activities	1.7	0.16	19		−2.2	1.8
Public administration and defense	1.0	0.01	21		−0.4	1.0
Education, health, and social work	1.0	0.08	19		−0.8	1.0
Other personal services	1.1	0.00	25		−2.6	1.2

continued on next page

Kazakhstan 3.4B *continued*

	Value (2018)	Score (0–1)	Rank (out of 25)	Distance to subregional average	10–year average growth rate (%)	10–year mean value
PRODUCTION LENGTH OF GLOBAL VALUE CHAINS						
Backward Measures of Average Production Length						
Production Length of Global Value Chain Activity (B)	0.4	0.11	23	▼	–3.8	0.5
Agriculture, hunting, forestry, and fishing	0.4	0.18	17		7.1	0.4
Mining and quarrying	0.4	0.22	17		–3.4	0.4
Light manufacturing	0.6	0.16	22		–1.7	0.7
Heavy manufacturing	0.4	0.00	25		–4.0	0.5
Utilities	0.5	0.11	23		–2.2	0.6
Construction	0.6	0.00	25		–2.2	0.6
Trade services	0.3	0.13	18		–1.8	0.3
Hotels and restaurants	0.5	0.18	21		2.3	0.5
Transport services	0.5	0.08	22		0.1	0.5
Telecommunications	0.4	0.11	20		–3.3	0.4
Financial intermediation	0.2	0.12	18		–10.0	0.4
Real estate, renting, and business activities	0.3	0.23	18		–5.8	0.3
Public administration and defense	0.5	0.31	13		–2.4	0.5
Education, health, and social work	0.6	0.49	9		1.0	0.6
Other personal services	0.3	0.14	19		–6.0	0.4
Forward Measures of Average Production Length						
Production Length of Global Value Chain Activity (F)	0.7	0.48	12	▲	–4.5	0.8
Agriculture, hunting, forestry, and fishing	0.2	0.09	21		–3.8	0.3
Mining and quarrying	2.8	0.72	3		–2.1	3.0
Light manufacturing	0.3	0.16	21		–4.6	0.4
Heavy manufacturing	2.0	0.71	8		–1.7	2.1
Utilities	0.8	0.28	10		0.7	0.9
Construction	0.2	0.23	6		–1.1	0.3
Trade services	1.4	0.65	5		–2.8	1.5
Hotels and restaurants	0.2	0.11	18		20.5	0.4
Transport services	1.1	0.44	11		–3.7	1.3
Telecommunications	0.4	0.16	18		–2.6	0.5
Financial intermediation	0.8	0.33	9		–5.9	1.1
Real estate, renting, and business activities	0.4	0.20	14		–1.5	0.5
Public administration and defense	0.0	0.00	23		–10.3	0.0
Education, health, and social work	0.0	0.12	12		17.6	0.0
Other personal services	0.1	0.02	24		37.0	0.1

Note: The scores of the economy in focus are shown in the horizontal bars with labels. The colored dots represent the indicator performance of the economy in focus compared to other economies in the region. The highest rank among economies is 1 while the lowest rank is 25. The indicators shown in the chart are selected from a broader set of indicators (see the technical appendix for more details).

Source: Asian Development Bank Multi-Regional Input–Output Database. https://mrio.adbx.online/ (accessed 4 August 2020).

3.5 Kyrgyz Republic

3.5A Internal Linkages

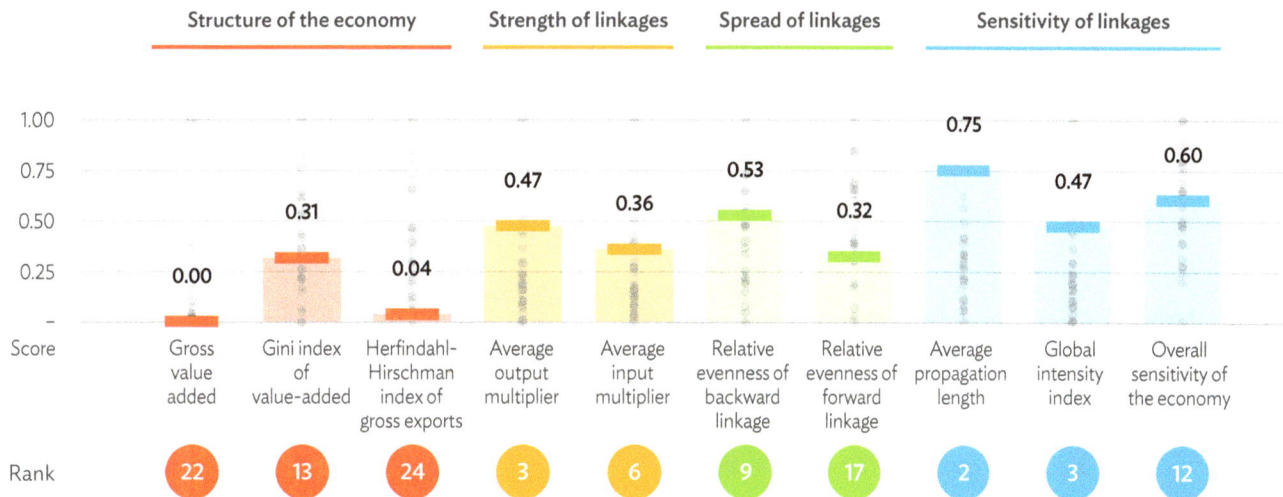

	Structure of the economy			Strength of linkages		Spread of linkages		Sensitivity of linkages		
Score	Gross value added	Gini index of value-added	Herfindahl-Hirschman index of gross exports	Average output multiplier	Average input multiplier	Relative evenness of backward linkage	Relative evenness of forward linkage	Average propagation length	Global intensity index	Overall sensitivity of the economy
(value)	0.00	0.31	0.04	0.47	0.36	0.53	0.32	0.75	0.47	0.60
Rank	22	13	24	3	6	9	17	2	3	12

Note: The scores of the economy in focus are shown in the horizontal bars with labels. The colored dots represent the indicator performance of the economy in focus compared to other economies in the region. The highest rank among economies is 1 while the lowest rank is 25. The indicators shown in the chart are selected from a broader set of indicators (see the technical appendix for more details).

Source: Asian Development Bank Multi-Regional Input–Output Database. https://mrio.adbx.online/ (accessed 4 August 2020).

		Value (2018)	Score (0–1)	Rank (out of 25)	Distance to subregional average	10–year average growth rate (%)	10–year mean value
STRUCTURE OF THE ECONOMY							
Economic Indicators							
Gross output	($)	**14,709**	**0.00**	**22**	▼	**3.7**	**12,976**
Gross value-added	($)	**6,342**	**0.00**	**22**	▼	**4.3**	**5,476**
Value-added content of domestic final demand		4,553	0.00	22		5.0	3,856
Value-added content of exports		1,789	0.00	22		3.4	1,620
Intermediate inputs	($)	**8,106**	**0.00**	**22**	▼	**3.3**	**7,249**
Domestic inputs		5,916	0.00	22		5.3	4,991
Foreign inputs		2,190	0.00	23		2.6	2,258
Direct production	($)	**8,793**	**0.00**	**22**	▼	**3.2**	**7,985**
Domestic final demand		6,309	0.00	22		4.0	5,597
Exports		2,484	0.00	23		2.1	2,388
Indirect production	($)	**5,916**	**0.00**	**22**	▼	**5.3**	**4,991**
Indirect production embedded in domestic final demand		4,087	0.00	20		6.1	3,338
Indirect production embedded in exports		1,829	0.00	21		4.5	1,653
Economic Diversification							
Gross output		**0.25**	**0.28**	**19**	▼	**−2.0**	**0.27**
Gini concentration index of gross output		0.43	0.34	19		−1.4	0.46
Herfindahl-Hirschman concentration index of gross output		0.05	0.19	18		−4.0	0.06
Theil concentration index of gross output		0.26	0.25	19		−2.6	0.30

continued on next page

Kyrgyz Republic 3.5A *continued*

	Value (2018)	Score (0–1)	Rank (out of 25)	Distance to subregional average	10–year average growth rate (%)	10–year mean value
Gross value-added	**0.24**	**0.25**	**13**	▼	**−2.3**	**0.26**
Gini concentration index of gross value added	0.42	0.31	13		−1.5	0.44
Herfindahl-Hirschman concentration index of gross value added	0.05	0.14	12		−4.5	0.05
Theil concentration index of gross value added	0.25	0.25	13		−3.0	0.28
Gross exports	**0.40**	**0.08**	**23**	▼	**0.1**	**0.44**
Gini concentration index of gross exports	0.61	0.16	23		−0.1	0.64
Herfindahl-Hirschman concentration index of gross exports	0.10	0.04	24		2.4	0.14
Theil concentration index of gross exports	0.50	0.13	23		0.1	0.53

Structural Changes

	Value (2018)	Score (0–1)	Rank (out of 25)	Distance to subregional average	10–year average growth rate (%)	10–year mean value
Changes in output due to technological changes	**−0.4%**	**0.71**	**18**	▲	**–**	**–**
Agriculture, hunting, forestry, and fishing	−1.3%	0.47	21			
Mining and quarrying	−7.6%	0.67	23			
Light manufacturing	−2.1%	0.22	24			
Heavy manufacturing	−3.6%	0.55	21			
Utilities	0.0%	0.54	10			
Construction	1.2%	0.29	3			
Trade services	1.4%	0.94	2			
Hotels and restaurants	0.5%	0.09	10			
Transport services	1.1%	0.79	2			
Telecommunications	0.9%	0.33	5			
Financial intermediation	1.7%	0.62	3			
Real estate, renting, and business activities	0.8%	0.75	7			
Public administration and defense	0.1%	0.39	7			
Education, health, and social work	0.1%	0.73	12			
Other personal services	1.1%	0.66	2			
Changes in output due to structural changes in consumption (%)	**2.3%**	**0.28**	**20**	▼	**–**	**–**
Agriculture, hunting, forestry, and fishing	3.8%	0.67	6			
Mining and quarrying	0.0%	0.02	23			
Light manufacturing	1.5%	0.27	17			
Heavy manufacturing	0.4%	0.13	20			
Utilities	1.0%	0.16	23			
Construction	−1.4%	0.10	24			
Trade services	4.6%	0.70	8			
Hotels and restaurants	7.3%	0.25	6			
Transport services	2.4%	0.39	13			
Telecommunications	2.3%	0.47	17			
Financial intermediation	4.5%	0.52	9			
Real estate, renting, and business activities	4.5%	0.22	10			
Public administration and defense	1.7%	0.19	23			
Education, health, and social work	3.9%	0.14	18			
Other personal services	−1.6%	0.05	24			
Changes in output due to structural changes in investment (%)	**1.6%**	**0.47**	**5**	▲	**–**	**–**
Agriculture, hunting, forestry, and fishing	0.1%	0.05	22			
Mining and quarrying	0.2%	0.11	18			
Light manufacturing	0.8%	0.23	8			

continued on next page

Kyrgyz Republic 3.5A *continued*

	Value (2018)	Score (0–1)	Rank (out of 25)	Distance to subregional average	10–year average growth rate (%)	10–year mean value
Heavy manufacturing	0.6%	0.17	17			
Utilities	3.2%	0.91	3			
Construction	11.8%	0.74	3			
Trade services	0.9%	0.28	12			
Hotels and restaurants	0.4%	0.46	8			
Transport services	0.6%	0.15	11			
Telecommunications	0.0%	0.09	24			
Financial intermediation	1.7%	0.40	3			
Real estate, renting, and business activities	−0.1%	0.16	22			
Public administration and defense	0.2%	0.28	4			
Education, health, and social work	1.6%	1.00	1			
Other personal services	1.6%	0.82	2			
Changes in output due to structural changes in stock (%)	**−0.4%**	**0.00**	**25**	▼	–	–
Agriculture, hunting, forestry, and fishing	0.3%	0.61	3			
Mining and quarrying	0.0%	0.38	11			
Light manufacturing	−0.1%	0.14	18			
Heavy manufacturing	0.0%	0.28	17			
Utilities	0.2%	0.23	6			
Construction	−0.3%	0.62	24			
Trade services	0.1%	0.36	8			
Hotels and restaurants	0.1%	0.51	4			
Transport services	0.0%	0.06	11			
Telecommunications	0.0%	0.49	7			
Financial intermediation	−5.2%	0.00	25			
Real estate, renting, and business activities	−0.1%	0.13	21			
Public administration and defense	−0.6%	0.45	24			
Education, health, and social work	−0.2%	0.11	24			
Other personal services	−0.1%	0.34	22			
Changes in output due to structural changes in export	**2.3%**	**0.52**	**8**	▲	–	–
Agriculture, hunting, forestry, and fishing	−4.8%	0.00	25			
Mining and quarrying	22.0%	1.00	1			
Light manufacturing	3.4%	0.36	7			
Heavy manufacturing	−0.4%	0.15	22			
Utilities	−0.9%	0.00	25			
Construction	1.0%	0.20	6			
Trade services	−0.3%	0.00	25			
Hotels and restaurants	0.3%	0.05	18			
Transport services	3.2%	0.71	6			
Telecommunications	0.9%	0.14	14			
Financial intermediation	3.7%	0.61	5			
Real estate, renting, and business activities	1.7%	0.51	8			
Public administration and defense	4.5%	1.00	1			
Education, health, and social work	0.2%	0.08	14			
Other personal services	0.3%	0.07	22			

continued on next page

Kyrgyz Republic 3.5A *continued*

	Value (2018)	Score (0–1)	Rank (out of 25)	Distance to subregional average	10-year average growth rate (%)	10-year mean value
Changes in output due to import substitution on intermediate demand	**1.2%**	**0.53**	**3**	▲	–	–
Agriculture, hunting, forestry, and fishing	3.5%	1.00	1			
Mining and quarrying	4.5%	0.35	4			
Light manufacturing	1.4%	0.90	2			
Heavy manufacturing	2.4%	0.36	5			
Utilities	1.5%	1.00	1			
Construction	0.1%	0.96	2			
Trade services	1.1%	1.00	1			
Hotels and restaurants	0.5%	1.00	1			
Transport services	0.4%	0.58	4			
Telecommunications	0.2%	1.00	1			
Financial intermediation	1.1%	1.00	1			
Real estate, renting, and business activities	0.7%	0.89	2			
Public administration and defense	0.0%	0.72	4			
Education, health, and social work	0.0%	0.65	2			
Other personal services	0.2%	0.60	2			
Changes in output due to import substitution on domestic final demand	**–0.8%**	**0.25**	**22**	▲	–	–
Agriculture, hunting, forestry, and fishing	1.0%	0.88	2			
Mining and quarrying	–0.4%	0.27	24			
Light manufacturing	–4.2%	0.00	25			
Heavy manufacturing	–0.5%	0.49	20			
Utilities	–0.3%	0.46	22			
Construction	–0.1%	0.64	20			
Trade services	–0.2%	0.79	19			
Hotels and restaurants	–0.3%	0.32	19			
Transport services	–2.6%	0.00	25			
Telecommunications	–0.8%	0.40	23			
Financial intermediation	–0.7%	0.50	23			
Real estate, renting, and business activities	–1.4%	0.05	24			
Public administration and defense	–1.2%	0.00	25			
Education, health, and social work	0.0%	0.85	19			
Other personal services	–0.2%	0.91	18			

STRENGTH OF LINKAGES

Demand-side Linkages

	Value (2018)	Score (0–1)	Rank (out of 25)	Distance to subregional average	10-year average growth rate (%)	10-year mean value
Direct backward linkage	**0.37**	**0.48**	**7**	▲	**3.2**	**0.34**
Agriculture, hunting, forestry, and fishing	0.62	1.00	1		2.2	0.57
Mining and quarrying	0.38	0.62	3		11.3	0.26
Light manufacturing	0.49	0.61	17		–0.1	0.47
Heavy manufacturing	0.46	0.46	9		4.3	0.45
Utilities	0.34	0.34	16		6.2	0.26
Construction	0.43	0.32	15		7.4	0.38
Trade services	0.20	0.15	19		–1.7	0.21
Hotels and restaurants	0.40	0.48	17		0.2	0.41
Transport services	0.25	0.40	20		19.8	0.21
Telecommunications	0.16	0.07	24		9.9	0.18

continued on next page

Kyrgyz Republic 3.5A *continued*

	Value (2018)	Score (0–1)	Rank (out of 25)	Distance to subregional average	10–year average growth rate (%)	10–year mean value
Financial intermediation	0.80	1.00	1		3.6	0.77
Real estate, renting, and business activities	0.28	0.59	10		3.5	0.26
Public administration and defense	0.23	0.41	18		0.7	0.23
Education, health, and social work	0.19	0.25	17		2.4	0.18
Other personal services	0.32	0.55	10		8.0	0.30
Total backward linkage	**1.77**	**0.47**	**3**	▲	**2.1**	**1.70**
Agriculture, hunting, forestry, and fishing	2.25	1.00	1		1.8	2.11
Mining and quarrying	1.55	0.44	7		2.4	1.37
Light manufacturing	1.83	0.40	11		–0.2	1.80
Heavy manufacturing	1.79	0.27	6		2.2	1.76
Utilities	1.51	0.19	16		1.7	1.39
Construction	1.69	0.17	15		2.3	1.60
Trade services	1.31	0.22	17		–0.9	1.33
Hotels and restaurants	1.65	0.34	15		0.0	1.68
Transport services	1.39	0.27	18		2.1	1.33
Telecommunications	1.23	0.04	24		0.9	1.28
Financial intermediation	4.81	1.00	1		13.2	4.28
Real estate, renting, and business activities	1.43	0.35	10		0.8	1.39
Public administration and defense	1.37	0.37	17		–0.1	1.37
Education, health, and social work	1.30	0.17	15		0.5	1.28
Other personal services	1.50	0.38	11		1.9	1.46
Normalized backward linkage	**–**	**–**	**–**	▬	**–**	**–**
Agriculture, hunting, forestry, and fishing	1.27	1.00	1		0.0	1.25
Mining and quarrying	0.87	0.40	14		0.9	0.81
Light manufacturing	1.03	0.31	23		–1.8	1.07
Heavy manufacturing	1.01	0.19	20		0.0	1.04
Utilities	0.85	0.05	23		–0.2	0.82
Construction	0.95	0.00	25		0.2	0.95
Trade services	0.74	0.00	25		–2.6	0.79
Hotels and restaurants	0.93	0.01	24		–1.8	0.99
Transport services	0.78	0.06	24		0.0	0.78
Telecommunications	0.70	0.00	25		–1.3	0.76
Financial intermediation	2.71	1.00	1		8.6	2.50
Real estate, renting, and business activities	0.81	0.20	23		–0.9	0.82
Public administration and defense	0.77	0.19	24		–1.7	0.81
Education, health, and social work	0.73	0.00	25		–1.1	0.76
Other personal services	0.84	0.12	22		–0.2	0.86
Net backward linkage	**1.00**	**0.83**	**2**	▲	**–0.4**	**1.00**
Agriculture, hunting, forestry, and fishing	1.09	1.00	1		3.8	1.00
Mining and quarrying	1.44	1.00	1		15.2	0.87
Light manufacturing	1.24	0.70	6		–1.2	1.19
Heavy manufacturing	0.96	0.60	12		0.5	0.98
Utilities	0.73	0.59	7		1.0	0.75
Construction	1.24	0.24	19		1.4	1.24
Trade services	0.64	0.17	21		–1.7	0.71

continued on next page

Kyrgyz Republic 3.5A *continued*

	Value (2018)	Score (0–1)	Rank (out of 25)	Distance to subregional average	10-year average growth rate (%)	10-year mean value
Hotels and restaurants	1.11	0.38	21		0.6	1.18
Transport services	0.84	0.37	14		−0.7	0.90
Telecommunications	0.73	0.37	15		−2.9	0.89
Financial intermediation	0.70	0.59	6		2.4	0.67
Real estate, renting, and business activities	0.70	0.61	18		−4.2	0.89
Public administration and defense	1.34	0.40	15		−0.3	1.36
Education, health, and social work	1.24	0.22	16		0.2	1.25
Other personal services	0.99	0.64	13		−1.6	1.09
Growth equalized output multipliers	**0.11**	**0.27**	**8**	▲	**0.9**	**0.11**
Agriculture, hunting, forestry, and fishing	0.35	1.00	2		−2.3	0.40
Mining and quarrying	0.02	0.05	13		13.8	0.01
Light manufacturing	0.11	0.17	19		−3.8	0.12
Heavy manufacturing	0.17	0.20	14		1.3	0.19
Utilities	0.05	0.24	7		5.2	0.05
Construction	0.24	0.42	5		8.0	0.18
Trade services	0.26	0.62	2		2.6	0.22
Hotels and restaurants	0.04	0.06	14		3.9	0.03
Transport services	0.08	0.36	14		3.5	0.08
Telecommunications	0.06	0.77	5		4.3	0.07
Financial intermediation	0.05	0.13	18		3.4	0.04
Real estate, renting, and business activities	0.07	0.16	20		3.0	0.06
Public administration and defense	0.07	0.40	11		3.3	0.07
Education, health, and social work	0.08	0.46	7		2.7	0.08
Other personal services	0.03	0.12	17		11.6	0.02
Supply-Side Linkages						
Direct forward linkage	**0.37**	**0.30**	**13**	▲	**3.6**	**0.35**
Agriculture, hunting, forestry, and fishing	0.52	0.50	13		−0.2	0.53
Mining and quarrying	0.07	0.07	22		14.1	0.37
Light manufacturing	0.32	0.21	18		4.8	0.34
Heavy manufacturing	0.46	0.59	16		4.7	0.44
Utilities	0.52	0.52	21		3.3	0.46
Construction	0.26	0.55	5		8.8	0.22
Trade services	0.51	0.65	8		1.3	0.47
Hotels and restaurants	0.33	0.63	7		5.4	0.29
Transport services	0.40	0.42	15		8.3	0.32
Telecommunications	0.41	0.35	20		21.8	0.30
Financial intermediation	0.85	0.96	3		2.9	0.83
Real estate, renting, and business activities	0.51	0.46	8		287.7	0.35
Public administration and defense	0.02	0.08	18		877.8	0.01
Education, health, and social work	0.04	0.14	13		20.4	0.03
Other personal services	0.34	0.37	7		34.2	0.25
Total forward linkage	**1.80**	**0.36**	**6**	▲	**2.5**	**1.72**
Agriculture, hunting, forestry, and fishing	1.99	0.43	10		0.2	2.03
Mining and quarrying	1.11	0.04	22		−2.1	1.58
Light manufacturing	1.50	0.14	16		1.6	1.51

continued on next page

Kyrgyz Republic 3.5A *continued*

	Value (2018)	Score (0–1)	Rank (out of 25)	Distance to subregional average	10–year average growth rate (%)	10–year mean value
Heavy manufacturing	1.82	0.39	10		2.6	1.76
Utilities	1.82	0.25	21		1.5	1.69
Construction	1.39	0.42	5		1.2	1.32
Trade services	1.88	0.46	7		0.5	1.80
Hotels and restaurants	1.55	0.45	7		1.0	1.46
Transport services	1.65	0.26	13		2.5	1.51
Telecommunications	1.65	0.30	19		4.1	1.46
Financial intermediation	5.24	1.00	1		12.4	4.69
Real estate, renting, and business activities	1.79	0.37	9		7.6	1.54
Public administration and defense	1.03	0.08	15		0.3	1.01
Education, health, and social work	1.06	0.16	14		0.4	1.04
Other personal services	1.54	0.41	9		4.1	1.37
Normalized forward linkage	–	–	–	▬	–	–
Agriculture, hunting, forestry, and fishing	1.11	0.44	13		–2.1	1.18
Mining and quarrying	0.63	0.00	25		–3.1	0.94
Light manufacturing	0.85	0.02	24		0.2	0.89
Heavy manufacturing	1.02	0.37	19		0.5	1.04
Utilities	1.02	0.21	24		–0.2	1.00
Construction	0.78	0.33	16		–0.8	0.78
Trade services	1.06	0.36	14		–0.8	1.06
Hotels and restaurants	0.87	0.34	12		–0.8	0.86
Transport services	0.93	0.11	22		0.9	0.89
Telecommunications	0.93	0.00	25		2.8	0.86
Financial intermediation	2.95	1.00	1		8.0	2.74
Real estate, renting, and business activities	1.01	0.23	18		5.4	0.91
Public administration and defense	0.58	0.18	23		–1.0	0.60
Education, health, and social work	0.60	0.25	23		–0.9	0.61
Other personal services	0.87	0.21	18		2.3	0.81
Net forward linkage	**0.73**	**0.23**	**21**	▼	**2.4**	**0.69**
Agriculture, hunting, forestry, and fishing	0.60	0.02	24		–2.4	0.64
Mining and quarrying	0.54	0.24	20		–1.1	0.78
Light manufacturing	0.46	0.33	15		5.1	0.44
Heavy manufacturing	0.70	0.76	6		5.6	0.64
Utilities	0.80	0.38	14		7.1	0.72
Construction	0.42	0.45	14		1.4	0.41
Trade services	1.16	0.56	11		1.2	1.10
Hotels and restaurants	0.62	0.41	8		2.6	0.56
Transport services	0.67	0.28	16		5.4	0.65
Telecommunications	0.88	0.31	20		5.5	0.73
Financial intermediation	0.70	0.00	25		7.6	0.61
Real estate, renting, and business activities	1.10	0.43	14		8.6	0.93
Public administration and defense	0.69	0.55	15		2.0	0.64
Education, health, and social work	0.79	0.61	8		1.0	0.76
Other personal services	0.77	0.40	15		3.6	0.70

continued on next page

Kyrgyz Republic 3.5A *continued*

	Value (2018)	Score (0–1)	Rank (out of 25)	Distance to subregional average	10–year average growth rate (%)	10–year mean value
Growth equalized input multipliers	**0.11**	**0.27**	**7**	▲	**0.6**	**0.11**
Agriculture, hunting, forestry, and fishing	0.29	0.60	4		–5.8	0.37
Mining and quarrying	0.02	0.03	16		11.7	0.01
Light manufacturing	0.07	0.18	20		–1.4	0.08
Heavy manufacturing	0.16	0.32	10		6.9	0.18
Utilities	0.06	0.26	8		11.3	0.05
Construction	0.14	0.23	4		9.0	0.11
Trade services	0.41	1.00	1		2.1	0.36
Hotels and restaurants	0.03	0.10	12		5.2	0.03
Transport services	0.08	0.37	17		3.9	0.07
Telecommunications	0.07	0.61	4		5.0	0.07
Financial intermediation	0.05	0.03	23		10.1	0.04
Real estate, renting, and business activities	0.10	0.15	21		10.9	0.08
Public administration and defense	0.07	0.37	9		3.3	0.06
Education, health, and social work	0.09	0.71	5		2.4	0.09
Other personal services	0.03	0.16	18		13.7	0.02

Impacts from Hypothetical Extraction

	Value (2018)	Score (0–1)	Rank (out of 25)	Distance to subregional average	10–year average growth rate (%)	10–year mean value
Changes in gross output due to hypothetical extraction	**–8.6%**	**0.93**	**5**	▼	**0.0**	**–0.08**
Agriculture, hunting, forestry, and fishing	–25.5%	0.13	24		–2.2	–28.2
Mining and quarrying	–2.2%	0.94	14		16.5	–1.2
Light manufacturing	–10.9%	0.78	7		–4.6	–12.3
Heavy manufacturing	–11.4%	0.79	12		–0.2	–13.4
Utilities	–4.2%	0.80	19		6.1	–3.6
Construction	–19.1%	0.57	19		6.9	–15.1
Trade services	–18.3%	0.61	21		0.7	–16.8
Hotels and restaurants	–3.6%	0.94	9		3.0	–3.3
Transport services	–6.5%	0.72	11		5.0	–6.0
Telecommunications	–4.0%	0.33	20		4.4	–5.1
Financial intermediation	–2.9%	0.92	5		0.7	–2.6
Real estate, renting, and business activities	–5.3%	0.85	5		1.9	–4.8
Public administration and defense	–6.1%	0.67	17		2.1	–5.8
Education, health, and social work	–6.3%	0.65	18		2.2	–6.6
Other personal services	–2.1%	0.91	10		11.9	–2.1

Impacts from Hypothetical Insertion

	Value (2018)	Score (0–1)	Rank (out of 25)	Distance to subregional average	10–year average growth rate (%)	10–year mean value
Changes in gross output due to hypothetical insertion	**5.1%**	**0.35**	**6**	▲	**3.8**	**0.05**
Agriculture, hunting, forestry, and fishing	26.1%	1.00	1		1.1	26.9
Mining and quarrying	0.8%	0.07	12		27.7	0.3
Light manufacturing	5.3%	0.15	19		–4.5	6.0
Heavy manufacturing	8.0%	0.12	14		9.6	9.1
Utilities	1.6%	0.17	12		14.8	1.1
Construction	9.9%	0.40	6		17.8	6.8
Trade services	4.8%	0.28	8		0.5	4.5
Hotels and restaurants	1.5%	0.08	18		3.6	1.4
Transport services	1.9%	0.23	19		36.6	1.5
Telecommunications	0.8%	0.20	15		13.5	1.2
Financial intermediation	10.9%	1.00	1		28.6	8.2

continued on next page

Kyrgyz Republic 3.5A *continued*

	Value (2018)	Score (0–1)	Rank (out of 25)	Distance to subregional average	10–year average growth rate (%)	10–year mean value
Real estate, renting, and business activities	1.7%	0.20	16		7.5	1.5
Public administration and defense	1.6%	0.39	13		2.9	1.6
Education, health, and social work	1.5%	0.23	11		5.3	1.5
Other personal services	0.8%	0.10	15		18.9	0.7

SPREAD OF ECONOMIC LINKAGES

Demand-side

	Value (2018)	Score (0–1)	Rank (out of 25)	Distance to subregional average	10–year average growth rate (%)	10–year mean value
Relative evenness of direct backward linkage	0.47	0.53	9	▼	–0.2	0.50
Relative evenness of total backward linkage	0.50	1.00	1	▲	14.9	0.44
		0.00				
Backward measure of concentration based on input coefficients	0.84	0.00	25	▼	–0.3	0.85
Agriculture, hunting, forestry, and fishing	0.67	0.00	25		2.4	0.61
Mining and quarrying	0.86	0.17	22		–1.0	0.90
Light manufacturing	0.94	0.86	2		1.2	0.93
Heavy manufacturing	0.61	0.40	24		0.2	0.60
Utilities	0.94	0.88	7		0.3	0.94
Construction	0.88	0.79	18		–0.2	0.90
Trade services	0.94	0.82	18		1.1	0.93
Hotels and restaurants	0.95	0.94	3		0.1	0.95
Transport services	0.93	0.68	10		–0.1	0.94
Telecommunications	0.95	0.84	6		0.5	0.94
Financial intermediation	0.16	0.00	25		0.2	0.25
Real estate, renting, and business activities	0.96	0.95	9		0.1	0.96
Public administration and defense	0.95	0.61	15		0.5	0.95
Education, health, and social work	0.97	0.95	3		0.3	0.97
Other personal services	0.96	0.92	10		0.0	0.96
Relative evenness of direct forward linkage	0.59	0.32	17	▼	–2.5	0.63
Relative evenness of total forward linkage	0.55	1.00	1	▲	10.0	0.51
Forward measure of concentration based on output coefficients	0.63	0.41	18	▼	–0.6	0.63
Agriculture, hunting, forestry, and fishing	0.18	0.00	25		–5.5	0.22
Mining and quarrying	0.62	0.86	4		1.0	0.65
Light manufacturing	0.72	0.76	10		–0.5	0.74
Heavy manufacturing	0.32	0.00	25		–1.6	0.30
Utilities	0.88	0.91	3		0.2	0.87
Construction	0.33	0.38	19		–4.1	0.48
Trade services	0.76	0.67	12		1.3	0.75
Hotels and restaurants	0.81	0.74	9		1.8	0.81
Transport services	0.86	1.00	1		0.1	0.86
Telecommunications	0.89	0.96	2		3.4	0.84
Financial intermediation	0.16	0.00	25		0.9	0.22
Real estate, renting, and business activities	0.86	0.77	9		1.5	0.84
Public administration and defense	0.48	0.52	18		49.0	0.41
Education, health, and social work	0.73	0.81	8		–0.3	0.71
Other personal services	0.80	0.75	8		0.6	0.78

continued on next page

Kyrgyz Republic 3.5A *continued*

	Value (2018)	Score (0–1)	Rank (out of 25)	Distance to subregional average	10–year average growth rate (%)	10–year mean value
SENSITIVITY OF ECONOMIC LINKAGES						
Economic Complexity						
Percentage intermediate transaction	0.40	0.42	8	▲	1.6	0.38
Average output multiplier	1.77	0.47	3	▲	2.1	1.70
Average of Leontief inverse	0.23	0.45	4	▲	2.5	0.21
Average technical coefficient	0.02	0.48	7	▲	3.2	0.02
Mean intermediate coefficient	0.37	0.48	7	▲	3.2	0.34
Percentage of above-average coefficients (%)	0.24	0.20	22	▼	1.0	0.24
Determinant of non-competitive Leontief inverse	30.16	1.00	1	▲	41.9	23.10
Determinant of competitive Leontief inverse	53.86	0.64	2	▲	33.0	49.00
Mean path length	1.67	0.27	8	▲	0.9	1.63
Cycling index	0.22	0.78	3	▲	2.5	0.21
Average propagation length	2.33	0.75	2	▲	3.2	2.18
Overall sensitivity of the economy	0.75	0.60	12	▲	2.3	0.71
Index of direct interrelatedness	0.56	0.33	12	▲	1.7	0.54
Index of indirect interrelatedness	0.18	0.75	5	▲	5.4	0.17
Global intensity index	26.61	0.47	3	▲	2.1	25.44

Note: The scores of the economy in focus are shown in the horizontal bars with labels. The colored dots represent the indicator performance of the economy in focus compared to other economies in the region. The highest rank among economies is 1 while the lowest rank is 25. The indicators shown in the chart are selected from a broader set of indicators (see the technical appendix for more details).

Source: Asian Development Bank Multi-Regional Input–Output Database. https://mrio.adbx.online/ (accessed 4 August 2020).

3.5B External Linkages

$ = United States dollars, GVC = global value chain.

Note: The scores of the economy in focus are shown in the horizontal bars with labels. The colored dots represent the indicator performance of the economy in focus compared to other economies in the region. The highest rank among economies is 1, while the lowest rank is 25. The indicators shown in the chart are selected from a broader set of indicators (see the technical appendix for more details).

Source: Asian Development Bank Multi-Regional Input–Output Database. https://mrio.adbx.online/ (accessed 4 August 2020).

		Value (2018)	Score (0–1)	Rank (out of 25)	Distance to subregional average	10–year average growth rate (%)	10–year mean value
PARTICIPATION IN GLOBAL VALUE CHAINS							
International Trade Coefficients							
Trade openness		1.05	0.39	9	▲	–1.5	1.18
Self-sufficiency ratio		0.85	0.18	24	▼	0.3	0.84
Regional supply percentage		0.71	0.32	20	▼	0.9	0.69
Regional purchase coefficient		0.80	0.63	16	▼	1.8	0.77
Sectoral purchase coefficient		0.73	0.75	21	▼	4.7	0.72
Simple location quotient of gross output		1.27	0.61	8	▲	–0.3	1.30
Fabrication effect		1.12	0.93	2	▲	–0.4	1.13
Exports	($)	**2,484**	**0.00**	**23**	▼	**2.1**	**2,388**
Export-to-output ratio		**0.19**	**0.65**	**7**	▲	**1.1**	**0.18**
Agriculture, hunting, forestry, and fishing		0.11	0.50	9		6.6	0.15
Mining and quarrying		0.91	1.00	1		53.2	0.46
Light manufacturing		0.41	0.77	4		12.2	0.27
Heavy manufacturing		0.50	0.59	6		–4.7	0.52
Utilities		0.00	0.01	15		–5.1	0.06
Construction		0.05	0.56	5		–6.6	0.05
Trade services		0.07	0.10	19		–8.9	0.10
Hotels and restaurants		0.01	0.01	18		–20.0	0.01
Transport services		0.27	0.35	9		–9.0	0.24
Telecommunications		0.12	0.35	10		–6.3	0.15

continued on next page

Kyrgyz Republic 3.5B *continued*

		Value (2018)	Score (0–1)	Rank (out of 25)	Distance to subregional average	10-year average growth rate (%)	10-year mean value
Financial intermediation		0.04	0.09	8		−6.5	0.03
Real estate, renting, and business activities		0.00	0.00	25		−0.1	0.18
Public administration and defense		0.40	1.00	1		−3.7	0.41
Education, health, and social work		0.01	0.09	11		−6.8	0.00
Other personal services		0.00	0.00	25		0.3	0.00
Imports	($)	**5,075**	**0.00**	**22**	▼	**3.6**	**4,903**
Import-to-input ratio		**0.15**	**0.64**	**8**	▲	**−2.3**	**0.19**
Agriculture, hunting, forestry, and fishing		0.07	0.19	12		2.8	0.11
Mining and quarrying		0.12	0.29	8		−4.9	0.23
Light manufacturing		0.18	0.31	9		−0.6	0.21
Heavy manufacturing		0.13	0.13	21		−1.0	0.17
Utilities		0.20	0.32	9		−4.2	0.28
Construction		0.24	0.54	5		−2.2	0.28
Trade services		0.16	0.63	4		3.5	0.16
Hotels and restaurants		0.17	0.56	5		−0.5	0.18
Transport services		0.32	0.62	5		2.8	0.37
Telecommunications		0.28	0.81	2		5.1	0.27
Financial intermediation		0.02	0.09	17		−1.2	0.06
Real estate, renting, and business activities		0.09	0.50	5		−2.9	0.12
Public administration and defense		0.09	0.53	7		−5.3	0.12
Education, health, and social work		0.06	0.29	14		−3.3	0.08
Other personal services		0.16	0.43	4		5.2	0.17
Total foreign factor content of consumption	($)	**908**	**0.00**	**22**	▼	**1.0**	**1,005**
Total foreign factor content of investment	($)	**681**	**0.00**	**21**	▼	**8.9**	**546**
Total foreign factor content of exports	($)	**618**	**0.00**	**23**	▼	**0.9**	**693**

Interregional Multipliers

		Value (2018)	Score (0–1)	Rank (out of 25)	Distance to subregional average	10-year average growth rate (%)	10-year mean value
Import Leakage Effects		**0.24**	**0.57**	**8**	▲	**−2.5**	**0.28**
Agriculture, hunting, forestry, and fishing		0.20	0.45	7		2.7	0.25
Mining and quarrying		0.20	0.43	7		−3.3	0.29
Light manufacturing		0.29	0.44	9		−0.7	0.34
Heavy manufacturing		0.25	0.23	17		−3.9	0.30
Utilities		0.29	0.40	9		−4.1	0.37
Construction		0.38	0.67	7		−1.3	0.41
Trade services		0.21	0.53	5		1.2	0.22
Hotels and restaurants		0.27	0.69	6		−1.7	0.30
Transport services		0.38	0.54	5		1.6	0.42
Telecommunications		0.32	0.60	4		2.1	0.33
Financial intermediation		0.12	0.36	4		−4.8	0.25
Real estate, renting, and business activities		0.16	0.53	5		−3.9	0.19
Public administration and defense		0.14	0.42	8		−4.4	0.18
Education, health, and social work		0.11	0.38	14		−3.7	0.13
Other personal services		0.24	0.58	4		−0.1	0.26
Intraregional transfer multiplier		**1.77**	**0.47**	**3**	▲	**2.1**	**1.70**
Agriculture, hunting, forestry, and fishing		2.25	1.00	1		1.8	2.11
Mining and quarrying		1.55	0.44	7		2.4	1.37

continued on next page

Kyrgyz Republic 3.5B *continued*

	Value (2018)	Score (0–1)	Rank (out of 25)	Distance to subregional average	10–year average growth rate (%)	10–year mean value
Light manufacturing	1.83	0.40	11		−0.2	1.80
Heavy manufacturing	1.79	0.27	6		2.2	1.76
Utilities	1.51	0.19	16		1.7	1.39
Construction	1.69	0.17	15		2.3	1.60
Trade services	1.31	0.22	17		−0.9	1.33
Hotels and restaurants	1.65	0.34	15		0.0	1.68
Transport services	1.39	0.27	18		2.1	1.33
Telecommunications	1.23	0.04	24		0.9	1.28
Financial intermediation	4.81	1.00	1		13.2	4.28
Real estate, renting, and business activities	1.43	0.35	10		0.8	1.39
Public administration and defense	1.37	0.37	17		−0.1	1.37
Education, health, and social work	1.30	0.17	15		0.5	1.28
Other personal services	1.50	0.38	11		1.9	1.46
Interregional spillover multiplier	**1.41**	**0.75**	**6**	▲	**−1.3**	**1.49**
Agriculture, hunting, forestry, and fishing	1.17	0.25	12		−0.1	1.24
Mining and quarrying	1.32	0.37	8		−2.3	1.59
Light manufacturing	1.45	0.36	7		−0.5	1.53
Heavy manufacturing	1.38	0.21	19		−2.3	1.46
Utilities	1.55	0.43	8		−2.2	1.75
Construction	1.65	0.66	5		−1.6	1.76
Trade services	1.44	0.82	3		0.8	1.42
Hotels and restaurants	1.44	0.59	5		−0.5	1.47
Transport services	1.88	0.77	4		0.4	2.00
Telecommunications	1.77	1.00	1		0.6	1.75
Financial intermediation	1.05	0.10	19		−3.2	1.13
Real estate, renting, and business activities	1.22	0.65	4		−1.5	1.31
Public administration and defense	1.23	0.50	6		−1.7	1.30
Education, health, and social work	1.15	0.34	13		−1.2	1.20
Other personal services	1.43	0.45	3		−0.7	1.45
Interregional feedback multiplier	**1.000**	**0.00**	**22**	▲	**0.0**	**1.00**
Agriculture, hunting, forestry, and fishing	1.000	0.00	22		0.0	1.00
Mining and quarrying	1.000	0.00	18		0.0	1.00
Light manufacturing	1.000	0.00	22		0.0	1.00
Heavy manufacturing	1.000	0.00	24		0.0	1.00
Utilities	1.000	0.00	22		0.0	1.00
Construction	1.000	0.00	22		0.0	1.00
Trade services	1.000	0.00	17		0.0	1.00
Hotels and restaurants	1.000	0.01	20		0.0	1.00
Transport services	1.000	0.00	20		0.0	1.00
Telecommunications	1.000	0.00	19		0.0	1.00
Financial intermediation	1.000	0.00	24		0.0	1.00
Real estate, renting, and business activities	1.000	0.00	18		0.0	1.00
Public administration and defense	1.000	0.00	18		0.0	1.00
Education, health, and social work	1.000	0.00	20		0.0	1.00
Other personal services	1.000	0.00	20		0.0	1.00

continued on next page

Kyrgyz Republic 3.5B *continued*

	Value (2018)	Score (0–1)	Rank (out of 25)	Distance to subregional average	10–year average growth rate (%)	10–year mean value
Global Value Chain (GVC) Participation Index						
Backward GVC Participation	24.9%	0.47	5	▲	–1.2	0.28
Simple GVCs	17.3%	0.95	3	▲	–0.4	0.19
Agriculture, hunting, forestry, and fishing	2.5	1.00	1		1.7	3.04
Mining and quarrying	0.0	0.10	13		84.8	0.05
Light manufacturing	0.8	0.15	18		–7.4	1.63
Heavy manufacturing	0.1	0.01	23		–45.1	0.23
Utilities	0.7	0.65	2		5.1	0.78
Construction	6.0	0.57	4		4.7	5.10
Trade services	2.3	1.00	1		5.5	2.05
Hotels and restaurants	0.6	0.33	6		2.0	0.65
Transport services	1.0	0.63	7		–0.6	1.37
Telecommunications	0.8	0.84	2		5.1	1.11
Financial intermediation	0.1	0.05	15		10.6	0.14
Real estate, renting, and business activities	0.5	0.29	11		11.9	0.50
Public administration and defense	0.6	0.15	12		12.1	0.73
Education, health, and social work	0.8	0.44	14		–2.5	1.01
Other personal services	0.4	0.32	6		10.0	0.46
Complex GVCs	7.5%	0.19	11	▲	–1.2	0.09
Agriculture, hunting, forestry, and fishing	1.1	1.00	1		12.1	1.59
Mining and quarrying	0.3	0.62	3		36.4	0.16
Light manufacturing	1.3	0.11	9		–1.7	1.29
Heavy manufacturing	0.8	0.04	13		3.4	1.31
Utilities	0.2	0.40	10		–1.7	0.24
Construction	1.6	0.36	5		5.9	1.55
Trade services	0.6	0.11	4		–2.0	0.72
Hotels and restaurants	0.2	0.02	14		1.9	0.17
Transport services	0.4	0.20	15		–26.6	0.52
Telecommunications	0.3	0.46	2		–0.6	0.50
Financial intermediation	0.0	0.01	14		19.1	0.05
Real estate, renting, and business activities	0.1	0.14	15		3.8	0.28
Public administration and defense	0.3	0.26	9		–4.9	0.46
Education, health, and social work	0.2	0.23	16		–2.6	0.27
Other personal services	0.1	0.24	11		16.0	0.13
Forward GVC Participation	16.1%	0.29	15	▲	1.0	0.17
Simple GVCs	9.8%	0.26	15	▲	0.6	0.11
Agriculture, hunting, forestry, and fishing	1.0	0.49	10		–5.9	1.95
Mining and quarrying	0.4	0.03	9		28.8	0.18
Light manufacturing	0.5	0.12	18		–0.1	0.48
Heavy manufacturing	2.9	0.26	7		–3.6	3.25
Utilities	0.2	0.02	13		1.8	0.22
Construction	0.3	0.08	6		1.7	0.27
Trade services	1.7	0.19	10		–0.3	1.74
Hotels and restaurants	0.1	0.01	17		2.1	0.05
Transport services	0.8	0.19	10		0.0	0.75
Telecommunications	0.4	0.29	5		–11.8	0.53

continued on next page

Kyrgyz Republic 3.5B *continued*

	Value (2018)	Score (0–1)	Rank (out of 25)	Distance to subregional average	10–year average growth rate (%)	10–year mean value
Financial intermediation	0.1	0.02	23		15.3	0.09
Real estate, renting, and business activities	0.3	0.04	18		–4.5	0.54
Public administration and defense	1.0	1.00	1		–4.3	0.92
Education, health, and social work	0.0	0.12	11		32.0	0.02
Other personal services	0.0	0.00	24		3.3	0.03
Complex GVCs	**6.3%**	**0.33**	**14**	▲	**1.8**	**0.06**
Agriculture, hunting, forestry, and fishing	0.6	0.35	6		1.7	1.13
Mining and quarrying	0.2	0.02	10		19.5	0.10
Light manufacturing	0.3	0.12	18		4.0	0.23
Heavy manufacturing	2.4	0.36	7		6.6	2.38
Utilities	0.1	0.03	13		6.8	0.12
Construction	0.1	0.05	6		6.3	0.10
Trade services	0.9	0.27	12		5.1	0.83
Hotels and restaurants	0.0	0.01	16		11.6	0.03
Transport services	0.5	0.30	9		8.7	0.39
Telecommunications	0.2	0.37	5		–7.9	0.25
Financial intermediation	0.1	0.03	23		22.4	0.05
Real estate, renting, and business activities	0.2	0.05	17		–0.4	0.26
Public administration and defense	0.6	1.00	1		–0.7	0.47
Education, health, and social work	0.0	0.16	11		29.6	0.01
Other personal services	0.0	0.00	25		8.1	0.01

SPECIALIZATION IN GLOBAL VALUE CHAINS

Vertical Specialization

	Value (2018)	Score (0–1)	Rank (out of 25)	Distance to subregional average	10–year average growth rate (%)	10–year mean value
Vertical Specialization Ratio	**24.9%**	**0.38**	**11**	▲	**–2.4**	**0.29**
Agriculture, hunting, forestry, and fishing	20.1%	0.45	7		2.7	0.25
Mining and quarrying	20.3%	0.43	7		–3.3	0.29
Light manufacturing	29.4%	0.44	9		–0.7	0.34
Heavy manufacturing	25.2%	0.23	17		–3.9	0.30
Utilities	29.1%	0.46	9		–13.9	0.33
Construction	37.9%	0.66	7		–1.3	0.41
Trade services	21.4%	0.53	5		1.2	0.22
Hotels and restaurants	26.8%	0.69	6		–1.7	0.30
Transport services	37.9%	0.54	5		1.6	0.43
Telecommunications	32.2%	0.60	4		2.1	0.33
Financial intermediation	12.5%	0.36	4		–4.8	0.25
Real estate, renting, and business activities	16.0%	0.53	5		–13.4	0.18
Public administration and defense	14.3%	0.42	8		–4.4	0.18
Education, health, and social work	10.5%	0.38	14		–12.5	0.11
Other personal services	24.2%	0.58	4		–30.6	0.17

Revealed Comparative Advantages

Traditional RCA Index						
Agriculture, hunting, forestry, and fishing	5.99	1.00	1	▲	–1.6	8.37
Mining and quarrying	1.07	0.10	7	▲	6.6	0.35
Light manufacturing	1.01	0.17	12	▼	24.3	0.71

continued on next page

Kyrgyz Republic 3.5B *continued*

	Value (2018)	Score (0–1)	Rank (out of 25)	Distance to subregional average	10–year average growth rate (%)	10–year mean value
Heavy manufacturing	0.67	0.37	12	▲	0.3	0.72
Utilities	0.15	0.00	15	▼	−27.6	1.64
Construction	5.75	0.73	3	▲	−8.6	6.51
Trade services	0.83	0.11	16	▼	−8.7	0.94
Hotels and restaurants	0.11	0.00	18	▼	−11.3	0.08
Transport services	1.38	0.32	8	▼	−6.5	1.08
Telecommunications	3.14	0.51	6	▲	−24.0	4.97
Financial intermediation	0.21	0.05	6	▲	0.7	0.14
Real estate, renting, and business activities	0.01	0.00	25	▼	−8.9	0.51
Public administration and defense	26.61	0.97	2	▲	−6.1	25.68
Education, health, and social work	0.49	0.06	10	▼	−17.4	0.31
Other personal services	0.00	0.00	25	▼	−14.0	0.01

New RCA Index (Based on Domestic Value Added)

	Value (2018)	Score (0–1)	Rank (out of 25)	Distance to subregional average	10–year average growth rate (%)	10–year mean value
Agriculture, hunting, forestry, and fishing	2.60	0.37	8	▲	−1.6	3.95
Mining and quarrying	0.54	0.08	10	▼	1.9	0.21
Light manufacturing	0.81	0.18	14	▼	16.4	0.63
Heavy manufacturing	1.08	0.48	6	▲	−1.5	1.13
Utilities	0.70	0.04	13	▼	−5.1	0.73
Construction	2.44	0.14	3	▼	−1.5	2.32
Trade services	1.32	0.38	10	▲	2.0	1.27
Hotels and restaurants	0.56	0.01	17	▼	23.9	0.44
Transport services	1.00	0.30	11	▼	−4.1	0.76
Telecommunications	2.24	0.60	5	▲	−10.2	2.85
Financial intermediation	0.18	0.00	23	▼	2.4	0.13
Real estate, renting, and business activities	0.24	0.10	18	▼	7.6	0.34
Public administration and defense	11.08	1.00	1	▲	−4.7	10.31
Education, health, and social work	0.60	0.12	12	▼	−1.5	0.37
Other personal services	0.17	0.01	23	▼	18.2	0.11

POSITION IN GLOBAL VALUE CHAINS

Upstreamness Index	**2.2**	**0.51**	**7**	▲	**2.1**	**2.1**
Agriculture, hunting, forestry, and fishing	2.2	0.44	11		0.0	2.4
Mining and quarrying	2.0	0.46	20		0.2	2.2
Light manufacturing	1.8	0.23	16		1.6	1.8
Heavy manufacturing	3.2	0.91	3		2.8	3.1
Utilities	2.0	0.08	23		0.6	2.0
Construction	1.5	0.41	7		1.3	1.4
Trade services	2.2	0.44	11		0.7	2.1
Hotels and restaurants	1.7	0.42	13		1.2	1.6
Transport services	2.3	0.46	16		1.1	2.1
Telecommunications	2.0	0.28	15		5.9	1.8
Financial intermediation	5.7	1.00	1		11.1	5.0
Real estate, renting, and business activities	2.0	0.33	12		2.4	1.9
Public administration and defense	1.6	0.90	3		0.8	1.5
Education, health, and social work	1.1	0.14	16		0.5	1.0
Other personal services	1.6	0.31	16		4.6	1.4

continued on next page

Kyrgyz Republic 3.5B *continued*

	Value (2018)	Score (0–1)	Rank (out of 25)	Distance to subregional average	10–year average growth rate (%)	10–year mean value
PRODUCTION LENGTH OF GLOBAL VALUE CHAINS						
Backward Measures of Average Production Length						
Production Length of Global Value Chain Activity (B)	1.0	0.62	5	▲	−2.4	1.2
Agriculture, hunting, forestry, and fishing	1.0	0.58	7		2.2	1.1
Mining and quarrying	0.8	0.49	7		−2.3	1.1
Light manufacturing	1.2	0.56	10		−0.8	1.4
Heavy manufacturing	1.1	0.33	16		−3.8	1.3
Utilities	1.2	0.44	9		−3.5	1.4
Construction	1.6	0.70	6		−0.6	1.7
Trade services	0.8	0.56	7		0.3	0.9
Hotels and restaurants	1.1	0.68	6		−1.9	1.2
Transport services	1.4	0.57	5		2.3	1.6
Telecommunications	1.3	0.70	3		1.6	1.3
Financial intermediation	0.8	0.79	2		−3.4	1.5
Real estate, renting, and business activities	0.7	0.60	4		−4.0	0.8
Public administration and defense	0.6	0.39	8		−4.3	0.7
Education, health, and social work	0.4	0.33	15		−3.6	0.5
Other personal services	1.0	0.65	3		−0.4	1.1
Forward Measures of Average Production Length						
Production Length of Global Value Chain Activity (F)	0.7	0.45	15	▲	2.2	0.7
Agriculture, hunting, forestry, and fishing	0.5	0.27	14		−0.5	0.7
Mining and quarrying	1.3	0.35	11		3.8	1.0
Light manufacturing	0.5	0.31	14		7.8	0.5
Heavy manufacturing	2.3	0.85	3		4.4	2.2
Utilities	0.4	0.12	19		0.8	0.5
Construction	0.2	0.17	8		3.5	0.2
Trade services	0.5	0.22	17		0.3	0.6
Hotels and restaurants	0.2	0.11	14		2.7	0.2
Transport services	1.0	0.39	12		−4.1	1.0
Telecommunications	0.6	0.27	14		−2.3	0.5
Financial intermediation	1.4	0.55	4		15.6	1.0
Real estate, renting, and business activities	0.4	0.20	16		−2.9	0.6
Public administration and defense	0.8	1.00	1		−6.3	0.7
Education, health, and social work	0.0	0.11	13		31.3	0.0
Other personal services	0.2	0.06	19		4.9	0.1

Note: The scores of the economy in focus are shown in the horizontal bars with labels. The colored dots represent the indicator performance of the economy in focus compared to other economies in the region. The highest rank among economies is 1 while the lowest rank is 25. The indicators shown in the chart are selected from a broader set of indicators (see the technical appendix for more details).

Source: Asian Development Bank Multi-Regional Input–Output Database. https://mrio.adbx.online/ (accessed 4 August 2020).

3.6 Maldives

3.6A Internal Linkages

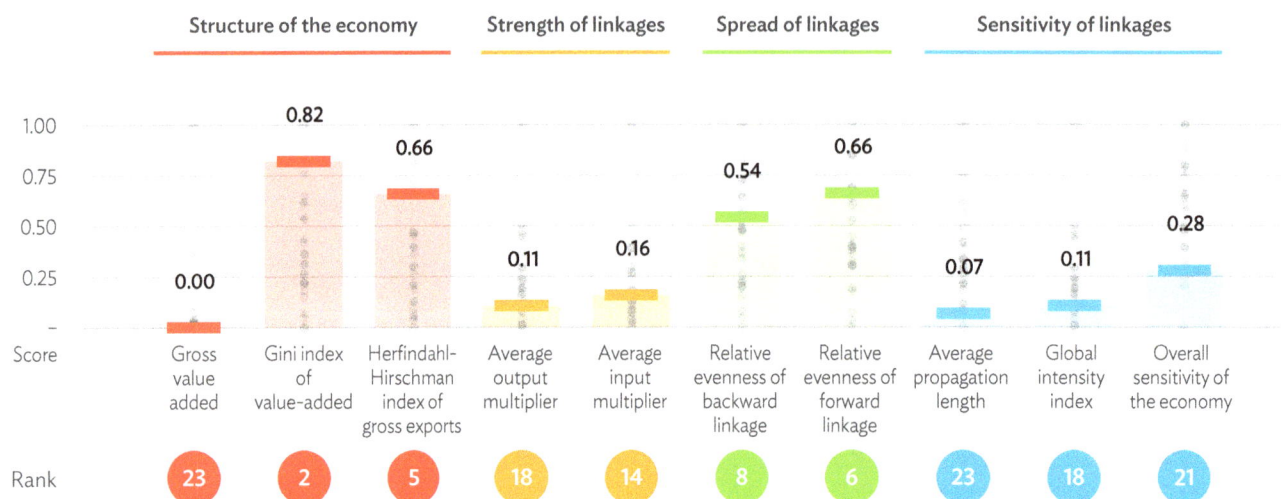

Note: The scores of the economy in focus are shown in the horizontal bars with labels. The colored dots represent the indicator performance of the economy in focus compared to other economies in the region. The highest rank among economies is 1 while the lowest rank is 25. The indicators shown in the chart are selected from a broader set of indicators (see the technical appendix for more details).

Source: Asian Development Bank Multi-Regional Input–Output Database. https://mrio.adbx.online/ (accessed 4 August 2020).

		Value (2018)	Score (0–1)	Rank (out of 25)	Distance to subregional average	10–year average growth rate (%)	10–year mean value
STRUCTURE OF THE ECONOMY							
Economic Indicators							
Gross output	($)	10,015	0.00	23	▼	8.5	6,834
Gross value-added	($)	4,237	0.00	23	▼	7.6	3,007
Value-added content of domestic final demand		2,168	0.00	24		8.5	1,380
Value-added content of exports		2,069	0.00	21		9.1	1,627
Intermediate inputs	($)	5,573	0.00	23	▼	9.1	3,742
Domestic inputs		3,286	0.00	23		9.0	2,274
Foreign inputs		2,287	0.00	22		11.3	1,468
Direct production	($)	6,728	0.00	23	▼	8.6	4,560
Domestic final demand		3,240	0.00	24		9.5	1,940
Exports		3,489	0.00	21		10.5	2,620
Indirect production	($)	3,286	0.00	23	▼	9.0	2,274
Indirect production embedded in domestic final demand		1,385	0.00	23		13.2	798
Indirect production embedded in exports		1,901	0.00	20		9.2	1,475
Economic Diversification							
Gross output		0.42	1.00	1	▲	2.5	0.35
Gini concentration index of gross output		0.61	1.00	1		1.7	0.53
Herfindahl-Hirschman concentration index of gross output		0.15	0.91	3		4.9	0.11
Theil concentration index of gross output		0.51	1.00	1		2.9	0.41

continued on next page

Maldives 3.6A *continued*

	Value (2018)	Score (0–1)	Rank (out of 25)	Distance to subregional average	10–year average growth rate (%)	10–year mean value
Gross value-added	**0.39**	**0.76**	**2**	▲	**2.9**	**0.31**
Gini concentration index of gross value added	0.58	0.82	2		2.1	0.50
Herfindahl-Hirschman concentration index of gross value added	0.12	0.56	2		5.9	0.08
Theil concentration index of gross value added	0.47	0.79	2		3.4	0.36
Gross exports	**0.71**	**0.73**	**6**	▲	**–0.4**	**0.75**
Gini concentration index of gross exports	0.82	0.79	7		0.0	0.83
Herfindahl-Hirschman concentration index of gross exports	0.52	0.66	5		–0.1	0.59
Theil concentration index of gross exports	0.80	0.82	6		–0.3	0.82
Structural Changes						
Changes in output due to technological changes	**–1.7%**	**0.54**	**24**	▲	**–**	**–**
Agriculture, hunting, forestry, and fishing	–8.6%	0.00	25			
Mining and quarrying	0.0%	0.74	7			
Light manufacturing	5.7%	0.80	2			
Heavy manufacturing	–16.4%	0.00	25			
Utilities	–3.7%	0.00	25			
Construction	6.1%	1.00	1			
Trade services	–1.3%	0.00	25			
Hotels and restaurants	0.0%	0.06	17			
Transport services	–3.6%	0.09	24			
Telecommunications	–0.9%	0.14	17			
Financial intermediation	0.2%	0.50	13			
Real estate, renting, and business activities	–4.8%	0.00	25			
Public administration and defense	2.6%	1.00	1			
Education, health, and social work	0.2%	0.79	7			
Other personal services	–0.8%	0.26	23			
Changes in output due to structural changes in consumption (%)	**3.3%**	**0.36**	**13**	▼	**–**	**–**
Agriculture, hunting, forestry, and fishing	0.1%	0.17	23			
Mining and quarrying	0.0%	0.03	20			
Light manufacturing	8.9%	1.00	1			
Heavy manufacturing	3.8%	0.60	3			
Utilities	6.3%	0.65	3			
Construction	12.2%	1.00	1			
Trade services	2.4%	0.43	15			
Hotels and restaurants	0.4%	0.05	23			
Transport services	1.1%	0.24	16			
Telecommunications	1.2%	0.38	23			
Financial intermediation	2.2%	0.33	21			
Real estate, renting, and business activities	1.1%	0.09	23			
Public administration and defense	6.2%	0.44	11			
Education, health, and social work	3.1%	0.12	21			
Other personal services	0.1%	0.15	22			
Changes in output due to structural changes in investment (%)	**0.4%**	**0.11**	**21**	▼	**–**	**–**
Agriculture, hunting, forestry, and fishing	0.0%	0.05	23			
Mining and quarrying	0.0%	0.06	21			
Light manufacturing	0.3%	0.10	18			

continued on next page

Maldives 3.6A *continued*

	Value (2018)	Score (0–1)	Rank (out of 25)	Distance to subregional average	10–year average growth rate (%)	10–year mean value
Heavy manufacturing	2.1%	0.32	8			
Utilities	−1.4%	0.00	25			
Construction	4.4%	0.29	18			
Trade services	−0.6%	0.00	25			
Hotels and restaurants	0.0%	0.30	22			
Transport services	0.1%	0.01	21			
Telecommunications	−0.5%	0.00	25			
Financial intermediation	0.5%	0.10	15			
Real estate, renting, and business activities	0.0%	0.17	21			
Public administration and defense	0.0%	0.03	13			
Education, health, and social work	0.0%	0.02	13			
Other personal services	0.4%	0.29	10			
Changes in output due to structural changes in stock (%)	**0.1%**	**0.35**	**8**	▲	–	–
Agriculture, hunting, forestry, and fishing	−0.1%	0.51	15			
Mining and quarrying	0.0%	0.38	13			
Light manufacturing	0.5%	0.35	4			
Heavy manufacturing	0.7%	0.77	2			
Utilities	−0.2%	0.00	25			
Construction	0.6%	1.00	1			
Trade services	0.5%	1.00	1			
Hotels and restaurants	−0.4%	0.00	25			
Transport services	−0.4%	0.00	25			
Telecommunications	−0.1%	0.41	22			
Financial intermediation	0.2%	0.94	5			
Real estate, renting, and business activities	0.0%	0.17	7			
Public administration and defense	0.1%	0.66	2			
Education, health, and social work	0.0%	0.24	5			
Other personal services	−0.1%	0.30	23			
Changes in output due to structural changes in export	**3.8%**	**0.81**	**3**	▲	–	–
Agriculture, hunting, forestry, and fishing	3.3%	0.71	4			
Mining and quarrying	0.0%	0.11	19			
Light manufacturing	11.3%	1.00	1			
Heavy manufacturing	3.6%	0.56	6			
Utilities	1.5%	0.08	10			
Construction	5.9%	1.00	1			
Trade services	2.1%	0.26	10			
Hotels and restaurants	7.2%	0.61	3			
Transport services	3.0%	0.68	7			
Telecommunications	4.1%	0.42	4			
Financial intermediation	6.1%	0.97	2			
Real estate, renting, and business activities	1.0%	0.37	14			
Public administration and defense	2.3%	0.56	2			
Education, health, and social work	0.3%	0.12	9			
Other personal services	4.8%	1.00	1			

continued on next page

Maldives 3.6A *continued*

	Value (2018)	Score (0–1)	Rank (out of 25)	Distance to subregional average	10-year average growth rate (%)	10-year mean value
Changes in output due to import substitution on intermediate demand	**0.7%**	**0.47**	**5**	▲	–	–
Agriculture, hunting, forestry, and fishing	−0.1%	0.67	11			
Mining and quarrying	0.0%	0.31	17			
Light manufacturing	−2.4%	0.65	24			
Heavy manufacturing	16.4%	1.00	1			
Utilities	1.4%	0.98	2			
Construction	−0.7%	0.00	25			
Trade services	−3.7%	0.00	25			
Hotels and restaurants	0.0%	0.97	13			
Transport services	1.5%	1.00	1			
Telecommunications	−0.2%	0.93	16			
Financial intermediation	0.2%	0.70	3			
Real estate, renting, and business activities	−1.8%	0.31	24			
Public administration and defense	−0.2%	0.00	25			
Education, health, and social work	−0.2%	0.14	24			
Other personal services	−0.3%	0.37	21			
Changes in output due to import substitution on domestic final demand	**−1.1%**	**0.07**	**24**	▲	–	–
Agriculture, hunting, forestry, and fishing	−1.7%	0.00	25			
Mining and quarrying	0.0%	0.49	12			
Light manufacturing	1.0%	1.00	1			
Heavy manufacturing	−1.8%	0.31	22			
Utilities	0.3%	0.95	3			
Construction	0.2%	0.78	3			
Trade services	−2.0%	0.03	24			
Hotels and restaurants	−0.1%	0.58	13			
Transport services	−1.6%	0.33	24			
Telecommunications	−1.6%	0.00	25			
Financial intermediation	−1.7%	0.00	25			
Real estate, renting, and business activities	−0.6%	0.34	19			
Public administration and defense	2.5%	1.00	1			
Education, health, and social work	−1.8%	0.31	24			
Other personal services	−7.0%	0.30	24			

STRENGTH OF LINKAGES

Demand-side Linkages

	Value (2018)	Score (0–1)	Rank (out of 25)	Distance to subregional average	10-year average growth rate (%)	10-year mean value
Direct backward linkage	**0.29**	**0.18**	**18**	▼	**2.7**	**0.27**
Agriculture, hunting, forestry, and fishing	0.24	0.30	14		−0.7	0.26
Mining and quarrying	0.00	0.00	23		0.0	0.00
Light manufacturing	0.54	0.69	12		16.0	0.48
Heavy manufacturing	0.21	0.00	25		17.8	0.23
Utilities	0.30	0.28	17		3.9	0.26
Construction	0.28	0.00	24		−2.1	0.33
Trade services	0.55	1.00	1		10.9	0.46
Hotels and restaurants	0.38	0.42	20		−0.4	0.40
Transport services	0.28	0.45	15		3.2	0.25
Telecommunications	0.38	0.58	9		7.2	0.34

continued on next page

Maldives 3.6A *continued*

	Value (2018)	Score (0–1)	Rank (out of 25)	Distance to subregional average	10–year average growth rate (%)	10–year mean value
Financial intermediation	0.18	0.16	18		74.0	0.16
Real estate, renting, and business activities	0.22	0.38	17		2.6	0.19
Public administration and defense	0.27	0.49	14		44.8	0.23
Education, health, and social work	0.18	0.24	18		6.7	0.16
Other personal services	0.29	0.49	13		3.9	0.26
Total backward linkage	**1.42**	**0.11**	**18**	▼	**0.6**	**1.39**
Agriculture, hunting, forestry, and fishing	1.37	0.24	12		–1.5	1.40
Mining and quarrying	1.00	0.00	23		0.0	1.00
Light manufacturing	1.77	0.37	14		3.3	1.72
Heavy manufacturing	1.31	0.00	25		0.1	1.34
Utilities	1.46	0.16	17		0.8	1.39
Construction	1.41	0.00	25		–0.8	1.49
Trade services	1.77	1.00	1		1.8	1.64
Hotels and restaurants	1.56	0.27	20		–0.2	1.60
Transport services	1.42	0.29	15		0.7	1.37
Telecommunications	1.55	0.41	10		1.9	1.49
Financial intermediation	1.26	0.04	18		0.7	1.22
Real estate, renting, and business activities	1.30	0.20	17		0.5	1.27
Public administration and defense	1.38	0.39	15		2.2	1.31
Education, health, and social work	1.26	0.14	20		0.9	1.22
Other personal services	1.44	0.32	13		0.8	1.37
Normalized backward linkage	–	–	–	▬	–	–
Agriculture, hunting, forestry, and fishing	0.97	0.40	9		–1.9	1.01
Mining and quarrying	0.70	0.08	23		–0.3	0.72
Light manufacturing	1.25	0.66	6		2.5	1.23
Heavy manufacturing	0.92	0.00	25		–0.7	0.96
Utilities	1.03	0.30	12		0.4	1.00
Construction	0.99	0.08	22		–1.3	1.08
Trade services	1.25	1.00	1		0.9	1.18
Hotels and restaurants	1.10	0.43	15		–0.7	1.15
Transport services	1.00	0.42	11		0.1	0.99
Telecommunications	1.09	0.78	6		1.3	1.07
Financial intermediation	0.88	0.10	14		0.0	0.88
Real estate, renting, and business activities	0.92	0.49	10		0.1	0.92
Public administration and defense	0.97	0.57	10		1.6	0.94
Education, health, and social work	0.89	0.49	16		0.5	0.88
Other personal services	1.01	0.62	8		0.4	0.99
Net backward linkage	**0.79**	**0.00**	**25**	▼	**0.8**	**0.73**
Agriculture, hunting, forestry, and fishing	0.34	0.13	24		–0.3	0.34
Mining and quarrying	0.00	0.00	23		0.0	0.00
Light manufacturing	1.02	0.47	15		8.3	0.69
Heavy manufacturing	0.87	0.49	14		0.1	0.88
Utilities	0.67	0.51	9		2.6	0.53
Construction	0.75	0.00	25		–0.5	0.82
Trade services	0.49	0.00	25		3.8	0.48

continued on next page

Maldives 3.6A *continued*

	Value (2018)	Score (0–1)	Rank (out of 25)	Distance to subregional average	10–year average growth rate (%)	10–year mean value
Hotels and restaurants	1.53	0.72	6		−0.2	1.56
Transport services	0.93	0.46	11		3.7	0.72
Telecommunications	0.75	0.40	14		2.4	0.69
Financial intermediation	0.14	0.00	25		24.5	0.17
Real estate, renting, and business activities	0.88	0.81	8		9.6	0.69
Public administration and defense	1.08	0.09	23		0.5	1.15
Education, health, and social work	1.09	0.08	22		0.7	1.03
Other personal services	1.35	0.91	3		2.2	1.18
Growth equalized output multipliers	**0.10**	**0.12**	**17**	▼	**0.1**	**0.10**
Agriculture, hunting, forestry, and fishing	0.04	0.12	19		−10.0	0.08
Mining and quarrying	0.00	0.00	23		0.0	0.00
Light manufacturing	0.09	0.15	21		27.4	0.08
Heavy manufacturing	0.00	0.00	25		−1.5	0.01
Utilities	0.04	0.14	14		−1.3	0.04
Construction	0.50	1.00	1		18.3	0.23
Trade services	0.05	0.00	25		−1.1	0.09
Hotels and restaurants	0.40	1.00	1		−1.7	0.48
Transport services	0.08	0.35	16		0.7	0.11
Telecommunications	0.04	0.55	6		1.0	0.06
Financial intermediation	0.03	0.04	23		2.2	0.04
Real estate, renting, and business activities	0.04	0.03	24		−4.5	0.08
Public administration and defense	0.12	0.71	3		7.3	0.12
Education, health, and social work	0.04	0.05	22		−3.4	0.06
Other personal services	0.01	0.03	22		−3.0	0.02
Supply-Side Linkages						
Direct forward linkage	**0.38**	**0.34**	**10**	▲	**0.2**	**0.42**
Agriculture, hunting, forestry, and fishing	0.75	0.85	2		0.1	0.76
Mining and quarrying	0.00	0.00	23		0.0	0.00
Light manufacturing	0.42	0.41	11		−2.9	0.60
Heavy manufacturing	0.34	0.41	20		0.4	0.34
Utilities	0.55	0.55	20		0.2	0.62
Construction	0.47	0.96	2		7.3	0.45
Trade services	0.72	1.00	1		3.0	0.70
Hotels and restaurants	0.02	0.02	24		49.8	0.02
Transport services	0.34	0.34	16		−0.3	0.47
Telecommunications	0.52	0.58	11		0.8	0.53
Financial intermediation	0.89	1.00	1		0.9	0.86
Real estate, renting, and business activities	0.33	0.19	18		−2.2	0.46
Public administration and defense	0.22	1.00	1		23.4	0.12
Education, health, and social work	0.14	0.50	3		36.6	0.16
Other personal services	0.06	0.03	22		20.9	0.15
Total forward linkage	**1.57**	**0.16**	**14**	▼	**0.0**	**1.62**
Agriculture, hunting, forestry, and fishing	2.02	0.44	9		0.1	2.07
Mining and quarrying	1.00	0.00	23		0.0	1.00
Light manufacturing	1.51	0.14	15		−1.7	1.78

continued on next page

Maldives 3.6A *continued*

	Value (2018)	Score (0–1)	Rank (out of 25)	Distance to subregional average	10–year average growth rate (%)	10–year mean value
Heavy manufacturing	1.57	0.26	20		0.2	1.57
Utilities	1.85	0.26	19		−0.1	2.01
Construction	1.69	0.75	3		1.5	1.65
Trade services	2.12	0.61	2		1.8	2.10
Hotels and restaurants	1.03	0.01	24		0.1	1.03
Transport services	1.50	0.18	17		−0.2	1.67
Telecommunications	1.78	0.43	12		0.2	1.84
Financial intermediation	2.26	0.26	8		0.5	2.22
Real estate, renting, and business activities	1.53	0.17	17		−1.6	1.76
Public administration and defense	1.34	1.00	1		2.1	1.19
Education, health, and social work	1.19	0.63	3		1.3	1.21
Other personal services	1.08	0.04	22		1.0	1.23
Normalized forward linkage	–	–	–	▬	–	–
Agriculture, hunting, forestry, and fishing	1.29	0.77	7		0.1	1.28
Mining and quarrying	0.70	0.07	23		−0.3	0.72
Light manufacturing	1.06	0.50	13		−2.3	1.28
Heavy manufacturing	1.11	0.49	15		−0.4	1.13
Utilities	1.30	0.53	18		−0.7	1.45
Construction	1.19	0.81	2		0.8	1.19
Trade services	1.49	1.00	1		1.2	1.51
Hotels and restaurants	0.72	0.08	23		−0.2	0.74
Transport services	1.06	0.36	15		−0.6	1.20
Telecommunications	1.26	0.61	7		−0.4	1.32
Financial intermediation	1.59	0.36	3		−0.3	1.59
Real estate, renting, and business activities	1.08	0.33	12		−2.5	1.27
Public administration and defense	0.94	1.00	1		1.7	0.86
Education, health, and social work	0.84	0.93	2		0.7	0.87
Other personal services	0.76	0.09	23		0.5	0.88
Net forward linkage	0.73	0.23	22	▼	−0.4	0.76
Agriculture, hunting, forestry, and fishing	0.80	0.18	23		3.8	0.81
Mining and quarrying	0.00	0.00	23		0.0	0.00
Light manufacturing	0.41	0.24	20		−5.8	0.59
Heavy manufacturing	0.76	0.83	5		2.8	0.72
Utilities	0.31	0.06	24		−3.8	0.42
Construction	0.68	0.99	2		6.5	0.59
Trade services	0.96	0.39	20		2.8	0.93
Hotels and restaurants	0.35	0.00	25		−1.1	0.37
Transport services	0.58	0.21	21		0.4	0.65
Telecommunications	0.92	0.34	16		−1.0	0.96
Financial intermediation	1.76	0.69	3		0.4	1.73
Real estate, renting, and business activities	1.09	0.41	15		−2.1	1.30
Public administration and defense	0.90	0.86	3		0.4	0.84
Education, health, and social work	0.93	0.90	3		1.4	0.94
Other personal services	0.44	0.00	25		−0.9	0.56

continued on next page

Maldives 3.6A *continued*

	Value (2018)	Score (0–1)	Rank (out of 25)	Distance to subregional average	10-year average growth rate (%)	10-year mean value
Growth equalized input multipliers	**0.10**	**0.14**	**17**	▼	**0.2**	**0.10**
Agriculture, hunting, forestry, and fishing	0.05	0.10	20		−8.3	0.09
Mining and quarrying	0.00	0.00	23		0.0	0.00
Light manufacturing	0.06	0.16	22		12.2	0.07
Heavy manufacturing	0.01	0.01	24		5.0	0.01
Utilities	0.02	0.04	23		−4.0	0.03
Construction	0.54	1.00	1		35.3	0.22
Trade services	0.08	0.02	24		−1.0	0.12
Hotels and restaurants	0.22	1.00	1		−2.5	0.27
Transport services	0.07	0.36	18		−0.6	0.11
Telecommunications	0.06	0.54	5		0.4	0.08
Financial intermediation	0.08	0.15	18		3.3	0.10
Real estate, renting, and business activities	0.07	0.04	24		−3.8	0.16
Public administration and defense	0.17	1.00	1		9.0	0.15
Education, health, and social work	0.06	0.35	14		−1.6	0.08
Other personal services	0.01	0.02	23		−2.2	0.02

Impacts from Hypothetical Extraction

	Value (2018)	Score (0–1)	Rank (out of 25)	Distance to subregional average	10-year average growth rate (%)	10-year mean value
Changes in gross output due to hypothetical extraction	**−9.0%**	**0.82**	**12**	▼	**−0.2**	**−0.09**
Agriculture, hunting, forestry, and fishing	−3.6%	0.88	7		−8.9	−7.0
Mining and quarrying	0.0%	1.00	1		0.0	0.0
Light manufacturing	−10.9%	0.78	6		33.0	−8.5
Heavy manufacturing	−0.4%	1.00	1		−0.9	−0.4
Utilities	−3.5%	0.85	13		−0.2	−3.9
Construction	−37.2%	0.00	25		14.4	−19.3
Trade services	−5.8%	1.00	1		1.1	−9.0
Hotels and restaurants	−42.1%	0.00	25		−2.1	−50.9
Transport services	−7.4%	0.65	14		1.3	−9.8
Telecommunications	−3.9%	0.36	19		1.9	−4.8
Financial intermediation	−2.3%	0.95	3		2.7	−2.8
Real estate, renting, and business activities	−3.5%	0.97	2		−4.1	−6.6
Public administration and defense	−10.4%	0.35	22		9.4	−10.3
Education, health, and social work	−3.5%	0.96	4		−2.4	−4.8
Other personal services	−1.0%	0.98	4		−1.4	−1.7

Impacts from Hypothetical Insertion

	Value (2018)	Score (0–1)	Rank (out of 25)	Distance to subregional average	10-year average growth rate (%)	10-year mean value
Changes in gross output due to hypothetical insertion	**3.2%**	**0.12**	**18**	▼	**0.9**	**0.03**
Agriculture, hunting, forestry, and fishing	1.0%	0.04	21		−7.3	2.6
Mining and quarrying	0.0%	0.00	23		20.0	0.0
Light manufacturing	4.9%	0.14	20		86.7	4.4
Heavy manufacturing	0.1%	0.00	25		9.6	0.1
Utilities	1.2%	0.11	15		3.4	1.1
Construction	13.7%	0.61	3		15.9	7.2
Trade services	2.6%	0.11	20		14.6	3.6
Hotels and restaurants	15.3%	1.00	1		−2.4	19.2
Transport services	2.3%	0.30	16		6.6	2.8
Telecommunications	1.6%	0.45	5		12.1	1.9
Financial intermediation	0.5%	0.02	22		58.1	0.6

continued on next page

Maldives 3.6A *continued*

	Value (2018)	Score (0–1)	Rank (out of 25)	Distance to subregional average	10–year average growth rate (%)	10–year mean value
Real estate, renting, and business activities	0.8%	0.05	23		−2.8	1.4
Public administration and defense	3.0%	0.70	7		51.8	2.6
Education, health, and social work	0.7%	0.08	22		1.8	0.9
Other personal services	0.3%	0.03	21		3.7	0.5

SPREAD OF ECONOMIC LINKAGES

Demand-side

	Value (2018)	Score (0–1)	Rank (out of 25)	Distance to subregional average	10–year average growth rate (%)	10–year mean value
Relative evenness of direct backward linkage	0.48	0.54	8	▼	1.1	0.53
Relative evenness of total backward linkage	0.14	0.10	13	▼	0.4	0.15
		0.00				
Backward measure of concentration based on input coefficients	0.89	0.43	21	▼	−0.3	0.91
Agriculture, hunting, forestry, and fishing	0.94	0.91	6		1.7	0.90
Mining and quarrying	1.04	1.00	1		0.0	1.04
Light manufacturing	0.90	0.62	15		0.1	0.89
Heavy manufacturing	0.95	0.97	4		0.6	0.93
Utilities	0.90	0.73	15		0.8	0.86
Construction	0.74	0.45	24		−2.3	0.90
Trade services	0.88	0.52	22		−0.1	0.92
Hotels and restaurants	0.89	0.69	17		−0.3	0.94
Transport services	0.95	0.83	4		0.2	0.94
Telecommunications	0.87	0.29	23		0.4	0.85
Financial intermediation	0.83	0.82	18		−0.9	0.91
Real estate, renting, and business activities	0.62	0.00	25		−1.6	0.73
Public administration and defense	0.92	0.46	22		−0.6	0.95
Education, health, and social work	0.91	0.31	24		−0.6	0.94
Other personal services	0.96	0.92	11		0.4	0.94
Relative evenness of direct forward linkage	0.71	0.66	6	▲	−0.2	0.68
Relative evenness of total forward linkage	0.25	0.20	12	▼	−0.4	0.26
Forward measure of concentration based on output coefficients	0.59	0.23	22	▼	−0.2	0.58
Agriculture, hunting, forestry, and fishing	0.29	0.24	18		−0.5	0.29
Mining and quarrying	0.00	0.00	23		0.0	0.00
Light manufacturing	0.36	0.08	24		−3.5	0.39
Heavy manufacturing	0.64	0.59	13		0.2	0.65
Utilities	0.83	0.82	10		0.0	0.82
Construction	0.61	0.71	12		−0.3	0.64
Trade services	0.68	0.34	18		−0.4	0.69
Hotels and restaurants	0.66	0.37	22		0.9	0.64
Transport services	0.62	0.28	23		0.6	0.60
Telecommunications	0.73	0.20	22		−0.2	0.71
Financial intermediation	0.67	0.71	20		1.5	0.64
Real estate, renting, and business activities	0.77	0.54	20		1.6	0.73
Public administration and defense	0.76	0.82	11		0.3	0.72
Education, health, and social work	0.45	0.43	19		−1.9	0.48
Other personal services	0.76	0.65	13		0.7	0.73

continued on next page

Maldives 3.6A *continued*

	Value (2018)	Score (0–1)	Rank (out of 25)	Distance to subregional average	10–year average growth rate (%)	10–year mean value
SENSITIVITY OF ECONOMIC LINKAGES						
Economic Complexity						
Percentage intermediate transaction	0.33	0.22	17	▼	0.4	0.33
Average output multiplier	1.42	0.11	18	▼	0.6	1.39
Average of Leontief inverse	0.18	0.11	19	▼	0.7	0.18
Average technical coefficient	0.02	0.18	18	▼	2.7	0.02
Mean intermediate coefficient	0.29	0.18	18	▼	2.7	0.27
Percentage of above-average coefficients (%)	0.27	0.44	10	▼	0.7	0.28
Determinant of non-competitive Leontief inverse	1.91	0.02	22	▼	–1.4	2.18
Determinant of competitive Leontief inverse	3.35	0.02	18	▼	–2.7	4.05
Mean path length	1.49	0.12	17	▼	0.1	1.50
Cycling index	0.09	0.23	17	▼	7.8	0.06
Average propagation length	1.48	0.07	23	▼	0.3	1.50
Overall sensitivity of the economy	0.65	0.28	21	▼	0.2	0.65
Index of direct interrelatedness	0.49	0.05	24	▼	0.7	0.49
Index of indirect interrelatedness	0.15	0.54	10	▼	1.2	0.16
Global intensity index	21.28	0.11	18	▼	0.6	20.83

Note: The scores of the economy in focus are shown in the horizontal bars with labels. The colored dots represent the indicator performance of the economy in focus compared to other economies in the region. The highest rank among economies is 1 while the lowest rank is 25. The indicators shown in the chart are selected from a broader set of indicators (see the technical appendix for more details).

Source: Asian Development Bank Multi-Regional Input–Output Database. https://mrio.adbx.online/ (accessed 4 August 2020).

3.6B External Linkages

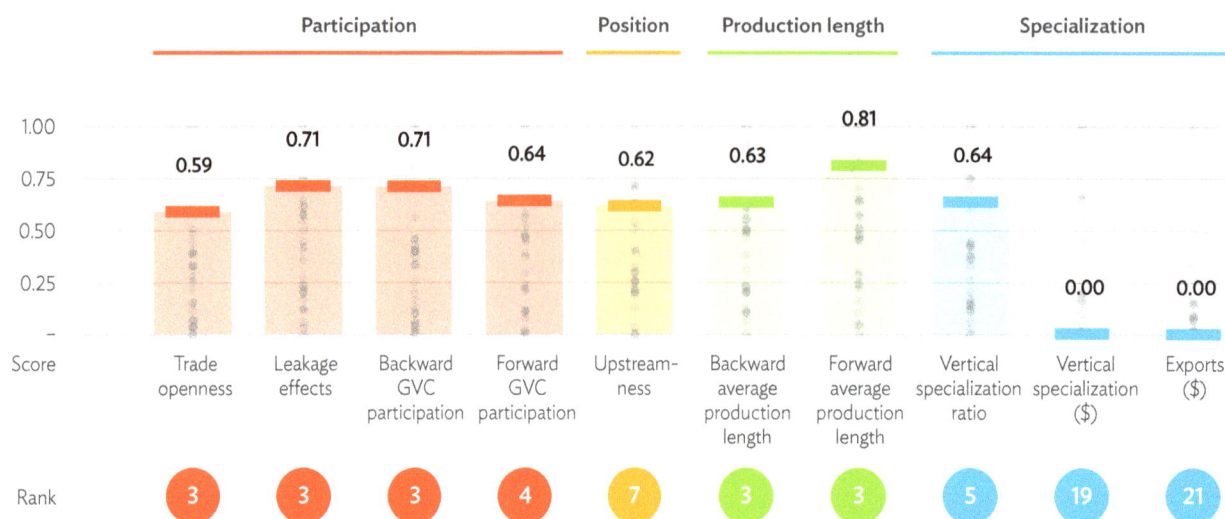

$ = United States dollars, GVC = global value chain.

Note: The scores of the economy in focus are shown in the horizontal bars with labels. The colored dots represent the indicator performance of the economy in focus compared to other economies in the region. The highest rank among economies is 1, while the lowest rank is 25. The indicators shown in the chart are selected from a broader set of indicators (see the technical appendix for more details).

Source: Asian Development Bank Multi-Regional Input–Output Database. https://mrio.adbx.online/ (accessed 4 August 2020).

		Value (2018)	Score (0–1)	Rank (out of 25)	Distance to subregional average	10-year average growth rate (%)	10-year mean value
PARTICIPATION IN GLOBAL VALUE CHAINS							
International Trade Coefficients							
Trade openness		1.44	0.59	3	▲	0.5	1.53
Self-sufficiency ratio		0.99	0.63	14	▲	1.0	1.05
Regional supply percentage		0.65	0.15	24	▼	0.5	0.65
Regional purchase coefficient		0.55	0.00	25	▼	−0.5	0.61
Sectoral purchase coefficient		0.00	0.00	24	▼	0.0	0.00
Simple location quotient of gross output		1.56	1.00	1	▲	−1.3	1.74
Fabrication effect		0.97	0.62	11	▲	0.9	0.94
Exports	($)	3,489	0.00	21	▼	10.5	2,620
Export-to-output ratio		0.24	0.81	3	▲	11.3	0.19
Agriculture, hunting, forestry, and fishing		0.14	0.64	7		18.1	0.08
Mining and quarrying		0.00	0.00	23		0.0	0.00
Light manufacturing		0.23	0.41	14		−6.6	0.20
Heavy manufacturing		0.15	0.16	18		20.7	0.13
Utilities		0.04	0.04	6		19.5	0.06
Construction		0.06	0.68	4		39.7	0.06
Trade services		0.10	0.14	16		5.3	0.09
Hotels and restaurants		0.94	0.98	2		0.6	0.93
Transport services		0.55	0.72	3		17.7	0.35
Telecommunications		0.32	1.00	1		9.1	0.27

continued on next page

Maldives 3.6B *continued*

		Value (2018)	Score (0–1)	Rank (out of 25)	Distance to subregional average	10–year average growth rate (%)	10–year mean value
Financial intermediation		0.09	0.21	3		8.6	0.10
Real estate, renting, and business activities		0.03	0.08	15		16.9	0.04
Public administration and defense		0.06	0.14	5		5.8	0.09
Education, health, and social work		0.00	0.03	17		8.3	0.03
Other personal services		0.82	1.00	1		14.3	0.47
Imports	($)	3,543	0.00	23	▼	9.2	2,301
Import-to-input ratio		0.19	0.81	5	▲	0.8	0.20
Agriculture, hunting, forestry, and fishing		0.34	0.98	2		3.7	0.34
Mining and quarrying		0.00	0.00	23		0.0	0.00
Light manufacturing		0.19	0.34	6		8.8	0.19
Heavy manufacturing		0.26	0.32	11		2.4	0.29
Utilities		0.53	1.00	1		2.3	0.53
Construction		0.29	0.68	2		1.5	0.29
Trade services		0.07	0.26	11		8.8	0.12
Hotels and restaurants		0.23	0.76	3		9.7	0.22
Transport services		0.30	0.60	6		0.0	0.34
Telecommunications		0.12	0.32	8		1.4	0.14
Financial intermediation		0.05	0.23	8		16.4	0.07
Real estate, renting, and business activities		0.06	0.33	9		4.4	0.07
Public administration and defense		0.07	0.41	11		11.2	0.07
Education, health, and social work		0.06	0.31	13		−4.0	0.08
Other personal services		0.20	0.54	3		2.5	0.24
Total foreign factor content of consumption	($)	771	0.00	23	▼	17.5	373
Total foreign factor content of investment	($)	265	0.00	23	▼	16.6	168
Total foreign factor content of exports	($)	1,251	0.00	19	▼	13.4	917

Interregional Multipliers

	Value (2018)	Score (0–1)	Rank (out of 25)	Distance to subregional average	10–year average growth rate (%)	10–year mean value
Import Leakage Effects	0.28	0.71	3	▲	1.1	0.28
Agriculture, hunting, forestry, and fishing	0.42	1.00	1		0.0	0.43
Mining and quarrying	0.00	0.00	23		0.0	0.00
Light manufacturing	0.40	0.66	5		4.8	0.37
Heavy manufacturing	0.32	0.34	12		0.0	0.36
Utilities	0.63	1.00	1		2.0	0.61
Construction	0.39	0.70	5		−0.1	0.41
Trade services	0.24	0.60	4		5.5	0.25
Hotels and restaurants	0.36	1.00	1		2.9	0.35
Transport services	0.39	0.56	4		0.1	0.42
Telecommunications	0.21	0.37	7		0.6	0.22
Financial intermediation	0.11	0.32	5		7.3	0.11
Real estate, renting, and business activities	0.14	0.45	9		3.7	0.13
Public administration and defense	0.15	0.46	7		11.4	0.13
Education, health, and social work	0.13	0.53	10		−0.4	0.14
Other personal services	0.28	0.69	3		1.4	0.31
Intraregional transfer multiplier	1.42	0.11	18	▼	0.6	1.39
Agriculture, hunting, forestry, and fishing	1.37	0.24	12		−1.5	1.40
Mining and quarrying	1.00	0.00	23		0.0	1.00

continued on next page

Maldives 3.6B *continued*

	Value (2018)	Score (0–1)	Rank (out of 25)	Distance to subregional average	10–year average growth rate (%)	10–year mean value
Light manufacturing	1.77	0.37	14		3.3	1.72
Heavy manufacturing	1.31	0.00	25		0.1	1.34
Utilities	1.46	0.16	17		0.8	1.39
Construction	1.41	0.00	25		−0.8	1.49
Trade services	1.77	1.00	1		1.8	1.64
Hotels and restaurants	1.56	0.27	20		−0.2	1.60
Transport services	1.42	0.29	15		0.7	1.37
Telecommunications	1.55	0.41	10		1.9	1.49
Financial intermediation	1.26	0.04	18		0.7	1.22
Real estate, renting, and business activities	1.30	0.20	17		0.5	1.27
Public administration and defense	1.38	0.39	15		2.2	1.31
Education, health, and social work	1.26	0.14	20		0.9	1.22
Other personal services	1.44	0.32	13		0.8	1.37
Interregional spillover multiplier	**1.39**	**0.72**	**8**	▲	**−0.2**	**1.43**
Agriculture, hunting, forestry, and fishing	1.64	0.97	2		0.4	1.66
Mining and quarrying	1.00	0.00	23		0.0	1.00
Light manufacturing	1.39	0.31	9		0.3	1.42
Heavy manufacturing	1.65	0.41	11		0.0	1.73
Utilities	2.13	1.00	1		0.6	2.13
Construction	1.68	0.70	3		−0.2	1.69
Trade services	1.14	0.26	14		0.2	1.27
Hotels and restaurants	1.51	0.69	3		1.2	1.48
Transport services	1.61	0.52	10		−0.4	1.70
Telecommunications	1.22	0.26	10		−0.6	1.26
Financial intermediation	1.10	0.25	8		0.4	1.13
Real estate, renting, and business activities	1.13	0.36	11		0.1	1.15
Public administration and defense	1.14	0.31	12		0.3	1.14
Education, health, and social work	1.13	0.28	16		−1.0	1.18
Other personal services	1.40	0.42	4		−0.3	1.47
Interregional feedback multiplier	**1.000**	**0.00**	**20**	▼	**0.0**	**1.00**
Agriculture, hunting, forestry, and fishing	1.000	0.01	18		0.0	1.00
Mining and quarrying	1.000	0.00	23		0.0	1.00
Light manufacturing	1.000	0.00	21		0.0	1.00
Heavy manufacturing	1.000	0.00	20		0.0	1.00
Utilities	1.000	0.01	16		0.0	1.00
Construction	1.000	0.00	21		0.0	1.00
Trade services	1.000	0.00	22		0.0	1.00
Hotels and restaurants	1.000	0.01	18		0.0	1.00
Transport services	1.000	0.00	22		0.0	1.00
Telecommunications	1.000	0.00	22		0.0	1.00
Financial intermediation	1.000	0.00	21		0.0	1.00
Real estate, renting, and business activities	1.000	0.00	21		0.0	1.00
Public administration and defense	1.000	0.00	20		0.0	1.00
Education, health, and social work	1.000	0.00	23		0.0	1.00
Other personal services	1.000	0.00	19		0.0	1.00

continued on next page

Maldives 3.6B *continued*

	Value (2018)	Score (0–1)	Rank (out of 25)	Distance to subregional average	10-year average growth rate (%)	10-year mean value
Global Value Chain (GVC) Participation Index						
Backward GVC Participation	33.2%	0.71	3	▲	1.8	0.31
Simple GVCs	16.6%	0.89	5	▲	2.7	0.13
Agriculture, hunting, forestry, and fishing	0.2	0.08	16		−14.2	0.72
Mining and quarrying	0.0	0.10	21		0.0	0.00
Light manufacturing	1.5	0.30	9		−7.1	0.78
Heavy manufacturing	0.1	0.00	25		−1.7	0.09
Utilities	1.1	1.00	1		6.0	0.96
Construction	10.0	1.00	1		12.7	4.90
Trade services	0.2	0.06	21		−16.4	0.55
Hotels and restaurants	0.7	0.34	5		−7.9	0.94
Transport services	0.4	0.19	19		4.3	0.95
Telecommunications	0.2	0.16	13		−2.0	0.29
Financial intermediation	0.0	0.00	25		−4.6	0.02
Real estate, renting, and business activities	0.4	0.22	12		−3.8	0.56
Public administration and defense	1.3	0.33	5		0.6	1.38
Education, health, and social work	0.5	0.28	18		−11.6	0.77
Other personal services	0.0	0.02	22		−20.0	0.30
Complex GVCs	16.6%	0.56	3	▲	3.6	0.17
Agriculture, hunting, forestry, and fishing	0.2	0.14	10		−7.3	0.35
Mining and quarrying	0.0	0.01	22		0.0	0.00
Light manufacturing	1.4	0.13	7		11.0	0.86
Heavy manufacturing	0.1	0.00	25		4.4	0.07
Utilities	0.4	1.00	1		0.2	0.37
Construction	4.0	1.00	1		19.6	2.07
Trade services	0.1	0.01	21		−7.7	0.22
Hotels and restaurants	8.3	1.00	1		−5.5	10.47
Transport services	1.0	0.47	3		2.2	1.33
Telecommunications	0.1	0.23	5		−15.9	0.20
Financial intermediation	0.0	0.00	25		−15.2	0.01
Real estate, renting, and business activities	0.1	0.15	14		−7.5	0.24
Public administration and defense	0.6	0.48	3		7.4	0.66
Education, health, and social work	0.2	0.19	18		−10.2	0.31
Other personal services	0.1	0.24	7		−21.2	0.21
Forward GVC Participation	30.8%	0.64	4	▲	0.3	0.33
Simple GVCs	19.4%	0.59	5	▲	0.1	0.21
Agriculture, hunting, forestry, and fishing	0.6	0.29	12		−6.5	1.16
Mining and quarrying	0.0	0.00	23		0.0	0.00
Light manufacturing	0.6	0.15	14		−13.2	0.78
Heavy manufacturing	0.0	0.00	25		−8.1	0.04
Utilities	0.1	0.01	17		1.1	0.22
Construction	3.8	1.00	1		8.5	1.71
Trade services	0.6	0.06	22		2.9	1.13
Hotels and restaurants	8.3	1.00	1		−3.0	9.45
Transport services	1.8	0.44	4		−0.1	1.93
Telecommunications	1.1	0.74	2		1.4	1.31

continued on next page

Maldives 3.6B *continued*

	Value (2018)	Score (0–1)	Rank (out of 25)	Distance to subregional average	10–year average growth rate (%)	10–year mean value
Financial intermediation	0.9	0.18	6		2.2	1.15
Real estate, renting, and business activities	0.4	0.06	16		–0.2	1.16
Public administration and defense	0.8	0.78	2		–0.3	0.69
Education, health, and social work	0.1	0.33	7		–17.9	0.17
Other personal services	0.3	0.44	5		34.6	0.30
Complex GVCs	**11.4%**	**0.65**	**6**	▲	**0.7**	**0.11**
Agriculture, hunting, forestry, and fishing	0.3	0.19	11		–10.5	0.60
Mining and quarrying	0.0	0.00	23		0.0	0.00
Light manufacturing	0.4	0.18	13		–7.4	0.41
Heavy manufacturing	0.0	0.00	25		0.6	0.02
Utilities	0.1	0.01	18		–2.4	0.11
Construction	2.3	1.00	1		8.7	0.96
Trade services	0.3	0.09	22		–0.1	0.61
Hotels and restaurants	5.3	1.00	1		1.5	5.36
Transport services	0.7	0.47	5		–2.2	0.81
Telecommunications	0.6	0.94	2		2.5	0.66
Financial intermediation	0.5	0.26	5		–1.5	0.65
Real estate, renting, and business activities	0.2	0.06	16		–0.1	0.61
Public administration and defense	0.5	0.80	2		2.3	0.36
Education, health, and social work	0.0	0.36	7		–20.0	0.08
Other personal services	0.2	1.00	1		33.9	0.17

Vertical Specialization

	Value (2018)	Score (0–1)	Rank (out of 25)	Distance to subregional average	10–year average growth rate (%)	10–year mean value
Vertical Specialization Ratio	**35.9%**	**0.64**	**5**	▲	**1.7**	**0.35**
Agriculture, hunting, forestry, and fishing	41.7%	1.00	1		0.0	0.43
Mining and quarrying	0.0%	0.00	23		0.0	0.00
Light manufacturing	39.7%	0.66	5		4.8	0.37
Heavy manufacturing	32.3%	0.34	12		0.0	0.36
Utilities	63.4%	1.00	1		2.1	0.61
Construction	39.5%	0.70	5		–0.1	0.41
Trade services	24.1%	0.60	4		5.5	0.25
Hotels and restaurants	36.3%	1.00	1		2.9	0.35
Transport services	38.6%	0.56	4		0.1	0.42
Telecommunications	21.2%	0.37	7		0.6	0.22
Financial intermediation	11.3%	0.32	5		7.3	0.11
Real estate, renting, and business activities	13.9%	0.45	9		3.7	0.13
Public administration and defense	15.5%	0.46	7		11.4	0.13
Education, health, and social work	13.5%	0.53	10		–0.4	0.14
Other personal services	28.2%	0.69	3		1.4	0.31

Revealed Comparative Advantages

	Value (2018)	Score (0–1)	Rank (out of 25)	Distance to subregional average	10–year average growth rate (%)	10–year mean value
Traditional RCA Index						
Agriculture, hunting, forestry, and fishing	0.48	0.08	16	▼	5.5	0.44
Mining and quarrying	0.00	0.00	23	▼	0.0	0.00
Light manufacturing	0.28	0.04	20	▼	0.3	0.18

continued on next page

Maldives 3.6B continued

	Value (2018)	Score (0–1)	Rank (out of 25)	Distance to subregional average	10–year average growth rate (%)	10–year mean value
Heavy manufacturing	0.00	0.00	25	▼	22.5	0.00
Utilities	0.46	0.01	9	▼	3.2	0.84
Construction	7.89	1.00	1	▲	59.9	4.21
Trade services	0.12	0.02	23	▼	4.7	0.18
Hotels and restaurants	59.05	1.00	1	▲	–1.2	70.58
Transport services	1.50	0.35	7	▼	9.8	1.19
Telecommunications	3.61	0.60	3	▲	11.6	3.94
Financial intermediation	0.16	0.04	10	▼	2.3	0.20
Real estate, renting, and business activities	0.03	0.01	22	▼	0.5	0.10
Public administration and defense	3.12	0.11	6	▼	1.0	4.94
Education, health, and social work	0.05	0.01	23	▼	–2.8	0.84
Other personal services	1.28	0.07	6	▼	5.4	1.16

New RCA Index (Based on Domestic Value Added)

	Value (2018)	Score (0–1)	Rank (out of 25)	Distance to subregional average	10–year average growth rate (%)	10–year mean value
Agriculture, hunting, forestry, and fishing	0.70	0.10	18	▼	–7.9	1.19
Mining and quarrying	0.00	0.00	23	▼	0.0	0.00
Light manufacturing	0.45	0.10	20	▼	–4.9	0.45
Heavy manufacturing	0.01	0.00	25	▼	0.3	0.01
Utilities	0.20	0.01	23	▼	–0.3	0.36
Construction	17.45	1.00	1	▲	21.8	7.43
Trade services	0.23	0.03	24	▼	1.4	0.41
Hotels and restaurants	34.39	1.00	1	▲	–5.2	39.23
Transport services	1.17	0.36	9	▼	2.2	1.22
Telecommunications	2.89	0.79	3	▲	–2.2	3.36
Financial intermediation	0.71	0.16	11	▲	–7.5	0.87
Real estate, renting, and business activities	0.13	0.04	23	▼	–5.7	0.38
Public administration and defense	4.61	0.42	4	▲	–7.2	4.19
Education, health, and social work	0.47	0.09	15	▼	–6.3	1.19
Other personal services	0.60	0.06	12	▼	13.1	0.63

POSITION IN GLOBAL VALUE CHAINS

	Value (2018)	Score (0–1)	Rank (out of 25)	Distance to subregional average	10–year average growth rate (%)	10–year mean value
Upstreamness Index	**2.2**	**0.48**	**9**	▲	**0.5**	**2.2**
Agriculture, hunting, forestry, and fishing	2.9	0.76	5		0.2	2.9
Mining and quarrying	0.0	0.00	23		0.0	0.0
Light manufacturing	2.1	0.41	9		–3.1	2.5
Heavy manufacturing	1.9	0.13	22		0.4	1.9
Utilities	2.2	0.18	21		–0.3	2.5
Construction	2.1	1.00	1		2.9	2.1
Trade services	2.8	0.89	3		1.4	2.9
Hotels and restaurants	2.4	0.93	2		0.9	2.3
Transport services	2.5	0.57	9		1.1	2.6
Telecommunications	2.9	0.96	2		1.1	2.9
Financial intermediation	3.2	0.45	5		–0.1	3.2
Real estate, renting, and business activities	1.9	0.24	15		–2.1	2.2
Public administration and defense	1.6	0.95	2		4.1	1.4
Education, health, and social work	1.2	0.58	3		1.9	1.3
Other personal services	2.5	0.86	2		7.0	2.1

continued on next page

Maldives 3.6B *continued*

	Value (2018)	Score (0–1)	Rank (out of 25)	Distance to subregional average	10-year average growth rate (%)	10-year mean value
PRODUCTION LENGTH OF GLOBAL VALUE CHAINS						
Backward Measures of Average Production Length						
Production Length of Global Value Chain Activity (B)	**1.0**	**0.63**	**3**	▲	**0.8**	**1.0**
Agriculture, hunting, forestry, and fishing	1.3	0.81	3		−1.9	1.4
Mining and quarrying	0.0	0.00	23		0.0	0.0
Light manufacturing	1.5	0.74	7		4.4	1.4
Heavy manufacturing	1.2	0.39	13		−0.4	1.4
Utilities	2.2	0.94	2		1.6	2.1
Construction	1.5	0.60	8		−0.8	1.5
Trade services	1.0	0.72	2		4.9	1.0
Hotels and restaurants	1.4	0.88	2		1.8	1.3
Transport services	1.3	0.52	9		0.1	1.5
Telecommunications	0.8	0.41	8		1.5	0.8
Financial intermediation	0.4	0.38	6		5.6	0.4
Real estate, renting, and business activities	0.6	0.50	10		3.5	0.5
Public administration and defense	0.6	0.43	7		11.8	0.5
Education, health, and social work	0.5	0.42	11		0.2	0.5
Other personal services	1.0	0.64	4		1.1	1.1
Forward Measures of Average Production Length						
Production Length of Global Value Chain Activity (F)	**1.1**	**0.81**	**3**	▲	**1.7**	**1.1**
Agriculture, hunting, forestry, and fishing	1.6	1.00	1		3.1	1.7
Mining and quarrying	0.0	0.00	23		0.0	0.0
Light manufacturing	1.1	0.72	6		−1.5	1.4
Heavy manufacturing	0.7	0.22	19		−2.7	0.7
Utilities	0.8	0.27	11		−1.9	1.1
Construction	0.9	1.00	1		7.3	0.9
Trade services	1.4	0.67	4		5.2	1.5
Hotels and restaurants	1.9	1.00	1		2.2	1.8
Transport services	1.7	0.66	6		2.8	1.6
Telecommunications	1.9	0.99	2		0.9	1.8
Financial intermediation	1.8	0.74	3		3.8	1.9
Real estate, renting, and business activities	0.7	0.32	10		3.6	0.9
Public administration and defense	0.5	0.62	3		1.0	0.3
Education, health, and social work	0.1	0.60	3		−8.2	0.2
Other personal services	2.1	1.00	1		24.6	1.3

Note: The scores of the economy in focus are shown in the horizontal bars with labels. The colored dots represent the indicator performance of the economy in focus compared to other economies in the region. The highest rank among economies is 1 while the lowest rank is 25. The indicators shown in the chart are selected from a broader set of indicators (see the technical appendix for more details).

Source: Asian Development Bank Multi-Regional Input–Output Database. https://mrio.adbx.online/ (accessed 4 August 2020).

3.7 Nepal

3.7A Internal Linkages

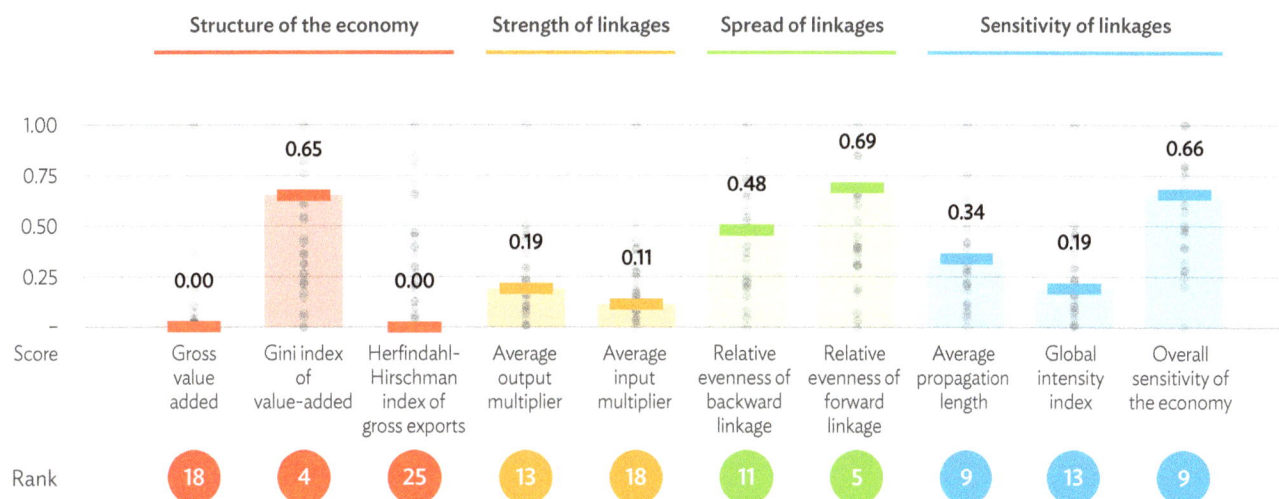

	Structure of the economy			Strength of linkages		Spread of linkages		Sensitivity of linkages		
Score	Gross value added	Gini index of value-added	Herfindahl-Hirschman index of gross exports	Average output multiplier	Average input multiplier	Relative evenness of backward linkage	Relative evenness of forward linkage	Average propagation length	Global intensity index	Overall sensitivity of the economy
	0.00	0.65	0.00	0.19	0.11	0.48	0.69	0.34	0.19	0.66
Rank	18	4	25	13	18	11	5	9	13	9

Note: The scores of the economy in focus are shown in the horizontal bars with labels. The colored dots represent the indicator performance of the economy in focus compared to other economies in the region. The highest rank among economies is 1 while the lowest rank is 25. The indicators shown in the chart are selected from a broader set of indicators (see the technical appendix for more details).

Source: Asian Development Bank Multi-Regional Input–Output Database. https://mrio.adbx.online/ (accessed 4 August 2020).

		Value (2018)	Score (0–1)	Rank (out of 25)	Distance to subregional average	10-year average growth rate (%)	10-year mean value
STRUCTURE OF THE ECONOMY							
Economic Indicators							
Gross output	($)	37,000	0.00	18	▼	7.5	27,493
Gross value-added	($)	20,471	0.00	18	▼	7.3	16,387
Value-added content of domestic final demand		19,413	0.00	17		7.8	15,446
Value-added content of exports		1,058	0.00	24		3.7	941
Intermediate inputs	($)	15,120	0.00	18	▼	7.6	10,380
Domestic inputs		11,315	0.00	18		7.6	7,878
Foreign inputs		3,805	0.00	18		9.7	2,502
Direct production	($)	25,685	0.00	18	▼	7.9	19,615
Domestic final demand		24,251	0.00	17		8.4	18,421
Exports		1,434	0.00	24		4.4	1,193
Indirect production	($)	11,315	0.00	18	▼	7.6	7,878
Indirect production embedded in domestic final demand		10,639	0.00	17		8.1	7,338
Indirect production embedded in exports		676	0.00	24		4.2	540
Economic Diversification							
Gross output		0.26	0.32	16	▼	–0.1	0.27
Gini concentration index of gross output		0.43	0.36	17		–0.1	0.45
Herfindahl-Hirschman concentration index of gross output		0.05	0.22	14		0.5	0.06
Theil concentration index of gross output		0.28	0.31	15		0.0	0.31

continued on next page

Nepal **3.7A** *continued*

	Value (2018)	Score (0–1)	Rank (out of 25)	Distance to subregional average	10–year average growth rate (%)	10–year mean value
Gross value-added	**0.33**	**0.57**	**4**	▲	**0.8**	**0.34**
Gini concentration index of gross value added	0.53	0.65	4		0.6	0.53
Herfindahl-Hirschman concentration index of gross value added	0.09	0.39	3		1.2	0.10
Theil concentration index of gross value added	0.38	0.58	4		0.9	0.39
Gross exports	**0.36**	**0.00**	**25**	▼	**0.4**	**0.36**
Gini concentration index of gross exports	0.57	0.05	24		0.2	0.56
Herfindahl-Hirschman concentration index of gross exports	0.08	0.00	25		1.1	0.08
Theil concentration index of gross exports	0.44	0.00	25		0.7	0.43
Structural Changes						
Changes in output due to technological changes	**0.6%**	**0.83**	**4**	▼	**–**	**–**
Agriculture, hunting, forestry, and fishing	0.2%	0.56	8			
Mining and quarrying	−0.1%	0.74	11			
Light manufacturing	0.7%	0.42	5			
Heavy manufacturing	7.0%	1.00	1			
Utilities	1.5%	0.75	3			
Construction	−0.7%	0.01	24			
Trade services	−0.6%	0.23	20			
Hotels and restaurants	0.8%	0.11	9			
Transport services	−0.5%	0.56	16			
Telecommunications	1.0%	0.34	4			
Financial intermediation	−0.1%	0.47	16			
Real estate, renting, and business activities	−0.4%	0.59	19			
Public administration and defense	0.0%	0.37	15			
Education, health, and social work	−0.1%	0.65	22			
Other personal services	−0.2%	0.38	18			
Changes in output due to structural changes in consumption (%)	**3.9%**	**0.42**	**8**	▲	**–**	**–**
Agriculture, hunting, forestry, and fishing	3.1%	0.57	10			
Mining and quarrying	3.4%	0.22	4			
Light manufacturing	4.4%	0.55	7			
Heavy manufacturing	3.3%	0.53	5			
Utilities	4.2%	0.45	10			
Construction	0.2%	0.20	16			
Trade services	3.4%	0.56	12			
Hotels and restaurants	6.2%	0.22	8			
Transport services	3.5%	0.51	8			
Telecommunications	5.1%	0.71	6			
Financial intermediation	6.3%	0.69	5			
Real estate, renting, and business activities	1.5%	0.10	21			
Public administration and defense	4.3%	0.33	18			
Education, health, and social work	6.1%	0.21	12			
Other personal services	3.0%	0.30	19			
Changes in output due to structural changes in investment (%)	**2.3%**	**0.69**	**3**	▲	**–**	**–**
Agriculture, hunting, forestry, and fishing	2.6%	0.55	3			
Mining and quarrying	3.2%	0.64	3			
Light manufacturing	1.6%	0.48	3			

continued on next page

Nepal 3.7A *continued*

	Value (2018)	Score (0–1)	Rank (out of 25)	Distance to subregional average	10-year average growth rate (%)	10-year mean value
Heavy manufacturing	2.9%	0.41	5			
Utilities	2.2%	0.72	4			
Construction	6.3%	0.41	12			
Trade services	3.3%	0.74	3			
Hotels and restaurants	0.9%	0.64	4			
Transport services	1.9%	0.52	2			
Telecommunications	1.3%	0.32	6			
Financial intermediation	0.5%	0.11	13			
Real estate, renting, and business activities	6.3%	1.00	1			
Public administration and defense	0.0%	0.05	10			
Education, health, and social work	0.3%	0.20	3			
Other personal services	1.2%	0.63	3			
Changes in output due to structural changes in stock (%)	**−0.2%**	**0.11**	**23**	▼	–	–
Agriculture, hunting, forestry, and fishing	−1.8%	0.00	25			
Mining and quarrying	−0.2%	0.36	22			
Light manufacturing	−0.5%	0.00	25			
Heavy manufacturing	−0.3%	0.10	23			
Utilities	−0.2%	0.01	23			
Construction	0.0%	0.73	21			
Trade services	−0.2%	0.07	23			
Hotels and restaurants	0.0%	0.42	21			
Transport services	−0.1%	0.04	23			
Telecommunications	−0.1%	0.39	23			
Financial intermediation	0.0%	0.90	18			
Real estate, renting, and business activities	−0.2%	0.05	24			
Public administration and defense	0.0%	0.64	18			
Education, health, and social work	0.0%	0.22	23			
Other personal services	0.0%	0.41	16			
Changes in output due to structural changes in export	**0.4%**	**0.12**	**19**	▼	–	–
Agriculture, hunting, forestry, and fishing	0.0%	0.43	22			
Mining and quarrying	0.2%	0.12	18			
Light manufacturing	0.2%	0.10	23			
Heavy manufacturing	0.4%	0.24	20			
Utilities	0.3%	0.04	21			
Construction	0.1%	0.04	17			
Trade services	0.3%	0.06	21			
Hotels and restaurants	0.2%	0.05	19			
Transport services	0.5%	0.42	19			
Telecommunications	0.6%	0.12	15			
Financial intermediation	0.1%	0.08	21			
Real estate, renting, and business activities	0.1%	0.18	19			
Public administration and defense	1.1%	0.33	4			
Education, health, and social work	0.0%	0.02	20			
Other personal services	1.1%	0.23	10			

continued on next page

Nepal 3.7A *continued*

	Value (2018)	Score (0–1)	Rank (out of 25)	Distance to subregional average	10–year average growth rate (%)	10–year mean value
Changes in output due to import substitution on intermediate demand	**−0.4%**	**0.34**	**18**	▼	–	–
Agriculture, hunting, forestry, and fishing	0.2%	0.69	5			
Mining and quarrying	−0.3%	0.31	21			
Light manufacturing	0.2%	0.82	8			
Heavy manufacturing	−5.5%	0.00	25			
Utilities	−0.4%	0.60	21			
Construction	0.0%	0.86	13			
Trade services	−0.1%	0.75	15			
Hotels and restaurants	0.0%	0.97	10			
Transport services	0.1%	0.47	11			
Telecommunications	0.0%	0.97	6			
Financial intermediation	−0.1%	0.60	14			
Real estate, renting, and business activities	0.0%	0.72	11			
Public administration and defense	0.0%	0.65	13			
Education, health, and social work	0.0%	0.59	10			
Other personal services	0.0%	0.51	12			
Changes in output due to import substitution on domestic final demand	**−0.7%**	**0.30**	**21**	▲	–	–
Agriculture, hunting, forestry, and fishing	−0.3%	0.46	15			
Mining and quarrying	−1.0%	0.00	25			
Light manufacturing	−2.0%	0.42	24			
Heavy manufacturing	−3.4%	0.07	24			
Utilities	−0.9%	0.00	25			
Construction	−0.1%	0.64	21			
Trade services	−0.5%	0.69	22			
Hotels and restaurants	−0.1%	0.54	14			
Transport services	−1.1%	0.51	23			
Telecommunications	−0.8%	0.41	22			
Financial intermediation	−0.2%	0.72	16			
Real estate, renting, and business activities	−0.2%	0.47	17			
Public administration and defense	−0.1%	0.30	22			
Education, health, and social work	0.0%	0.86	18			
Other personal services	−0.1%	0.92	13			

STRENGTH OF LINKAGES

Demand-side Linkages

Direct backward linkage	**0.34**	**0.36**	**12**	▲	**0.7**	**0.31**
Agriculture, hunting, forestry, and fishing	0.23	0.29	16		0.7	0.21
Mining and quarrying	0.15	0.25	16		1.8	0.14
Light manufacturing	0.54	0.70	11		−0.6	0.56
Heavy manufacturing	0.34	0.25	19		−2.2	0.41
Utilities	0.46	0.55	5		5.8	0.32
Construction	0.31	0.07	22		−1.0	0.33
Trade services	0.22	0.19	17		3.9	0.18
Hotels and restaurants	0.62	0.97	2		2.1	0.56
Transport services	0.08	0.05	24		−1.0	0.17
Telecommunications	0.53	0.94	2		2.3	0.42

continued on next page

Nepal 3.7A *continued*

	Value (2018)	Score (0–1)	Rank (out of 25)	Distance to subregional average	10–year average growth rate (%)	10–year mean value
Financial intermediation	0.20	0.18	17		3.7	0.19
Real estate, renting, and business activities	0.34	0.76	5		1.4	0.30
Public administration and defense	0.33	0.60	9		8.2	0.29
Education, health, and social work	0.31	0.57	6		2.5	0.28
Other personal services	0.36	0.67	8		4.2	0.27
Total backward linkage	**1.50**	**0.19**	**13**	▲	**0.1**	**1.45**
Agriculture, hunting, forestry, and fishing	1.34	0.22	16		0.0	1.30
Mining and quarrying	1.24	0.19	16		–0.2	1.21
Light manufacturing	1.80	0.38	13		–0.4	1.80
Heavy manufacturing	1.51	0.11	18		–1.1	1.63
Utilities	1.69	0.29	7		1.9	1.46
Construction	1.50	0.05	20		–0.6	1.52
Trade services	1.30	0.20	18		0.1	1.25
Hotels and restaurants	1.92	0.55	7		0.9	1.80
Transport services	1.12	0.04	24		–1.4	1.23
Telecommunications	1.81	0.71	3		0.9	1.61
Financial intermediation	1.31	0.06	15		0.4	1.28
Real estate, renting, and business activities	1.51	0.44	6		0.1	1.45
Public administration and defense	1.49	0.50	9		0.4	1.43
Education, health, and social work	1.44	0.30	8		0.2	1.39
Other personal services	1.55	0.43	8		1.2	1.40
Normalized backward linkage	–	–	–	▬	–	–
Agriculture, hunting, forestry, and fishing	0.89	0.25	17		0.0	0.89
Mining and quarrying	0.82	0.30	19		–0.3	0.84
Light manufacturing	1.20	0.57	15		–0.4	1.24
Heavy manufacturing	1.01	0.18	21		–1.2	1.12
Utilities	1.12	0.42	8		1.9	1.01
Construction	1.00	0.08	21		–0.7	1.05
Trade services	0.87	0.25	20		–0.1	0.86
Hotels and restaurants	1.28	0.86	3		1.1	1.24
Transport services	0.75	0.00	25		–1.7	0.85
Telecommunications	1.20	1.00	1		0.8	1.11
Financial intermediation	0.87	0.09	16		0.5	0.88
Real estate, renting, and business activities	1.00	0.71	3		0.0	1.00
Public administration and defense	1.00	0.61	8		–0.1	0.98
Education, health, and social work	0.96	0.70	6		0.0	0.96
Other personal services	1.03	0.69	6		1.2	0.96
Net backward linkage	**0.97**	**0.73**	**6**	▲	**–0.1**	**0.97**
Agriculture, hunting, forestry, and fishing	0.95	0.84	4		0.0	0.98
Mining and quarrying	0.32	0.22	14		4.7	0.29
Light manufacturing	0.86	0.30	20		–1.8	0.97
Heavy manufacturing	0.46	0.00	25		–2.4	0.55
Utilities	0.37	0.16	16		–1.0	0.40
Construction	1.27	0.26	17		0.1	1.28
Trade services	0.96	0.54	3		2.2	0.86

continued on next page

Nepal 3.7A *continued*

	Value (2018)	Score (0–1)	Rank (out of 25)	Distance to subregional average	10–year average growth rate (%)	10–year mean value
Hotels and restaurants	1.38	0.60	11		0.8	1.38
Transport services	0.67	0.20	21		−2.4	0.78
Telecommunications	1.06	0.80	2		−0.8	1.08
Financial intermediation	1.08	1.00	1		0.8	1.08
Real estate, renting, and business activities	0.92	0.86	5		1.1	0.84
Public administration and defense	1.47	0.54	8		0.4	1.41
Education, health, and social work	1.37	0.35	9		0.2	1.32
Other personal services	1.47	1.00	1		1.3	1.33
Growth equalized output multipliers	**0.10**	**0.09**	**19**	▼	**−0.2**	**0.09**
Agriculture, hunting, forestry, and fishing	0.35	1.00	1		−0.1	0.37
Mining and quarrying	0.01	0.01	19		−0.3	0.01
Light manufacturing	0.15	0.24	15		−1.8	0.15
Heavy manufacturing	0.05	0.05	19		−1.8	0.05
Utilities	0.02	0.05	20		−0.9	0.02
Construction	0.13	0.18	11		0.4	0.13
Trade services	0.17	0.35	14		1.3	0.15
Hotels and restaurants	0.04	0.07	12		2.9	0.04
Transport services	0.11	0.56	10		−2.0	0.12
Telecommunications	0.04	0.46	7		0.4	0.03
Financial intermediation	0.05	0.15	14		0.6	0.05
Real estate, renting, and business activities	0.14	0.50	8		0.8	0.12
Public administration and defense	0.03	0.08	23		2.4	0.03
Education, health, and social work	0.11	0.73	3		1.0	0.10
Other personal services	0.05	0.24	7		0.8	0.04
Supply-Side Linkages						
Direct forward linkage	**0.35**	**0.23**	**17**	▼	**0.5**	**0.33**
Agriculture, hunting, forestry, and fishing	0.29	0.17	22		2.0	0.24
Mining and quarrying	0.74	0.75	9		−1.1	0.76
Light manufacturing	0.52	0.61	6		1.9	0.46
Heavy manufacturing	0.69	0.93	2		1.5	0.66
Utilities	0.78	0.84	6		1.8	0.73
Construction	0.15	0.31	12		−0.9	0.16
Trade services	0.26	0.24	23		−3.7	0.31
Hotels and restaurants	0.28	0.52	10		1.0	0.23
Transport services	0.40	0.43	14		2.3	0.36
Telecommunications	0.41	0.35	19		4.5	0.33
Financial intermediation	0.17	0.00	25		3.9	0.16
Real estate, renting, and business activities	0.39	0.29	15		−0.8	0.42
Public administration and defense	0.02	0.08	17		3.1	0.02
Education, health, and social work	0.05	0.17	11		0.4	0.05
Other personal services	0.05	0.03	23		5.7	0.05
Total forward linkage	**1.51**	**0.11**	**18**	▼	**0.0**	**1.48**
Agriculture, hunting, forestry, and fishing	1.44	0.12	21		0.2	1.35
Mining and quarrying	2.10	0.36	9		−0.7	2.12
Light manufacturing	1.77	0.33	7		0.7	1.66

continued on next page

Nepal **3.7A** *continued*

	Value (2018)	Score (0–1)	Rank (out of 25)	Distance to subregional average	10-year average growth rate (%)	10-year mean value
Heavy manufacturing	2.12	0.54	2		0.6	2.08
Utilities	2.16	0.37	15		0.9	2.05
Construction	1.23	0.26	11		−0.7	1.25
Trade services	1.39	0.15	22		−1.4	1.46
Hotels and restaurants	1.38	0.31	12		0.2	1.32
Transport services	1.57	0.22	15		0.4	1.51
Telecommunications	1.58	0.24	21		1.1	1.46
Financial intermediation	1.23	0.00	25		−0.2	1.22
Real estate, renting, and business activities	1.56	0.19	16		−0.5	1.58
Public administration and defense	1.02	0.06	18		0.0	1.02
Education, health, and social work	1.06	0.19	12		−0.1	1.07
Other personal services	1.07	0.03	23		−0.2	1.07
Normalized forward linkage	–	–	–		–	–
Agriculture, hunting, forestry, and fishing	0.95	0.17	21		0.1	0.91
Mining and quarrying	1.40	0.67	9		−0.7	1.46
Light manufacturing	1.18	0.76	8		0.7	1.15
Heavy manufacturing	1.41	0.92	3		0.5	1.43
Utilities	1.44	0.68	13		0.8	1.41
Construction	0.82	0.37	11		−0.8	0.86
Trade services	0.93	0.16	23		−1.5	1.00
Hotels and restaurants	0.92	0.43	11		0.2	0.91
Transport services	1.04	0.33	17		0.3	1.04
Telecommunications	1.05	0.23	20		0.9	1.01
Financial intermediation	0.82	0.00	25		−0.4	0.84
Real estate, renting, and business activities	1.04	0.27	15		−0.6	1.09
Public administration and defense	0.68	0.41	15		0.1	0.70
Education, health, and social work	0.71	0.57	12		0.0	0.73
Other personal services	0.71	0.03	24		−0.1	0.73
Net forward linkage	**0.75**	**0.26**	**20**	▼	**−1.2**	**0.81**
Agriculture, hunting, forestry, and fishing	0.99	0.33	16		−0.2	0.99
Mining and quarrying	1.54	0.68	7		−0.6	1.62
Light manufacturing	0.46	0.32	16		0.0	0.46
Heavy manufacturing	0.46	0.48	16		0.2	0.48
Utilities	0.73	0.33	18		−4.4	1.02
Construction	0.55	0.72	8		−0.8	0.58
Trade services	1.04	0.45	16		−1.5	1.15
Hotels and restaurants	0.37	0.04	24		−2.8	0.45
Transport services	0.77	0.38	8		0.4	0.78
Telecommunications	0.58	0.08	24		−1.3	0.70
Financial intermediation	0.87	0.11	23		−0.8	0.89
Real estate, renting, and business activities	0.93	0.19	24		−1.0	1.02
Public administration and defense	0.61	0.43	18		2.1	0.65
Education, health, and social work	0.66	0.36	19		0.1	0.71
Other personal services	0.62	0.21	24		−1.9	0.73

continued on next page

Nepal 3.7A *continued*

	Value (2018)	Score (0–1)	Rank (out of 25)	Distance to subregional average	10–year average growth rate (%)	10–year mean value
Growth equalized input multipliers	**0.09**	**0.07**	**20**	▼	**−0.3**	**0.09**
Agriculture, hunting, forestry, and fishing	0.44	0.90	2		0.2	0.44
Mining and quarrying	0.01	0.02	19		−0.5	0.01
Light manufacturing	0.08	0.22	17		−1.3	0.08
Heavy manufacturing	0.03	0.05	22		−1.2	0.03
Utilities	0.02	0.06	22		−5.1	0.03
Construction	0.09	0.14	10		0.2	0.09
Trade services	0.22	0.43	16		0.1	0.21
Hotels and restaurants	0.02	0.04	21		2.0	0.02
Transport services	0.11	0.59	8		−1.2	0.11
Telecommunications	0.03	0.13	14		−0.8	0.03
Financial intermediation	0.06	0.07	22		0.5	0.05
Real estate, renting, and business activities	0.16	0.34	12		0.3	0.15
Public administration and defense	0.02	0.06	23		2.0	0.02
Education, health, and social work	0.09	0.72	4		0.6	0.09
Other personal services	0.04	0.22	13		−0.7	0.04

Impacts from Hypothetical Extraction

	Value (2018)	Score (0–1)	Rank (out of 25)	Distance to subregional average	10–year average growth rate (%)	10–year mean value
Changes in gross output due to hypothetical extraction	**−9.1%**	**0.81**	**13**	▲	**−0.1**	**−0.09**
Agriculture, hunting, forestry, and fishing	−29.2%	0.00	25		0.2	−31.4
Mining and quarrying	−0.6%	0.99	7		−0.3	−0.6
Light manufacturing	−15.4%	0.68	11		−2.0	−16.2
Heavy manufacturing	−3.8%	0.93	7		−2.5	−4.3
Utilities	−2.6%	0.92	8		1.1	−2.1
Construction	−13.8%	0.74	15		0.0	−13.5
Trade services	−14.8%	0.72	16		1.6	−13.4
Hotels and restaurants	−5.3%	0.90	18		3.6	−4.4
Transport services	−8.5%	0.57	15		−3.0	−9.9
Telecommunications	−4.6%	0.23	21		1.5	−3.6
Financial intermediation	−4.6%	0.82	14		1.3	−4.3
Real estate, renting, and business activities	−13.4%	0.32	21		0.9	−11.7
Public administration and defense	−3.4%	0.87	3		4.0	−3.1
Education, health, and social work	−10.9%	0.15	24		1.5	−9.9
Other personal services	−4.9%	0.75	20		2.2	−4.4

Impacts from Hypothetical Insertion

	Value (2018)	Score (0–1)	Rank (out of 25)	Distance to subregional average	10–year average growth rate (%)	10–year mean value
Changes in gross output due to hypothetical insertion	**3.0%**	**0.10**	**19**	▼	**0.5**	**0.03**
Agriculture, hunting, forestry, and fishing	8.3%	0.32	2		0.7	7.8
Mining and quarrying	0.1%	0.01	20		3.7	0.1
Light manufacturing	8.1%	0.23	15		−2.3	8.6
Heavy manufacturing	1.7%	0.02	19		−4.0	2.2
Utilities	1.1%	0.11	16		5.8	0.7
Construction	4.6%	0.11	18		−0.3	4.7
Trade services	3.5%	0.18	15		7.5	2.7
Hotels and restaurants	2.6%	0.15	9		4.8	2.0
Transport services	1.0%	0.07	23		−0.3	2.0
Telecommunications	2.1%	0.60	4		3.8	1.4
Financial intermediation	1.1%	0.07	14		4.9	0.9

continued on next page

Nepal 3.7A *continued*

	Value (2018)	Score (0–1)	Rank (out of 25)	Distance to subregional average	10–year average growth rate (%)	10–year mean value
Real estate, renting, and business activities	4.9%	0.72	4		3.2	3.8
Public administration and defense	1.1%	0.26	19		19.7	0.9
Education, health, and social work	3.4%	0.63	4		6.4	2.8
Other personal services	1.8%	0.23	6		5.8	1.3

SPREAD OF ECONOMIC LINKAGES

Demand-side

	Value (2018)	Score (0–1)	Rank (out of 25)	Distance to subregional average	10–year average growth rate (%)	10–year mean value
Relative evenness of direct backward linkage	0.45	0.48	11	▼	3.8	0.44
Relative evenness of total backward linkage	0.15	0.13	11	▼	2.3	0.14
		0.00				
Backward measure of concentration based on input coefficients	0.90	0.60	13	▲	0.1	0.90
Agriculture, hunting, forestry, and fishing	0.91	0.81	12		0.0	0.92
Mining and quarrying	0.89	0.31	19		0.3	0.88
Light manufacturing	0.87	0.46	20		–0.2	0.88
Heavy manufacturing	0.79	0.70	18		–0.7	0.82
Utilities	0.95	0.91	5		0.0	0.95
Construction	0.87	0.77	20		–0.2	0.88
Trade services	0.87	0.46	23		0.1	0.86
Hotels and restaurants	0.88	0.67	18		0.0	0.89
Transport services	0.95	0.82	5		0.2	0.94
Telecommunications	0.93	0.73	12		0.0	0.93
Financial intermediation	0.90	0.91	13		0.5	0.88
Real estate, renting, and business activities	0.92	0.84	20		0.8	0.87
Public administration and defense	0.91	0.42	23		–0.2	0.91
Education, health, and social work	0.94	0.63	17		0.1	0.94
Other personal services	0.95	0.90	13		0.1	0.94
Relative evenness of direct forward linkage	0.72	0.69	5	▲	1.0	0.74
Relative evenness of total forward linkage	0.25	0.20	13	▼	0.7	0.25
Forward measure of concentration based on output coefficients	0.65	0.51	16	▲	–0.1	0.65
Agriculture, hunting, forestry, and fishing	0.60	0.97	2		0.7	0.57
Mining and quarrying	0.33	0.45	18		–0.2	0.33
Light manufacturing	0.73	0.78	8		0.8	0.69
Heavy manufacturing	0.63	0.56	14		0.3	0.61
Utilities	0.91	1.00	1		0.0	0.91
Construction	0.14	0.16	23		–5.5	0.22
Trade services	0.79	0.77	7		0.3	0.77
Hotels and restaurants	0.80	0.72	10		–0.1	0.81
Transport services	0.81	0.84	5		–0.2	0.84
Telecommunications	0.82	0.62	14		–0.1	0.84
Financial intermediation	0.69	0.73	19		1.5	0.68
Real estate, renting, and business activities	0.82	0.67	14		–0.4	0.83
Public administration and defense	0.48	0.53	17		–1.0	0.50
Education, health, and social work	0.65	0.71	9		–0.3	0.67
Other personal services	0.50	0.08	23		–0.5	0.54

continued on next page

Nepal 3.7A *continued*

	Value (2018)	Score (0–1)	Rank (out of 25)	Distance to subregional average	10–year average growth rate (%)	10–year mean value
SENSITIVITY OF ECONOMIC LINKAGES						
Economic Complexity						
Percentage intermediate transaction	0.31	0.15	19	▼	0.1	0.29
Average output multiplier	1.50	0.19	13	▲	0.1	1.45
Average of Leontief inverse	0.19	0.15	16	▼	0.0	0.18
Average technical coefficient	0.02	0.36	12	▲	0.7	0.02
Mean intermediate coefficient	0.34	0.36	12	▲	0.7	0.31
Percentage of above-average coefficients (%)	0.25	0.24	18	▼	0.5	0.25
Determinant of non-competitive Leontief inverse	2.12	0.03	21	▼	–0.1	2.09
Determinant of competitive Leontief inverse	3.93	0.03	17	▼	0.2	3.70
Mean path length	1.44	0.09	19	▼	–0.2	1.41
Cycling index	0.06	0.13	21	▼	–0.4	0.06
Average propagation length	1.82	0.34	9	▲	–0.1	1.78
Overall sensitivity of the economy	0.76	0.66	9	▲	–0.1	0.76
Index of direct interrelatedness	0.55	0.26	16	▼	–0.2	0.55
Index of indirect interrelatedness	0.22	1.00	1	▲	0.3	0.21
Global intensity index	22.52	0.19	13	▲	0.1	21.78

Note: The scores of the economy in focus are shown in the horizontal bars with labels. The colored dots represent the indicator performance of the economy in focus compared to other economies in the region. The highest rank among economies is 1 while the lowest rank is 25. The indicators shown in the chart are selected from a broader set of indicators (see the technical appendix for more details).

Source: Asian Development Bank Multi-Regional Input–Output Database. https://mrio.adbx.online/ (accessed 4 August 2020).

3.7B External Linkages

$ = United States dollars, GVC = global value chain.

Note: The scores of the economy in focus are shown in the horizontal bars with labels. The colored dots represent the indicator performance of the economy in focus compared to other economies in the region. The highest rank among economies is 1, while the lowest rank is 25. The indicators shown in the chart are selected from a broader set of indicators (see the technical appendix for more details).

Source: Asian Development Bank Multi-Regional Input–Output Database. https://mrio.adbx.online/ (accessed 4 August 2020).

	Value (2018)	Score (0–1)	Rank (out of 25)	Distance to subregional average	10-year average growth rate (%)	10-year mean value
PARTICIPATION IN GLOBAL VALUE CHAINS						
International Trade Coefficients						
Trade openness	0.51	0.12	18	▼	3.5	0.41
Self-sufficiency ratio	0.79	0.00	25	▼	−1.2	0.84
Regional supply percentage	0.76	0.47	12	▼	−1.0	0.81
Regional purchase coefficient	0.86	0.77	8	▲	−0.2	0.87
Sectoral purchase coefficient	0.88	0.90	11	▲	−0.2	0.89
Simple location quotient of gross output	1.32	0.68	4	▲	−0.1	1.32
Fabrication effect	0.98	0.64	9	▲	1.3	0.87
Exports ($)	1,434	0.00	24	▼	4.4	1,193
Export-to-output ratio	0.06	0.09	21	▼	−1.2	0.06
Agriculture, hunting, forestry, and fishing	0.01	0.01	23		7.2	0.01
Mining and quarrying	0.02	0.02	20		6.1	0.02
Light manufacturing	0.06	0.05	24		−4.9	0.07
Heavy manufacturing	0.07	0.06	23		−2.9	0.08
Utilities	0.01	0.01	11		−3.9	0.01
Construction	0.01	0.17	10		4.6	0.02
Trade services	0.04	0.05	21		7.4	0.04
Hotels and restaurants	0.01	0.01	17		10.7	0.02
Transport services	0.10	0.12	20		−0.3	0.10
Telecommunications	0.07	0.19	16		0.5	0.07

continued on next page

Nepal 3.7B *continued*

		Value (2018)	Score (0–1)	Rank (out of 25)	Distance to subregional average	10-year average growth rate (%)	10-year mean value
Financial intermediation		0.00	0.00	25		–4.0	0.00
Real estate, renting, and business activities		0.00	0.00	24		–3.6	0.01
Public administration and defense		0.19	0.47	2		3.7	0.20
Education, health, and social work		0.00	0.02	19		–2.1	0.00
Other personal services		0.26	0.32	4		–0.5	0.29
Imports	($)	**11,159**	**0.00**	**18**	▼	**13.6**	**6,500**
Import-to-input ratio		**0.11**	**0.44**	**12**	▲	**3.0**	**0.10**
Agriculture, hunting, forestry, and fishing		0.05	0.13	17		2.2	0.04
Mining and quarrying		0.09	0.21	12		2.2	0.08
Light manufacturing		0.14	0.24	11		2.6	0.13
Heavy manufacturing		0.31	0.40	8		2.2	0.28
Utilities		0.15	0.22	14		2.9	0.14
Construction		0.18	0.39	10		1.8	0.17
Trade services		0.02	0.09	21		1.7	0.02
Hotels and restaurants		0.09	0.26	11		5.1	0.07
Transport services		0.35	0.69	3		4.8	0.27
Telecommunications		0.07	0.17	15		2.3	0.07
Financial intermediation		0.06	0.29	5		11.6	0.06
Real estate, renting, and business activities		0.04	0.21	16		1.7	0.04
Public administration and defense		0.06	0.36	12		20.8	0.06
Education, health, and social work		0.05	0.23	16		3.1	0.04
Other personal services		0.03	0.08	19		1.2	0.03
Total foreign factor content of consumption	($)	**2,122**	**0.00**	**18**	▼	**8.7**	**1,480**
Total foreign factor content of investment	($)	**1,307**	**0.00**	**17**	▼	**14.5**	**690**
Total foreign factor content of exports	($)	**281**	**0.00**	**24**	▼	**6.7**	**200**
Interregional Multipliers							
Import Leakage Effects		**0.18**	**0.36**	**14**	▲	**2.4**	**0.15**
Agriculture, hunting, forestry, and fishing		0.09	0.16	18		2.0	0.07
Mining and quarrying		0.11	0.24	13		1.7	0.10
Light manufacturing		0.22	0.29	14		1.9	0.20
Heavy manufacturing		0.42	0.48	9		1.0	0.39
Utilities		0.23	0.30	15		4.2	0.19
Construction		0.26	0.36	14		1.2	0.24
Trade services		0.08	0.14	16		3.1	0.06
Hotels and restaurants		0.17	0.37	13		4.9	0.14
Transport services		0.36	0.52	6		3.4	0.29
Telecommunications		0.16	0.26	12		2.9	0.14
Financial intermediation		0.10	0.26	8		7.8	0.09
Real estate, renting, and business activities		0.11	0.35	12		1.5	0.10
Public administration and defense		0.11	0.33	11		8.0	0.10
Education, health, and social work		0.10	0.36	17		2.5	0.08
Other personal services		0.10	0.22	15		4.5	0.08
Intraregional transfer multiplier		**1.50**	**0.19**	**13**	▲	**0.1**	**1.45**
Agriculture, hunting, forestry, and fishing		1.34	0.22	16		0.0	1.30
Mining and quarrying		1.24	0.19	16		–0.2	1.21

continued on next page

Nepal 3.7B *continued*

	Value (2018)	Score (0–1)	Rank (out of 25)	Distance to subregional average	10–year average growth rate (%)	10–year mean value
Light manufacturing	1.80	0.38	13		−0.4	1.80
Heavy manufacturing	1.51	0.11	18		−1.1	1.63
Utilities	1.69	0.29	7		1.9	1.46
Construction	1.50	0.05	20		−0.6	1.52
Trade services	1.30	0.20	18		0.1	1.25
Hotels and restaurants	1.92	0.55	7		0.9	1.80
Transport services	1.12	0.04	24		−1.4	1.23
Telecommunications	1.81	0.71	3		0.9	1.61
Financial intermediation	1.31	0.06	15		0.4	1.28
Real estate, renting, and business activities	1.51	0.44	6		0.1	1.45
Public administration and defense	1.49	0.50	9		0.4	1.43
Education, health, and social work	1.44	0.30	8		0.2	1.39
Other personal services	1.55	0.43	8		1.2	1.40
Interregional spillover multiplier	**1.30**	**0.53**	**11**	▲	**0.5**	**1.26**
Agriculture, hunting, forestry, and fishing	1.14	0.19	15		0.2	1.11
Mining and quarrying	1.24	0.27	11		0.3	1.21
Light manufacturing	1.36	0.28	10		0.6	1.32
Heavy manufacturing	1.87	0.58	7		0.9	1.77
Utilities	1.42	0.30	11		0.8	1.40
Construction	1.49	0.48	9		0.5	1.45
Trade services	1.05	0.10	21		−0.1	1.05
Hotels and restaurants	1.20	0.25	11		0.6	1.17
Transport services	1.96	0.84	3		2.0	1.73
Telecommunications	1.16	0.17	15		0.1	1.17
Financial intermediation	1.16	0.41	4		0.6	1.15
Real estate, renting, and business activities	1.11	0.31	15		0.1	1.10
Public administration and defense	1.15	0.32	11		0.6	1.14
Education, health, and social work	1.14	0.29	15		0.3	1.11
Other personal services	1.09	0.08	19		0.1	1.08
Interregional feedback multiplier	**1.000**	**0.00**	**24**	▼	**0.0**	**1.00**
Agriculture, hunting, forestry, and fishing	1.000	0.00	24		0.0	1.00
Mining and quarrying	1.000	0.00	21		0.0	1.00
Light manufacturing	1.000	0.00	24		0.0	1.00
Heavy manufacturing	1.000	0.00	23		0.0	1.00
Utilities	1.000	0.00	24		0.0	1.00
Construction	1.000	0.00	24		0.0	1.00
Trade services	1.000	0.00	24		0.0	1.00
Hotels and restaurants	1.000	0.00	24		0.0	1.00
Transport services	1.000	0.00	24		0.0	1.00
Telecommunications	1.000	0.00	24		0.0	1.00
Financial intermediation	1.000	0.00	22		0.0	1.00
Real estate, renting, and business activities	1.000	0.00	24		0.0	1.00
Public administration and defense	1.000	0.00	23		0.0	1.00
Education, health, and social work	1.000	0.00	24		0.0	1.00
Other personal services	1.000	0.00	25		0.0	1.00

continued on next page

Nepal 3.7B *continued*

	Value (2018)	Score (0–1)	Rank (out of 25)	Distance to subregional average	10–year average growth rate (%)	10–year mean value
Global Value Chain (GVC) Participation Index						
Backward GVC Participation	14.7%	0.17	16	▼	1.5	0.13
Simple GVCs	10.7%	0.42	13	▲	2.5	0.09
Agriculture, hunting, forestry, and fishing	1.7	0.66	2		2.3	1.48
Mining and quarrying	0.0	0.11	12		8.9	0.01
Light manufacturing	1.1	0.21	15		0.0	1.10
Heavy manufacturing	0.4	0.06	16		2.9	0.35
Utilities	0.1	0.06	20		1.9	0.08
Construction	2.2	0.17	15		2.9	1.84
Trade services	0.7	0.27	11		7.0	0.45
Hotels and restaurants	0.4	0.21	12		6.8	0.30
Transport services	1.6	1.00	1		2.4	1.36
Telecommunications	0.2	0.25	8		2.4	0.21
Financial intermediation	0.3	0.30	5		9.4	0.26
Real estate, renting, and business activities	0.7	0.42	9		3.5	0.50
Public administration and defense	0.2	0.06	20		13.5	0.19
Education, health, and social work	0.8	0.46	13		5.0	0.60
Other personal services	0.3	0.21	13		8.5	0.17
Complex GVCs	4.0%	0.05	19	▼	−0.3	0.04
Agriculture, hunting, forestry, and fishing	0.6	0.53	5		0.9	0.56
Mining and quarrying	0.0	0.03	15		5.4	0.01
Light manufacturing	0.5	0.03	21		−3.1	0.51
Heavy manufacturing	0.2	0.01	21		−2.2	0.23
Utilities	0.0	0.05	21		−0.3	0.03
Construction	0.8	0.14	15		0.6	0.73
Trade services	0.2	0.03	14		6.1	0.18
Hotels and restaurants	0.1	0.01	17		5.5	0.10
Transport services	0.7	0.31	5		−1.7	0.70
Telecommunications	0.1	0.14	11		1.2	0.07
Financial intermediation	0.1	0.09	5		7.0	0.10
Real estate, renting, and business activities	0.3	0.29	6		1.7	0.20
Public administration and defense	0.1	0.07	20		14.1	0.07
Education, health, and social work	0.3	0.34	10		2.3	0.23
Other personal services	0.1	0.24	10		5.2	0.08
Forward GVC Participation	3.6%	0.00	25	▼	−1.7	0.04
Simple GVCs	2.7%	0.00	24	▼	−1.7	0.03
Agriculture, hunting, forestry, and fishing	0.3	0.15	18		−3.7	0.32
Mining and quarrying	0.0	0.00	22		−4.5	0.01
Light manufacturing	0.2	0.03	24		−3.5	0.17
Heavy manufacturing	0.1	0.01	22		−3.7	0.10
Utilities	0.0	0.00	22		−1.2	0.04
Construction	0.1	0.01	13		4.9	0.08
Trade services	0.3	0.03	24		−1.6	0.40
Hotels and restaurants	0.0	0.00	20		11.1	0.03
Transport services	0.5	0.11	16		0.0	0.49
Telecommunications	0.1	0.05	17		−0.3	0.10

continued on next page

Nepal 3.7B *continued*

	Value (2018)	Score (0–1)	Rank (out of 25)	Distance to subregional average	10–year average growth rate (%)	10–year mean value
Financial intermediation	0.0	0.00	25		8.3	0.04
Real estate, renting, and business activities	0.1	0.01	24		2.0	0.15
Public administration and defense	0.2	0.20	4		7.1	0.23
Education, health, and social work	0.0	0.10	12		27.1	0.03
Other personal services	0.6	1.00	1		1.7	0.68
Complex GVCs	**0.9%**	**0.00**	**25**	▼	**–1.9**	**0.01**
Agriculture, hunting, forestry, and fishing	0.1	0.05	21		–2.4	0.09
Mining and quarrying	0.0	0.00	22		–5.6	0.00
Light manufacturing	0.1	0.01	24		0.0	0.05
Heavy manufacturing	0.0	0.00	24		–2.4	0.03
Utilities	0.0	0.00	24		2.1	0.02
Construction	0.0	0.01	15		8.3	0.03
Trade services	0.2	0.04	24		–1.3	0.21
Hotels and restaurants	0.0	0.00	24		11.9	0.01
Transport services	0.2	0.06	19		–1.9	0.17
Telecommunications	0.0	0.04	22		0.5	0.04
Financial intermediation	0.0	0.00	25		4.5	0.01
Real estate, renting, and business activities	0.0	0.00	24		2.4	0.06
Public administration and defense	0.1	0.20	4		6.0	0.11
Education, health, and social work	0.0	0.04	20		23.9	0.01
Other personal services	0.1	0.65	5		–2.5	0.17

SPECIALIZATION IN GLOBAL VALUE CHAINS

Vertical Specialization

Vertical Specialization Ratio	**19.6%**	**0.26**	**15**	▲	**1.9**	**0.17**
Agriculture, hunting, forestry, and fishing	8.7%	0.16	18		2.0	0.07
Mining and quarrying	11.3%	0.24	13		1.7	0.10
Light manufacturing	22.2%	0.29	14		1.9	0.20
Heavy manufacturing	42.0%	0.48	9		1.0	0.39
Utilities	23.4%	0.37	15		4.2	0.19
Construction	25.8%	0.36	14		1.2	0.24
Trade services	7.6%	0.14	16		3.1	0.06
Hotels and restaurants	17.1%	0.36	13		4.9	0.14
Transport services	36.5%	0.52	6		3.4	0.29
Telecommunications	16.1%	0.26	12		2.9	0.14
Financial intermediation	9.7%	0.26	9		7.8	0.09
Real estate, renting, and business activities	11.0%	0.35	12		1.5	0.10
Public administration and defense	11.3%	0.33	11		8.0	0.10
Education, health, and social work	10.1%	0.36	17		2.5	0.08
Other personal services	10.5%	0.22	15		4.5	0.08

Revealed Comparative Advantages

Traditional RCA Index						
Agriculture, hunting, forestry, and fishing	2.13	0.36	7	▼	–3.2	2.86
Mining and quarrying	0.03	0.00	18	▼	3.0	0.03
Light manufacturing	1.00	0.17	13	▼	–1.8	1.14

continued on next page

Nepal 3.7B *continued*

	Value (2018)	Score (0–1)	Rank (out of 25)	Distance to subregional average	10–year average growth rate (%)	10–year mean value
Heavy manufacturing	0.13	0.07	16	▼	−2.0	0.14
Utilities	0.63	0.01	6	▼	−2.3	0.91
Construction	4.86	0.61	4	▲	−6.3	7.58
Trade services	1.46	0.19	7	▲	−0.8	1.33
Hotels and restaurants	0.78	0.01	12	▼	−0.6	0.81
Transport services	3.36	0.79	2	▲	0.4	3.15
Telecommunications	5.97	1.00	1	▲	2.3	5.17
Financial intermediation	0.02	0.00	25	▼	0.1	0.04
Real estate, renting, and business activities	0.09	0.03	18	▼	1.7	0.18
Public administration and defense	27.47	1.00	1	▲	−0.2	26.56
Education, health, and social work	0.65	0.08	8	▼	1.2	1.18
Other personal services	17.38	1.00	1	▲	−0.9	17.04

New RCA Index (Based on Domestic Value Added)

	Value (2018)	Score (0–1)	Rank (out of 25)	Distance to subregional average	10–year average growth rate (%)	10–year mean value
Agriculture, hunting, forestry, and fishing	2.83	0.41	5	▲	−1.9	3.06
Mining and quarrying	0.06	0.01	19	▼	1.9	0.06
Light manufacturing	0.91	0.20	11	▼	−1.6	0.97
Heavy manufacturing	0.16	0.07	16	▼	2.5	0.15
Utilities	0.47	0.03	17	▼	−1.5	0.53
Construction	2.43	0.14	4	▼	0.2	2.73
Trade services	1.21	0.34	12	▲	1.3	1.23
Hotels and restaurants	0.81	0.02	13	▼	2.5	0.80
Transport services	2.70	0.93	2	▲	2.3	2.44
Telecommunications	2.07	0.54	6	▲	2.2	2.01
Financial intermediation	0.17	0.00	25	▼	2.2	0.19
Real estate, renting, and business activities	0.31	0.15	15	▼	1.8	0.34
Public administration and defense	9.53	0.86	2	▲	6.5	9.10
Education, health, and social work	1.08	0.24	5	▼	2.6	1.28
Other personal services	7.49	1.00	1	▲	0.9	8.13

POSITION IN GLOBAL VALUE CHAINS

	Value (2018)	Score (0–1)	Rank (out of 25)	Distance to subregional average	10–year average growth rate (%)	10–year mean value
Upstreamness Index	**1.6**	**0.00**	**24**	▼	**−0.3**	**1.6**
Agriculture, hunting, forestry, and fishing	1.5	0.05	24		0.0	1.4
Mining and quarrying	2.2	0.49	19		−0.9	2.2
Light manufacturing	1.9	0.24	15		0.5	1.7
Heavy manufacturing	2.2	0.34	17		−0.1	2.2
Utilities	2.3	0.18	20		0.8	2.2
Construction	1.3	0.22	13		−0.8	1.3
Trade services	1.5	0.00	25		−1.7	1.6
Hotels and restaurants	1.4	0.27	19		0.1	1.4
Transport services	1.8	0.18	22		0.1	1.7
Telecommunications	1.8	0.08	23		0.8	1.6
Financial intermediation	1.3	0.00	25		−0.4	1.2
Real estate, renting, and business activities	1.6	0.10	21		−0.6	1.6
Public administration and defense	1.3	0.56	4		−0.9	1.4
Education, health, and social work	1.1	0.15	14		−0.1	1.1
Other personal services	1.5	0.25	17		−0.9	1.5

continued on next page

Nepal 3.7B *continued*

	Value (2018)	Score (0–1)	Rank (out of 25)	Distance to subregional average	10–year average growth rate (%)	10–year mean value
PRODUCTION LENGTH OF GLOBAL VALUE CHAINS						
Backward Measures of Average Production Length						
Production Length of Global Value Chain Activity (B)	0.7	0.38	14	▲	2.3	0.6
Agriculture, hunting, forestry, and fishing	0.4	0.17	18		2.1	0.3
Mining and quarrying	0.5	0.27	13		1.6	0.4
Light manufacturing	0.9	0.37	14		1.9	0.8
Heavy manufacturing	1.8	0.62	9		0.8	1.7
Utilities	1.0	0.36	14		4.7	0.8
Construction	1.1	0.35	14		1.0	1.0
Trade services	0.3	0.18	16		3.4	0.3
Hotels and restaurants	0.7	0.39	13		5.2	0.6
Transport services	1.4	0.53	8		2.9	1.1
Telecommunications	0.7	0.34	11		3.2	0.6
Financial intermediation	0.4	0.33	7		6.8	0.4
Real estate, renting, and business activities	0.5	0.45	11		1.6	0.4
Public administration and defense	0.5	0.33	11		5.9	0.4
Education, health, and social work	0.4	0.33	14		2.7	0.4
Other personal services	0.5	0.28	14		5.0	0.3
Forward Measures of Average Production Length						
Production Length of Global Value Chain Activity (F)	0.2	0.05	23	▼	–1.2	0.2
Agriculture, hunting, forestry, and fishing	0.1	0.00	25		–1.9	0.1
Mining and quarrying	0.1	0.03	22		–5.0	0.1
Light manufacturing	0.2	0.00	25		–1.4	0.1
Heavy manufacturing	0.2	0.05	23		–4.6	0.3
Utilities	0.2	0.03	23		4.3	0.2
Construction	0.0	0.04	17		4.0	0.1
Trade services	0.1	0.03	24		–3.1	0.2
Hotels and restaurants	0.1	0.05	23		4.6	0.1
Transport services	0.3	0.09	22		–0.4	0.3
Telecommunications	0.3	0.09	22		1.3	0.3
Financial intermediation	0.0	0.00	25		5.6	0.1
Real estate, renting, and business activities	0.1	0.01	24		0.5	0.1
Public administration and defense	0.5	0.61	4		3.3	0.5
Education, health, and social work	0.0	0.05	19		15.6	0.0
Other personal services	0.7	0.31	6		0.8	0.7

Note: The scores of the economy in focus are shown in the horizontal bars with labels. The colored dots represent the indicator performance of the economy in focus compared to other economies in the region. The highest rank among economies is 1 while the lowest rank is 25. The indicators shown in the chart are selected from a broader set of indicators (see the technical appendix for more details).

Source: Asian Development Bank Multi-Regional Input–Output Database. https://mrio.adbx.online/ (accessed 4 August 2020).

3.8 Pakistan

3.8A Internal Linkages

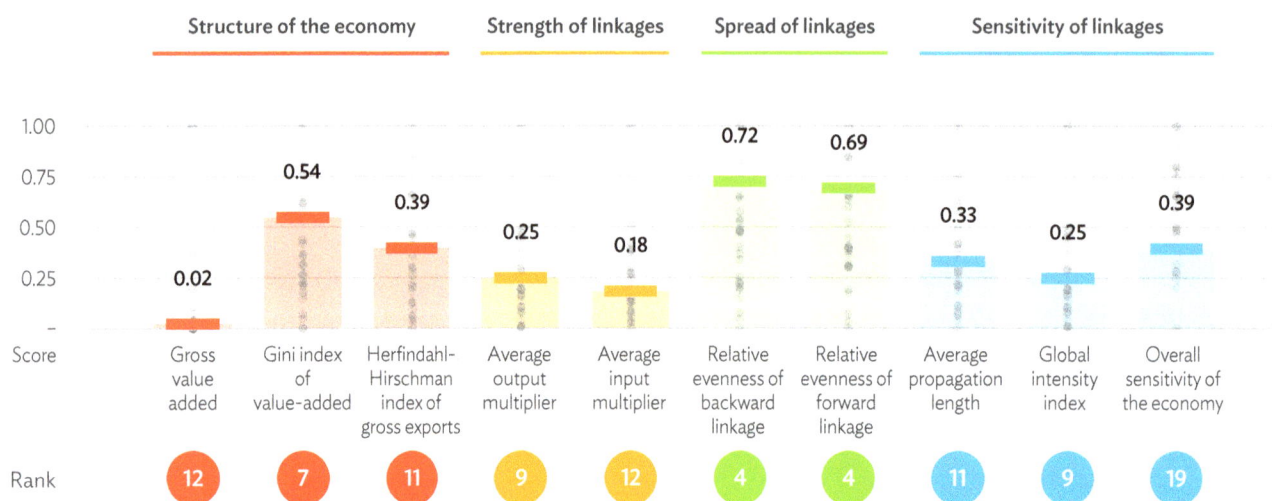

Note: The scores of the economy in focus are shown in the horizontal bars with labels. The colored dots represent the indicator performance of the economy in focus compared to other economies in the region. The highest rank among economies is 1 while the lowest rank is 25. The indicators shown in the chart are selected from a broader set of indicators (see the technical appendix for more details).

Source: Asian Development Bank Multi-Regional Input–Output Database. https://mrio.adbx.online/ (accessed 4 August 2020).

		Value (2018)	Score (0–1)	Rank (out of 25)	Distance to subregional average	10-year average growth rate (%)	10-year mean value
STRUCTURE OF THE ECONOMY							
Economic Indicators							
Gross output	($)	489,307	0.01	13	▼	6.2	404,863
Gross value-added	($)	265,837	0.02	12	▼	6.5	216,974
Value-added content of domestic final demand		243,713	0.02	9		6.6	194,071
Value-added content of exports		22,123	0.01	15		6.9	22,903
Intermediate inputs	($)	214,010	0.01	13	▼	5.7	182,445
Domestic inputs		186,096	0.01	13		5.8	159,538
Foreign inputs		27,914	0.02	13		5.6	22,908
Direct production	($)	303,211	0.02	13	▼	6.6	245,326
Domestic final demand		278,225	0.02	9		6.7	219,728
Exports		24,986	0.01	15		7.0	25,598
Indirect production	($)	186,096	0.01	13	▼	5.8	159,538
Indirect production embedded in domestic final demand		168,132	0.01	10		6.1	140,718
Indirect production embedded in exports		17,964	0.00	15		4.1	18,820
Economic Diversification							
Gross output		0.26	0.33	15	▼	−0.4	0.27
Gini concentration index of gross output		0.45	0.41	14		−0.3	0.46
Herfindahl-Hirschman concentration index of gross output		0.05	0.19	17		−0.8	0.05
Theil concentration index of gross output		0.28	0.30	16		−0.4	0.29

continued on next page

Pakistan **3.8A** *continued*

	Value (2018)	Score (0–1)	Rank (out of 25)	Distance to subregional average	10–year average growth rate (%)	10–year mean value
Gross value-added	**0.30**	**0.46**	**7**	▲	**0.1**	**0.31**
Gini concentration index of gross value added	0.49	0.54	7		0.1	0.50
Herfindahl-Hirschman concentration index of gross value added	0.07	0.28	6		0.2	0.07
Theil concentration index of gross value added	0.34	0.46	7		0.1	0.35
Gross exports	**0.61**	**0.51**	**11**	▲	**0.4**	**0.61**
Gini concentration index of gross exports	0.76	0.63	14		0.0	0.77
Herfindahl-Hirschman concentration index of gross exports	0.34	0.39	11		7.0	0.34
Theil concentration index of gross exports	0.71	0.62	13		0.3	0.71
Structural Changes						
Changes in output due to technological changes	**−0.2%**	**0.73**	**16**	▼	**–**	**–**
Agriculture, hunting, forestry, and fishing	0.2%	0.56	7			
Mining and quarrying	−2.3%	0.72	21			
Light manufacturing	−0.1%	0.37	10			
Heavy manufacturing	−0.8%	0.66	14			
Utilities	0.7%	0.64	8			
Construction	0.1%	0.13	15			
Trade services	−0.4%	0.29	18			
Hotels and restaurants	−0.1%	0.06	18			
Transport services	−0.3%	0.58	14			
Telecommunications	0.1%	0.25	9			
Financial intermediation	−1.2%	0.37	22			
Real estate, renting, and business activities	0.4%	0.70	11			
Public administration and defense	0.0%	0.37	12			
Education, health, and social work	0.1%	0.77	9			
Other personal services	0.4%	0.51	9			
Changes in output due to structural changes in consumption (%)	**5.0%**	**0.51**	**6**	▲	**–**	**–**
Agriculture, hunting, forestry, and fishing	5.3%	0.86	3			
Mining and quarrying	2.4%	0.16	7			
Light manufacturing	4.8%	0.59	6			
Heavy manufacturing	3.6%	0.57	4			
Utilities	4.3%	0.46	9			
Construction	0.1%	0.20	19			
Trade services	5.3%	0.79	3			
Hotels and restaurants	5.0%	0.19	12			
Transport services	3.9%	0.55	7			
Telecommunications	3.5%	0.57	11			
Financial intermediation	1.3%	0.24	24			
Real estate, renting, and business activities	6.9%	0.32	4			
Public administration and defense	11.3%	0.73	4			
Education, health, and social work	9.8%	0.32	5			
Other personal services	7.7%	0.56	8			
Changes in output due to structural changes in investment (%)	**1.0%**	**0.29**	**16**	▼	**–**	**–**
Agriculture, hunting, forestry, and fishing	0.3%	0.11	13			
Mining and quarrying	0.8%	0.20	14			
Light manufacturing	0.4%	0.14	16			

continued on next page

Pakistan 3.8A *continued*

	Value (2018)	Score (0–1)	Rank (out of 25)	Distance to subregional average	10–year average growth rate (%)	10–year mean value
Heavy manufacturing	2.1%	0.32	9			
Utilities	0.3%	0.35	16			
Construction	7.5%	0.48	9			
Trade services	0.5%	0.22	17			
Hotels and restaurants	0.0%	0.31	21			
Transport services	0.3%	0.07	17			
Telecommunications	0.4%	0.16	16			
Financial intermediation	0.5%	0.10	16			
Real estate, renting, and business activities	0.4%	0.23	16			
Public administration and defense	0.0%	0.01	20			
Education, health, and social work	0.0%	0.03	9			
Other personal services	1.1%	0.57	4			
Changes in output due to structural changes in stock (%)	**0.0%**	**0.31**	**11**	▼	–	–
Agriculture, hunting, forestry, and fishing	0.1%	0.55	8			
Mining and quarrying	0.0%	0.38	18			
Light manufacturing	0.0%	0.18	11			
Heavy manufacturing	0.3%	0.49	8			
Utilities	0.0%	0.12	11			
Construction	0.1%	0.79	5			
Trade services	0.0%	0.32	9			
Hotels and restaurants	0.0%	0.45	11			
Transport services	0.0%	0.06	12			
Telecommunications	0.0%	0.48	8			
Financial intermediation	0.0%	0.90	8			
Real estate, renting, and business activities	0.0%	0.16	10			
Public administration and defense	0.0%	0.64	10			
Education, health, and social work	0.0%	0.23	8			
Other personal services	0.0%	0.40	17			
Changes in output due to structural changes in export	**0.2%**	**0.09**	**22**	▼	–	–
Agriculture, hunting, forestry, and fishing	0.3%	0.44	18			
Mining and quarrying	0.3%	0.12	15			
Light manufacturing	0.3%	0.11	20			
Heavy manufacturing	0.2%	0.22	21			
Utilities	0.1%	0.03	23			
Construction	0.0%	0.03	24			
Trade services	0.3%	0.06	22			
Hotels and restaurants	0.0%	0.03	22			
Transport services	0.1%	0.38	21			
Telecommunications	0.1%	0.08	22			
Financial intermediation	0.1%	0.09	20			
Real estate, renting, and business activities	0.2%	0.19	18			
Public administration and defense	0.0%	0.12	19			
Education, health, and social work	0.5%	0.19	5			
Other personal services	0.3%	0.07	21			

continued on next page

Pakistan 3.8A *continued*

	Value (2018)	Score (0–1)	Rank (out of 25)	Distance to subregional average	10–year average growth rate (%)	10–year mean value
Changes in output due to import substitution on intermediate demand	**0.0%**	**0.38**	**12**	▼	–	–
Agriculture, hunting, forestry, and fishing	−0.1%	0.67	12			
Mining and quarrying	0.5%	0.32	10			
Light manufacturing	0.0%	0.81	12			
Heavy manufacturing	−0.1%	0.25	17			
Utilities	0.0%	0.67	12			
Construction	0.0%	0.86	10			
Trade services	0.0%	0.76	11			
Hotels and restaurants	0.0%	0.97	9			
Transport services	0.0%	0.43	15			
Telecommunications	−0.2%	0.93	17			
Financial intermediation	−0.1%	0.57	18			
Real estate, renting, and business activities	0.0%	0.71	12			
Public administration and defense	0.0%	0.66	7			
Education, health, and social work	0.0%	0.59	14			
Other personal services	−0.2%	0.42	19			
Changes in output due to import substitution on domestic final demand	**−0.1%**	**0.71**	**14**	▼	–	–
Agriculture, hunting, forestry, and fishing	−0.1%	0.53	12			
Mining and quarrying	−0.3%	0.32	23			
Light manufacturing	−0.1%	0.78	9			
Heavy manufacturing	−0.2%	0.52	18			
Utilities	−0.2%	0.59	19			
Construction	0.0%	0.65	18			
Trade services	−0.1%	0.86	13			
Hotels and restaurants	0.0%	0.71	6			
Transport services	0.0%	0.87	11			
Telecommunications	−0.2%	0.67	14			
Financial intermediation	−0.4%	0.62	21			
Real estate, renting, and business activities	−0.1%	0.52	11			
Public administration and defense	0.0%	0.34	8			
Education, health, and social work	0.0%	0.86	15			
Other personal services	−0.2%	0.91	16			

STRENGTH OF LINKAGES

Demand-side Linkages

	Value (2018)	Score (0–1)	Rank (out of 25)	Distance to subregional average	10–year average growth rate (%)	10–year mean value
Direct backward linkage	**0.36**	**0.43**	**8**	▲	**−0.1**	**0.36**
Agriculture, hunting, forestry, and fishing	0.26	0.34	11		−0.1	0.26
Mining and quarrying	0.15	0.25	17		−0.2	0.16
Light manufacturing	0.65	0.86	4		−0.2	0.65
Heavy manufacturing	0.44	0.43	11		−1.1	0.48
Utilities	0.72	0.98	2		0.9	0.71
Construction	0.50	0.48	9		−0.9	0.53
Trade services	0.16	0.05	22		−0.3	0.17
Hotels and restaurants	0.61	0.95	3		−0.1	0.61
Transport services	0.40	0.70	7		−0.2	0.41
Telecommunications	0.41	0.64	7		0.1	0.41

continued on next page

Pakistan 3.8A *continued*

	Value (2018)	Score (0–1)	Rank (out of 25)	Distance to subregional average	10-year average growth rate (%)	10-year mean value
Financial intermediation	0.18	0.15	20		3.6	0.17
Real estate, renting, and business activities	0.10	0.00	24		0.9	0.10
Public administration and defense	0.40	0.72	4		0.7	0.40
Education, health, and social work	0.17	0.21	19		0.6	0.17
Other personal services	0.19	0.23	21		–0.2	0.19
Total backward linkage	**1.55**	**0.25**	**9**	▲	**–0.1**	**1.57**
Agriculture, hunting, forestry, and fishing	1.36	0.24	13		–0.1	1.37
Mining and quarrying	1.22	0.17	18		–0.1	1.22
Light manufacturing	1.94	0.47	9		–0.1	1.97
Heavy manufacturing	1.70	0.22	9		–0.5	1.77
Utilities	2.41	0.70	2		0.9	2.41
Construction	1.80	0.24	11		–0.5	1.86
Trade services	1.24	0.10	22		–0.2	1.25
Hotels and restaurants	1.98	0.60	3		–0.3	2.01
Transport services	1.61	0.45	9		–0.2	1.64
Telecommunications	1.54	0.40	12		0.0	1.54
Financial intermediation	1.23	0.04	20		0.0	1.23
Real estate, renting, and business activities	1.13	0.00	25		0.1	1.13
Public administration and defense	1.63	0.64	5		0.1	1.64
Education, health, and social work	1.27	0.14	19		–0.1	1.28
Other personal services	1.25	0.13	21		0.0	1.26
Normalized backward linkage	**–**	**–**	**–**	▬	**–**	**–**
Agriculture, hunting, forestry, and fishing	0.88	0.22	19		0.1	0.87
Mining and quarrying	0.78	0.23	20		0.1	0.78
Light manufacturing	1.25	0.66	8		0.0	1.25
Heavy manufacturing	1.09	0.37	11		–0.5	1.13
Utilities	1.55	1.00	1		1.0	1.53
Construction	1.16	0.39	11		–0.4	1.19
Trade services	0.80	0.12	23		–0.1	0.80
Hotels and restaurants	1.28	0.85	4		–0.2	1.28
Transport services	1.04	0.47	9		–0.1	1.04
Telecommunications	0.99	0.58	13		0.0	0.98
Financial intermediation	0.79	0.05	24		0.1	0.78
Real estate, renting, and business activities	0.73	0.00	25		0.2	0.72
Public administration and defense	1.05	0.71	6		0.1	1.04
Education, health, and social work	0.82	0.26	22		0.0	0.81
Other personal services	0.81	0.01	24		0.1	0.80
Net backward linkage	**1.00**	**0.82**	**3**	▲	**–0.2**	**1.02**
Agriculture, hunting, forestry, and fishing	0.46	0.28	21		0.6	0.45
Mining and quarrying	0.18	0.13	19		1.9	0.21
Light manufacturing	1.52	1.00	1		0.0	1.55
Heavy manufacturing	0.78	0.39	18		–0.1	0.79
Utilities	0.77	0.63	6		1.4	0.83
Construction	1.72	0.48	4		–0.6	1.79
Trade services	0.73	0.28	17		0.8	0.72

continued on next page

Pakistan 3.8A *continued*

	Value (2018)	Score (0–1)	Rank (out of 25)	Distance to subregional average	10–year average growth rate (%)	10–year mean value
Hotels and restaurants	1.87	1.00	1		−0.2	1.89
Transport services	1.22	0.75	2		−0.5	1.24
Telecommunications	0.87	0.56	7		−1.3	0.90
Financial intermediation	0.49	0.37	17		−3.7	0.55
Real estate, renting, and business activities	0.63	0.52	22		0.4	0.62
Public administration and defense	1.62	0.72	5		0.1	1.64
Education, health, and social work	1.14	0.13	20		0.6	1.15
Other personal services	0.95	0.61	18		1.8	0.94
Growth equalized output multipliers	**0.11**	**0.22**	**10**	▲	**−0.3**	**0.11**
Agriculture, hunting, forestry, and fishing	0.30	0.86	3		0.5	0.30
Mining and quarrying	0.02	0.05	11		−2.3	0.03
Light manufacturing	0.30	0.50	6		−1.5	0.32
Heavy manufacturing	0.11	0.13	15		−1.5	0.12
Utilities	0.09	0.47	3		0.9	0.10
Construction	0.06	0.02	22		−0.2	0.05
Trade services	0.20	0.44	9		−0.9	0.21
Hotels and restaurants	0.04	0.06	15		−1.1	0.04
Transport services	0.17	0.97	2		1.2	0.17
Telecommunications	0.02	0.19	18		1.4	0.02
Financial intermediation	0.02	0.02	24		−5.6	0.03
Real estate, renting, and business activities	0.12	0.39	12		1.0	0.10
Public administration and defense	0.10	0.58	6		4.7	0.08
Education, health, and social work	0.04	0.03	23		4.1	0.03
Other personal services	0.03	0.16	13		2.8	0.03
Supply-Side Linkages						
Direct forward linkage	**0.37**	**0.29**	**15**	▲	**0.2**	**0.36**
Agriculture, hunting, forestry, and fishing	0.66	0.71	9		−0.3	0.67
Mining and quarrying	0.85	0.86	7		0.3	0.83
Light manufacturing	0.21	0.00	25		−0.3	0.21
Heavy manufacturing	0.54	0.70	7		−0.3	0.55
Utilities	0.68	0.72	15		0.3	0.66
Construction	0.04	0.09	21		3.9	0.04
Trade services	0.41	0.49	14		−1.1	0.43
Hotels and restaurants	0.05	0.09	22		−0.3	0.06
Transport services	0.24	0.20	22		1.0	0.24
Telecommunications	0.43	0.39	17		2.6	0.42
Financial intermediation	0.60	0.61	15		3.9	0.55
Real estate, renting, and business activities	0.44	0.36	12		−0.2	0.45
Public administration and defense	0.00	0.01	22		34.2	0.00
Education, health, and social work	0.10	0.35	4		7.1	0.10
Other personal services	0.24	0.25	15		−0.2	0.25
Total forward linkage	**1.59**	**0.18**	**12**	▲	**0.0**	**1.59**
Agriculture, hunting, forestry, and fishing	1.99	0.42	11		−0.1	2.00
Mining and quarrying	2.67	0.54	5		0.5	2.62
Light manufacturing	1.30	0.00	25		−0.1	1.31

continued on next page

Pakistan 3.8A *continued*

	Value (2018)	Score (0–1)	Rank (out of 25)	Distance to subregional average	10–year average growth rate (%)	10–year mean value
Heavy manufacturing	1.81	0.38	12		–0.3	1.86
Utilities	2.29	0.42	8		0.4	2.24
Construction	1.05	0.06	22		0.1	1.05
Trade services	1.61	0.29	13		–0.5	1.64
Hotels and restaurants	1.09	0.06	22		0.0	1.09
Transport services	1.35	0.11	23		0.2	1.37
Telecommunications	1.66	0.31	18		0.8	1.66
Financial intermediation	1.90	0.17	14		1.6	1.83
Real estate, renting, and business activities	1.66	0.27	12		–0.2	1.69
Public administration and defense	1.00	0.01	22		0.0	1.00
Education, health, and social work	1.13	0.40	8		–0.8	1.13
Other personal services	1.36	0.27	15		–0.9	1.39
Normalized forward linkage	–	–	–	▬	–	–
Agriculture, hunting, forestry, and fishing	1.25	0.69	8		–0.1	1.26
Mining and quarrying	1.72	0.94	3		0.5	1.66
Light manufacturing	0.84	0.00	25		0.0	0.83
Heavy manufacturing	1.16	0.57	12		–0.2	1.18
Utilities	1.47	0.71	10		0.4	1.43
Construction	0.68	0.20	21		0.2	0.67
Trade services	1.04	0.32	17		–0.4	1.04
Hotels and restaurants	0.70	0.04	24		0.1	0.70
Transport services	0.87	0.00	25		0.3	0.87
Telecommunications	1.07	0.26	18		0.9	1.05
Financial intermediation	1.22	0.19	19		1.7	1.16
Real estate, renting, and business activities	1.07	0.32	13		–0.1	1.08
Public administration and defense	0.64	0.33	19		0.1	0.64
Education, health, and social work	0.73	0.61	11		–0.7	0.72
Other personal services	0.88	0.22	16		–1.0	0.89
Net forward linkage	**0.93**	**0.57**	**7**	▲	**0.1**	**0.93**
Agriculture, hunting, forestry, and fishing	1.42	0.67	6		–0.1	1.43
Mining and quarrying	2.22	0.98	2		0.5	2.18
Light manufacturing	0.37	0.17	21		–0.1	0.37
Heavy manufacturing	0.47	0.49	14		–0.3	0.48
Utilities	0.35	0.09	23		1.5	0.33
Construction	0.36	0.33	19		–0.2	0.36
Trade services	1.27	0.64	4		–0.5	1.30
Hotels and restaurants	0.38	0.04	23		0.0	0.38
Transport services	0.67	0.28	17		0.3	0.67
Telecommunications	0.92	0.34	17		0.8	0.91
Financial intermediation	1.52	0.53	9		1.6	1.47
Real estate, renting, and business activities	1.48	0.98	2		–0.3	1.52
Public administration and defense	0.51	0.30	22		0.2	0.51
Education, health, and social work	0.89	0.82	4		–0.6	0.89
Other personal services	1.08	0.78	5		–0.9	1.11

continued on next page

Pakistan 3.8A *continued*

	Value (2018)	Score (0–1)	Rank (out of 25)	Distance to subregional average	10–year average growth rate (%)	10–year mean value
Growth equalized input multipliers	**0.11**	**0.23**	**10**	▲	**−0.3**	**0.11**
Agriculture, hunting, forestry, and fishing	0.49	1.00	1		0.5	0.49
Mining and quarrying	0.06	0.09	10		−2.1	0.08
Light manufacturing	0.13	0.35	12		−1.5	0.14
Heavy manufacturing	0.06	0.11	16		−1.7	0.07
Utilities	0.03	0.13	15		3.3	0.04
Construction	0.03	0.01	24		−0.3	0.02
Trade services	0.29	0.63	7		−1.3	0.31
Hotels and restaurants	0.02	0.02	24		−1.1	0.02
Transport services	0.13	0.73	4		1.7	0.13
Telecommunications	0.02	0.07	20		2.3	0.02
Financial intermediation	0.04	0.01	24		−4.2	0.05
Real estate, renting, and business activities	0.20	0.45	7		0.7	0.18
Public administration and defense	0.06	0.28	15		4.9	0.05
Education, health, and social work	0.04	0.09	22		3.9	0.03
Other personal services	0.04	0.26	12		1.5	0.04

Impacts from Hypothetical Extraction

	Value (2018)	Score (0–1)	Rank (out of 25)	Distance to subregional average	10–year average growth rate (%)	10–year mean value
Changes in gross output due to hypothetical extraction	**−9.5%**	**0.71**	**19**	▲	**−0.2**	**−0.10**
Agriculture, hunting, forestry, and fishing	−20.4%	0.30	23		0.5	−20.5
Mining and quarrying	−1.8%	0.95	12		−2.0	−2.3
Light manufacturing	−32.9%	0.30	22		−1.2	−34.9
Heavy manufacturing	−10.3%	0.81	11		−1.5	−11.1
Utilities	−7.7%	0.54	23		0.7	−9.1
Construction	−6.6%	0.97	3		−0.5	−6.0
Trade services	−14.8%	0.72	15		−0.7	−15.6
Hotels and restaurants	−4.5%	0.92	14		−1.1	−4.7
Transport services	−15.9%	0.01	24		1.3	−15.8
Telecommunications	−1.9%	0.76	9		1.4	−1.9
Financial intermediation	−1.7%	0.99	2		−5.3	−2.2
Real estate, renting, and business activities	−7.7%	0.69	10		1.4	−6.8
Public administration and defense	−10.0%	0.38	21		5.2	−7.8
Education, health, and social work	−3.1%	1.00	1		4.5	−2.5
Other personal services	−2.5%	0.89	12		3.1	−2.1

Impacts from Hypothetical Insertion

	Value (2018)	Score (0–1)	Rank (out of 25)	Distance to subregional average	10–year average growth rate (%)	10–year mean value
Changes in gross output due to hypothetical insertion	**3.9%**	**0.20**	**11**	▲	**−0.4**	**0.04**
Agriculture, hunting, forestry, and fishing	6.7%	0.26	4		0.6	6.8
Mining and quarrying	0.3%	0.03	16		−2.3	0.4
Light manufacturing	17.3%	0.48	8		−1.5	18.8
Heavy manufacturing	4.8%	0.07	15		−2.2	5.7
Utilities	7.5%	1.00	1		4.0	8.9
Construction	3.0%	0.02	22		−0.9	2.8
Trade services	3.0%	0.14	17		−0.9	3.3
Hotels and restaurants	2.3%	0.13	11		−1.3	2.4
Transport services	6.4%	1.00	1		1.1	6.6
Telecommunications	0.7%	0.17	18		1.5	0.7
Financial intermediation	0.3%	0.00	23		−0.7	0.4

continued on next page

Pakistan 3.8A *continued*

	Value (2018)	Score (0–1)	Rank (out of 25)	Distance to subregional average	10-year average growth rate (%)	10-year mean value
Real estate, renting, and business activities	0.9%	0.07	21		2.2	0.8
Public administration and defense	3.8%	0.91	3		6.3	3.1
Education, health, and social work	0.7%	0.07	23		6.4	0.5
Other personal services	0.5%	0.06	18		2.9	0.4

SPREAD OF ECONOMIC LINKAGES

Demand-side

	Value (2018)	Score (0–1)	Rank (out of 25)	Distance to subregional average	10-year average growth rate (%)	10-year mean value
Relative evenness of direct backward linkage	**0.56**	**0.72**	**4**	▲	**0.3**	**0.57**
Relative evenness of total backward linkage	**0.24**	**0.35**	**3**	▲	**0.6**	**0.24**
		0.00				
Backward measure of concentration based on input coefficients	**0.89**	**0.51**	**19**	▼	**−0.1**	**0.90**
Agriculture, hunting, forestry, and fishing	0.71	0.14	24		−0.7	0.72
Mining and quarrying	0.91	0.41	15		−0.1	0.92
Light manufacturing	0.79	0.00	25		−0.4	0.80
Heavy manufacturing	0.96	0.98	3		0.1	0.95
Utilities	0.83	0.49	21		−0.1	0.83
Construction	0.95	0.96	4		0.0	0.95
Trade services	0.96	0.90	9		0.0	0.96
Hotels and restaurants	0.94	0.90	4		0.0	0.94
Transport services	0.95	0.79	6		0.1	0.94
Telecommunications	0.87	0.28	24		−0.2	0.88
Financial intermediation	0.88	0.88	16		−0.2	0.89
Real estate, renting, and business activities	0.88	0.74	24		−0.1	0.89
Public administration and defense	0.97	0.69	10		0.0	0.96
Education, health, and social work	0.95	0.68	15		0.1	0.94
Other personal services	0.88	0.64	24		−0.1	0.89
Relative evenness of direct forward linkage	**0.72**	**0.69**	**4**	▲	**0.4**	**0.71**
Relative evenness of total forward linkage	**0.30**	**0.33**	**4**	▲	**0.7**	**0.29**
Forward measure of concentration based on output coefficients	**0.68**	**0.68**	**7**	▲	**−0.1**	**0.68**
Agriculture, hunting, forestry, and fishing	0.39	0.49	13		1.6	0.38
Mining and quarrying	0.50	0.69	7		−0.3	0.49
Light manufacturing	0.79	0.89	4		0.3	0.78
Heavy manufacturing	0.77	0.83	5		0.2	0.77
Utilities	0.55	0.17	24		−0.1	0.53
Construction	0.21	0.25	21		−0.9	0.24
Trade services	0.75	0.64	13		0.5	0.74
Hotels and restaurants	0.71	0.48	18		0.0	0.70
Transport services	0.77	0.71	13		0.1	0.76
Telecommunications	0.90	1.00	1		0.0	0.90
Financial intermediation	0.88	0.99	2		0.0	0.88
Real estate, renting, and business activities	0.94	1.00	1		0.0	0.94
Public administration and defense	0.58	0.63	15		−0.9	0.61
Education, health, and social work	0.58	0.61	15		−0.9	0.61
Other personal services	0.90	0.97	2		0.0	0.90

continued on next page

Pakistan 3.8A *continued*

	Value (2018)	Score (0–1)	Rank (out of 25)	Distance to subregional average	10-year average growth rate (%)	10-year mean value
SENSITIVITY OF ECONOMIC LINKAGES						
Economic Complexity						
Percentage intermediate transaction	0.38	0.36	10	▲	–0.4	0.39
Average output multiplier	1.55	0.25	9	▲	–0.1	1.57
Average of Leontief inverse	0.20	0.21	12	▲	–0.1	0.20
Average technical coefficient	0.02	0.43	8	▲	–0.1	0.02
Mean intermediate coefficient	0.36	0.43	8	▲	–0.1	0.36
Percentage of above-average coefficients (%)	0.26	0.36	12	▼	0.0	0.26
Determinant of non-competitive Leontief inverse	3.21	0.07	14	▼	0.9	3.25
Determinant of competitive Leontief inverse	4.09	0.03	15	▼	0.8	4.18
Mean path length	1.61	0.22	10	▲	–0.3	1.65
Cycling index	0.10	0.27	15	▼	0.2	0.10
Average propagation length	1.81	0.33	11	▲	0.0	1.83
Overall sensitivity of the economy	0.68	0.39	19	▼	0.1	0.67
Index of direct interrelatedness	0.56	0.29	14	▲	0.1	0.55
Index of indirect interrelatedness	0.13	0.33	19	▼	0.4	0.13
Global intensity index	23.31	0.25	9	▲	–0.1	23.59

Note: The scores of the economy in focus are shown in the horizontal bars with labels. The colored dots represent the indicator performance of the economy in focus compared to other economies in the region. The highest rank among economies is 1 while the lowest rank is 25. The indicators shown in the chart are selected from a broader set of indicators (see the technical appendix for more details).

Source: Asian Development Bank Multi-Regional Input–Output Database. https://mrio.adbx.online/ (accessed 4 August 2020).

3.8B External Linkages

$ = United States dollars, GVC = global value chain.

Note: The scores of the economy in focus are shown in the horizontal bars with labels. The colored dots represent the indicator performance of the economy in focus compared to other economies in the region. The highest rank among economies is 1, while the lowest rank is 25. The indicators shown in the chart are selected from a broader set of indicators (see the technical appendix for more details).

Source: Asian Development Bank Multi-Regional Input–Output Database. https://mrio.adbx.online/ (accessed 4 August 2020).

		Value (2018)	Score (0–1)	Rank (out of 25)	Distance to subregional average	10-year average growth rate (%)	10-year mean value
PARTICIPATION IN GLOBAL VALUE CHAINS							
International Trade Coefficients							
Trade openness		0.29	0.00	25	▼	–1.0	0.31
Self-sufficiency ratio		0.94	0.46	22	▲	0.0	0.96
Regional supply percentage		0.89	0.85	4	▲	0.1	0.90
Regional purchase coefficient		0.87	0.80	7	▲	0.1	0.87
Sectoral purchase coefficient		0.94	0.97	3	▲	0.1	0.94
Simple location quotient of gross output		1.22	0.56	11	▼	0.1	1.22
Fabrication effect		0.82	0.29	20	▼	0.0	0.82
Exports	($)	24,986	0.01	15	▼	7.0	25,598
Export-to-output ratio		0.03	0.00	25	▼	3.5	0.04
Agriculture, hunting, forestry, and fishing		0.02	0.07	20		–2.6	0.02
Mining and quarrying		0.03	0.03	18		–16.9	0.03
Light manufacturing		0.17	0.27	16		–2.6	0.19
Heavy manufacturing		0.04	0.03	24		–9.1	0.05
Utilities		0.00	0.00	24		–19.7	0.00
Construction		0.00	0.02	20		–2.5	0.00
Trade services		0.05	0.07	20		–3.2	0.07
Hotels and restaurants		0.00	0.00	23		–3.3	0.00
Transport services		0.03	0.04	23		–0.9	0.04
Telecommunications		0.02	0.03	23		–2.3	0.03

continued on next page

Pakistan 3.8B *continued*

		Value (2018)	Score (0–1)	Rank (out of 25)	Distance to subregional average	10–year average growth rate (%)	10–year mean value
Financial intermediation		0.01	0.01	24		−7.2	0.01
Real estate, renting, and business activities		0.01	0.04	20		−3.7	0.02
Public administration and defense		0.00	0.00	15		20.9	0.00
Education, health, and social work		0.07	0.91	2		3.3	0.11
Other personal services		0.05	0.05	11		−0.4	0.07
Imports	($)	**56,121**	**0.03**	**14**	▼	**6.0**	**43,005**
Import-to-input ratio		**0.06**	**0.15**	**23**	▼	**0.2**	**0.06**
Agriculture, hunting, forestry, and fishing		0.02	0.05	23		−1.4	0.02
Mining and quarrying		0.01	0.02	22		4.9	0.01
Light manufacturing		0.05	0.03	23		−0.1	0.05
Heavy manufacturing		0.18	0.20	17		−0.2	0.18
Utilities		0.13	0.17	18		−3.1	0.14
Construction		0.10	0.18	19		3.6	0.09
Trade services		0.03	0.12	18		3.5	0.03
Hotels and restaurants		0.04	0.11	22		1.1	0.04
Transport services		0.09	0.15	21		−0.3	0.09
Telecommunications		0.03	0.05	22		11.3	0.03
Financial intermediation		0.02	0.06	22		−9.0	0.02
Real estate, renting, and business activities		0.01	0.00	25		1.8	0.01
Public administration and defense		0.08	0.51	8		3.5	0.09
Education, health, and social work		0.04	0.16	18		4.9	0.04
Other personal services		0.01	0.02	24		−0.2	0.01
Total foreign factor content of consumption	($)	**21,018**	**0.04**	**13**	▼	**5.8**	**17,034**
Total foreign factor content of investment	($)	**4,445**	**0.01**	**14**	▼	**5.1**	**3,479**
Total foreign factor content of exports	($)	**2,048**	**0.01**	**17**	▼	**6.1**	**2,123**
Interregional Multipliers							
Import Leakage Effects		**0.09**	**0.06**	**23**	▼	**−1.0**	**0.09**
Agriculture, hunting, forestry, and fishing		0.04	0.03	22		−1.8	0.04
Mining and quarrying		0.02	0.04	22		0.4	0.02
Light manufacturing		0.08	0.00	25		−1.2	0.08
Heavy manufacturing		0.23	0.19	20		−0.9	0.24
Utilities		0.25	0.32	14		−2.8	0.26
Construction		0.15	0.09	19		1.0	0.15
Trade services		0.04	0.05	22		1.3	0.05
Hotels and restaurants		0.09	0.11	22		−2.6	0.10
Transport services		0.13	0.10	21		−1.1	0.13
Telecommunications		0.05	0.01	23		5.7	0.05
Financial intermediation		0.02	0.00	25		−9.5	0.03
Real estate, renting, and business activities		0.01	0.00	25		0.7	0.01
Public administration and defense		0.13	0.38	9		0.4	0.13
Education, health, and social work		0.06	0.15	23		0.7	0.06
Other personal services		0.02	0.00	24		−1.3	0.02
Intraregional transfer multiplier		**1.55**	**0.25**	**9**	▲	**−0.1**	**1.57**
Agriculture, hunting, forestry, and fishing		1.36	0.24	13		−0.1	1.37
Mining and quarrying		1.22	0.17	18		−0.1	1.22

continued on next page

Pakistan 3.8B *continued*

	Value (2018)	Score (0–1)	Rank (out of 25)	Distance to subregional average	10–year average growth rate (%)	10–year mean value
Light manufacturing	1.94	0.47	9		−0.1	1.97
Heavy manufacturing	1.70	0.22	9		−0.5	1.77
Utilities	2.41	0.70	2		0.9	2.41
Construction	1.80	0.24	11		−0.5	1.86
Trade services	1.24	0.10	22		−0.2	1.25
Hotels and restaurants	1.98	0.60	3		−0.3	2.01
Transport services	1.61	0.45	9		−0.2	1.64
Telecommunications	1.54	0.40	12		0.0	1.54
Financial intermediation	1.23	0.04	20		0.0	1.23
Real estate, renting, and business activities	1.13	0.00	25		0.1	1.13
Public administration and defense	1.63	0.64	5		0.1	1.64
Education, health, and social work	1.27	0.14	19		−0.1	1.28
Other personal services	1.25	0.13	21		0.0	1.26
Interregional spillover multiplier	**1.14**	**0.17**	**23**	▼	**−0.1**	**1.14**
Agriculture, hunting, forestry, and fishing	1.05	0.06	23		−0.1	1.05
Mining and quarrying	1.02	0.02	22		0.0	1.02
Light manufacturing	1.11	0.04	24		0.0	1.11
Heavy manufacturing	1.46	0.27	17		0.0	1.45
Utilities	1.30	0.19	18		−0.9	1.32
Construction	1.26	0.22	19		0.5	1.23
Trade services	1.07	0.13	18		0.0	1.07
Hotels and restaurants	1.10	0.10	22		0.0	1.09
Transport services	1.25	0.19	20		−0.1	1.23
Telecommunications	1.07	0.05	22		0.0	1.07
Financial intermediation	1.03	0.07	22		0.3	1.05
Real estate, renting, and business activities	1.01	0.00	24		0.0	1.01
Public administration and defense	1.21	0.46	7		−0.1	1.21
Education, health, and social work	1.10	0.20	17		0.0	1.11
Other personal services	1.03	0.02	24		0.0	1.03
Interregional feedback multiplier	**1.000**	**0.01**	**17**	▼	**0.0**	**1.00**
Agriculture, hunting, forestry, and fishing	1.000	0.00	20		0.0	1.00
Mining and quarrying	1.000	0.00	20		0.0	1.00
Light manufacturing	1.000	0.01	18		0.0	1.00
Heavy manufacturing	1.000	0.01	15		0.0	1.00
Utilities	1.000	0.01	17		0.0	1.00
Construction	1.000	0.01	17		0.0	1.00
Trade services	1.000	0.01	16		0.0	1.00
Hotels and restaurants	1.000	0.01	16		0.0	1.00
Transport services	1.000	0.01	15		0.0	1.00
Telecommunications	1.000	0.00	20		0.0	1.00
Financial intermediation	1.000	0.00	17		0.0	1.00
Real estate, renting, and business activities	1.000	0.00	20		0.0	1.00
Public administration and defense	1.000	0.02	13		0.0	1.00
Education, health, and social work	1.000	0.01	17		0.0	1.00
Other personal services	1.000	0.00	23		0.0	1.00

continued on next page

Pakistan 3.8B *continued*

	Value (2018)	Score (0–1)	Rank (out of 25)	Distance to subregional average	10-year average growth rate (%)	10-year mean value
Global Value Chain (GVC) Participation Index						
Backward GVC Participation	9.3%	0.01	24	▼	−1.1	0.09
Simple GVCs	6.5%	0.09	23	▼	−0.9	0.07
Agriculture, hunting, forestry, and fishing	0.3	0.11	12		−0.4	0.27
Mining and quarrying	0.0	0.10	17		−1.3	0.01
Light manufacturing	1.2	0.25	13		−1.9	1.27
Heavy manufacturing	0.8	0.16	14		−1.8	0.84
Utilities	0.5	0.49	5		−3.0	0.76
Construction	0.6	0.00	25		0.1	0.56
Trade services	0.3	0.11	18		0.8	0.36
Hotels and restaurants	0.2	0.13	17		−3.9	0.28
Transport services	1.2	0.76	4		−0.6	1.19
Telecommunications	0.0	0.03	22		5.9	0.05
Financial intermediation	0.0	0.01	24		11.8	0.03
Real estate, renting, and business activities	0.1	0.00	25		2.4	0.05
Public administration and defense	0.9	0.22	8		4.4	0.77
Education, health, and social work	0.1	0.04	24		6.7	0.12
Other personal services	0.0	0.01	23		5.3	0.03
Complex GVCs	2.8%	0.00	25	▼	−1.4	0.03
Agriculture, hunting, forestry, and fishing	0.1	0.09	17		−1.4	0.10
Mining and quarrying	0.0	0.02	19		3.8	0.00
Light manufacturing	0.6	0.05	18		−2.8	0.67
Heavy manufacturing	0.4	0.02	17		−1.1	0.40
Utilities	0.2	0.45	8		−3.4	0.24
Construction	0.3	0.00	25		0.3	0.24
Trade services	0.1	0.02	19		1.6	0.15
Hotels and restaurants	0.1	0.01	20		−3.5	0.10
Transport services	0.5	0.23	12		−2.0	0.52
Telecommunications	0.0	0.02	22		5.1	0.02
Financial intermediation	0.0	0.00	24		6.5	0.01
Real estate, renting, and business activities	0.0	0.00	25		1.1	0.02
Public administration and defense	0.4	0.31	7		3.2	0.33
Education, health, and social work	0.1	0.04	24		2.8	0.06
Other personal services	0.0	0.03	23		2.7	0.01
Forward GVC Participation	4.6%	0.02	23	▼	−0.9	0.06
Simple GVCs	3.0%	0.02	23	▼	−0.4	0.04
Agriculture, hunting, forestry, and fishing	1.0	0.49	9		−1.2	1.23
Mining and quarrying	0.1	0.00	16		8.9	0.11
Light manufacturing	0.6	0.15	15		−2.6	0.76
Heavy manufacturing	0.1	0.01	21		1.7	0.14
Utilities	0.0	0.00	25		0.8	0.03
Construction	0.0	0.00	25		18.9	0.00
Trade services	0.6	0.06	21		1.9	0.89
Hotels and restaurants	0.0	0.00	25		−3.1	0.00
Transport services	0.2	0.02	24		18.8	0.26
Telecommunications	0.0	0.00	25		9.3	0.03

continued on next page

Pakistan 3.8B *continued*

	Value (2018)	Score (0–1)	Rank (out of 25)	Distance to subregional average	10–year average growth rate (%)	10–year mean value
Financial intermediation	0.0	0.00	24		18.5	0.07
Real estate, renting, and business activities	0.2	0.02	21		14.9	0.26
Public administration and defense	0.0	0.00	22		18.7	0.00
Education, health, and social work	0.0	0.25	9		1.2	0.06
Other personal services	0.1	0.08	16		4.4	0.10
Complex GVCs	**1.6%**	**0.05**	**23**	▼	**–1.7**	**0.02**
Agriculture, hunting, forestry, and fishing	0.5	0.30	8		–1.8	0.62
Mining and quarrying	0.0	0.00	17		8.8	0.05
Light manufacturing	0.3	0.15	15		–2.5	0.40
Heavy manufacturing	0.1	0.01	20		0.3	0.07
Utilities	0.0	0.00	25		0.2	0.02
Construction	0.0	0.00	25		18.1	0.00
Trade services	0.4	0.10	20		0.1	0.52
Hotels and restaurants	0.0	0.00	25		–3.3	0.00
Transport services	0.1	0.01	24		9.8	0.10
Telecommunications	0.0	0.00	25		8.7	0.02
Financial intermediation	0.0	0.01	24		12.5	0.03
Real estate, renting, and business activities	0.1	0.02	21		10.9	0.15
Public administration and defense	0.0	0.00	21		30.3	0.00
Education, health, and social work	0.0	0.17	10		3.4	0.02
Other personal services	0.0	0.04	21		2.0	0.03

SPECIALIZATION IN GLOBAL VALUE CHAINS

Vertical Specialization

Vertical Specialization Ratio	8.2%	0.00	25	▼	–1.2	0.08
Agriculture, hunting, forestry, and fishing	3.6%	0.03	22		–1.7	0.04
Mining and quarrying	1.7%	0.04	22		0.5	0.02
Light manufacturing	8.4%	0.00	25		–1.2	0.08
Heavy manufacturing	22.5%	0.20	20		–0.9	0.23
Utilities	24.9%	0.39	14		–2.8	0.26
Construction	15.0%	0.09	19		1.1	0.14
Trade services	4.3%	0.05	22		1.3	0.04
Hotels and restaurants	9.2%	0.10	22		–2.6	0.10
Transport services	13.1%	0.10	21		–1.1	0.13
Telecommunications	4.5%	0.01	23		5.7	0.05
Financial intermediation	2.2%	0.00	25		–9.4	0.03
Real estate, renting, and business activities	1.1%	0.00	25		0.7	0.01
Public administration and defense	12.8%	0.38	9		0.5	0.13
Education, health, and social work	5.8%	0.15	23		0.7	0.06
Other personal services	2.1%	0.00	24		–1.2	0.02

Revealed Comparative Advantages

Traditional RCA Index						
Agriculture, hunting, forestry, and fishing	3.36	0.56	4	▲	7.2	2.91
Mining and quarrying	0.12	0.01	13	▼	30.1	0.10
Light manufacturing	3.86	0.69	2	▲	3.0	3.78

continued on next page

Pakistan 3.8B *continued*

	Value (2018)	Score (0–1)	Rank (out of 25)	Distance to subregional average	10-year average growth rate (%)	10-year mean value
Heavy manufacturing	0.12	0.07	17	▼	7.0	0.11
Utilities	0.09	0.00	17	▼	−14.4	0.34
Construction	0.19	0.02	19	▼	−5.4	0.25
Trade services	1.46	0.19	6	▲	−6.7	1.70
Hotels and restaurants	0.06	0.00	20	▼	9.5	0.05
Transport services	1.06	0.24	9	▼	−6.6	1.22
Telecommunications	0.57	0.08	17	▼	−5.4	0.72
Financial intermediation	0.05	0.01	23	▼	−11.4	0.11
Real estate, renting, and business activities	0.24	0.07	10	▼	−4.6	0.29
Public administration and defense	0.55	0.02	11	▼	−0.8	0.45
Education, health, and social work	7.74	1.00	1	▲	−7.2	8.46
Other personal services	1.44	0.08	5	▼	−5.0	1.43

New RCA Index (Based on Domestic Value Added)

	Value (2018)	Score (0–1)	Rank (out of 25)	Distance to subregional average	10-year average growth rate (%)	10-year mean value
Agriculture, hunting, forestry, and fishing	6.95	1.00	1	▲	3.1	6.75
Mining and quarrying	0.22	0.03	13	▼	8.9	0.22
Light manufacturing	2.22	0.50	5	▲	2.8	2.19
Heavy manufacturing	0.17	0.07	15	▼	4.1	0.15
Utilities	0.30	0.01	21	▼	−0.8	0.32
Construction	0.08	0.00	24	▼	−0.8	0.08
Trade services	1.51	0.43	6	▲	−4.4	1.69
Hotels and restaurants	0.09	0.00	25	▼	−0.4	0.10
Transport services	0.76	0.21	15	▼	−5.1	0.85
Telecommunications	0.43	0.05	21	▼	−3.5	0.48
Financial intermediation	0.18	0.00	24	▼	−6.9	0.25
Real estate, renting, and business activities	0.34	0.17	12	▼	−2.4	0.37
Public administration and defense	0.14	0.01	19	▼	0.2	0.12
Education, health, and social work	4.36	1.00	1	▲	−5.5	4.34
Other personal services	0.94	0.11	8	▼	−3.7	0.92

POSITION IN GLOBAL VALUE CHAINS

	Value (2018)	Score (0–1)	Rank (out of 25)	Distance to subregional average	10-year average growth rate (%)	10-year mean value
Upstreamness Index	**1.7**	**0.03**	**23**	▼	**−0.1**	**1.7**
Agriculture, hunting, forestry, and fishing	2.1	0.39	13		−0.3	2.2
Mining and quarrying	2.8	0.63	14		0.4	2.8
Light manufacturing	1.5	0.00	25		−0.3	1.6
Heavy manufacturing	1.9	0.13	23		−0.4	2.0
Utilities	2.3	0.21	18		0.3	2.3
Construction	1.1	0.04	24		0.1	1.1
Trade services	1.7	0.17	23		−0.6	1.8
Hotels and restaurants	1.1	0.01	24		0.0	1.1
Transport services	1.4	0.00	25		0.2	1.4
Telecommunications	1.7	0.06	24		0.7	1.7
Financial intermediation	2.0	0.16	22		1.7	1.9
Real estate, renting, and business activities	1.7	0.16	18		−0.3	1.8
Public administration and defense	1.0	0.01	22		0.0	1.0
Education, health, and social work	1.2	0.40	4		−1.1	1.2
Other personal services	1.4	0.20	19		−1.1	1.5

continued on next page

Pakistan 3.8B *continued*

	Value (2018)	Score (0–1)	Rank (out of 25)	Distance to subregional average	10–year average growth rate (%)	10–year mean value
PRODUCTION LENGTH OF GLOBAL VALUE CHAINS						
Backward Measures of Average Production Length						
Production Length of Global Value Chain Activity (B)	0.4	0.07	24	▼	–1.1	0.4
Agriculture, hunting, forestry, and fishing	0.1	0.02	22		–0.1	0.1
Mining and quarrying	0.1	0.04	22		0.5	0.1
Light manufacturing	0.3	0.00	25		–0.3	0.4
Heavy manufacturing	0.9	0.24	21		–0.1	0.9
Utilities	1.1	0.40	11		–0.7	1.1
Construction	0.6	0.05	19		1.2	0.6
Trade services	0.2	0.05	23		0.4	0.2
Hotels and restaurants	0.4	0.13	22		–0.4	0.4
Transport services	0.6	0.12	21		1.9	0.5
Telecommunications	0.2	0.00	24		1.4	0.2
Financial intermediation	0.1	0.00	25		1.3	0.1
Real estate, renting, and business activities	0.0	0.00	25		0.9	0.0
Public administration and defense	0.5	0.36	9		0.1	0.6
Education, health, and social work	0.2	0.13	23		–0.2	0.3
Other personal services	0.1	0.00	25		–0.5	0.1
Forward Measures of Average Production Length						
Production Length of Global Value Chain Activity (F)	0.1	0.00	25	▼	0.3	0.2
Agriculture, hunting, forestry, and fishing	0.3	0.15	18		–3.3	0.3
Mining and quarrying	0.2	0.06	19		1.4	0.3
Light manufacturing	0.3	0.13	23		–3.5	0.4
Heavy manufacturing	0.2	0.03	24		–2.4	0.2
Utilities	0.1	0.00	25		–2.0	0.1
Construction	0.0	0.00	25		10.6	0.0
Trade services	0.2	0.06	23		–1.5	0.3
Hotels and restaurants	0.0	0.00	25		–3.3	0.0
Transport services	0.1	0.00	24		1.0	0.1
Telecommunications	0.1	0.00	25		1.5	0.1
Financial intermediation	0.1	0.03	24		2.4	0.2
Real estate, renting, and business activities	0.1	0.02	23		–0.2	0.2
Public administration and defense	0.0	0.00	22		2.3	0.0
Education, health, and social work	0.1	0.35	9		–0.9	0.1
Other personal services	0.1	0.04	21		0.8	0.2

Note: The scores of the economy in focus are shown in the horizontal bars with labels. The colored dots represent the indicator performance of the economy in focus compared to other economies in the region. The highest rank among economies is 1 while the lowest rank is 25. The indicators shown in the chart are selected from a broader set of indicators (see the technical appendix for more details).

Source: Asian Development Bank Multi-Regional Input–Output Database. https://mrio.adbx.online/ (accessed 4 August 2020).

3.9 Sri Lanka

3.9A Internal Linkages

Structure of the economy | Strength of linkages | Spread of linkages | Sensitivity of linkages

Score:

	Gross value added	Gini index of value-added	Herfindahl-Hirschman index of gross exports	Average output multiplier	Average input multiplier	Relative evenness of backward linkage	Relative evenness of forward linkage	Average propagation length	Global intensity index	Overall sensitivity of the economy
Score	0.01	0.15	0.21	0.08	0.08	0.48	0.64	0.29	0.08	0.64
Rank	16	21	17	20	20	12	8	13	20	11

Note: The scores of the economy in focus are shown in the horizontal bars with labels. The colored dots represent the indicator performance of the economy in focus compared to other economies in the region. The highest rank among economies is 1 while the lowest rank is 25. The indicators shown in the chart are selected from a broader set of indicators (see the technical appendix for more details).

Source: Asian Development Bank Multi-Regional Input–Output Database. https://mrio.adbx.online/ (accessed 4 August 2020).

		Value (2018)	Score (0–1)	Rank (out of 25)	Distance to subregional average	10-year average growth rate (%)	10-year mean value
STRUCTURE OF THE ECONOMY							
Economic Indicators							
Gross output	($)	135,332	0.00	16	▼	6.6	110,634
Gross value-added	($)	80,354	0.01	16	▼	7.1	64,641
Value-added content of domestic final demand		67,906	0.01	16		7.2	54,600
Value-added content of exports		12,447	0.00	16		7.7	10,041
Intermediate inputs	($)	52,158	0.00	16	▼	6.4	43,885
Domestic inputs		40,319	0.00	16		7.1	34,010
Foreign inputs		11,839	0.01	16		5.3	9,874
Direct production	($)	95,013	0.01	16	▼	6.6	76,624
Domestic final demand		79,984	0.01	16		6.7	64,424
Exports		15,028	0.01	16		7.4	12,200
Indirect production	($)	40,319	0.00	16	▼	7.1	34,010
Indirect production embedded in domestic final demand		33,170	0.00	16		7.2	28,063
Indirect production embedded in exports		7,149	0.00	16		8.1	5,947
Economic Diversification							
Gross output		0.22	0.15	22	▼	−0.4	0.24
Gini concentration index of gross output		0.39	0.20	22		−0.2	0.42
Herfindahl-Hirschman concentration index of gross output		0.04	0.09	23		−0.6	0.04
Theil concentration index of gross output		0.22	0.12	22		−0.6	0.25

continued on next page

Sri Lanka 3.9A *continued*

	Value (2018)	Score (0–1)	Rank (out of 25)	Distance to subregional average	10–year average growth rate (%)	10–year mean value
Gross value-added	**0.20**	**0.12**	**21**	▼	**0.1**	**0.22**
Gini concentration index of gross value added	0.37	0.15	21		0.0	0.39
Herfindahl-Hirschman concentration index of gross value added	0.03	0.04	21		−0.1	0.03
Theil concentration index of gross value added	0.21	0.14	21		0.3	0.22
Gross exports	**0.52**	**0.32**	**18**	▼	**0.6**	**0.52**
Gini concentration index of gross exports	0.71	0.45	18		0.2	0.71
Herfindahl-Hirschman concentration index of gross exports	0.22	0.21	17		2.7	0.23
Theil concentration index of gross exports	0.63	0.43	18		0.6	0.63
Structural Changes						
Changes in output due to technological changes	**0.0%**	**0.75**	**11**	▼	**–**	**–**
Agriculture, hunting, forestry, and fishing	−1.4%	0.46	22			
Mining and quarrying	−0.9%	0.73	15			
Light manufacturing	−0.2%	0.36	15			
Heavy manufacturing	0.8%	0.73	4			
Utilities	−1.8%	0.28	24			
Construction	0.6%	0.20	8			
Trade services	−0.6%	0.23	19			
Hotels and restaurants	−0.2%	0.05	22			
Transport services	0.6%	0.72	7			
Telecommunications	1.7%	0.42	3			
Financial intermediation	1.2%	0.59	7			
Real estate, renting, and business activities	−1.0%	0.51	23			
Public administration and defense	0.0%	0.37	10			
Education, health, and social work	0.6%	1.00	1			
Other personal services	0.2%	0.47	12			
Changes in output due to structural changes in consumption (%)	**3.6%**	**0.39**	**11**	▼	**–**	**–**
Agriculture, hunting, forestry, and fishing	3.5%	0.62	7			
Mining and quarrying	4.6%	0.28	3			
Light manufacturing	0.6%	0.18	23			
Heavy manufacturing	2.4%	0.40	9			
Utilities	2.0%	0.25	19			
Construction	2.5%	0.36	4			
Trade services	3.3%	0.54	13			
Hotels and restaurants	4.7%	0.18	13			
Transport services	2.2%	0.36	14			
Telecommunications	1.8%	0.43	19			
Financial intermediation	4.4%	0.52	11			
Real estate, renting, and business activities	6.3%	0.29	5			
Public administration and defense	5.3%	0.39	15			
Education, health, and social work	4.5%	0.16	17			
Other personal services	5.6%	0.45	10			
Changes in output due to structural changes in investment (%)	**1.5%**	**0.44**	**6**	▲	**–**	**–**
Agriculture, hunting, forestry, and fishing	0.5%	0.15	8			
Mining and quarrying	1.9%	0.40	5			
Light manufacturing	0.2%	0.07	23			

continued on next page

Sri Lanka 3.9A *continued*

	Value (2018)	Score (0–1)	Rank (out of 25)	Distance to subregional average	10–year average growth rate (%)	10–year mean value
Heavy manufacturing	2.7%	0.38	6			
Utilities	0.6%	0.41	9			
Construction	7.0%	0.45	10			
Trade services	0.5%	0.21	18			
Hotels and restaurants	0.0%	0.32	18			
Transport services	0.7%	0.17	10			
Telecommunications	5.1%	1.00	1			
Financial intermediation	1.3%	0.30	5			
Real estate, renting, and business activities	1.0%	0.30	9			
Public administration and defense	0.0%	0.01	17			
Education, health, and social work	0.0%	0.02	11			
Other personal services	0.3%	0.23	13			
Changes in output due to structural changes in stock (%)	**0.6%**	**0.73**	**2**	▲	–	–
Agriculture, hunting, forestry, and fishing	1.6%	1.00	1			
Mining and quarrying	5.8%	1.00	1			
Light manufacturing	0.9%	0.50	2			
Heavy manufacturing	0.7%	0.77	3			
Utilities	1.1%	0.65	2			
Construction	–1.7%	0.00	25			
Trade services	0.3%	0.70	4			
Hotels and restaurants	0.0%	0.46	7			
Transport services	0.2%	0.09	6			
Telecommunications	0.1%	0.59	5			
Financial intermediation	0.0%	0.90	16			
Real estate, renting, and business activities	0.0%	0.17	8			
Public administration and defense	0.0%	0.64	6			
Education, health, and social work	0.0%	0.24	3			
Other personal services	0.1%	0.47	5			
Changes in output due to structural changes in export	**0.8%**	**0.21**	**17**	▼	–	–
Agriculture, hunting, forestry, and fishing	0.9%	0.51	11			
Mining and quarrying	1.0%	0.15	13			
Light manufacturing	1.0%	0.17	15			
Heavy manufacturing	–0.6%	0.13	23			
Utilities	0.8%	0.06	18			
Construction	–0.2%	0.00	25			
Trade services	1.6%	0.21	12			
Hotels and restaurants	4.0%	0.36	7			
Transport services	1.4%	0.52	14			
Telecommunications	–0.8%	0.00	25			
Financial intermediation	1.5%	0.29	11			
Real estate, renting, and business activities	0.2%	0.20	17			
Public administration and defense	0.0%	0.12	20			
Education, health, and social work	0.1%	0.03	19			
Other personal services	0.7%	0.15	16			

continued on next page

Sri Lanka 3.9A *continued*

	Value (2018)	Score (0–1)	Rank (out of 25)	Distance to subregional average	10–year average growth rate (%)	10–year mean value
Changes in output due to import substitution on intermediate demand	**–0.1%**	**0.37**	**15**	▼	–	–
Agriculture, hunting, forestry, and fishing	0.1%	0.69	7			
Mining and quarrying	–2.9%	0.29	22			
Light manufacturing	0.4%	0.83	5			
Heavy manufacturing	0.4%	0.27	11			
Utilities	0.0%	0.68	11			
Construction	0.0%	0.87	7			
Trade services	0.1%	0.78	8			
Hotels and restaurants	0.0%	0.97	11			
Transport services	0.2%	0.50	9			
Telecommunications	–0.1%	0.93	13			
Financial intermediation	0.1%	0.65	6			
Real estate, renting, and business activities	0.4%	0.80	3			
Public administration and defense	0.0%	0.66	9			
Education, health, and social work	0.0%	0.61	4			
Other personal services	0.0%	0.52	9			
Changes in output due to import substitution on domestic final demand	**0.1%**	**0.88**	**3**	▼	–	–
Agriculture, hunting, forestry, and fishing	0.0%	0.55	10			
Mining and quarrying	0.6%	0.77	5			
Light manufacturing	–0.2%	0.76	15			
Heavy manufacturing	0.7%	0.66	3			
Utilities	0.1%	0.79	7			
Construction	0.0%	0.68	6			
Trade services	0.2%	0.97	2			
Hotels and restaurants	–0.2%	0.45	16			
Transport services	0.4%	1.00	1			
Telecommunications	0.2%	0.87	4			
Financial intermediation	0.1%	0.87	4			
Real estate, renting, and business activities	0.1%	0.58	2			
Public administration and defense	0.0%	0.33	13			
Education, health, and social work	0.0%	0.86	12			
Other personal services	0.0%	0.93	9			

STRENGTH OF LINKAGES

Demand-side Linkages

	Value	Score	Rank	Distance	growth	mean
Direct backward linkage	**0.28**	**0.14**	**19**	▼	**0.5**	**0.28**
Agriculture, hunting, forestry, and fishing	0.18	0.19	22		0.3	0.18
Mining and quarrying	0.15	0.25	18		3.3	0.14
Light manufacturing	0.39	0.45	23		–0.1	0.41
Heavy manufacturing	0.30	0.16	21		6.2	0.34
Utilities	0.36	0.37	15		2.3	0.37
Construction	0.35	0.15	20		–0.7	0.38
Trade services	0.19	0.12	21		4.5	0.18
Hotels and restaurants	0.45	0.58	14		1.6	0.42
Transport services	0.34	0.57	13		2.6	0.31
Telecommunications	0.42	0.68	6		3.8	0.43

continued on next page

Sri Lanka 3.9A *continued*

	Value (2018)	Score (0–1)	Rank (out of 25)	Distance to subregional average	10–year average growth rate (%)	10–year mean value
Financial intermediation	0.27	0.28	10		19.3	0.20
Real estate, renting, and business activities	0.20	0.33	18		–1.1	0.22
Public administration and defense	0.06	0.10	24		6.6	0.07
Education, health, and social work	0.09	0.00	25		–4.0	0.10
Other personal services	0.40	0.77	5		–1.2	0.40
Total backward linkage	**1.40**	**0.08**	**20**	▼	**0.1**	**1.41**
Agriculture, hunting, forestry, and fishing	1.25	0.14	21		0.0	1.27
Mining and quarrying	1.22	0.18	17		0.5	1.22
Light manufacturing	1.55	0.24	22		0.1	1.58
Heavy manufacturing	1.43	0.07	20		1.9	1.54
Utilities	1.52	0.19	15		0.7	1.55
Construction	1.49	0.05	21		–0.2	1.53
Trade services	1.28	0.16	19		0.4	1.27
Hotels and restaurants	1.63	0.32	17		0.5	1.61
Transport services	1.49	0.35	13		0.8	1.46
Telecommunications	1.62	0.49	7		0.9	1.64
Financial intermediation	1.40	0.08	10		1.9	1.29
Real estate, renting, and business activities	1.30	0.19	18		–0.3	1.32
Public administration and defense	1.09	0.09	24		–1.2	1.10
Education, health, and social work	1.11	0.00	25		–1.1	1.13
Other personal services	1.59	0.47	7		–0.7	1.60
Normalized backward linkage	–	–	–	▬	–	–
Agriculture, hunting, forestry, and fishing	0.89	0.25	16		–0.1	0.90
Mining and quarrying	0.88	0.40	13		0.4	0.87
Light manufacturing	1.11	0.43	19		0.0	1.12
Heavy manufacturing	1.02	0.22	18		1.2	1.09
Utilities	1.09	0.37	10		0.6	1.10
Construction	1.07	0.22	20		–0.3	1.09
Trade services	0.91	0.35	12		0.3	0.90
Hotels and restaurants	1.17	0.58	9		0.4	1.14
Transport services	1.07	0.52	6		0.7	1.04
Telecommunications	1.16	0.91	3		0.7	1.16
Financial intermediation	1.00	0.15	4		1.8	0.92
Real estate, renting, and business activities	0.93	0.51	9		–0.3	0.94
Public administration and defense	0.78	0.21	23		–1.4	0.78
Education, health, and social work	0.79	0.19	24		–1.2	0.81
Other personal services	1.14	1.00	1		–0.7	1.14
Net backward linkage	**0.93**	**0.53**	**14**	▼	**0.3**	**0.91**
Agriculture, hunting, forestry, and fishing	0.85	0.72	8		1.9	0.75
Mining and quarrying	0.82	0.57	5		24.3	0.52
Light manufacturing	1.05	0.50	14		–1.2	1.09
Heavy manufacturing	0.51	0.06	23		–0.7	0.53
Utilities	0.27	0.04	23		–4.2	0.31
Construction	1.36	0.30	15		–0.7	1.43
Trade services	0.90	0.46	9		0.2	0.84

continued on next page

Sri Lanka 3.9A *continued*

	Value (2018)	Score (0–1)	Rank (out of 25)	Distance to subregional average	10-year average growth rate (%)	10-year mean value
Hotels and restaurants	1.52	0.71	7		3.7	1.45
Transport services	0.99	0.52	7		−0.2	1.00
Telecommunications	0.82	0.48	10		−1.7	0.93
Financial intermediation	0.55	0.44	12		2.0	0.50
Real estate, renting, and business activities	0.90	0.85	6		0.1	0.91
Public administration and defense	1.06	0.07	24		−1.4	1.08
Education, health, and social work	1.02	0.01	24		−0.8	1.05
Other personal services	1.26	0.84	5		2.3	1.23
Growth equalized output multipliers	**0.09**	**0.07**	**20**	▼	**0.0**	**0.10**
Agriculture, hunting, forestry, and fishing	0.10	0.29	15		−0.4	0.10
Mining and quarrying	0.03	0.06	10		3.5	0.03
Light manufacturing	0.26	0.45	10		−0.6	0.30
Heavy manufacturing	0.07	0.08	18		2.6	0.08
Utilities	0.02	0.00	25		−2.3	0.02
Construction	0.14	0.20	10		2.8	0.13
Trade services	0.13	0.24	19		−0.7	0.13
Hotels and restaurants	0.03	0.04	20		5.0	0.03
Transport services	0.17	1.00	1		0.7	0.19
Telecommunications	0.02	0.21	16		4.3	0.02
Financial intermediation	0.07	0.25	8		4.0	0.06
Real estate, renting, and business activities	0.09	0.27	17		0.4	0.09
Public administration and defense	0.06	0.27	15		−2.9	0.06
Education, health, and social work	0.04	0.07	21		−1.8	0.05
Other personal services	0.18	1.00	1		0.5	0.17

Supply-Side Linkages

	Value (2018)	Score (0–1)	Rank (out of 25)	Distance to subregional average	10-year average growth rate (%)	10-year mean value
Direct forward linkage	**0.33**	**0.17**	**20**	▼	**−0.7**	**0.35**
Agriculture, hunting, forestry, and fishing	0.32	0.21	19		0.1	0.41
Mining and quarrying	0.33	0.33	18		−7.6	0.57
Light manufacturing	0.32	0.21	19		3.7	0.31
Heavy manufacturing	0.64	0.85	4		1.8	0.65
Utilities	0.82	0.89	4		2.3	0.80
Construction	0.09	0.18	19		8.9	0.07
Trade services	0.30	0.30	20		0.9	0.33
Hotels and restaurants	0.07	0.12	21		−10.7	0.10
Transport services	0.34	0.33	17		3.2	0.31
Telecommunications	0.50	0.53	13		5.1	0.43
Financial intermediation	0.61	0.61	14		0.3	0.61
Real estate, renting, and business activities	0.30	0.16	20		0.2	0.31
Public administration and defense	0.02	0.10	15		25.8	0.02
Education, health, and social work	0.08	0.28	8		12.9	0.07
Other personal services	0.21	0.22	17		−5.3	0.23
Total forward linkage	**1.48**	**0.08**	**20**	▼	**−0.2**	**1.51**
Agriculture, hunting, forestry, and fishing	1.45	0.12	20		0.0	1.58
Mining and quarrying	1.40	0.13	20		−3.7	1.73
Light manufacturing	1.45	0.10	19		1.1	1.44

continued on next page

Sri Lanka 3.9A *continued*

	Value (2018)	Score (0–1)	Rank (out of 25)	Distance to subregional average	10–year average growth rate (%)	10–year mean value
Heavy manufacturing	1.99	0.48	5		1.5	2.04
Utilities	2.23	0.40	11		1.0	2.22
Construction	1.12	0.13	20		0.5	1.09
Trade services	1.43	0.17	20		0.4	1.48
Hotels and restaurants	1.09	0.07	21		−2.8	1.14
Transport services	1.49	0.18	18		1.0	1.47
Telecommunications	1.76	0.40	14		1.7	1.66
Financial intermediation	1.86	0.16	15		0.1	1.87
Real estate, renting, and business activities	1.44	0.10	21		−0.4	1.45
Public administration and defense	1.03	0.08	16		0.1	1.02
Education, health, and social work	1.10	0.32	9		−0.3	1.10
Other personal services	1.31	0.23	16		−2.0	1.34
Normalized forward linkage	–	–	–	▬	–	–
Agriculture, hunting, forestry, and fishing	0.98	0.22	18		0.2	1.05
Mining and quarrying	1.00	0.32	19		−3.6	1.24
Light manufacturing	1.04	0.44	15		1.0	1.02
Heavy manufacturing	1.42	0.93	2		1.2	1.45
Utilities	1.60	0.85	3		1.0	1.58
Construction	0.80	0.35	14		0.6	0.78
Trade services	1.02	0.30	18		0.3	1.05
Hotels and restaurants	0.78	0.18	19		−2.8	0.81
Transport services	1.07	0.37	14		0.8	1.04
Telecommunications	1.26	0.61	8		1.6	1.18
Financial intermediation	1.33	0.24	14		0.0	1.33
Real estate, renting, and business activities	1.03	0.25	16		−0.4	1.04
Public administration and defense	0.73	0.53	12		0.2	0.73
Education, health, and social work	0.79	0.78	4		−0.3	0.78
Other personal services	0.94	0.29	11		−2.1	0.96
Net forward linkage	**0.87**	**0.48**	**11**	▼	**−0.5**	**0.90**
Agriculture, hunting, forestry, and fishing	1.06	0.39	15		−0.3	1.16
Mining and quarrying	1.13	0.50	13		−3.8	1.41
Light manufacturing	0.72	0.81	2		2.0	0.67
Heavy manufacturing	0.40	0.41	18		−0.1	0.53
Utilities	1.16	0.61	3		0.5	1.10
Construction	0.56	0.74	6		1.9	0.51
Trade services	1.10	0.50	14		0.1	1.14
Hotels and restaurants	0.54	0.29	14		−3.2	0.58
Transport services	0.82	0.42	7		1.3	0.81
Telecommunications	0.62	0.11	22		0.5	0.55
Financial intermediation	1.30	0.39	15		−1.4	1.42
Real estate, renting, and business activities	1.07	0.39	17		0.2	1.06
Public administration and defense	0.95	0.93	2		2.3	0.93
Education, health, and social work	0.98	1.00	1		1.4	0.94
Other personal services	0.68	0.29	22		0.8	0.68

continued on next page

Sri Lanka 3.9A *continued*

	Value (2018)	Score (0–1)	Rank (out of 25)	Distance to subregional average	10–year average growth rate (%)	10–year mean value
Growth equalized input multipliers	**0.09**	**0.06**	**21**	▼	**−0.1**	**0.10**
Agriculture, hunting, forestry, and fishing	0.13	0.26	17		−1.4	0.14
Mining and quarrying	0.04	0.06	13		−1.2	0.04
Light manufacturing	0.22	0.64	5		0.9	0.24
Heavy manufacturing	0.03	0.07	18		−5.8	0.05
Utilities	0.02	0.06	21		−2.4	0.03
Construction	0.09	0.14	9		4.3	0.08
Trade services	0.17	0.29	20		−1.0	0.18
Hotels and restaurants	0.02	0.04	20		0.9	0.02
Transport services	0.17	1.00	1		1.7	0.18
Telecommunications	0.02	0.01	24		4.1	0.01
Financial intermediation	0.11	0.26	12		2.3	0.09
Real estate, renting, and business activities	0.12	0.19	18		0.0	0.11
Public administration and defense	0.06	0.33	12		−1.3	0.06
Education, health, and social work	0.05	0.22	18		−0.9	0.05
Other personal services	0.14	1.00	1		0.7	0.14

Impacts from Hypothetical Extraction

	Value (2018)	Score (0–1)	Rank (out of 25)	Distance to subregional average	10–year average growth rate (%)	10–year mean value
Changes in gross output due to hypothetical extraction	**−8.8%**	**0.88**	**10**	▼	**0.1**	**−0.09**
Agriculture, hunting, forestry, and fishing	−8.8%	0.70	12		−0.3	−8.7
Mining and quarrying	−2.6%	0.93	16		4.0	−2.2
Light manufacturing	−24.2%	0.49	15		−1.0	−27.8
Heavy manufacturing	−6.2%	0.89	8		1.9	−6.7
Utilities	−1.6%	0.99	3		−1.2	−2.0
Construction	−14.5%	0.72	16		2.5	−14.0
Trade services	−11.4%	0.82	9		−0.3	−11.4
Hotels and restaurants	−3.5%	0.95	6		5.7	−3.1
Transport services	−16.0%	0.00	25		0.6	−17.0
Telecommunications	−2.5%	0.65	13		5.1	−2.1
Financial intermediation	−7.0%	0.68	20		5.6	−4.9
Real estate, renting, and business activities	−8.0%	0.67	12		0.3	−7.9
Public administration and defense	−4.4%	0.79	7		−3.8	−4.5
Education, health, and social work	−3.3%	0.98	3		−2.3	−3.5
Other personal services	−17.8%	0.00	25		1.4	−16.8

Impacts from Hypothetical Insertion

	Value (2018)	Score (0–1)	Rank (out of 25)	Distance to subregional average	10–year average growth rate (%)	10–year mean value
Changes in gross output due to hypothetical insertion	**2.9%**	**0.08**	**20**	▼	**0.8**	**0.03**
Agriculture, hunting, forestry, and fishing	1.8%	0.07	16		0.1	1.9
Mining and quarrying	0.5%	0.04	13		7.9	0.4
Light manufacturing	10.2%	0.28	11		0.1	12.1
Heavy manufacturing	2.2%	0.03	18		30.4	3.2
Utilities	0.6%	0.03	21		1.3	0.8
Construction	4.8%	0.12	17		2.4	4.9
Trade services	2.5%	0.11	21		5.6	2.4
Hotels and restaurants	1.3%	0.07	20		7.1	1.2
Transport services	6.0%	0.93	2		4.0	6.0
Telecommunications	1.0%	0.26	8		9.6	0.8
Financial intermediation	2.1%	0.17	8		25.3	1.1

continued on next page

Sri Lanka 3.9A *continued*

	Value (2018)	Score (0–1)	Rank (out of 25)	Distance to subregional average	10-year average growth rate (%)	10-year mean value
Real estate, renting, and business activities	1.9%	0.23	15		−0.2	2.0
Public administration and defense	0.4%	0.08	24		5.8	0.4
Education, health, and social work	0.3%	0.00	25		−5.2	0.4
Other personal services	7.3%	1.00	1		−0.8	7.1

SPREAD OF ECONOMIC LINKAGES

Demand-side

	Value (2018)	Score (0–1)	Rank (out of 25)	Distance to subregional average	10-year average growth rate (%)	10-year mean value
Relative evenness of direct backward linkage	0.45	0.48	12	▼	2.5	0.49
Relative evenness of total backward linkage	0.13	0.08	20	▼	2.7	0.14
		0.00				
Backward measure of concentration based on input coefficients	0.94	0.97	3	▲	0.1	0.94
Agriculture, hunting, forestry, and fishing	0.96	0.95	3		0.5	0.94
Mining and quarrying	0.93	0.49	13		−0.1	0.92
Light manufacturing	0.91	0.68	10		−0.2	0.91
Heavy manufacturing	0.86	0.81	13		−0.9	0.89
Utilities	0.96	0.98	2		0.3	0.96
Construction	0.95	0.95	7		0.0	0.94
Trade services	0.94	0.83	15		−0.2	0.95
Hotels and restaurants	0.92	0.83	8		−0.2	0.93
Transport services	0.92	0.58	14		−0.3	0.93
Telecommunications	0.96	0.94	3		0.0	0.96
Financial intermediation	0.94	0.95	7		0.6	0.92
Real estate, renting, and business activities	0.97	1.00	1		0.1	0.97
Public administration and defense	0.96	0.66	11		0.3	0.95
Education, health, and social work	0.93	0.53	21		0.3	0.94
Other personal services	0.96	0.93	8		0.8	0.95
Relative evenness of direct forward linkage	0.70	0.64	8	▲	0.9	0.70
Relative evenness of total forward linkage	0.24	0.16	16	▼	0.9	0.25
Forward measure of concentration based on output coefficients	0.61	0.30	20	▼	−0.2	0.60
Agriculture, hunting, forestry, and fishing	0.41	0.53	9		3.4	0.34
Mining and quarrying	0.30	0.42	19		−2.7	0.34
Light manufacturing	0.70	0.71	13		0.3	0.68
Heavy manufacturing	0.82	0.92	2		1.2	0.77
Utilities	0.85	0.86	6		−0.2	0.84
Construction	0.40	0.46	17		−4.7	0.47
Trade services	0.82	0.89	4		1.4	0.76
Hotels and restaurants	0.52	0.00	25		−1.9	0.54
Transport services	0.75	0.65	18		−0.8	0.75
Telecommunications	0.78	0.44	17		0.0	0.79
Financial intermediation	0.72	0.77	17		−1.1	0.72
Real estate, renting, and business activities	0.58	0.00	25		−1.1	0.60
Public administration and defense	0.15	0.16	21		7.2	0.14
Education, health, and social work	0.56	0.58	16		9.1	0.51
Other personal services	0.73	0.59	17		1.6	0.71

continued on next page

Sri Lanka 3.9A *continued*

	Value (2018)	Score (0–1)	Rank (out of 25)	Distance to subregional average	10–year average growth rate (%)	10–year mean value
SENSITIVITY OF ECONOMIC LINKAGES						
Economic Complexity						
Percentage intermediate transaction	0.30	0.13	20	▼	0.2	0.31
Average output multiplier	1.40	0.08	20	▼	0.1	1.41
Average of Leontief inverse	0.18	0.08	20	▼	0.1	0.18
Average technical coefficient	0.02	0.14	19	▼	0.5	0.02
Mean intermediate coefficient	0.28	0.14	19	▼	0.5	0.28
Percentage of above-average coefficients (%)	0.31	0.80	2	▲	0.1	0.30
Determinant of non-competitive Leontief inverse	2.16	0.03	20	▼	1.0	2.21
Determinant of competitive Leontief inverse	3.30	0.02	19	▼	1.5	3.24
Mean path length	1.42	0.07	20	▼	0.0	1.44
Cycling index	0.07	0.18	19	▼	0.9	0.08
Average propagation length	1.75	0.29	13	▼	0.1	1.77
Overall sensitivity of the economy	0.76	0.64	11	▲	–0.2	0.76
Index of direct interrelatedness	0.55	0.26	16	▼	–0.6	0.56
Index of indirect interrelatedness	0.21	0.96	2	▲	1.3	0.20
Global intensity index	20.96	0.08	20	▼	0.1	21.10

Note: The scores of the economy in focus are shown in the horizontal bars with labels. The colored dots represent the indicator performance of the economy in focus compared to other economies in the region. The highest rank among economies is 1 while the lowest rank is 25. The indicators shown in the chart are selected from a broader set of indicators (see the technical appendix for more details).

Source: Asian Development Bank Multi-Regional Input–Output Database. https://mrio.adbx.online/ (accessed 4 August 2020).

3.9B External Linkages

$ = United States dollars, GVC = global value chain.

Note: The scores of the economy in focus are shown in the horizontal bars with labels. The colored dots represent the indicator performance of the economy in focus compared to other economies in the region. The highest rank among economies is 1, while the lowest rank is 25. The indicators shown in the chart are selected from a broader set of indicators (see the technical appendix for more details).

Source: Asian Development Bank Multi-Regional Input–Output Database. https://mrio.adbx.online/ (accessed 4 August 2020).

		Value (2018)	Score (0–1)	Rank (out of 25)	Distance to subregional average	10-year average growth rate (%)	10-year mean value
PARTICIPATION IN GLOBAL VALUE CHAINS							
International Trade Coefficients							
Trade openness		0.42	0.07	20	▼	−0.5	0.44
Self-sufficiency ratio		0.95	0.48	20	▲	0.2	0.95
Regional supply percentage		0.84	0.71	7	▲	0.2	0.84
Regional purchase coefficient		0.86	0.77	9	▲	0.2	0.86
Sectoral purchase coefficient		0.90	0.93	9	▲	0.1	0.90
Simple location quotient of gross output		1.24	0.58	9	▼	0.5	1.21
Fabrication effect		0.75	0.13	21	▼	−0.4	0.75
Exports	($)	**15,028**	**0.01**	**16**	▼	**7.4**	**12,200**
Export-to-output ratio		**0.08**	**0.20**	**17**	▼	**2.5**	**0.08**
Agriculture, hunting, forestry, and fishing		0.07	0.28	15		0.5	0.07
Mining and quarrying		0.06	0.07	16		0.5	0.07
Light manufacturing		0.27	0.49	11		1.2	0.25
Heavy manufacturing		0.07	0.06	22		0.4	0.10
Utilities		0.00	0.00	22		0.3	0.01
Construction		0.00	0.06	14		0.5	0.01
Trade services		0.18	0.24	12		0.5	0.17
Hotels and restaurants		0.23	0.24	7		0.5	0.16
Transport services		0.16	0.20	14		−0.6	0.15
Telecommunications		0.08	0.23	12		0.5	0.14

continued on next page

Sri Lanka 3.9B *continued*

		Value (2018)	Score (0–1)	Rank (out of 25)	Distance to subregional average	10–year average growth rate (%)	10–year mean value
Financial intermediation		0.05	0.11	6		0.5	0.04
Real estate, renting, and business activities		0.02	0.08	17		–4.2	0.03
Public administration and defense		0.00	0.00	20		0.5	0.01
Education, health, and social work		0.00	0.01	20		–12.2	0.00
Other personal services		0.03	0.04	16		0.7	0.03
Imports	($)	**22,315**	**0.01**	**16**	▼	**5.5**	**18,568**
Import-to-input ratio		**0.09**	**0.32**	**16**	▼	**1.8**	**0.09**
Agriculture, hunting, forestry, and fishing		0.08	0.23	8		2.9	0.08
Mining and quarrying		0.03	0.07	19		–2.5	0.04
Light manufacturing		0.10	0.15	19		–1.4	0.11
Heavy manufacturing		0.44	0.60	2		10.1	0.34
Utilities		0.09	0.10	19		1.2	0.11
Construction		0.11	0.22	17		3.9	0.12
Trade services		0.03	0.11	20		19.0	0.04
Hotels and restaurants		0.05	0.13	20		7.4	0.06
Transport services		0.09	0.15	22		–4.6	0.11
Telecommunications		0.18	0.50	6		8.2	0.19
Financial intermediation		0.02	0.06	21		7.2	0.03
Real estate, renting, and business activities		0.03	0.16	18		0.3	0.04
Public administration and defense		0.01	0.06	23		4.0	0.02
Education, health, and social work		0.02	0.05	23		–1.9	0.03
Other personal services		0.05	0.12	15		–4.7	0.06
Total foreign factor content of consumption	($)	**5,916**	**0.01**	**16**	▼	**3.9**	**5,291**
Total foreign factor content of investment	($)	**2,699**	**0.00**	**16**	▼	**6.9**	**2,311**
Total foreign factor content of exports	($)	**2,135**	**0.01**	**16**	▼	**7.4**	**1,821**

Interregional Multipliers

		Value (2018)	Score (0–1)	Rank (out of 25)	Distance to subregional average	10–year average growth rate (%)	10–year mean value
Import Leakage Effects		**0.14**	**0.23**	**17**	▼	**1.2**	**0.14**
Agriculture, hunting, forestry, and fishing		0.12	0.25	11		0.9	0.12
Mining and quarrying		0.07	0.15	19		1.3	0.07
Light manufacturing		0.16	0.15	19		–0.9	0.16
Heavy manufacturing		0.54	0.66	4		5.9	0.43
Utilities		0.17	0.18	18		1.8	0.17
Construction		0.17	0.15	18		0.4	0.18
Trade services		0.05	0.08	20		7.4	0.06
Hotels and restaurants		0.11	0.17	21		2.8	0.12
Transport services		0.14	0.13	20		–2.8	0.16
Telecommunications		0.26	0.48	6		6.1	0.26
Financial intermediation		0.05	0.10	17		7.9	0.05
Real estate, renting, and business activities		0.06	0.18	20		0.2	0.07
Public administration and defense		0.02	0.06	24		–1.3	0.03
Education, health, and social work		0.03	0.00	25		–4.8	0.04
Other personal services		0.11	0.23	14		–3.3	0.11
Intraregional transfer multiplier		**1.40**	**0.08**	**20**	▼	**0.1**	**1.41**
Agriculture, hunting, forestry, and fishing		1.25	0.14	21		0.0	1.27
Mining and quarrying		1.22	0.18	17		0.5	1.22

continued on next page

Sri Lanka 3.9B *continued*

	Value (2018)	Score (0–1)	Rank (out of 25)	Distance to subregional average	10–year average growth rate (%)	10–year mean value
Light manufacturing	1.55	0.24	22		0.1	1.58
Heavy manufacturing	1.43	0.07	20		1.9	1.54
Utilities	1.52	0.19	15		0.7	1.55
Construction	1.49	0.05	21		–0.2	1.53
Trade services	1.28	0.16	19		0.4	1.27
Hotels and restaurants	1.63	0.32	17		0.5	1.61
Transport services	1.49	0.35	13		0.8	1.46
Telecommunications	1.62	0.49	7		0.9	1.64
Financial intermediation	1.40	0.08	10		1.9	1.29
Real estate, renting, and business activities	1.30	0.19	18		–0.3	1.32
Public administration and defense	1.09	0.09	24		–1.2	1.10
Education, health, and social work	1.11	0.00	25		–1.1	1.13
Other personal services	1.59	0.47	7		–0.7	1.60
Interregional spillover multiplier	**1.22**	**0.36**	**17**	▼	**0.1**	**1.23**
Agriculture, hunting, forestry, and fishing	1.23	0.33	8		0.3	1.22
Mining and quarrying	1.08	0.10	18		–0.3	1.10
Light manufacturing	1.24	0.17	20		–0.4	1.26
Heavy manufacturing	2.10	0.75	3		3.4	1.85
Utilities	1.24	0.13	19		0.1	1.28
Construction	1.28	0.25	18		0.0	1.29
Trade services	1.06	0.12	19		0.2	1.08
Hotels and restaurants	1.11	0.12	20		0.1	1.13
Transport services	1.24	0.18	22		–1.1	1.29
Telecommunications	1.45	0.57	6		1.4	1.47
Financial intermediation	1.04	0.07	21		–0.3	1.06
Real estate, renting, and business activities	1.08	0.21	17		0.1	1.09
Public administration and defense	1.02	0.05	23		–0.6	1.05
Education, health, and social work	1.06	0.07	23		–0.5	1.08
Other personal services	1.13	0.13	13		–0.7	1.15
Interregional feedback multiplier	**1.000**	**0.01**	**19**	▼	**0.0**	**1.00**
Agriculture, hunting, forestry, and fishing	1.000	0.01	17		0.0	1.00
Mining and quarrying	1.000	0.00	19		0.0	1.00
Light manufacturing	1.000	0.01	19		0.0	1.00
Heavy manufacturing	1.000	0.01	16		0.0	1.00
Utilities	1.000	0.00	20		0.0	1.00
Construction	1.000	0.00	20		0.0	1.00
Trade services	1.000	0.00	19		0.0	1.00
Hotels and restaurants	1.000	0.00	21		0.0	1.00
Transport services	1.000	0.00	21		0.0	1.00
Telecommunications	1.000	0.01	16		0.0	1.00
Financial intermediation	1.000	0.00	19		0.0	1.00
Real estate, renting, and business activities	1.000	0.00	16		0.0	1.00
Public administration and defense	1.000	0.00	22		0.0	1.00
Education, health, and social work	1.000	0.00	19		0.0	1.00
Other personal services	1.000	0.00	18		0.0	1.00

continued on next page

Sri Lanka 3.9B *continued*

	Value (2018)	Score (0–1)	Rank (out of 25)	Distance to subregional average	10–year average growth rate (%)	10–year mean value
Global Value Chain (GVC) Participation Index						
Backward GVC Participation	12.4%	0.10	19	▼	–1.1	0.13
Simple GVCs	8.1%	0.22	18	▼	–0.6	0.08
Agriculture, hunting, forestry, and fishing	0.6	0.23	7		1.3	0.48
Mining and quarrying	0.1	0.16	5		10.5	0.05
Light manufacturing	1.3	0.28	10		–0.8	1.72
Heavy manufacturing	0.9	0.18	12		23.3	0.59
Utilities	0.0	0.01	24		–5.8	0.05
Construction	1.7	0.12	18		–2.4	1.71
Trade services	0.3	0.09	20		0.8	0.32
Hotels and restaurants	0.2	0.09	20		2.2	0.18
Transport services	1.0	0.62	8		–2.4	1.26
Telecommunications	0.2	0.20	10		9.4	0.16
Financial intermediation	0.1	0.09	12		16.8	0.09
Real estate, renting, and business activities	0.3	0.16	17		–1.8	0.32
Public administration and defense	0.1	0.02	24		2.9	0.17
Education, health, and social work	0.1	0.00	25		2.8	0.13
Other personal services	1.1	1.00	1		–0.7	1.14
Complex GVCs	4.3%	0.06	18	▼	–1.9	0.05
Agriculture, hunting, forestry, and fishing	0.3	0.28	6		1.7	0.27
Mining and quarrying	0.0	0.11	9		34.3	0.03
Light manufacturing	1.3	0.12	8		–2.0	1.54
Heavy manufacturing	0.5	0.02	14		1.3	0.40
Utilities	0.0	0.00	25		–3.9	0.03
Construction	0.6	0.10	18		0.6	0.65
Trade services	0.1	0.01	20		2.5	0.14
Hotels and restaurants	0.1	0.01	16		18.5	0.11
Transport services	0.5	0.24	10		–4.8	0.70
Telecommunications	0.1	0.14	10		10.2	0.08
Financial intermediation	0.0	0.03	12		12.4	0.03
Real estate, renting, and business activities	0.1	0.12	16		3.6	0.12
Public administration and defense	0.0	0.03	24		–5.0	0.07
Education, health, and social work	0.0	0.00	25		–8.1	0.06
Other personal services	0.4	1.00	1		0.8	0.44
Forward GVC Participation	8.0%	0.10	21	▼	0.3	0.08
Simple GVCs	5.2%	0.09	20	▼	0.4	0.05
Agriculture, hunting, forestry, and fishing	0.3	0.16	16		2.1	0.37
Mining and quarrying	0.1	0.01	15		1.1	0.11
Light manufacturing	1.2	0.32	6		0.0	1.14
Heavy manufacturing	0.1	0.01	19		–2.3	0.19
Utilities	0.0	0.00	21		–1.7	0.05
Construction	0.0	0.01	18		0.9	0.05
Trade services	1.2	0.13	13		–0.7	1.25
Hotels and restaurants	0.1	0.01	14		0.8	0.06
Transport services	1.1	0.27	8		–4.4	1.12
Telecommunications	0.1	0.03	21		9.9	0.09

continued on next page

Sri Lanka 3.9B *continued*

	Value (2018)	Score (0–1)	Rank (out of 25)	Distance to subregional average	10-year average growth rate (%)	10-year mean value
Financial intermediation	0.4	0.08	11		6.7	0.32
Real estate, renting, and business activities	0.2	0.02	22		–3.5	0.21
Public administration and defense	0.0	0.00	23		9.4	0.00
Education, health, and social work	0.0	0.05	20		6.1	0.01
Other personal services	0.3	0.38	6		1.7	0.23
Complex GVCs	**2.8%**	**0.12**	**21**	▼	**0.1**	**0.03**
Agriculture, hunting, forestry, and fishing	0.2	0.10	15		2.1	0.22
Mining and quarrying	0.1	0.00	15		5.9	0.06
Light manufacturing	0.6	0.29	7		1.5	0.60
Heavy manufacturing	0.1	0.01	21		–2.0	0.11
Utilities	0.0	0.00	21		0.8	0.03
Construction	0.0	0.01	21		3.5	0.02
Trade services	0.9	0.27	13		3.9	0.78
Hotels and restaurants	0.0	0.01	15		4.3	0.03
Transport services	0.5	0.28	11		–3.2	0.42
Telecommunications	0.0	0.04	23		13.1	0.03
Financial intermediation	0.2	0.11	13		10.6	0.16
Real estate, renting, and business activities	0.1	0.02	22		–0.9	0.12
Public administration and defense	0.0	0.00	23		9.5	0.00
Education, health, and social work	0.0	0.05	18		8.5	0.01
Other personal services	0.1	0.47	7		3.5	0.09

SPECIALIZATION IN GLOBAL VALUE CHAINS

Vertical Specialization

	Value (2018)	Score (0–1)	Rank (out of 25)	Distance to subregional average	10-year average growth rate (%)	10-year mean value
Vertical Specialization Ratio	**14.2%**	**0.14**	**20**	▼	**–1.0**	**0.15**
Agriculture, hunting, forestry, and fishing	12.2%	0.25	11		0.9	0.12
Mining and quarrying	6.8%	0.15	19		1.3	0.07
Light manufacturing	15.6%	0.15	19		–0.9	0.16
Heavy manufacturing	54.3%	0.66	4		5.9	0.43
Utilities	16.6%	0.26	18		1.8	0.17
Construction	17.2%	0.14	18		0.4	0.18
Trade services	5.2%	0.08	21		7.4	0.06
Hotels and restaurants	11.1%	0.17	21		2.8	0.12
Transport services	14.4%	0.13	20		–2.8	0.16
Telecommunications	26.2%	0.48	6		6.1	0.26
Financial intermediation	5.0%	0.10	17		7.8	0.05
Real estate, renting, and business activities	6.2%	0.18	20		0.2	0.07
Public administration and defense	2.0%	0.06	24		–15.8	0.03
Education, health, and social work	3.0%	0.00	25		–4.8	0.04
Other personal services	10.7%	0.23	14		–3.3	0.11

Revealed Comparative Advantages

Traditional RCA Index

	Value (2018)	Score (0–1)	Rank (out of 25)	Distance to subregional average	10-year average growth rate (%)	10-year mean value
Agriculture, hunting, forestry, and fishing	1.82	0.30	9	▼	1.0	1.78
Mining and quarrying	0.17	0.02	12	▼	9.5	0.14
Light manufacturing	2.97	0.53	5	▲	0.8	3.01

continued on next page

Sri Lanka 3.9B *continued*

	Value (2018)	Score (0–1)	Rank (out of 25)	Distance to subregional average	10–year average growth rate (%)	10–year mean value
Heavy manufacturing	0.07	0.04	19	▼	9.6	0.10
Utilities	0.01	0.00	23	▼	–10.4	0.17
Construction	0.61	0.08	14	▼	–7.6	2.06
Trade services	1.84	0.24	4	▲	0.0	1.86
Hotels and restaurants	3.52	0.06	7	▼	–1.7	2.70
Transport services	3.03	0.71	3	▲	–4.9	2.99
Telecommunications	1.49	0.23	13	▼	8.2	2.09
Financial intermediation	0.73	0.21	3	▲	9.3	0.46
Real estate, renting, and business activities	0.19	0.06	12	▼	–6.4	0.27
Public administration and defense	0.08	0.00	18	▼	0.1	0.77
Education, health, and social work	0.07	0.01	20	▼	–15.1	0.29
Other personal services	2.79	0.16	2	▼	–1.1	2.35
New RCA Index (Based on Domestic Value Added)						
Agriculture, hunting, forestry, and fishing	1.84	0.26	13	▼	2.7	2.05
Mining and quarrying	0.17	0.02	16	▼	4.5	0.20
Light manufacturing	3.44	0.78	3	▲	–0.5	3.39
Heavy manufacturing	0.09	0.04	19	▼	–2.9	0.14
Utilities	0.41	0.02	19	▼	–1.8	0.48
Construction	0.53	0.03	14	▼	5.6	0.73
Trade services	1.41	0.41	7	▲	0.8	1.47
Hotels and restaurants	2.01	0.06	8	▼	–2.7	1.59
Transport services	2.47	0.84	3	▲	–3.8	2.45
Telecommunications	0.63	0.11	18	▼	9.0	0.67
Financial intermediation	1.00	0.25	6	▲	7.7	0.78
Real estate, renting, and business activities	0.19	0.07	20	▼	–3.3	0.22
Public administration and defense	0.06	0.01	21	▼	2.4	0.38
Education, health, and social work	0.33	0.06	19	▼	0.3	0.42
Other personal services	1.86	0.24	3	▲	1.6	1.71

POSITION IN GLOBAL VALUE CHAINS

	Value (2018)	Score (0–1)	Rank (out of 25)	Distance to subregional average	10–year average growth rate (%)	10–year mean value
Upstreamness Index	**1.6**	**0.00**	**25**	▼	**–0.4**	**1.7**
Agriculture, hunting, forestry, and fishing	1.6	0.10	22		–0.3	1.7
Mining and quarrying	1.5	0.34	22		–3.8	1.9
Light manufacturing	1.7	0.13	22		1.0	1.7
Heavy manufacturing	2.2	0.29	19		0.9	2.3
Utilities	2.4	0.23	16		1.0	2.4
Construction	1.1	0.11	20		0.3	1.1
Trade services	1.8	0.22	21		0.2	1.9
Hotels and restaurants	1.2	0.12	22		–2.3	1.3
Transport services	1.8	0.19	21		1.1	1.7
Telecommunications	2.0	0.26	16		–0.1	2.0
Financial intermediation	2.1	0.19	17		0.4	2.1
Real estate, renting, and business activities	1.5	0.05	23		–0.5	1.6
Public administration and defense	1.0	0.04	18		0.1	1.0
Education, health, and social work	1.1	0.25	10		–0.3	1.1
Other personal services	1.4	0.17	21		–1.9	1.4

continued on next page

Sri Lanka 3.9B *continued*

	Value (2018)	Score (0–1)	Rank (out of 25)	Distance to subregional average	10-year average growth rate (%)	10-year mean value
PRODUCTION LENGTH OF GLOBAL VALUE CHAINS						
Backward Measures of Average Production Length						
Production Length of Global Value Chain Activity (B)	0.6	0.24	16	▼	1.3	0.6
Agriculture, hunting, forestry, and fishing	0.5	0.26	11		1.1	0.5
Mining and quarrying	0.3	0.18	19		2.3	0.3
Light manufacturing	0.6	0.19	19		−0.7	0.7
Heavy manufacturing	2.0	0.75	5		5.8	1.6
Utilities	0.7	0.21	19		2.4	0.7
Construction	0.7	0.09	18		0.1	0.7
Trade services	0.2	0.09	21		5.0	0.2
Hotels and restaurants	0.5	0.19	19		2.2	0.5
Transport services	0.6	0.16	20		−2.1	0.7
Telecommunications	1.1	0.58	6		5.8	1.1
Financial intermediation	0.2	0.15	15		7.5	0.2
Real estate, renting, and business activities	0.3	0.22	20		0.8	0.3
Public administration and defense	0.1	0.06	24		−2.8	0.1
Education, health, and social work	0.1	0.00	25		−5.4	0.2
Other personal services	0.5	0.28	15		−2.4	0.5
Forward Measures of Average Production Length						
Production Length of Global Value Chain Activity (F)	0.3	0.10	22	▼	−0.4	0.3
Agriculture, hunting, forestry, and fishing	0.2	0.11	20		1.6	0.3
Mining and quarrying	0.2	0.05	21		−0.4	0.3
Light manufacturing	0.4	0.19	19		1.5	0.4
Heavy manufacturing	0.4	0.10	22		−0.3	0.4
Utilities	0.3	0.08	21		0.9	0.3
Construction	0.0	0.02	22		2.4	0.0
Trade services	0.6	0.26	15		0.2	0.6
Hotels and restaurants	0.2	0.11	15		1.4	0.2
Transport services	0.5	0.16	19		−0.6	0.4
Telecommunications	0.4	0.15	20		1.3	0.5
Financial intermediation	0.4	0.15	17		−0.3	0.4
Real estate, renting, and business activities	0.1	0.04	22		−2.0	0.2
Public administration and defense	0.0	0.00	24		6.6	0.0
Education, health, and social work	0.0	0.08	16		5.6	0.0
Other personal services	0.1	0.04	22		2.5	0.1

Note: The scores of the economy in focus are shown in the horizontal bars with labels. The colored dots represent the indicator performance of the economy in focus compared to other economies in the region. The highest rank among economies is 1 while the lowest rank is 25. The indicators shown in the chart are selected from a broader set of indicators (see the technical appendix for more details).

Source: Asian Development Bank Multi-Regional Input–Output Database. https://mrio.adbx.online/ (accessed 4 August 2020).

PART 4

ECONOMY-SPECIFIC INPUT–OUTPUT TABLES FOR 2000 AND 2018

4.1A Input–Output Table for Bangladesh, 2000
(at current prices, $ million)

Sector	Code	Agriculture, Hunting, Forestry, and Fishing AHF	Mining and Quarrying MIN	Light Manufacturing LMF	Heavy Manufacturing HMF	Utilities UTL	Construction CON	Trade Services TRD	Hotels and Restaurants HRS	Transport Services TSP
Agriculture, hunting, forestry, and fishing	AHF	1,499	–	2,022	0	–	801	–	242	–
Mining and quarrying	MIN	8	3	117	48	69	119	–	8	101
Light manufacturing	LMF	359	5	4,040	128	36	1,080	165	120	172
Heavy manufacturing	HMF	264	5	260	440	40	606	34	7	72
Utilities	UTL	63	10	261	87	15	97	4	2	80
Construction	CON	313	8	315	68	12	1,186	132	25	363
Trade services	TRD	524	4	1,242	172	47	491	47	91	112
Hotels and restaurants	HRS	8	–	150	51	10	70	90	0	30
Transport services	TSP	205	6	515	142	54	162	51	45	74
Telecommunications	TEL	9	0	118	49	6	15	32	4	23
Financial intermediation	FIN	45	1	325	67	7	163	62	5	58
Real estate, renting, and business activities	BUS	29	4	198	84	63	89	97	12	87
Public administration and defense	PAD	36	1	87	20	4	55	32	1	32
Education, health, and social work	EHS	7	–	12	–	–	–	–	–	–
Other personal services	OSV	84	3	295	96	41	113	286	19	63
Total imports	**IMP**	**406**	**12**	**1,262**	**337**	**61**	**633**	**86**	**90**	**248**
Total intermediate consumption	**r60**	**3,859**	**62**	**11,218**	**1,788**	**463**	**5,681**	**1,116**	**674**	**1,513**
Taxes less subsidies on products	r99	35	4	160	74	11	124	32	16	91
CIF / FOB adjustments on exports	r61	–	–	–	–	–	–	–	–	–
Direct purchases abroad by residents	r62	–	–	–	–	–	–	–	–	–
Domestic purchases by nonresidents	r63	–	–	–	–	–	–	–	–	–
Value-added at basic prices	r64	11,195	443	5,263	1,419	589	3,379	5,601	281	3,471
International transport margins	trs	–	–	–	–	–	–	–	–	–
Gross output	**r69**	**15,089**	**509**	**16,641**	**3,282**	**1,063**	**9,185**	**6,749**	**970**	**5,075**

– = magnitude equals zero; 0 = magnitude is less than half of unit employed; $ = United States dollars; ( ) = negative; CIF = cost, insurance, and freight; FOB = free on board.

Source: Asian Development Bank Multi-Regional Input–Output Database. https://mrio.adbx.online/ (accessed 4 August 2020).

4.1A Input–Output Table for Bangladesh, 2000
(*continued*)

Telecommunications	Financial Intermediation	Real Estate, Renting, and Business Activities	Public Administration and Defense	Education, Health, and Social Work	Other Personal Services	Final Consumption Expenditure by Households	Final Consumption Expenditure by Nonprofit Organizations Serving Households	Final Consumption Expenditure by Government	Gross Fixed Capital Formation	Changes in Inventories and Valuables	Exports	Gross Output
TEL	FIN	BUS	PAD	EHS	OSV	F1	F2	F3	F4	F5	EXP	
–	–	11	–	9	7	10,372	–	–	5	–	120	15,089
–	–	2	0	0	0	33	–	–	–	–	1	509
16	47	58	25	81	166	4,691	–	–	688	–	4,763	16,641
4	6	7	6	106	12	329	–	–	981	–	102	3,282
4	12	4	3	6	4	391	–	–	22	–	1	1,063
15	18	161	12	9	42	–	–	–	6,500	–	6	9,185
6	14	21	10	77	45	3,063	–	–	504	–	279	6,749
19	24	35	8	7	37	428	–	–	–	–	5	970
8	19	23	20	43	33	3,545	–	–	71	–	59	5,075
6	23	7	4	11	10	128	–	–	–	–	29	475
12	17	34	14	4	37	169	–	–	–	–	2	1,020
10	31	41	10	24	46	3,769	–	–	–	–	2	4,595
1	7	10	9	4	9	–	–	1,293	–	–	2	1,603
–	–	–	217	–	18	1,581	–	764	–	–	1	2,601
21	34	87	13	14	37	3,212	–	19	–	–	64	4,500
26	45	26	43	134	68	2,952	–	2	1,418	–	–	7,851
148	296	528	394	528	570	34,665	–	2,078	10,188	–	5,436	81,207
11	25	13	13	9	27	596	–	0	328	–	–	1,568
–	–	–	–	–	–	–	–	–	–	–	–	–
–	–	–	–	–	–	–	–	–	–	–	–	–
–	–	–	–	–	–	–	–	–	–	–	–	–
316	700	4,054	1,196	2,064	3,902	–	–	–	–	–	–	43,871
–	–	–	–	–	–	–	–	–	–	–	–	–
475	1,020	4,595	1,603	2,601	4,500	35,260	–	2,079	10,515	–	5,436	126,646

4.1B Input–Output Table for Bangladesh, 2018
(at current prices, $ million)

Sector	Code	Agriculture, Hunting, Forestry, and Fishing AHF	Mining and Quarrying MIN	Light Manufacturing LMF	Heavy Manufacturing HMF	Utilities UTL	Construction CON	Trade Services TRD	Hotels and Restaurants HRS	Transport Services TSP
Agriculture, hunting, forestry, and fishing	AHF	4,949	–	12,339	2	–	1,551	–	2,221	–
Mining and quarrying	MIN	45	49	1,439	454	682	1,346	–	125	1,060
Light manufacturing	LMF	1,758	58	27,095	1,203	238	8,898	816	1,343	1,112
Heavy manufacturing	HMF	1,122	51	1,803	2,461	222	3,148	234	92	522
Utilities	UTL	214	81	1,711	624	86	758	27	21	491
Construction	CON	648	51	1,597	388	53	7,387	728	180	1,870
Trade services	TRD	1,256	24	5,131	673	164	3,741	298	723	673
Hotels and restaurants	HRS	35	–	1,376	313	80	496	780	3	243
Transport services	TSP	753	52	3,865	1,299	342	1,528	277	449	479
Telecommunications	TEL	26	1	604	304	28	84	174	33	106
Financial intermediation	FIN	312	18	4,864	903	82	2,388	829	99	735
Real estate, renting, and business activities	BUS	126	41	1,775	1,067	475	672	602	160	731
Public administration and defense	PAD	144	7	711	199	28	393	289	12	236
Education, health, and social work	EHS	23	–	89	–	–	–	–	–	–
Other personal services	OSV	190	16	1,225	361	122	579	957	212	359
Total imports	**IMP**	**1,774**	**72**	**11,438**	**2,189**	**418**	**4,728**	**571**	**616**	**1,672**
Total intermediate consumption	**r60**	**13,376**	**521**	**77,063**	**12,440**	**3,020**	**37,696**	**6,583**	**6,288**	**10,289**
Taxes less subsidies on products	r99	853	113	859	312	85	492	811	64	521
CIF / FOB adjustments on exports	r61	–	–	–	–	–	–	–	–	–
Direct purchases abroad by residents	r62	–	–	–	–	–	–	–	–	–
Domestic purchases by nonresidents	r63	–	–	–	–	–	–	–	–	–
Value-added at basic prices	r64	35,252	4,659	35,531	12,889	3,515	20,350	33,525	2,651	21,556
International transport margins	trs	–	–	–	–	–	–	–	–	–
Gross output	**r69**	**49,480**	**5,292**	**113,453**	**25,641**	**6,619**	**58,538**	**40,919**	**9,003**	**32,366**

– = magnitude equals zero; 0 = magnitude is less than half of unit employed; $ = United States dollars; ( ) = negative; CIF = cost, insurance, and freight; FOB = free on board.

Source: Asian Development Bank Multi-Regional Input–Output Database. https://mrio.adbx.online/ (accessed 4 August 2020).

4.1B Input–Output Table for Bangladesh, 2018
(continued)

Telecommunications	Financial Intermediation	Real Estate, Renting, and Business Activities	Public Administration and Defense	Education, Health, and Social Work	Other Personal Services	Final Consumption Expenditure by Households	Final Consumption Expenditure by Nonprofit Organizations Serving Households	Final Consumption Expenditure by Government	Gross Fixed Capital Formation	Changes in Inventories and Valuables	Exports	Gross Output
TEL	FIN	BUS	PAD	EHS	OSV	F1	F2	F3	F4	F5	EXP	
–	–	60	–	45	43	27,884	–	–	74	–	312	49,480
–	–	23	0	1	0	59	–	–	–	–	8	5,292
105	603	284	266	542	958	28,514	–	–	6,221	–	33,439	113,453
42	113	46	98	725	67	1,962	–	–	12,436	–	495	25,641
35	153	23	38	33	15	2,212	–	–	99	–	–	6,619
95	184	684	113	47	273	0	–	–	43,976	–	264	58,538
31	156	67	69	241	145	23,148	–	–	4,374	–	6	40,919
194	410	248	117	59	194	4,453	–	–	–	–	1	9,003
69	239	139	226	254	187	20,515	–	–	1,620	–	74	32,366
39	232	34	38	51	31	1,878	–	–	–	–	569	4,232
205	491	379	362	55	428	1,844	–	–	–	–	111	14,104
105	563	311	183	208	427	18,145	–	–	–	–	732	26,321
9	109	65	137	32	49	–	–	10,973	–	–	2,479	15,871
–	–	–	2,644	–	134	8,226	–	5,457	–	–	2	16,576
129	275	229	100	54	39	24,207	–	90	–	–	31	29,176
142	302	195	409	910	446	20,997	–	3	13,038	–	–	59,920
1,200	3,830	2,788	4,800	3,257	3,435	184,044	–	16,524	81,838	–	38,523	507,513
72	243	556	261	315	460	5,617	–	504	2,498	–	–	14,635
–	–	–	–	–	–	–	–	–	–	–	–	–
–	–	–	–	–	–	–	–	–	–	–	–	–
–	–	–	–	–	–	–	–	–	–	–	–	–
2,961	10,031	22,978	10,810	13,004	25,281	–	–	–	–	–	–	254,992
–	–	–	–	–	–	–	–	–	–	–	–	–
4,232	14,104	26,321	15,871	16,576	29,176	189,661	–	17,028	84,336	–	38,523	777,140

4.2A Input–Output Table for Bhutan, 2000
(at current prices, $ million)

Sector	Code	Agriculture, Hunting, Forestry, and Fishing AHF	Mining and Quarrying MIN	Light Manufacturing LMF	Heavy Manufacturing HMF	Utilities UTL	Construction CON	Trade Services TRD	Hotels and Restaurants HRS	Transport Services TSP
Agriculture, hunting, forestry, and fishing	AHF	6	–	3	–	–	12	–	1	0
Mining and quarrying	MIN	–	–	4	2	–	1	–	–	–
Light manufacturing	LMF	1	0	2	1	0	21	0	0	1
Heavy manufacturing	HMF	0	0	1	1	0	3	–	0	0
Utilities	UTL	0	1	10	4	0	0	0	0	0
Construction	CON	0	0	0	0	0	2	0	0	0
Trade services	TRD	0	0	2	1	0	4	0	0	1
Hotels and restaurants	HRS	–	–	–	–	0	0	0	–	0
Transport services	TSP	1	0	2	1	0	8	1	0	2
Telecommunications	TEL	0	0	1	0	0	1	0	0	2
Financial intermediation	FIN	1	0	2	1	0	2	0	0	5
Real estate, renting, and business activities	BUS	–	0	0	0	0	–	2	0	1
Public administration and defense	PAD	–	0	1	1	–	1	0	0	0
Education, health, and social work	EHS	–	–	–	–	–	–	–	–	–
Other personal services	OSV	0	0	0	0	0	0	0	0	0
Total imports	IMP	4	1	4	4	0	45	1	0	9
Total intermediate consumption	r60	14	2	31	16	0	101	5	1	21
Taxes less subsidies on products	r99	0	0	0	0	0	2	0	0	0
CIF / FOB adjustments on exports	r61	–	–	–	–	–	–	–	–	–
Direct purchases abroad by residents	r62	–	–	–	–	–	–	–	–	–
Domestic purchases by nonresidents	r63	–	–	–	–	–	–	–	–	–
Value-added at basic prices	r64	118	7	24	12	50	61	20	2	32
International transport margins	trs	–	–	–	–	–	–	–	–	–
Gross output	r69	131	9	55	29	51	164	24	3	53

– = magnitude equals zero; 0 = magnitude is less than half of unit employed; $ = United States dollars; ( ) = negative; CIF = cost, insurance, and freight; FOB = free on board.

Source: Asian Development Bank Multi-Regional Input–Output Database. https://mrio.adbx.online/ (accessed 4 August 2020).

4.2A Input–Output Table for Bhutan, 2000
(continued)

Telecommunications	Financial Intermediation	Real Estate, Renting, and Business Activities	Public Administration and Defense	Education, Health, and Social Work	Other Personal Services	Final Consumption Expenditure by Households	Final Consumption Expenditure by Nonprofit Organizations Serving Households	Final Consumption Expenditure by Government	Gross Fixed Capital Formation	Changes in Inventories and Valuables	Exports	Gross Output
TEL	FIN	BUS	PAD	EHS	OSV	F1	F2	F3	F4	F5	EXP	
–	–	–	1	0	0	115	–	–	0	(12)	6	131
–	–	–	–	–	–	1	–	–	0	(2)	2	9
1	0	0	1	3	0	14	–	–	1	2	8	55
0	–	0	0	1	0	3	–	–	12	4	4	29
1	0	0	1	0	0	2	–	–	3	–	27	51
1	0	0	7	0	–	1	–	–	148	–	5	164
0	0	0	0	1	0	5	–	–	5	–	5	24
0	0	–	–	2	0	0	–	–	–	–	1	3
0	1	0	2	3	0	13	–	–	10	–	9	53
0	0	0	2	1	0	5	–	–	0	–	1	14
0	0	0	3	–	–	5	–	–	–	–	1	19
0	1	–	3	0	0	7	–	–	–	–	0	14
0	0	–	0	0	0	2	–	59	–	–	3	68
–	0	–	2	1	0	3	–	33	–	–	0	40
0	0	0	0	1	0	1	–	–	–	–	1	4
2	**0**	**0**	**5**	**4**	**0**	**32**	**–**	**5**	**39**	**0**	**–**	**158**
6	**2**	**0**	**28**	**16**	**2**	**210**	**–**	**96**	**220**	**(8)**	**74**	**837**
0	0	0	0	0	0	3	–	–	2	(0)	–	8
–	–	–	–	–	–	–	–	–	–	–	–	–
–	–	–	–	–	–	–	–	–	–	–	–	–
–	–	–	–	–	–	–	–	–	–	–	–	–
9	17	14	40	23	2	–	–	–	–	–	–	430
–	–	–	–	–	–	–	–	–	–	–	–	–
14	**19**	**14**	**68**	**40**	**4**	**212**	**–**	**96**	**222**	**(8)**	**74**	**1,275**

4.2B Input–Output Table for Bhutan, 2018
(at current prices, $ million)

Sector	Code	Agriculture, Hunting, Forestry, and Fishing AHF	Mining and Quarrying MIN	Light Manufacturing LMF	Heavy Manufacturing HMF	Utilities UTL	Construction CON	Trade Services TRD	Hotels and Restaurants HRS	Transport Services TSP
Agriculture, hunting, forestry, and fishing	AHF	17	–	21	–	–	40	–	7	0
Mining and quarrying	MIN	–	–	33	33	–	17	–	–	–
Light manufacturing	LMF	4	1	9	8	13	80	0	0	8
Heavy manufacturing	HMF	2	1	4	5	22	21	–	0	3
Utilities	UTL	0	18	44	50	5	3	0	1	0
Construction	CON	0	9	0	1	12	45	0	0	0
Trade services	TRD	3	1	10	8	11	33	0	1	13
Hotels and restaurants	HRS	–	–	–	–	3	0	1	–	4
Transport services	TSP	3	1	10	8	14	69	19	1	25
Telecommunications	TEL	0	1	1	1	2	2	2	0	6
Financial intermediation	FIN	5	1	5	4	1	10	3	0	36
Real estate, renting, and business activities	BUS	0	4	1	1	12	5	11	4	5
Public administration and defense	PAD	–	1	1	1	–	1	0	0	0
Education, health, and social work	EHS	–	–	–	–	–	–	–	–	–
Other personal services	OSV	0	0	0	0	0	0	0	0	0
Total imports	IMP	15	9	33	41	63	200	7	4	94
Total intermediate consumption	r60	50	46	172	161	158	527	44	18	196
Taxes less subsidies on products	r99	2	1	6	7	2	30	1	0	7
CIF / FOB adjustments on exports	r61	–	–	–	–	–	–	–	–	–
Direct purchases abroad by residents	r62	–	–	–	–	–	–	–	–	–
Domestic purchases by nonresidents	r63	–	–	–	–	–	–	–	–	–
Value-added at basic prices	r64	448	109	122	65	341	409	211	54	184
International transport margins	trs	–	–	–	–	–	–	–	–	–
Gross output	r69	500	156	300	233	501	966	256	73	387

– = magnitude equals zero; 0 = magnitude is less than half of unit employed; $ = United States dollars; ( ) = negative; CIF = cost, insurance, and freight; FOB = free on board.

Source: Asian Development Bank Multi-Regional Input–Output Database. https://mrio.adbx.online/ (accessed 4 August 2020).

4.2B Input–Output Table for Bhutan, 2018
(continued)

Telecommunications	Financial Intermediation	Real Estate, Renting, and Business Activities	Public Administration and Defense	Education, Health, and Social Work	Other Personal Services	Final Consumption Expenditure by Households	Final Consumption Expenditure by Nonprofit Organizations Serving Households	Final Consumption Expenditure by Government	Gross Fixed Capital Formation	Changes in Inventories and Valuables	Exports	Gross Output
TEL	FIN	BUS	PAD	EHS	OSV	F1	F2	F3	F4	F5	EXP	
–	–	0	2	0	1	360	–	–	0	0	52	500
–	–	–	–	–	–	11	–	–	2	(1)	62	156
3	0	1	3	2	0	114	–	–	2	0	50	300
0	–	0	0	1	0	44	–	–	76	(1)	53	233
5	0	2	8	1	1	20	–	–	65	–	276	501
6	0	2	66	1	–	86	–	–	722	–	16	966
1	0	1	1	1	0	82	–	–	40	–	51	256
0	0	4	–	6	1	4	–	–	–	–	50	73
1	4	2	8	3	0	86	–	–	38	–	94	387
0	1	2	3	0	1	35	–	–	0	–	18	77
0	0	0	11	–	–	57	–	–	–	–	4	137
3	3	–	9	2	0	35	–	–	5	–	3	103
0	0	0	0	0	0	5	–	274	–	–	16	300
–	0	0	1	0	0	4	–	101	–	–	5	111
0	0	1	1	0	0	10	–	–	–	–	5	17
7	3	10	27	9	2	361	–	64	337	0	–	1,284
26	12	26	139	26	7	1,314	–	439	1,288	(2)	754	5,402
1	0	1	1	1	0	47	–	–	32	(0)	–	139
–	–	–	–	–	–	–	–	–	–	–	–	–
–	–	–	–	–	–	–	–	–	–	–	–	–
–	–	–	–	–	–	–	–	–	–	–	–	–
50	124	77	159	84	10	–	–	–	–	–	–	2,448
–	–	–	–	–	–	–	–	–	–	–	–	–
77	137	103	300	111	17	1,361	–	439	1,319	(2)	754	7,989

4.3A Input–Output Table for India, 2000
(at current prices, $ million)

Sector	Code	Agriculture, Hunting, Forestry, and Fishing AHF	Mining and Quarrying MIN	Light Manufacturing LMF	Heavy Manufacturing HMF	Utilities UTL	Construction CON	Trade Services TRD	Hotels and Restaurants HRS	Transport Services TSP
Agriculture, hunting, forestry, and fishing	AHF	20,287	0	25,643	595	4	1,715	1	4,467	1,031
Mining and quarrying	MIN	–	24	665	10,570	960	318	–	1	2
Light manufacturing	LMF	1,363	135	23,813	5,348	351	10,400	820	2,663	3,105
Heavy manufacturing	HMF	3,746	816	10,666	51,743	3,311	10,067	1,195	336	11,768
Utilities	UTL	1,632	357	4,292	5,027	7,915	1,316	727	313	1,455
Construction	CON	755	230	1,792	988	719	9,073	331	349	824
Trade services	TRD	4,507	119	12,143	8,335	1,310	4,660	374	1,296	3,007
Hotels and restaurants	HRS	54	22	3	–	132	18	685	490	3,265
Transport services	TSP	1,572	298	7,718	5,646	1,081	2,933	3,010	522	1,704
Telecommunications	TEL	14	13	456	1,241	201	58	199	43	725
Financial intermediation	FIN	944	156	3,925	4,703	1,482	1,782	2,868	352	938
Real estate, renting, and business activities	BUS	26	37	678	892	20	222	185	31	344
Public administration and defense	PAD	–	–	–	–	–	–	–	–	–
Education, health, and social work	EHS	0	28	–	–	–	0	–	–	87
Other personal services	OSV	37	110	2,386	1,218	90	37	10	55	166
Total imports	IMP	**1,223**	**319**	**7,828**	**26,449**	**1,592**	**3,954**	**881**	**661**	**2,768**
Total intermediate consumption	r60	**36,160**	**2,665**	**102,007**	**122,754**	**19,168**	**46,553**	**11,285**	**11,578**	**31,190**
Taxes less subsidies on products	r99	(3,660)	285	1,893	9,716	619	3,510	663	53	5,055
CIF / FOB adjustments on exports	r61	–	–	–	–	–	–	–	–	–
Direct purchases abroad by residents	r62	–	–	–	–	–	–	–	–	–
Domestic purchases by nonresidents	r63	–	–	–	–	–	–	–	–	–
Value-added at basic prices	r64	102,570	10,214	36,169	32,038	10,717	26,699	58,853	5,881	27,174
International transport margins	trs	103	16	557	2,201	128	242	20	43	95
Gross output	r69	**135,173**	**13,179**	**140,627**	**166,709**	**30,631**	**77,004**	**70,822**	**17,556**	**63,514**

– = magnitude equals zero; 0 = magnitude is less than half of unit employed; $ = United States dollars; ( ) = negative; CIF = cost, insurance, and freight; FOB = free on board.

Source: Asian Development Bank Multi-Regional Input–Output Database. https://mrio.adbx.online/ (accessed 4 August 2020).

4.3A Input–Output Table for India, 2000
(continued)

Telecommunications	Financial Intermediation	Real Estate, Renting, and Business Activities	Public Administration and Defense	Education, Health, and Social Work	Other Personal Services	Final Consumption Expenditure by Households	Final Consumption Expenditure by Nonprofit Organizations Serving Households	Final Consumption Expenditure by Government	Gross Fixed Capital Formation	Changes in Inventories and Valuables	Exports	Gross Output
TEL	FIN	BUS	PAD	EHS	OSV	F1	F2	F3	F4	F5	EXP	
0	0	8	–	145	16	78,671	–	767	120	(1,322)	3,025	**135,173**
–	–	0	–	–	0	19	–	13	–	(1,224)	1,831	**13,179**
62	370	158	–	479	525	54,976	–	2,714	4,338	6,610	22,397	**140,627**
499	507	395	–	1,929	462	26,139	–	2,196	27,815	93	13,027	**166,709**
145	719	633	–	75	148	3,769	–	2,110	–	–	0	**30,631**
52	404	1,329	–	413	138	423	–	926	57,827	–	430	**77,004**
36	82	54	–	186	83	28,311	–	766	2,173	–	3,380	**70,822**
10	584	408	–	907	75	10,687	–	215	–	–	1	**17,556**
58	682	124	–	869	193	29,200	–	1,278	1,764	–	4,864	**63,514**
39	904	167	–	173	254	2,463	–	587	–	–	660	**8,198**
15	1,569	580	–	649	602	9,338	–	774	–	–	283	**30,959**
11	79	980	–	32	115	31,211	–	512	633	–	9,563	**45,571**
–	–	–	–	–	–	–	–	40,564	–	–	0	**40,564**
21	54	288	–	60	–	27,650	–	4,586	–	–	0	**32,773**
14	99	120	–	47	1,138	6,689	–	1,671	–	–	2,610	**16,497**
320	**437**	**1,749**	**–**	**827**	**766**	**7,812**	**–**	**1,693**	**6,535**	**1,309**	**–**	**67,123**
1,281	**6,489**	**6,993**	**–**	**6,790**	**4,513**	**317,359**	**–**	**61,372**	**101,205**	**5,466**	**62,071**	**956,900**
119	350	298	–	389	493	6,855	–	1,688	5,478	–	–	**33,804**
–	–	–	–	–	–	–	–	–	–	–	–	**–**
–	–	–	–	–	–	–	–	–	–	–	–	**–**
–	–	–	–	–	–	–	–	–	–	–	–	**–**
6,777	24,104	38,268	40,564	25,536	11,470	–	–	–	–	–	–	**457,035**
21	15	13	–	58	21	198	–	24	462	94	–	**4,311**
8,198	**30,959**	**45,571**	**40,564**	**32,773**	**16,497**	**324,411**	**–**	**63,085**	**107,145**	**5,560**	**62,071**	**1,452,050**

4.3B Input–Output Table for India, 2018
(at current prices, $ million)

Sector	Code	Agriculture, Hunting, Forestry, and Fishing AHF	Mining and Quarrying MIN	Light Manufacturing LMF	Heavy Manufacturing HMF	Utilities UTL	Construction CON	Trade Services TRD	Hotels and Restaurants HRS	Transport Services TSP
Agriculture, hunting, forestry, and fishing	AHF	54,449	1	105,511	2,450	6	7,301	2	15,050	1,566
Mining and quarrying	MIN	–	125	2,087	59,118	1,246	918	–	2	2
Light manufacturing	LMF	5,512	1,788	172,249	39,815	1,533	57,042	7,491	13,977	7,205
Heavy manufacturing	HMF	12,053	8,412	60,396	288,049	8,923	52,903	8,844	1,355	22,732
Utilities	UTL	4,438	3,166	18,200	25,799	17,391	6,253	4,440	1,062	2,520
Construction	CON	1,804	1,841	6,740	4,695	1,473	39,860	1,810	1,073	1,258
Trade services	TRD	28,309	2,465	118,289	94,205	6,693	52,919	5,249	10,281	10,981
Hotels and restaurants	HRS	143	364	18	–	553	169	7,812	3,137	9,951
Transport services	TSP	5,527	3,598	52,382	39,120	3,428	19,642	24,803	2,420	4,383
Telecommunications	TEL	29	117	2,244	6,996	450	289	1,228	147	1,331
Financial intermediation	FIN	3,230	1,752	25,413	33,601	4,132	10,989	22,031	1,517	2,061
Real estate, renting, and business activities	BUS	132	1,268	12,626	18,465	255	4,916	5,187	374	2,949
Public administration and defense	PAD	–	–	–	–	–	–	–	–	–
Education, health, and social work	EHS	5	1,024	–	–	–	0	–	–	303
Other personal services	OSV	74	1,314	13,006	7,816	267	243	82	252	422
Total imports	**IMP**	**2,774**	**1,570**	**38,239**	**148,845**	**16,778**	**24,230**	**102**	**21,073**	**96,270**
Total intermediate consumption	**r60**	**118,478**	**28,806**	**627,400**	**768,973**	**63,128**	**277,675**	**89,082**	**71,719**	**163,935**
Taxes less subsidies on products	r99	(15,629)	1,727	15,770	70,586	2,098	25,783	5,200	386	34,712
CIF / FOB adjustments on exports	r61	–	–	–	–	–	–	–	–	–
Direct purchases abroad by residents	r62	–	–	–	–	–	–	–	–	–
Domestic purchases by nonresidents	r63	–	–	–	–	–	–	–	–	–
Value-added at basic prices	r64	363,318	44,380	173,452	185,355	44,595	161,054	531,655	35,591	147,132
International transport margins	trs	–	–	–	–	–	–	–	–	–
Gross output	**r69**	**466,167**	**74,913**	**816,622**	**1,024,914**	**109,821**	**464,513**	**625,937**	**107,695**	**345,779**

– = magnitude equals zero; 0 = magnitude is less than half of unit employed; $ = United States dollars; ( ) = negative; CIF = cost, insurance, and freight; FOB = free on board.

Source: Asian Development Bank Multi-Regional Input–Output Database. https://mrio.adbx.online/ (accessed 4 August 2020).

4.3B Input–Output Table for India, 2018
(continued)

Telecommunications	Financial Intermediation	Real Estate, Renting, and Business Activities	Public Administration and Defense	Education, Health, and Social Work	Other Personal Services	Final Consumption Expenditure by Households	Final Consumption Expenditure by Nonprofit Organizations Serving Households	Final Consumption Expenditure by Government	Gross Fixed Capital Formation	Changes in Inventories and Valuables	Exports	Gross Output
TEL	FIN	BUS	PAD	EHS	OSV	F1	F2	F3	F4	F5	EXP	
0	1	74	–	550	39	262,379	–	2,198	839	(119)	13,869	466,167
–	–	1	–	–	0	39	–	23	–	1,000	10,351	74,913
377	1,838	2,977	–	3,293	3,214	283,486	–	12,060	58,768	54,873	89,124	816,622
2,040	1,790	3,830	–	8,862	1,289	112,084	–	7,822	201,361	55,071	167,098	1,024,914
411	2,211	4,531	–	289	383	12,802	–	5,779	–	–	145	109,821
134	1,087	10,291	–	1,470	321	1,348	–	2,555	386,045	–	708	464,513
236	601	1,073	–	1,657	495	229,261	–	5,378	36,899	–	20,947	625,937
53	3,401	7,107	–	6,527	362	66,708	–	1,161	–	–	229	107,695
226	2,906	1,292	–	4,848	696	142,517	–	5,476	17,331	–	15,184	345,779
111	2,836	1,545	–	680	664	8,278	–	1,709	–	–	2,374	31,028
55	5,988	5,913	–	3,272	1,956	39,942	–	2,867	–	–	1,117	165,839
107	945	27,607	–	507	1,476	206,231	–	22,535	13,208	–	77,354	396,139
–	–	–	–	–	–	–	–	195,158	–	–	14	195,172
207	305	5,119	–	983	–	166,573	–	24,457	–	–	89	199,066
53	398	1,343	–	244	3,932	38,732	–	8,385	–	–	11,903	88,466
430	**690**	**2,957**	**–**	**2,634**	**347**	**12,189**	**–**	**12,003**	**38,669**	**8,035**	**–**	**427,834**
4,440	**24,997**	**75,657**	**–**	**35,817**	**15,176**	**1,582,568**	**–**	**309,567**	**753,121**	**118,860**	**410,506**	**5,539,905**
548	1,661	2,946	–	2,082	1,701	43,586	–	10,976	45,307	–	–	249,440
–	–	–	–	–	–	–	–	–	–	–	–	-
–	–	–	–	–	–	–	–	–	–	–	–	-
–	–	–	–	–	–	–	–	–	–	–	–	-
26,040	139,180	317,536	195,172	161,167	71,590	–	–	–	–	–	–	2,597,216
–	–	–	–	–	–	–	–	–	–	–	–	-
31,028	**165,839**	**396,139**	**195,172**	**199,066**	**88,466**	**1,626,154**	**–**	**320,543**	**798,428**	**118,860**	**410,506**	**8,386,561**

4.4A Input–Output Table for Kazakhstan, 2000
(at current prices, $ million)

Sector	Code	Agriculture, Hunting, Forestry, and Fishing AHF	Mining and Quarrying MIN	Light Manufacturing LMF	Heavy Manufacturing HMF	Utilities UTL	Construction CON	Trade Services TRD	Hotels and Restaurants HRS	Transport Services TSP
Agriculture, hunting, forestry, and fishing	AHF	255	0	211	3	0	1	1	7	0
Mining and quarrying	MIN	94	664	54	2,263	89	3	2	0	43
Light manufacturing	LMF	19	25	414	55	10	150	57	13	56
Heavy manufacturing	HMF	192	1,101	303	5,343	281	323	47	4	538
Utilities	UTL	12	94	62	128	80	3	40	6	56
Construction	CON	5	17	2	11	18	75	48	0	39
Trade services	TRD	83	168	140	767	38	32	72	4	67
Hotels and restaurants	HRS	0	3	0	2	0	1	2	0	1
Transport services	TSP	29	200	66	223	18	11	317	3	96
Telecommunications	TEL	1	13	8	9	3	2	27	1	10
Financial intermediation	FIN	4	63	10	31	6	3	95	1	28
Real estate, renting, and business activities	BUS	8	239	45	58	18	12	107	5	145
Public administration and defense	PAD	–	–	–	–	–	–	–	–	–
Education, health, and social work	EHS	0	0	0	0	0	0	0	0	0
Other personal services	OSV	0	1	0	0	0	0	0	0	0
Total imports	IMP	129	580	366	1,347	119	172	245	12	331
Total intermediate consumption	r60	831	3,169	1,682	10,239	681	788	1,059	55	1,411
Taxes less subsidies on products	r99	(3)	103	22	38	13	59	137	4	42
CIF / FOB adjustments on exports	r61	–	–	–	–	–	–	–	–	–
Direct purchases abroad by residents	r62	–	–	–	–	–	–	–	–	–
Domestic purchases by nonresidents	r63	–	–	–	–	–	–	–	–	–
Value-added at basic prices	r64	1,080	1,855	1,356	6,049	540	501	1,730	64	1,269
International transport margins	trs	–	–	–	–	–	–	–	–	–
Gross output	r69	1,907	5,128	3,060	16,326	1,233	1,348	2,926	124	2,722

– = magnitude equals zero; 0 = magnitude is less than half of unit employed; $ = United States dollars; ( ) = negative; CIF = cost, insurance, and freight; FOB = free on board.

Source: Asian Development Bank Multi-Regional Input–Output Database. https://mrio.adbx.online/ (accessed 4 August 2020).

4.4A Input–Output Table for Kazakhstan, 2000
(continued)

Telecommunications	Financial Intermediation	Real Estate, Renting, and Business Activities	Public Administration and Defense	Education, Health, and Social Work	Other Personal Services	Final Consumption Expenditure by Households	Final Consumption Expenditure by Nonprofit Organizations Serving Households	Final Consumption Expenditure by Government	Gross Fixed Capital Formation	Changes in Inventories and Valuables	Exports	Gross Output
TEL	FIN	BUS	PAD	EHS	OSV	F1	F2	F3	F4	F5	EXP	
0	1	4	73	26	1	878	–	144	42	(2)	265	1,907
0	0	2	1	4	1	69	–	–	–	8	1,829	5,128
10	6	29	3	103	9	1,808	–	–	17	27	249	3,060
18	4	66	70	103	17	1,471	–	–	464	306	5,674	16,326
6	4	112	13	74	27	388	–	82	–	(2)	50	1,233
5	9	150	0	50	2	125	–	5	775	10	3	1,348
8	4	23	20	44	4	748	–	–	131	3	571	2,926
0	0	15	2	2	0	93	–	–	–	–	0	124
6	15	34	14	16	6	1,178	–	101	20	4	365	2,722
11	4	57	6	13	5	185	–	1	6	0	6	368
12	22	93	16	11	1	125	–	–	–	–	11	532
23	54	501	76	40	11	1,398	0	65	130	–	29	2,966
–	–	–	0	–	–	52	–	651	–	–	10	713
0	0	0	0	0	0	157	1	1,007	–	–	2	1,167
0	0	2	2	1	2	118	104	31	1	–	3	267
47	54	514	86	183	22	2,277	4	157	1,463	52	–	8,161
147	178	1,603	382	672	108	11,071	108	2,242	3,049	407	9,065	48,947
11	13	51	9	16	3	177	0	6	179	(6)	–	874
–	–	–	–	–	–	–	–	–	–	–	–	–
–	–	–	–	–	–	–	–	–	–	–	–	–
–	–	–	–	–	–	–	–	–	–	–	–	–
210	341	1,311	322	480	156	–	–	–	–	–	–	17,264
–	–	–	–	–	–	–	–	–	–	–	–	–
368	532	2,966	713	1,167	267	11,248	108	2,248	3,228	401	9,065	67,084

4.4B Input–Output Table for Kazakhstan, 2018
(at current prices, $ million)

Sector	Code	Agriculture, Hunting, Forestry, and Fishing AHF	Mining and Quarrying MIN	Light Manufacturing LMF	Heavy Manufacturing HMF	Utilities UTL	Construction CON	Trade Services TRD	Hotels and Restaurants HRS	Transport Services TSP
Agriculture, hunting, forestry, and fishing	AHF	2,414	3	2,238	1	1	3	26	187	5
Mining and quarrying	MIN	2	5,255	260	6,585	250	609	63	1	151
Light manufacturing	LMF	404	245	941	34	82	1,527	314	325	125
Heavy manufacturing	HMF	426	2,714	325	3,354	1,100	3,060	629	15	2,236
Utilities	UTL	55	702	307	36	499	47	748	14	219
Construction	CON	35	393	15	30	193	511	615	7	93
Trade services	TRD	839	2,766	1,255	3,509	383	1,471	554	154	1,382
Hotels and restaurants	HRS	0	93	2	6	4	4	19	4	38
Transport services	TSP	291	2,338	445	1,566	151	581	2,639	48	757
Telecommunications	TEL	0	44	2	0	18	1	447	1	206
Financial intermediation	FIN	467	186	58	79	81	124	1,493	9	717
Real estate, renting, and business activities	BUS	173	1,601	45	51	58	614	2,650	42	602
Public administration and defense	PAD	–	–	1	0	0	0	0	0	0
Education, health, and social work	EHS	0	45	0	1	2	1	2	0	43
Other personal services	OSV	5	52	1	2	4	1	14	1	7
Total imports	IMP	1,041	2,602	1,509	1,379	550	1,827	2,173	196	2,210
Total intermediate consumption	r60	6,152	19,039	7,405	16,633	3,376	10,379	12,386	1,002	8,792
Taxes less subsidies on products	r99	116	256	(47)	336	32	95	53	7	283
CIF / FOB adjustments on exports	r61	–	–	–	–	–	–	–	–	–
Direct purchases abroad by residents	r62	–	–	–	–	–	–	–	–	–
Domestic purchases by nonresidents	r63	–	–	–	–	–	–	–	–	–
Value-added at basic prices	r64	8,549	25,040	6,768	13,575	3,464	8,675	29,959	1,384	13,475
International transport margins	trs	–	–	–	–	–	–	–	–	–
Gross output	r69	14,818	44,335	14,125	30,544	6,873	19,150	42,399	2,394	22,550

– = magnitude equals zero; 0 = magnitude is less than half of unit employed; $ = United States dollars; ( ) = negative; CIF = cost, insurance, and freight; FOB = free on board.

Source: Asian Development Bank Multi-Regional Input–Output Database. https://mrio.adbx.online/ (accessed 4 August 2020).

4.4B Input–Output Table for Kazakhstan, 2018
(continued)

	TEL	FIN	BUS	PAD	EHS	OSV	F1	F2	F3	F4	F5	EXP	Gross Output
	0	6	14	367	8	17	7,781	–	296	482	(130)	1,099	14,818
	0	0	73	1	1	3	496	–	–	–	4,834	25,750	44,335
	76	11	363	37	184	90	7,991	–	–	89	62	1,224	14,125
	388	81	709	185	317	132	855	–	–	1,254	824	11,940	30,544
	90	9	308	248	416	368	2,455	–	123	–	(1)	230	6,873
	25	3	1,130	151	972	41	439	–	75	14,236	–	185	19,150
	153	52	949	161	469	148	11,042	–	–	5,476	–	11,638	42,399
	5	4	109	20	3	190	1,895	–	–	–	–	1	2,394
	75	249	805	748	553	54	6,894	–	864	564	–	2,927	22,550
	163	108	100	145	26	19	2,787	–	4	358	(10)	145	4,564
	70	671	557	587	744	54	1,121	–	–	–	–	75	7,092
	280	359	1,678	1,431	376	908	17,719	0	449	2,083	(0)	433	31,552
	0	–	18	0	0	0	207	–	8,070	–	–	0	8,297
	2	1	59	2	59	10	2,108	33	7,889	–	–	0	10,257
	19	13	31	18	99	8	4,438	1,802	282	116	(0)	302	7,217
	296	301	1,699	679	1,058	296	10,409	0	0	9,651	2,314	–	40,189
	1,644	**1,867**	**8,602**	**4,780**	**5,285**	**2,339**	**78,636**	**1,835**	**18,051**	**34,308**	**7,893**	**55,950**	**306,354**
	9	317	99	108	115	62	4,431	–	–	2,130	–	–	8,401
	–	–	–	–	–	–			–			–	-
	–	–	–	–	–	–	1,888	–	–	–	–	–	1,888
	–	–	–	–	–	–	(2,180)	–	–	–	–	–	(2,180)
	2,911	4,908	22,850	3,410	4,857	4,816	–	–	–	–	–	–	154,644
	–	–	–	–	–	–	–	–	–	–	–	–	-
	4,564	**7,092**	**31,552**	**8,297**	**10,257**	**7,217**	**82,776**	**1,835**	**18,051**	**36,438**	**7,893**	**55,950**	**469,108**

4.5A Input–Output Table for the Kyrgyz Republic, 2000
(at current prices, $ million)

Sector	Code	Agriculture, Hunting, Forestry, and Fishing AHF	Mining and Quarrying MIN	Light Manufacturing LMF	Heavy Manufacturing HMF	Utilities UTL	Construction CON	Trade Services TRD	Hotels and Restaurants HRS	Transport Services TSP
Agriculture, hunting, forestry, and fishing	AHF	571	1	151	66	4	7	44	4	1
Mining and quarrying	MIN	0	0	3	4	4	0	0	0	0
Light manufacturing	LMF	7	1	52	21	15	39	5	4	1
Heavy manufacturing	HMF	17	1	17	114	26	17	4	0	6
Utilities	UTL	7	1	13	22	80	5	6	1	2
Construction	CON	2	0	4	11	29	7	8	1	1
Trade services	TRD	90	1	35	28	31	9	12	2	2
Hotels and restaurants	HRS	1	0	7	0	0	0	0	1	0
Transport services	TSP	5	0	6	7	5	2	4	0	1
Telecommunications	TEL	0	0	1	1	0	0	0	0	0
Financial intermediation	FIN	4	0	3	2	1	0	1	0	0
Real estate, renting, and business activities	BUS	0	0	0	1	0	0	1	0	0
Public administration and defense	PAD	0	0	0	0	0	0	0	0	0
Education, health, and social work	EHS	0	0	0	0	0	0	0	0	0
Other personal services	OSV	0	0	0	0	0	0	0	0	0
Total imports	IMP	23	2	33	58	21	45	23	5	28
Total intermediate consumption	r60	726	8	324	334	216	134	109	18	43
Taxes less subsidies on products	r99	5	0	5	5	2	6	5	1	2
CIF / FOB adjustments on exports	r61	–	–	–	–	–	–	–	–	–
Direct purchases abroad by residents	r62	–	–	–	–	–	–	–	–	–
Domestic purchases by nonresidents	r63	–	–	–	–	–	–	–	–	–
Value-added at basic prices	r64	467	8	105	142	87	57	165	10	31
International transport margins	trs	–	–	–	–	–	–	–	–	–
Gross output	r69	1,198	16	434	481	304	197	279	29	76

– = magnitude equals zero; 0 = magnitude is less than half of unit employed; $ = United States dollars; ( ) = negative; CIF = cost, insurance, and freight; FOB = free on board.

Source: Asian Development Bank Multi-Regional Input–Output Database. https://mrio.adbx.online/ (accessed 4 August 2020).

4.5A Input–Output Table for the Kyrgyz Republic, 2000
(continued)

Telecommunications	Financial Intermediation	Real Estate, Renting, and Business Activities	Public Administration and Defense	Education, Health, and Social Work	Other Personal Services	Final Consumption Expenditure by Households	Final Consumption Expenditure by Nonprofit Organizations Serving Households	Final Consumption Expenditure by Government	Gross Fixed Capital Formation	Changes in Inventories and Valuables	Exports	Gross Output
TEL	FIN	BUS	PAD	EHS	OSV	F1	F2	F3	F4	F5	EXP	
0	1	2	10	2	0	207	2	14	5	(0)	107	1,198
0	–	0	0	0	0	0	–	0	0	(0)	4	16
0	2	2	8	6	2	142	2	6	16	12	93	434
0	3	1	1	1	0	17	2	2	3	1	249	481
0	8	6	2	4	2	64	3	12	55	2	12	304
0	1	4	1	3	1	36	0	0	67	5	15	197
0	1	2	5	2	1	53	0	0	5	(2)	2	279
0	1	0	1	1	0	15	0	0	0	(0)	1	29
0	0	1	0	0	0	31	0	3	4	(0)	6	76
0	0	0	0	0	0	19	0	1	12	0	1	38
0	8	1	0	0	0	11	2	0	1	0	4	39
0	0	1	0	0	0	26	–	24	3	3	10	70
0	0	0	0	0	0	2	2	85	0	(0)	3	92
0	0	0	0	1	0	8	–	91	–	0	2	101
0	0	0	0	0	0	2	19	3	–	(0)	3	29
16	7	8	10	8	6	186	5	33	70	5	–	594
16	32	29	38	29	13	818	38	275	241	27	509	3,976
2	1	2	1	1	1	43	0	(0)	6	0	–	89
–	–	–	–	–	–	–	–	–	–	–	–	–
–	–	–	–	–	–	–	–	–	–	–	–	–
–	–	–	–	–	–	–	–	–	–	–	–	–
20	6	39	52	71	15	–	–	–	–	–	–	1,275
–	–	–	–	–	–	–	–	–	–	–	–	–
38	39	70	92	101	29	861	38	274	247	27	509	5,339

4.5B Input–Output Table for the Kyrgyz Republic, 2018
(at current prices, $ million)

Sector	Code	Agriculture, Hunting, Forestry, and Fishing AHF	Mining and Quarrying MIN	Light Manufacturing LMF	Heavy Manufacturing HMF	Utilities UTL	Construction CON	Trade Services TRD	Hotels and Restaurants HRS	Transport Services TSP
Agriculture, hunting, forestry, and fishing	AHF	1,400	1	119	0	–	0	2	16	–
Mining and quarrying	MIN	0	1	1	3	6	2	0	0	0
Light manufacturing	LMF	4	0	54	4	7	100	68	18	9
Heavy manufacturing	HMF	9	4	9	547	15	65	15	1	13
Utilities	UTL	1	6	29	27	45	34	20	15	5
Construction	CON	0	0	7	3	2	434	58	4	4
Trade services	TRD	429	13	117	54	34	134	154	39	53
Hotels and restaurants	HRS	23	1	16	1	1	11	25	9	2
Transport services	TSP	35	9	31	25	26	60	37	5	31
Telecommunications	TEL	10	3	26	9	8	42	22	3	13
Financial intermediation	FIN	0	0	4	0	3	0	4	2	6
Real estate, renting, and business activities	BUS	2	41	38	8	3	14	43	17	45
Public administration and defense	PAD	–	–	4	–	–	–	–	0	0
Education, health, and social work	EHS	0	0	1	1	3	1	2	0	1
Other personal services	OSV	0	1	2	1	1	13	8	6	3
Total imports	IMP	216	25	166	200	91	504	359	57	229
Total intermediate consumption	r60	2,129	105	625	884	245	1,412	816	192	414
Taxes less subsidies on products	r99	14	2	27	28	11	53	42	7	17
CIF / FOB adjustments on exports	r61	–	–	–	–	–	–	–	–	–
Direct purchases abroad by residents	r62	–	–	–	–	–	–	–	–	–
Domestic purchases by nonresidents	r63	–	–	–	–	–	–	–	–	–
Value-added at basic prices	r64	924	103	289	575	202	641	1,385	134	294
International transport margins	trs	–	–	–	–	–	–	–	–	–
Gross output	r69	3,067	211	941	1,486	458	2,106	2,243	333	725

– = magnitude equals zero; 0 = magnitude is less than half of unit employed; $ = United States dollars; ( ) = negative; CIF = cost, insurance, and freight; FOB = free on board.

Source: Asian Development Bank Multi-Regional Input–Output Database. https://mrio.adbx.online/ (accessed 4 August 2020).

4.5B Input–Output Table for the Kyrgyz Republic, 2018
(continued)

Telecommunications	Financial Intermediation	Real Estate, Renting, and Business Activities	Public Administration and Defense	Education, Health, and Social Work	Other Personal Services	Final Consumption Expenditure by Households	Final Consumption Expenditure by Nonprofit Organizations Serving Households	Final Consumption Expenditure by Government	Gross Fixed Capital Formation	Changes in Inventories and Valuables	Exports	Gross Output
TEL	FIN	BUS	PAD	EHS	OSV	F1	F2	F3	F4	F5	EXP	
–	–	1	26	19	0	1,106	0	8	10	7	352	3,067
0	–	0	0	1	0	3	–	–	0	(0)	192	211
4	0	10	14	8	3	234	0	0	19	(2)	386	941
5	0	2	1	1	1	53	0	–	7	(10)	747	1,486
4	1	9	15	20	5	100	0	1	112	6	2	458
0	0	25	–	15	6	0	–	0	1,482	(29)	95	2,106
20	1	21	43	25	6	907	1	1	32	(8)	168	2,243
2	1	4	11	5	1	214	–	–	5	0	3	333
9	0	5	7	6	4	174	0	1	68	(0)	195	725
20	0	18	19	3	8	180	0	0	57	0	58	502
2	333	2	2	1	2	26	–	7	10	2	17	423
10	–	47	1	16	17	194	–	78	20	(0)	1	596
0	–	4	3	–	0	0	–	368	50	(33)	261	657
1	0	2	5	13	2	72	–	533	92	(0)	5	733
3	0	18	1	4	15	46	47	39	19	(0)	0	226
141	**10**	**53**	**57**	**44**	**37**	**2,461**	**15**	**188**	**287**	**(66)**	**–**	**5,075**
220	**347**	**222**	**206**	**180**	**109**	**5,771**	**64**	**1,223**	**2,270**	**(134)**	**2,484**	**19,784**
14	18	9	8	7	4	476	2	16	116	6	–	877
–	–	–	–	–	–	–	–	–	–	–	–	–
–	–	–	–	–	–	–	–	–	–	–	–	–
–	–	–	–	–	–	–	–	–	–	–	–	–
268	57	366	443	546	114	–	–	–	–	–	–	6,342
–	–	–	–	–	–	–	–	–	–	–	–	–
502	**423**	**596**	**657**	**733**	**226**	**6,247**	**66**	**1,239**	**2,386**	**(127)**	**2,484**	**27,002**

4.6A Input–Output Table for Maldives, 2000
(at current prices, $ million)

Sector	Code	Agriculture, Hunting, Forestry, and Fishing AHF	Mining and Quarrying MIN	Light Manufacturing LMF	Heavy Manufacturing HMF	Utilities UTL	Construction CON	Trade Services TRD	Hotels and Restaurants HRS	Transport Services TSP
Agriculture, hunting, forestry, and fishing	AHF	0	–	4	–	–	–	0	11	–
Mining and quarrying	MIN	–	–	0	–	–	0	–	0	–
Light manufacturing	LMF	0	0	7	0	0	1	0	15	1
Heavy manufacturing	HMF	0	0	0	0	0	0	0	0	0
Utilities	UTL	–	0	2	0	0	1	2	1	2
Construction	CON	1	0	2	0	0	14	0	1	1
Trade services	TRD	1	0	2	0	2	2	3	7	4
Hotels and restaurants	HRS	0	0	2	0	1	0	1	0	2
Transport services	TSP	0	0	2	0	0	3	3	7	14
Telecommunications	TEL	0	0	2	0	0	2	3	5	4
Financial intermediation	FIN	0	0	0	0	0	0	6	15	1
Real estate, renting, and business activities	BUS	0	0	4	1	0	4	3	16	5
Public administration and defense	PAD	–	–	0	0	–	0	1	1	0
Education, health, and social work	EHS	–	0	0	0	0	0	1	0	0
Other personal services	OSV	–	0	0	0	0	0	0	0	0
Total imports	**IMP**	**5**	**0**	**23**	**0**	**8**	**24**	**4**	**81**	**17**
Total intermediate consumption	**r60**	**7**	**0**	**49**	**2**	**12**	**52**	**26**	**160**	**50**
Taxes less subsidies on products	r99	1	0	2	0	1	3	0	11	2
CIF / FOB adjustments on exports	r61	–	–	–	–	–	–	–	–	–
Direct purchases abroad by residents	r62	–	–	–	–	–	–	–	–	–
Domestic purchases by nonresidents	r63	–	–	–	–	–	–	–	–	–
Value-added at basic prices	r64	31	0	29	1	11	30	19	165	43
International transport margins	trs	–	–	–	–	–	–	–	–	–
Gross output	**r69**	**38**	**0**	**80**	**3**	**24**	**85**	**46**	**336**	**95**

– = magnitude equals zero; 0 = magnitude is less than half of unit employed; $ = United States dollars; ( ) = negative; CIF = cost, insurance, and freight; FOB = free on board.

Source: Asian Development Bank Multi-Regional Input–Output Database. https://mrio.adbx.online/ (accessed 4 August 2020).

4.6A Input-Output Table for Maldives, 2000
(continued)

	Telecommunications	Financial Intermediation	Real Estate, Renting, and Business Activities	Public Administration and Defense	Education, Health, and Social Work	Other Personal Services	Final Consumption Expenditure by Households	Final Consumption Expenditure by Nonprofit Organizations Serving Households	Final Consumption Expenditure by Government	Gross Fixed Capital Formation	Changes in Inventories and Valuables	Exports	Gross Output
	TEL	FIN	BUS	PAD	EHS	OSV	F1	F2	F3	F4	F5	EXP	
	–	–	–	–	–	–	7	–	–	–	0	17	38
	–	0	0	–	–	–	0	–	–	–	(0)	0	0
	0	1	0	2	1	0	15	–	0	1	0	35	80
	0	0	0	0	0	0	0	–	0	2	0	0	3
	1	1	1	6	1	0	4	–	0	–	(0)	1	24
	0	0	1	0	0	0	12	–	17	31	(0)	6	85
	0	0	0	1	0	0	1	–	0	2	(0)	21	46
	1	0	1	0	1	0	4	–	5	1	(0)	319	336
	0	1	0	1	1	0	6	–	2	0	0	55	95
	3	4	1	2	1	0	4	–	–	–	(0)	10	41
	0	37	0	0	0	0	2	–	0	0	1	1	64
	0	3	1	4	2	0	37	–	0	0	0	2	83
	–	0	0	1	0	0	0	–	68	–	0	2	73
	0	0	0	3	0	0	4	–	26	–	0	0	34
	0	0	0	0	1	0	0	–	1	–	0	4	7
	2	2	4	7	2	1	81	–	14	101	(0)	–	377
	9	50	8	28	10	2	178	–	132	137	1	473	1,387
	0	0	1	0	0	0	11	–	0	14	(1)	–	45
	–	–	–	–	–	–	–	–	–	–	–	–	–
	–	–	–	–	–	–	–	–	–	–	–	–	–
	–	–	–	–	–	–	–	–	–	–	–	–	–
	32	14	74	45	24	5	–	–	–	–	–	–	523
	–	–	–	–	–	–	–	–	–	–	–	–	–
	41	64	83	73	34	7	189	–	132	151	0	473	1,954

4.6B Input–Output Table for Maldives, 2018
(at current prices, $ million)

Sector	Code	Agriculture, Hunting, Forestry, and Fishing AHF	Mining and Quarrying MIN	Light Manufacturing LMF	Heavy Manufacturing HMF	Utilities UTL	Construction CON	Trade Services TRD	Hotels and Restaurants HRS	Transport Services TSP
Agriculture, hunting, forestry, and fishing	AHF	6	–	130	1	0	0	–	68	0
Mining and quarrying	MIN	–	–	–	–	–	–	–	–	–
Light manufacturing	LMF	7	–	18	0	1	37	1	199	2
Heavy manufacturing	HMF	0	–	0	0	2	4	2	1	1
Utilities	UTL	2	–	28	0	9	17	12	9	5
Construction	CON	13	–	99	2	22	646	88	473	30
Trade services	TRD	19	–	22	2	28	84	2	47	31
Hotels and restaurants	HRS	0	–	2	0	0	2	7	10	7
Transport services	TSP	6	–	10	1	9	65	8	63	19
Telecommunications	TEL	6	–	5	0	1	13	6	34	32
Financial intermediation	FIN	4	–	8	0	2	39	11	68	9
Real estate, renting, and business activities	BUS	1	–	8	0	1	9	27	19	8
Public administration and defense	PAD	1	–	13	1	1	23	19	33	5
Education, health, and social work	EHS	0	–	0	0	0	4	1	1	1
Other personal services	OSV	0	–	0	0	0	0	0	1	1
Total imports	**IMP**	**93**	**–**	**120**	**8**	**133**	**977**	**22**	**623**	**166**
Total intermediate consumption	**r60**	**158**	**–**	**463**	**15**	**208**	**1,920**	**206**	**1,650**	**318**
Taxes less subsidies on products	r99	7	–	(0)	2	0	68	(23)	150	16
CIF / FOB adjustments on exports	r61	–	–	–	–	–	–	–	–	–
Direct purchases abroad by residents	r62	–	–	–	–	–	–	–	–	–
Domestic purchases by nonresidents	r63	–	–	–	–	–	–	–	–	–
Value-added at basic prices	r64	107	–	175	16	42	1,351	153	913	210
International transport margins	trs	–	–	–	–	–	–	–	–	–
Gross output	**r69**	**272**	**–**	**637**	**33**	**251**	**3,339**	**336**	**2,713**	**545**

– = magnitude equals zero; 0 = magnitude is less than half of unit employed; $ = United States dollars; ( ) = negative; CIF = cost, insurance, and freight; FOB = free on board.

Source: Asian Development Bank Multi-Regional Input–Output Database. https://mrio.adbx.online/ (accessed 4 August 2020).

4.6B Input–Output Table for Maldives, 2018
(continued)

	Telecommunications	Financial Intermediation	Real Estate, Renting, and Business Activities	Public Administration and Defense	Education, Health, and Social Work	Other Personal Services	Final Consumption Expenditure by Households	Final Consumption Expenditure by Nonprofit Organizations Serving Households	Final Consumption Expenditure by Government	Gross Fixed Capital Formation	Changes in Inventories and Valuables	Exports	Gross Output
	TEL	FIN	BUS	PAD	EHS	OSV	F1	F2	F3	F4	F5	EXP	
	–	–	0	–	–	0	28	–	–	–	0	39	272
	–	–	–	–	–	–	–	–	–	–	–	–	–
	1	0	0	2	1	0	218	–	0	0	(1)	150	637
	0	–	0	0	0	0	12	–	–	4	(0)	5	33
	11	4	1	24	14	1	105	–	0	0	(0)	9	251
	9	20	47	84	19	3	936	–	2	664	0	184	3,339
	0	0	0	1	2	3	54	–	0	5	0	34	336
	0	0	1	20	1	1	109	–	0	0	(0)	2,550	2,713
	0	0	0	3	1	2	58	–	0	2	0	298	545
	41	1	2	5	2	4	47	–	1	0	(0)	94	294
	0	8	2	20	1	1	4	–	0	–	(0)	18	195
	5	0	3	3	1	4	176	–	0	0	0	7	273
	42	0	2	24	6	1	17	–	548	–	0	43	779
	0	3	0	25	4	0	140	–	102	0	0	1	280
	1	0	0	0	0	0	9	–	0	0	(0)	56	69
	35	**10**	**17**	**52**	**18**	**14**	**664**	**–**	**126**	**430**	**36**	**–**	**3,543**
	146	**46**	**75**	**264**	**69**	**34**	**2,576**	**–**	**779**	**1,106**	**34**	**3,489**	**13,558**
	(3)	(3)	3	(11)	(7)	6	143	–	(3)	306	7	–	658
	–	–	–	–	–	–	–	–	–	–	–	–	–
	–	–	–	–	–	–	–	–	–	–	–	–	–
	–	–	–	–	–	–	–	–	–	–	–	–	–
	151	152	195	526	218	28	–	–	–	–	–	–	4,237
	–	–	–	–	–	–	–	–	–	–	–	–	–
	294	**195**	**273**	**779**	**280**	**69**	**2,719**	**–**	**777**	**1,412**	**41**	**3,489**	**18,452**

4.7A Input–Output Table for Nepal, 2000
(at current prices, $ million)

Sector	Code	Agriculture, Hunting, Forestry, and Fishing AHF	Mining and Quarrying MIN	Light Manufacturing LMF	Heavy Manufacturing HMF	Utilities UTL	Construction CON	Trade Services TRD	Hotels and Restaurants HRS	Transport Services TSP
Agriculture, hunting, forestry, and fishing	AHF	334	–	418	8	7	–	–	70	–
Mining and quarrying	MIN	–	–	15	2	–	11	–	0	–
Light manufacturing	LMF	156	2	240	20	3	116	4	22	11
Heavy manufacturing	HMF	34	0	31	107	2	52	1	0	14
Utilities	UTL	9	1	18	6	3	9	22	11	2
Construction	CON	7	0	7	3	2	1	3	0	5
Trade services	TRD	111	1	143	40	3	48	4	14	95
Hotels and restaurants	HRS	2	0	5	1	1	1	1	8	15
Transport services	TSP	24	0	32	10	3	8	144	4	40
Telecommunications	TEL	2	0	3	1	1	1	28	3	11
Financial intermediation	FIN	0	–	1	0	–	–	11	2	27
Real estate, renting, and business activities	BUS	102	4	18	8	9	15	98	1	27
Public administration and defense	PAD	0	0	–	–	0	0	0	0	1
Education, health, and social work	EHS	4	0	1	0	1	0	1	0	3
Other personal services	OSV	1	0	1	0	2	1	9	0	7
Total imports	IMP	126	2	140	120	16	105	33	8	129
Total intermediate consumption	r60	914	11	1,073	326	51	368	357	144	387
Taxes less subsidies on products	r99	27	0	30	22	3	15	3	5	16
CIF / FOB adjustments on exports	r61	–	–	–	–	–	–	–	–	–
Direct purchases abroad by residents	r62	–	–	–	–	–	–	–	–	–
Domestic purchases by nonresidents	r63	–	–	–	–	–	–	–	–	–
Value-added at basic prices	r64	1,631	23	354	88	69	437	754	100	289
International transport margins	trs	–	–	–	–	–	–	–	–	–
Gross output	r69	2,571	34	1,457	435	123	820	1,115	249	693

– = magnitude equals zero; 0 = magnitude is less than half of unit employed; $ = United States dollars; ( ) = negative; CIF = cost, insurance, and freight; FOB = free on board.

Source: Asian Development Bank Multi-Regional Input–Output Database. https://mrio.adbx.online/ (accessed 4 August 2020).

4.7A Input–Output Table for Nepal, 2000
(continued)

	Financial Intermediation	Real Estate, Renting, and Business Activities	Public Administration and Defense	Education, Health, and Social Work	Other Personal Services	Final Consumption Expenditure by Households	Final Consumption Expenditure by Nonprofit Organizations Serving Households	Final Consumption Expenditure by Government	Gross Fixed Capital Formation	Changes in Inventories and Valuables	Exports	Gross Output
TEL	FIN	BUS	PAD	EHS	OSV	F1	F2	F3	F4	F5	EXP	
39	–	–	15	70	–	1,231	2	–	82	181	114	2,571
0	–	0	–	–	–	4	–	–	–	0	2	34
17	3	9	16	6	4	509	0	1	3	14	300	1,457
0	1	3	0	4	1	92	0	0	14	1	78	435
10	2	3	1	4	3	15	0	–	0	0	3	123
0	1	130	1	3	2	11	0	9	574	–	63	820
9	3	10	8	15	2	415	1	–	63	–	131	1,115
7	4	11	0	8	11	146	16	2	1	–	9	249
8	4	9	4	18	14	226	11	6	14	–	114	693
3	4	9	0	4	4	80	2	0	0	–	26	181
2	2	4	0	4	3	137	–	–	–	–	1	194
2	24	28	5	20	20	196	0	2	81	–	9	670
0	0	0	0	0	2	10	0	82	–	–	28	125
0	1	11	1	5	5	72	21	316	1	–	1	444
1	1	2	2	4	4	16	2	77	3	–	106	238
8	10	29	4	20	8	519	2	6	57	9	–	1,352
107	58	256	59	184	83	3,679	59	500	895	206	984	10,702
2	2	5	0	1	2	136	1	2	39	0	–	314
–	–	–	–	–	–	–	–	–	–	–	–	–
–	–	–	–	–	–	–	–	–	–	–	–	–
–	–	–	–	–	–	–	–	–	–	–	–	–
72	134	409	65	258	153	–	–	–	–	–	–	4,836
–	–	–	–	–	–	–	–	–	–	–	–	–
181	194	670	125	444	238	3,816	60	502	934	206	984	15,852

4.7B Input–Output Table for Nepal, 2018
(at current prices, $ million)

Sector	Code	Agriculture, Hunting, Forestry, and Fishing AHF	Mining and Quarrying MIN	Light Manufacturing LMF	Heavy Manufacturing HMF	Utilities UTL	Construction CON	Trade Services TRD	Hotels and Restaurants HRS	Transport Services TSP
Agriculture, hunting, forestry, and fishing	AHF	764	–	919	12	48	–	–	310	–
Mining and quarrying	MIN	–	–	46	7	–	69	–	0	–
Light manufacturing	LMF	430	5	535	35	25	478	13	98	27
Heavy manufacturing	HMF	125	1	79	256	16	277	4	1	4
Utilities	UTL	33	3	40	10	35	34	71	69	10
Construction	CON	7	0	5	1	4	1	2	0	1
Trade services	TRD	271	3	289	56	21	137	10	67	15
Hotels and restaurants	HRS	4	0	9	1	6	2	2	39	30
Transport services	TSP	100	2	83	17	30	31	417	21	58
Telecommunications	TEL	8	0	8	1	8	5	102	26	39
Financial intermediation	FIN	0	–	5	1	–	–	41	16	10
Real estate, renting, and business activities	BUS	331	11	37	13	85	41	244	5	33
Public administration and defense	PAD	0	0	–	–	1	0	1	0	0
Education, health, and social work	EHS	13	0	2	0	4	0	1	1	2
Other personal services	OSV	4	0	0	0	0	0	19	2	0
Total imports	IMP	461	14	530	372	93	618	96	90	998
Total intermediate consumption	r60	2,553	39	2,586	784	376	1,692	1,024	746	1,228
Taxes less subsidies on products	r99	258	4	219	154	31	205	47	32	227
CIF / FOB adjustments on exports	r61	–	–	–	–	–	–	–	–	–
Direct purchases abroad by residents	r62	–	–	–	–	–	–	–	–	–
Domestic purchases by nonresidents	r63	–	–	–	–	–	–	–	–	–
Value-added at basic prices	r64	6,169	121	971	262	206	1,530	3,175	285	1,415
International transport margins	trs	–	–	–	–	–	–	–	–	–
Gross output	r69	8,980	165	3,776	1,201	612	3,428	4,247	1,063	2,870

– = magnitude equals zero; 0 = magnitude is less than half of unit employed; $ = United States dollars; ( ) = negative; CIF = cost, insurance, and freight; FOB = free on board.

Source: Asian Development Bank Multi-Regional Input–Output Database. https://mrio.adbx.online/ (accessed 4 August 2020).

4.7B Input–Output Table for Nepal, 2018
(continued)

Telecommunications	Financial Intermediation	Real Estate, Renting, and Business Activities	Public Administration and Defense	Education, Health, and Social Work	Other Personal Services	Final Consumption Expenditure by Households	Final Consumption Expenditure by Nonprofit Organizations Serving Households	Final Consumption Expenditure by Government	Gross Fixed Capital Formation	Changes in Inventories and Valuables	Exports	Gross Output
TEL	FIN	BUS	PAD	EHS	OSV	F1	F2	F3	F4	F5	EXP	
176	–	–	87	312	–	3,803	14	–	1,680	782	73	8,980
0	–	0	–	–	–	39	–	–	–	1	3	165
88	20	65	86	36	27	1,437	1	6	44	99	221	3,776
1	6	17	1	39	7	215	0	1	57	11	83	1,201
68	13	32	9	32	21	111	0	–	17	0	5	612
0	1	480	0	5	4	8	1	15	2,844	–	46	3,428
46	13	53	35	77	8	2,014	4	–	958	–	170	4,247
39	18	51	1	38	56	628	93	9	22	–	14	1,063
59	28	75	25	115	92	967	104	40	332	–	273	2,870
27	29	72	3	32	39	458	37	0	8	–	64	969
0	12	71	1	38	30	1,087	–	–	–	–	1	1,313
12	115	208	23	109	111	518	1	14	1,607	–	10	3,530
0	0	1	0	2	10	135	2	523	–	–	155	831
1	4	52	3	28	26	437	137	2,087	36	–	4	2,838
0	0	10	0	25	0	206	14	478	109	–	311	1,179
67	83	147	49	146	40	6,457	39	48	785	25	–	11,159
585	344	1,334	324	1,034	470	18,520	447	3,221	8,499	918	1,434	48,159
29	39	86	14	37	26	1,934	22	25	589	18	–	3,998
–	–	–	–	–	–	–	–	–	–	–	–	–
–	–	–	–	–	–	–	–	–	–	–	–	–
–	–	–	–	–	–	–	–	–	–	–	–	–
355	931	2,109	493	1,767	683	–	–	–	–	–	–	20,471
–	–	–	–	–	–	–	–	–	–	–	–	–
969	1,313	3,530	831	2,838	1,179	20,454	468	3,246	9,088	937	1,434	72,628

4.8A Input–Output Table for Pakistan, 2000
(at current prices, $ million)

Sector	Code	Agriculture, Hunting, Forestry, and Fishing AHF	Mining and Quarrying MIN	Light Manufacturing LMF	Heavy Manufacturing HMF	Utilities UTL	Construction CON	Trade Services TRD	Hotels and Restaurants HRS	Transport Services TSP
Agriculture, hunting, forestry, and fishing	AHF	4,207	8	9,741	57	60	56	21	384	830
Mining and quarrying	MIN	8	7	207	474	812	37	2	28	73
Light manufacturing	LMF	222	29	1,884	549	420	646	432	309	703
Heavy manufacturing	HMF	494	5	352	1,124	1,032	354	242	20	1,505
Utilities	UTL	93	15	787	638	8,271	117	7	253	74
Construction	CON	–	–	–	–	–	62	26	–	–
Trade services	TRD	970	11	2,476	778	860	430	239	170	920
Hotels and restaurants	HRS	67	0	41	1	41	1	1	17	27
Transport services	TSP	36	17	518	522	901	469	444	60	678
Telecommunications	TEL	23	38	72	128	15	2	21	48	143
Financial intermediation	FIN	45	16	145	46	43	94	241	80	53
Real estate, renting, and business activities	BUS	125	123	369	304	97	160	407	190	355
Public administration and defense	PAD	–	0	0	0	0	–	0	0	0
Education, health, and social work	EHS	–	0	9	8	0	–	24	1	3
Other personal services	OSV	10	15	39	187	6	111	231	71	159
Total imports	**IMP**	**375**	**14**	**846**	**1,253**	**898**	**252**	**339**	**90**	**836**
Total intermediate consumption	**r60**	**6,676**	**298**	**17,488**	**6,067**	**13,455**	**2,794**	**2,677**	**1,721**	**6,359**
Taxes less subsidies on products	r99	69	11	514	1,140	25	203	294	19	170
CIF / FOB adjustments on exports	r61	–	–	–	–	–	–	–	–	–
Direct purchases abroad by residents	r62	–	–	–	–	–	–	–	–	–
Domestic purchases by nonresidents	r63	–	–	–	–	–	–	–	–	–
Value-added at basic prices	r64	17,216	1,511	7,284	2,461	2,603	1,629	10,677	914	6,550
International transport margins	trs	–	–	–	–	–	–	–	–	–
Gross output	**r69**	**23,961**	**1,820**	**25,286**	**9,668**	**16,083**	**4,625**	**13,648**	**2,655**	**13,078**

– = magnitude equals zero; 0 = magnitude is less than half of unit employed; $ = United States dollars; ( ) = negative; CIF = cost, insurance, and freight; FOB = free on board.

Source: Asian Development Bank Multi-Regional Input–Output Database. https://mrio.adbx.online/ (accessed 4 August 2020).

4.8A Input–Output Table for Pakistan, 2000
(*continued*)

Telecommunications	Financial Intermediation	Real Estate, Renting, and Business Activities	Public Administration and Defense	Education, Health, and Social Work	Other Personal Services	Final Consumption Expenditure by Households	Final Consumption Expenditure by Nonprofit Organizations Serving Households	Final Consumption Expenditure by Government	Gross Fixed Capital Formation	Changes in Inventories and Valuables	Exports	Gross Output
TEL	FIN	BUS	PAD	EHS	OSV	F1	F2	F3	F4	F5	EXP	
0	2	2	72	17	4	7,589	–	–	258	249	406	**23,961**
10	3	4	36	6	9	39	–	–	3	12	51	**1,820**
53	11	20	265	34	43	14,140	–	305	630	385	4,206	**25,286**
27	13	9	752	150	20	758	–	–	2,386	110	315	**9,668**
13	2	19	376	76	42	5,282	–	2	–	4	10	**16,083**
–	–	–	–	–	–	–	–	–	4,516	10	11	**4,625**
22	7	9	393	75	20	3,232	–	–	1,400	–	1,636	**13,648**
0	2	4	2	–	8	2,437	–	–	–	(0)	5	**2,655**
4	1	7	562	0	17	7,581	–	–	0	(0)	1,261	**13,078**
76	23	23	90	23	52	799	–	–	27	(0)	71	**1,676**
57	43	83	153	53	83	92	–	–	–	0	22	**1,347**
253	120	175	301	137	212	306	–	–	70	(0)	168	**3,873**
0	0	0	151	–	0	3,766	–	3,786	–	0	4	**7,708**
0	3	1	48	–	3	1,925	–	1,019	–	0	193	**3,237**
181	11	11	72	11	299	1,607	–	809	122	2	285	**4,237**
35	**28**	**31**	**315**	**62**	**17**	**2,976**	–	**226**	**1,205**	**126**	**–**	**9,925**
731	**269**	**397**	**3,589**	**644**	**827**	**52,527**	–	**6,147**	**10,617**	**898**	**8,647**	**142,829**
21	12	15	13	2	8	1,231	–	17	705	66	–	**4,534**
–	–	–	–	–	–	–	–	–	–	–	–	**–**
–	–	–	–	–	–	–	–	–	–	–	–	**–**
–	–	–	–	–	–	–	–	–	–	–	–	**–**
925	1,066	3,461	4,106	2,591	3,403	–	–	–	–	–	–	**66,396**
–	–	–	–	–	–	–	–	–	–	–	–	**–**
1,676	**1,347**	**3,873**	**7,708**	**3,237**	**4,237**	**53,758**	**–**	**6,164**	**11,322**	**964**	**8,647**	**213,758**

4.8B Input–Output Table for Pakistan, 2018
(at current prices, $ million)

Sector	Code	Agriculture, Hunting, Forestry, and Fishing AHF	Mining and Quarrying MIN	Light Manufacturing LMF	Heavy Manufacturing HMF	Utilities UTL	Construction CON	Trade Services TRD	Hotels and Restaurants HRS	Transport Services TSP
Agriculture, hunting, forestry, and fishing	AHF	16,716	38	36,242	238	114	330	107	1,924	3,779
Mining and quarrying	MIN	15	16	504	1,659	3,440	254	4	114	162
Light manufacturing	LMF	711	122	5,979	1,819	718	2,310	1,868	1,242	2,822
Heavy manufacturing	HMF	1,443	19	1,132	3,704	1,349	1,434	1,082	67	4,697
Utilities	UTL	345	68	2,580	1,110	10,256	189	32	1,144	116
Construction	CON	–	–	–	–	–	587	215	–	–
Trade services	TRD	3,314	45	8,017	2,528	1,395	1,672	1,067	711	3,698
Hotels and restaurants	HRS	201	0	111	4	58	5	5	62	93
Transport services	TSP	113	65	1,539	1,633	1,177	1,450	1,689	220	2,636
Telecommunications	TEL	72	147	221	411	22	8	85	180	507
Financial intermediation	FIN	105	46	341	106	48	256	1,051	131	146
Real estate, renting, and business activities	BUS	383	483	1,129	1,308	140	712	1,979	899	1,638
Public administration and defense	PAD	–	0	4	3	0	–	13	1	1
Education, health, and social work	EHS	–	2	89	81	1	–	308	15	29
Other personal services	OSV	46	91	187	402	14	58	196	121	322
Total imports	**IMP**	**2,001**	**67**	**4,243**	**5,926**	**3,273**	**1,821**	**1,773**	**467**	**4,721**
Total intermediate consumption	**r60**	**25,464**	**1,210**	**62,320**	**20,934**	**22,005**	**11,086**	**11,474**	**7,298**	**25,367**
Taxes less subsidies on products	r99	254	35	1,835	4,071	63	1,053	1,101	68	668
CIF / FOB adjustments on exports	r61	–	–	–	–	–	–	–	–	–
Direct purchases abroad by residents	r62	–	–	–	–	–	–	–	–	–
Domestic purchases by non-residents	r63	–	–	–	–	–	–	–	–	–
Value-added at basic prices	r64	64,937	6,199	25,879	8,743	3,948	6,343	47,291	3,871	25,337
International transport margins	trs	–	–	–	–	–	–	–	–	–
Gross output	**r69**	**90,655**	**7,444**	**90,033**	**33,748**	**26,016**	**18,482**	**59,867**	**11,237**	**51,373**

– = magnitude equals zero; 0 = magnitude is less than half of unit employed; $ = United States dollars; ( ) = negative; CIF = cost, insurance, and freight; FOB = free on board.

Source: Asian Development Bank Multi-Regional Input–Output Database. https://mrio.adbx.online/ (accessed 4 August 2020).

4.8B Input–Output Table for Pakistan, 2018

(continued)

Telecommunications	Financial Intermediation	Real Estate, Renting, and Business Activities	Public Administration and Defense	Education, Health, and Social Work	Other Personal Services	Final Consumption Expenditure by Households	Final Consumption Expenditure by Nonprofit Organizations Serving Households	Final Consumption Expenditure by Government	Gross Fixed Capital Formation	Changes in Inventories and Valuables	Exports	Gross Output
TEL	FIN	BUS	PAD	EHS	OSV	F1	F2	F3	F4	F5	EXP	
2	10	21	326	72	11	27,035	–	–	709	991	1,990	**90,655**
25	10	23	78	12	13	913	–	–	4	(15)	212	**7,444**
226	65	203	1,033	127	110	52,916	–	356	1,444	1,067	14,898	**90,033**
91	62	90	2,432	495	48	6,480	–	–	6,589	1,142	1,391	**33,748**
60	14	219	1,158	315	119	8,273	–	2	–	4	13	**26,016**
–	–	–	–	–	–	–	–	–	17,511	138	32	**18,482**
93	42	94	1,522	280	51	28,106	–	–	4,263	–	2,967	**59,867**
0	10	34	6	–	18	10,611	–	–	–	(0)	19	**11,237**
14	2	69	1,904	0	37	37,325	–	–	0	(0)	1,498	**51,373**
288	115	224	315	81	121	3,529	–	–	55	(0)	107	**6,491**
313	167	605	429	140	327	2,718	–	–	–	0	40	**6,967**
1,341	608	1,647	1,881	471	890	18,962	–	–	150	(0)	452	**35,073**
0	2	2	22	–	1	322	–	29,557	–	0	54	**29,980**
1	42	42	526	–	23	7,195	–	2,787	–	0	864	**12,003**
182	89	159	390	57	86	5,912	–	783	403	(10)	449	**9,937**
196	**109**	**228**	**2,493**	**473**	**123**	**16,994**	**–**	**1,598**	**8,891**	**724**	**–**	**56,121**
2,831	**1,347**	**3,658**	**14,514**	**2,522**	**1,978**	**227,289**	**–**	**35,083**	**40,019**	**4,042**	**24,986**	**545,428**
83	32	75	70	12	41	5,069	–	83	3,453	266	–	**18,332**
–	–	–	–	–	–	–	–	–	–	–	–	**–**
–	–	–	–	–	–	–	–	–	–	–	–	**–**
–	–	–	–	–	–	–	–	–	–	–	–	**–**
3,577	5,588	31,339	15,396	9,469	7,919	–	–	–	–	–	–	**265,837**
–	–	–	–	–	–	–	–	–	–	–	–	**–**
6,491	**6,967**	**35,073**	**29,980**	**12,003**	**9,937**	**232,358**	**–**	**35,166**	**43,472**	**4,308**	**24,986**	**829,597**

4.9A Input–Output Table for Sri Lanka, 2000
(at current prices, $ million)

Sector	Code	Agriculture, Hunting, Forestry, and Fishing AHF	Mining and Quarrying MIN	Light Manufacturing LMF	Heavy Manufacturing HMF	Utilities UTL	Construction CON	Trade Services TRD	Hotels and Restaurants HRS	Transport Services TSP
Agriculture, hunting, forestry, and fishing	AHF	69	11	0	0	1	13	8	51	11
Mining and quarrying	MIN	2	0	0	0	9	491	1	0	0
Light manufacturing	LMF	25	2	0	0	5	46	15	11	25
Heavy manufacturing	HMF	19	4	0	0	2	9	0	0	1
Utilities	UTL	21	57	5	1	36	6	5	18	12
Construction	CON	1	0	0	0	0	36	0	5	0
Trade services	TRD	102	12	11	5	13	286	24	21	94
Hotels and restaurants	HRS	0	0	0	0	0	0	4	0	1
Transport services	TSP	47	8	7	2	31	139	82	9	155
Telecommunications	TEL	15	3	0	0	5	0	5	0	12
Financial intermediation	FIN	14	2	3	0	19	257	70	5	101
Real estate, renting, and business activities	BUS	29	5	0	0	10	1	16	1	24
Public administration and defense	PAD	–	–	–	–	–	–	0	–	0
Education, health, and social work	EHS	0	0	0	0	0	0	4	0	3
Other personal services	OSV	64	12	0	0	21	0	26	2	52
Total imports	IMP	600	77	108	36	96	1,374	141	63	714
Total intermediate consumption	r60	1,007	192	135	44	248	2,659	401	186	1,205
Taxes less subsidies on products	r99	26	2	91	16	32	106	36	8	78
CIF / FOB adjustments on exports	r61	–	–	–	–	–	–	–	–	–
Direct purchases abroad by residents	r62	–	–	–	–	–	–	–	–	–
Domestic purchases by non–residents	r63	–	–	–	–	–	–	–	–	–
Value-added at basic prices	r64	2,908	844	217	28	195	2,649	1,475	203	1,595
International transport margins	trs	–	–	–	–	–	–	–	–	–
Gross output	r69	3,940	1,038	443	89	475	5,414	1,913	397	2,878

– = magnitude equals zero; 0 = magnitude is less than half of unit employed; $ = United States dollars; ( ) = negative; CIF = cost, insurance, and freight; FOB = free on board.

Source: Asian Development Bank Multi-Regional Input–Output Database. https://mrio.adbx.online/ (accessed 4 August 2020).

4.9A Input–Output Table for Sri Lanka, 2000
(continued)

	Telecommunications	Financial Intermediation	Real Estate, Renting, and Business Activities	Public Administration and Defense	Education, Health, and Social Work	Other Personal Services	Final Consumption Expenditure by Households	Final Consumption Expenditure by Nonprofit Organizations Serving Households	Final Consumption Expenditure by Government	Gross Fixed Capital Formation	Changes in Inventories and Valuables	Exports	Gross Output
	TEL	FIN	BUS	PAD	EHS	OSV	F1	F2	F3	F4	F5	EXP	
	1	2	2	0	4	16	2,670	–	–	23	(0)	1,059	**3,940**
	0	0	4	0	0	1	68	–	–	0	(0)	460	**1,038**
	2	4	4	2	1	27	4	–	–	24	0	248	**443**
	0	0	0	0	0	0	11	–	–	2	2	39	**89**
	11	13	21	5	3	20	240	–	–	1	0	1	**475**
	0	0	29	0	0	66	3,435	–	–	1,817	(0)	24	**5,414**
	11	7	22	3	4	64	247	–	–	262	0	725	**1,913**
	0	0	2	2	0	16	213	–	–	–	–	158	**397**
	7	4	15	8	3	106	1,333	–	–	118	(0)	804	**2,878**
	6	14	9	2	0	32	65	–	–	52	–	39	**257**
	4	13	10	0	5	14	207	–	19	0	(0)	40	**784**
	11	34	38	2	0	209	802	–	–	104	0	90	**1,374**
	0	–	1	–	18	–	81	–	737	–	–	2	**838**
	0	0	1	0	16	17	132	–	516	0	–	2	**692**
	25	51	38	9	1	198	651	–	412	127	(0)	971	**2,661**
	75	**42**	**122**	**21**	**21**	**371**	**1,086**	–	**4**	**1,583**	**(2)**	–	**6,532**
	156	**184**	**316**	**54**	**75**	**1,154**	**11,246**	–	**1,688**	**4,112**	**1**	**4,661**	**29,726**
	21	16	33	3	1	97	522	–	29	466	–	–	**1,581**
	–	–	–	–	–	–	–	–	–	–	–	–	**–**
	–	–	–	–	–	–	–	–	–	–	–	–	**–**
	–	–	–	–	–	–	–	–	–	–	–	–	**–**
	81	584	1,025	781	616	1,410	–	–	–	–	–	–	**14,612**
	–	–	–	–	–	–	–	–	–	–	–	–	**–**
	257	**784**	**1,374**	**838**	**692**	**2,661**	**11,767**	–	**1,717**	**4,579**	**1**	**4,661**	**45,918**

4.9B Input–Output Table for Sri Lanka, 2018
(at current prices, $ million)

Sector	Code	Agriculture, Hunting, Forestry, and Fishing AHF	Mining and Quarrying MIN	Light Manufacturing LMF	Heavy Manufacturing HMF	Utilities UTL	Construction CON	Trade Services TRD	Hotels and Restaurants HRS	Transport Services TSP
Agriculture, hunting, forestry, and fishing	AHF	155	30	2,231	15	3	29	40	367	64
Mining and quarrying	MIN	3	0	183	2	17	702	7	1	0
Light manufacturing	LMF	253	25	3,701	177	37	974	422	381	475
Heavy manufacturing	HMF	418	118	416	1,016	118	726	119	53	742
Utilities	UTL	43	142	362	12	78	11	22	111	57
Construction	CON	4	2	15	14	0	85	3	44	3
Trade services	TRD	269	37	1,002	210	36	600	157	173	575
Hotels and restaurants	HRS	0	1	3	1	0	1	30	0	7
Transport services	TSP	210	21	935	458	77	550	473	63	1,872
Telecommunications	TEL	52	12	53	23	19	0	97	2	86
Financial intermediation	FIN	57	8	480	14	81	960	690	69	1,318
Real estate, renting, and business activities	BUS	62	14	96	27	23	1	104	6	109
Public administration and defense	PAD	–	–	–	–	–	–	1	–	1
Education, health, and social work	EHS	0	0	27	16	0	0	30	1	5
Other personal services	OSV	166	36	181	70	60	0	168	18	281
Total imports	**IMP**	**801**	**90**	**2,520**	**3,070**	**141**	**1,507**	**340**	**136**	**1,466**
Total intermediate consumption	**r60**	**2,492**	**534**	**12,206**	**5,126**	**692**	**6,144**	**2,703**	**1,426**	**7,062**
Taxes less subsidies on products	r99	80	15	488	382	51	456	164	37	354
CIF / FOB adjustments on exports	r61	–	–	–	–	–	–	–	–	–
Direct purchases abroad by residents	r62	–	–	–	–	–	–	–	–	–
Domestic purchases by non–residents	r63	–	–	–	–	–	–	–	–	–
Value-added at basic prices	r64	7,091	2,353	12,404	1,402	802	6,649	9,498	1,421	9,119
International transport margins	trs	–	–	–	–	–	–	–	–	–
Gross output	**r69**	**9,664**	**2,901**	**25,098**	**6,910**	**1,544**	**13,249**	**12,366**	**2,884**	**16,535**

– = magnitude equals zero; 0 = magnitude is less than half of unit employed; $ = United States dollars; ( ) = negative; CIF = cost, insurance, and freight; FOB = free on board.

Source: Asian Development Bank Multi-Regional Input–Output Database. https://mrio.adbx.online/ (accessed 4 August 2020).

4.9B Input-Output Table for Sri Lanka, 2018
(continued)

Telecommunications	Financial Intermediation	Real Estate, Renting, and Business Activities	Public Administration and Defense	Education, Health, and Social Work	Other Personal Services	Final Consumption Expenditure by Households	Final Consumption Expenditure by Nonprofit Organizations Serving Households	Final Consumption Expenditure by Government	Gross Fixed Capital Formation	Changes in Inventories and Valuables	Exports	Gross Output
TEL	FIN	BUS	PAD	EHS	OSV	F1	F2	F3	F4	F5	EXP	
9	17	11	1	17	98	4,561	–	–	376	988	650	**9,664**
0	0	25	0	0	6	800	–	–	0	970	183	**2,901**
73	247	323	58	13	891	6,850	–	0	1,165	2,137	6,896	**25,098**
170	26	107	21	31	347	613	–	–	427	960	480	**6,910**
73	109	105	28	12	108	227	–	–	4	38	1	**1,544**
1	2	215	1	0	791	1,920	–	–	10,241	(154)	61	**13,249**
93	76	148	23	19	286	4,898	–	–	992	522	2,250	**12,366**
1	5	12	18	2	119	2,028	–	–	–	(0)	655	**2,884**
54	36	90	56	12	647	7,418	–	–	703	277	2,584	**16,535**
73	220	85	34	1	316	294	–	–	631	(0)	168	**2,166**
56	230	97	1	43	145	2,302	–	100	2	(0)	352	**7,004**
84	346	258	10	2	1,474	5,369	–	–	462	(2)	216	**8,660**
3	–	6	–	114	–	177	–	5,142	–	(0)	5	**5,449**
2	1	7	0	92	142	2,000	–	1,818	0	(0)	5	**4,147**
218	580	266	63	6	1,391	11,317	–	209	1,200	0	523	**16,756**
387	117	280	54	88	843	4,517	–	1	4,663	1,295	–	**22,315**
1,300	2,012	2,035	369	453	7,605	55,292	–	7,270	20,867	7,032	15,028	**157,647**
96	86	149	14	14	436	2,670	–	168	1,889	329	–	**7,875**
–	–	–	–	–	–	–	–	–	–	–	–	**–**
–	–	–	–	–	–	–	–	–	–	–	–	**–**
770	4,906	6,476	5,066	3,680	8,716	–	–	–	–	–	–	**80,354**
–	–	–	–	–	–	–	–	–	–	–	–	**–**
2,166	**7,004**	**8,660**	**5,449**	**4,147**	**16,756**	**57,962**	**–**	**7,437**	**22,755**	**7,361**	**15,028**	**245,877**

AGGREGATION OF SECTORS USED

The Asian Development Bank's Multi-Regional Input–Output Tables follow the 35-sector classification used in the 2013 release of the World Input–Output Database, which was based on the United Nations International Standard Industrial Classification of All Economic Activities (ISIC) Rev. 3.1. Table A1.1 presents these sectors and how they correspond to the more recent ISIC Rev. 4 classifications.

Table A1.1:   Multi-Regional Input–Output 35-Sector Classification

Code	MRIO Sector	Short Name	ISIC Rev. 4
c1	Agriculture, hunting, forestry, and fishing	Agriculture	A
c2	Mining and quarrying	Mining	B
c3	Food, beverages, and tobacco	Food and beverages	C10-C12
c4	Textiles and textile products	Textiles	C13-C14
c5	Leather, leather products, and footwear	Leather	C15
c6	Wood and products of wood and cork	Wood	C16
c7	Pulp, paper, printing, and publishing	Paper	C17-C18, J58
c8	Coke, refined petroleum, and nuclear fuel	Refined fuels	C19
c9	Chemicals and chemical products	Chemicals	C20-C21
c10	Rubber and plastics	Rubber	C22
c11	Other nonmetallic mineral	Minerals n.e.c.	C23
c12	Basic metals and fabricated metal	Metals	C24-C25
c13	Machinery, not elsewhere classified	Machinery n.e.c.	C28, C33
c14	Electrical and optical equipment	Electricals	C26-C27
c15	Transport equipment	Transport equipment	C29-C30
c16	Manufacturing, not elsewhere classified; recycling	Manufacturing n.e.c.	C31-C32
c17	Electricity, gas, and water supply	Utilities	D, E36
c18	Construction	Construction	F
c19	Sale and repair of motor vehicles and motorcycles; retail sale of fuel	Sale of motor vehicles	G45
c20	Wholesale trade, except of motor vehicles and motorcycles	Wholesale trade	G46
c21	Retail trade and repair, except of motor vehicles and motorcycles	Retail trade	G47
c22	Hotels and restaurants	Hotels and restaurants	I
c23	Inland transport	Inland transport	H49
c24	Water transport	Water transport	H50
c25	Air transport	Air transport	H51

continued on next page

Table A1.1 *continued*

Code	MRIO Sector	Short Name	ISIC Rev. 4
c26	Other supporting transport activities	Transport activities n.e.c.	H52, N79
c27	Post and telecommunications	Telecommunications	H53, J61
c28	Financial intermediation	Finance	K
c29	Real estate activities	Real estate	L
c30	Renting of machinery and equipment and other business activities	Business activities n.e.c.	J (exc. 61), M, N (exc. 79)
c31	Public administration and defense; compulsory social security	Public administration	O
c32	Education	Education	P
c33	Health and social work	Social work	Q
c34	Other community, social, and personal services	Personal services n.e.c.	E37-E39, R, S
c35	Private households with employed persons	Private households	T

exc. = excluding, MRIO = multi-regional input–output, n.e.c. = not elsewhere classified.

Source: E. Timmer, E. Dietzenbacher, B. Los, R. Stehrer, and G. de Vries. 2015. An Illustrated User Guide to the World Input–Output Database: the Case of Global Automotive Production. *Review of International Economics*. 23 (3). pp. 575–605.

For most data tables, figures, and analyses in the report, closely related sectors were integrated under a broader 15-sector classification. The relationship between the original 35-sector classification and the adjusted 15-sector classification are detailed in Table A1.2.

Table A1.2: Multi-Regional Input–Output 15-Sector Classification

15-Sector Classification		35-Sector Classification	
Code	Sector	Code	Sector
AHF	Agriculture, hunting, forestry, and fishing	c1	Agriculture, hunting, forestry, and fishing
MIN	Mining and quarrying	c2	Mining and quarrying
LMF	Light manufacturing	c3	Food, beverages, and tobacco
		c4	Textiles and textile products
		c5	Leather, leather products, and footwear
		c6	Wood and products of wood and cork
		c7	Pulp, paper, paper products, printing, and publishing
		c10	Rubber and plastics
		c11	Other nonmetallic minerals
		c16	Manufacturing n.e.c.; recycling
HMF	Heavy manufacturing	c8	Coke, refined petroleum, and nuclear fuel
		c9	Chemicals and chemical products
		c12	Basic metals and fabricated metal
		c13	Machinery n.e.c.
		c14	Electrical and optical equipment
		c15	Transport equipment

continued on next page

Table A1.2 *continued*

15-Sector Classification		35-Sector Classification	
Code	**Sector**	**Code**	**Sector**
UTL	Utilities	c17	Electricity, gas, and water supply
CON	Construction	c18	Construction
TRD	Trade services	c19	Sale, maintenance, and repair of motor vehicles and motorcycles; retail sale of fuel
		c20	Wholesale trade and commission trade, except of motor vehicles and motorcycles
		c21	Retail trade, except of motor vehicles and motorcycles; repair of household goods
HRS	Hotels and restaurants	c22	Hotels and restaurants
TSP	Transport services	c23	Inland transport
		c24	Water transport
		c25	Air transport
		c26	Other supporting and auxiliary transport activities; activities of travel agencies
TEL	Telecommunications	c27	Post and telecommunications
FIN	Financial intermediation	c28	Financial intermediation
BUS	Real estate, renting, and business activities	c29	Real estate activities
		c30	Renting of M&Eq and other business activities
PAD	Public administration and defense	c31	Public administration and defense; compulsory social security
EHS	Education, health, and social work	c32	Education
		c33	Health and social work
OSV	Other personal services	c34	Other community, social, and personal services
		c35	Private households with employed persons

M&Eq = machinery and equipment, n.e.c. = not elsewhere classified.

Source: Asian Development Bank. Multi-Regional Input–Output Database.

In select figures, results were aggregated at 5-sector levels. The relationship between the original 35-sector classification and the 5-sector aggregation is provided in Table A1.3.

Table A1.3:   Multi-Regional Input–Output 5-Sector Aggregation

5-Sector Aggregation	Code	35-Sector Classification Sector
Primary	c1	Agriculture, hunting, forestry, and fishing
	c2	Mining and quarrying
Low tech manufacturing	c3	Food, beverages, and tobacco
	c4	Textiles and textile products
	c5	Leather, leather products, and footwear
	c6	Wood and products of wood and cork
	c7	Pulp, paper, paper products, printing, and publishing
	c10	Rubber and plastics
	c16	Manufacturing n.e.c.; recycling
	c17	Electricity, gas, and water supply
	c18	Construction
High and medium tech manufacturing	c8	Coke, refined petroleum, and nuclear fuel
	c9	Chemicals and chemical products
	c11	Other nonmetallic minerals
	c12	Basic metals and fabricated metal
	c13	Machinery n.e.c.
	c14	Electrical and optical equipment
	c15	Transport equipment
Business services	c19	Sale, maintenance, and repair of motor vehicles and motorcycles; retail sale of fuel
	c20	Wholesale trade and commission trade, except of motor vehicles and motorcycles
	c21	Retail trade, except of motor vehicles and motorcycles; repair of household goods
	c22	Hotels and restaurants
	c23	Inland transport
	c24	Water transport
	c25	Air transport
	c26	Other supporting and auxiliary transport activities; activities of travel agencies
	c27	Post and telecommunications
	c28	Financial intermediation
	c29	Real estate activities
	c30	Renting of machinery and equipment; other business activities
Public and welfare services	c31	Public administration and defense; compulsory social security
	c32	Education
	c33	Health and social work
	c34	Other community, social, and personal services
	c35	Private households with employed persons

n.e.c. = not elsewhere classified.

Source: Asian Development Bank. Multi-Regional Input–Output Database.

SUBREGIONAL GROUPING OF ECONOMIES

The report covers 25 economies in Asia and the Pacific, which are grouped into three subregions: East Asia, South and Central Asia, and Southeast Asia and the Pacific. The economies and their respective subregional groupings are detailed in Table A2.

Table A2: Subregional Grouping of Economies

Subregion	Code	Economy
East Asia	HKG	Hong Kong, China
	JPN	Japan
	KOR	Republic of Korea
	MON	Mongolia
	PRC	People's Republic of China
	TAP	Taipei,China
South and Central Asia	BAN	Bangladesh
	BHU	Bhutan
	IND	India
	KAZ	Kazakhstan
	KGZ	Kyrgyz Republic
	MLD	Maldives
	NEP	Nepal
	PAK	Pakistan
	SRI	Sri Lanka
Southeast Asia and the Pacific	BRU	Brunei Darussalam
	CAM	Cambodia
	FIJ	Fiji
	INO	Indonesia
	LAO	Lao People's Democratic Republic
	MAL	Malaysia
	PHI	Philippines
	SIN	Singapore
	THA	Thailand
	VIE	Viet Nam

TECHNICAL NOTE

Indicators	Description	Formula and Notations	Reference
Basic Economic Indicators			
Gross output (current $ million)	Gross output is a broad measure of total economic activity. It includes sales and receipts to final users and other industries as intermediate inputs.	x_j^r is the gross output x of sector j in economy r.	United Nations (2018)
Gross value-added (current $ million)	Gross value-added is the difference between the gross output and intermediate inputs or consumption of a given sector.	v_j^r is the gross value added v of sector j in economy r.	United Nations (2018)
Domestic final demand (current $ million)	Domestic final demand refers to the sales or receipts of domestic producers to final users in the economy. It is the sum of household final consumption expenditure, final consumption of nonprofit institutions serving households (NPISHs), government final consumption expenditure, gross fixed capital formation, and changes in inventories.	f_j^{rr} is the final consumption of *product i* in economy r.	United Nations (2018)
Exports (current $ million)	Exports are the total goods and services produced in economy s and purchased by a resident of another economy r. An export may be sold to final users or other industries in another economy. This amount is measured in millions of current United States (US) dollars.	e_j^{rs} is the sale of products from sector i in economy r to another economy s.	United Nations (2018)
Imports (current $ million)	Imports are the total goods and services purchased by a resident in economy s and produced in another economy r. An import may be used by final users or other industries in the purchasing economy as intermediate inputs.	m_i^{rs} is the sale of products from sector i in economy s to economy r.	United Nations (2018)

Indicators	Description	Formula and Notations	Reference
Intermediate inputs (*current $ million*)	Used interchangeably with intermediate consumption, intermediate inputs refer to the total amount of purchases of products or services of a given sector for use in the production process. These flows are also known as interindustry transactions.	$\sum_{i}^{n} z_{i,j}^{r}$ is the sum of n intermediate inputs z by sector j in economy r.	United Nations (2018)
Domestic inputs (*current $ million*)	Domestic inputs refer to intermediate inputs purchased from domestic sectors. This amount is measured in millions of current US dollars.	$\sum_{i}^{n} z_{i,j}^{rr}$ is the sum of n intermediate inputs purchased by sector j from domestic sectors in economy r.	United Nations (2018)
Foreign inputs (*current $ million*)	Foreign inputs, otherwise called imported inputs, refer to intermediate inputs purchased from foreign sectors.	$\sum_{i}^{n} z_{i,j}^{sr}$ is the sum of n intermediate inputs purchased by sector j in economy r from sectors in economy s.	United Nations (2018)
Indirect production embedded in domestic final demand (*current $ million*)	Indirect production embedded in domestic final demand is the measure of intermediate production processes attributable to the production of goods and services for domestic final demand.	Derived from the matrix equation $\mathbf{L}f^{rr}-f^{rr}$ where $\mathbf{L}$ is the Leontief inverse.	
Indirect production embedded in exports (*current $ million*)	Indirect production embedded in exports is a measure of intermediate production processes attributable to the production of goods and services for exports. This amount is measured in millions of current US dollars.	Derived from the matrix equation $\mathbf{L}e^{rs}-e^{rs}$ where $\mathbf{L}$ is the Leontief inverse and $e^{s,r}$ is the vector of economy r's exports to rest of the world s.	
Gross value-added to output ratio (*GVAR*)	GVAR is the ratio of sector j's total gross value-added to its gross output.	Calculated simply as v_{j}^{r}/x_{j}^{r}	
Gross value-added shares (*%*)	A crude measure of a sector's relative importance to the economy, the gross value-added share is calculated as the value-added contribution of sector j as a percentage of the economy-wide gross value-added.	$v_{j}^{r}/\sum_{j}^{n} v_{j}^{r}$ where n is the number of sectors in the economy r.	

Indicators	Description	Formula and Notations	Reference
Economic Diversification			
Gini concentration index	The Gini concentration index is an aggregate measure of the concentration of economic variables: gross output, gross exports, and gross value-added. It ranges between 0 and 1, where 0 implies a homogenously diversified economy wherein all sectors have a perfectly equal share of output, exports, or value-added to the total economy; and 1 implies an extremely concentrated economy with only one sector. Gini indexes are more sensitive to the middle portion of the distribution.	$Gini_t = 1 - \frac{1}{n_{r,t}} \sum_{n=1}^{n_{r,t}} (S_{i-1}^r + S_i^r)$ where S_i^r is the cumulative share of (a) gross output, or (b) gross exports, or (c) gross value added of sector i in the economy r, $n_{r,t}$ is the number of sectors in economy r at period t.	Ugarte (2014)
Herfindahl-Hirschman concentration index (HHI)	The HHI is an aggregate measure of the concentration of economic variables: gross output, gross exports, and gross value-added. It ranges between $1/n_{c,t}$ and 1. Like the Gini index, the HHI increases with the degree of concentration, but is more sensitive to the top portion of the distribution.	$HH_t = \sum_{n=1}^{n_{r,t}} (S_i^r)^2$ where S_i^r is the share of value-added of sector i in the economy r, $n_{r,t}$ is the number of sectors in economy r at period t.	Hirschman (1958)
Theil concentration index	The Theil concentration index is also an aggregate measure of the concentration of economic variables: gross output, gross exports, and gross value-added. The Theil index is normalized to ensure that its values range from 0 to 1, with values increasing with the degree of concentration. Unlike the Gini index, it is more sensitive to the bottom of the distribution.	$Theil_t = \frac{1}{n_{r,t}} \sum_{n=1}^{n_{r,t}} \left(\frac{S_i}{\bar{S}}\right) * log\left(\frac{S_i}{\bar{S}}\right)$ which is further normalized using $\overline{Theil}_t = 1 - \exp(-Theil_t)$.	Ugarte (2014)
Structural Changes			
Change in output of sector i due to technology changes in sector j (%)	Measures the average effects of technology change in sector j to the output of sector I between two periods. Technology change is analogous with intermediate demand which defines the technical coefficient of an industry. The changes between two periods were transformed to compound annual average rates.	In matrix terms, $(1/2) [\mathbf{L}^t (\Delta\mathbf{A}^j) \mathbf{L}^{t-p}](\mathbf{f}^t + \mathbf{f}^{t-p})$ where $\mathbf{L}$ is the Leontief inverse at period t, $\mathbf{f}$ is the vector of final demand of period t; $t-p$ is the index for the previous comparator period. Further, $\Delta\mathbf{A}^j$ is the matrix of $\Delta\mathbf{A}^j - \mathbf{A}^{t-p}$, where only the column of sector j is shown with zeroes elsewhere.	Miller and Blair (2009)

Indicators	Description	Formula and Notations	Reference
Change in output of sector i due to demand levels (%)	Measures the *average* effects of total amount of all expenditures in final demand (*level*) to the output of sector *i* between two periods. The changes between two periods were transformed to compound annual average rates.	In matrix terms, $(1/4)(\mathbf{L}^t + \mathbf{L}^{t-p})(\Delta f)(\mathbf{P}^{t-p}\mathbf{d}^{t-p} + \mathbf{P}^t\mathbf{d}^t)$ where $\mathbf{L}$ is the Leontief inverse at period t, Δf is scalar of change in total final demand between periods t and $t-p$. Further, $\mathbf{d}$ is the matrix of distribution of final demand across different categories (e.g. household demand, government consumption, etc.), while $\mathbf{P}$ is the product mix matrix which shows the shares of each product in the total column of each final demand category.	Miller and Blair (2009)
Change in output of sector i due to demand mix (%)	Measures the *average* effects of changes of product mix of final demand (i.e. the proportions of each product in the total final demand) to the output of sector *i* between two periods. The changes between two periods were transformed to compound annual average rates.	In matrix terms, $(1/4)(\mathbf{L}^t + \mathbf{L}^{t-p})[f^{t-p}(\Delta\mathbf{P})\mathbf{d}^t + f^t(\Delta\mathbf{P})\mathbf{d}^{t-p}]$ where $\mathbf{L}$ is the Leontief inverse at period t, f is scalar sum of all final demand elements, $\mathbf{d}$ is the matrix of distribution of final demand across different categories (e.g. household demand, government consumption, etc.), while $\mathbf{P}$ is the product mix matrix which shows the shares of each product in the total column of each final demand category; t and $t-p$ are time indexes for two periods under study.	Miller and Blair (2009)
Change in value added due to coefficient changes (%)	Measures the change in value added between two periods due to the value-added coefficient (GVAR) change.	In matrix terms, $(1/2)(\Delta\hat{\mathbf{v}}_c)(\mathbf{L}^t f^t + \mathbf{L}^{t-p} f^{t-p})$ where $\hat{\mathbf{v}}_c$ is the diagonalized vector of value-added to gross output coefficients.	Miller and Blair (2009)
Change in value added due to technology changes (%)	Measures the change in value added between two periods due to technology change (i.e. intermediate demand).	In matrix terms, $(1/2)[\hat{\mathbf{v}}_c^t(\Delta\mathbf{L})f^t + \hat{\mathbf{v}}_c^{t-p}(\Delta\mathbf{L})f^{t-p}]$, see description of notations above.	Miller and Blair (2009)
Change in value added due to demand changes (%)	Measures the change in value added between two periods due to final demand change.	In matrix terms, $(1/2)[\hat{\mathbf{v}}_c^t\mathbf{L}^t + \hat{\mathbf{v}}_c^{t-p}\mathbf{L}^{t-p}\Delta f]$, see description of notations above.	Miller and Blair (2009)

Indicators	Description	Formula and Notations	Reference
Changes in output due to structural changes in consumption (%)	Measures the average change in gross output due to combined changes in demand of households, NPISHs, and government. The changes are transformed to compound annual average rates.	In matrix terms, $\mathbf{L}_t^d (1-\hat{\mathbf{M}}_t^F)\Delta\mathbf{c}$ where $\mathbf{L}$ is the Leontief inverse using the input coefficients matrix of domestically produced goods d, $\hat{\mathbf{M}}$ is the matrix of import dependency ratios of final demand, and $\mathbf{c}$ is the vector of final demand aggregated across categories of household final consumption expenditure, NPISH final consumption expenditure, and government final consumption expenditure. The import dependency ratios are defined as $\overline{m}_{it}^F = f_{it} - f_{it}^d / f_{it}$ where f_{it} is the total final consumption of product i regardless of whether it is domestically produced or imported, while f_{it}^d makes the distinction for domestically produced commodities.	Dervis et al. (1985); Syrquin (1988); Jian (1996)
Changes in output due to structural changes in investment (%)	Measures the average change in gross output due to changes in gross fixed capital formation. The changes are transformed to compound annual average rates.	In matrix terms, $\mathbf{L}_t^d (1 - \hat{\mathbf{M}}_t^F)\Delta\mathbf{GFCF}$ where $\mathbf{GFCF}$ is the vector of gross fixed capital formation.	Syrquin (1988); Jian (1996)
Changes in output due to structural changes in stock (%)	Measures the average change in gross output due to changes in inventories. The changes are transformed to compound annual average rates.	In matrix terms, $\mathbf{L}_t^d (1 - \hat{\mathbf{M}}_t^F)\Delta\mathbf{INVT}$ where $\mathbf{INVT}$ is the vector of changes in inventories.	Syrquin (1988); Jian (1996)
Changes in output due to structural changes in export	Measures the average change in gross output due to changes in gross exports. The changes are transformed to compound annual average rates.	In matrix terms, $\mathbf{L}_t^d \Delta\mathbf{E}$ where $\mathbf{E}$ is the vector of gross exports.	Syrquin (1988); Jian (1996)
Changes in output due to import substitution on domestic final demand	Measures the average change in gross output due to import substitution on domestic final demand. The changes are transformed to compound annual average rates.	In matrix terms, $\mathbf{L}_t^d (\hat{\mathbf{M}}_t^F - \mathbf{M}_{t-p}^F)\mathbf{D}_t$. See description of notations above.	Syrquin (1988); Jian (1996)

Indicators	Description	Formula and Notations	Reference
Changes in output due to import substitution on intermediate demand	Measures the average change in gross output due to import substitution on intermediate demand. The changes are transformed to compound annual average rates.	In matrix terms, $\mathbf{L}_t^d\,(\hat{\mathbf{M}}_t^F - \mathbf{M}_{t-p}^F)$ $\mathbf{D}_t$. See description of notations above.	Syrquin (1988); Jian (1996)

Strength of Linkages

Demand-side

Indicators	Description	Formula and Notations	Reference
Direct backward linkage	Direct backward linkage is defined as the first round of economy-wide impacts induced by a change in final demand of sector *i*.	Direct backward linkages are measured as the column sums of input coefficients matrix, formulaically expressed as $DBL_j = \sum_{i=1}^{n} a_{ij}$ where a_{ij} is ratio of an intermediate transaction from sector *i* to *j* to the gross output of sector *j*.	United Nations (2018)
Total backward linkage	Total backward linkage is defined as the total economy-wide impacts induced by a change in final demand of sector *i*. This linkage measure is analogous to simple output multipliers.	Total backward linkages are measured as the column sums of Leontief inverse matrix, formulaically expressed as $TBL_j = \sum_{i=1}^{n} l_{ij}$ where l_{ij} are elements of the Leontief inverse matrix.	United Nations (2018)
Normalized backward linkage	Normalized backward linkage is a measure of an industry's total backward linkage relative to the average of the economy. Values above one (1) indicate a stronger-than-average demand-pulling effects of a final demand change in sector *i* to the economy.	Normalized backward linkages are formulaically expressed as $$\overline{BL}_j = \frac{TBL_j}{\frac{1}{n}\sum_{j=1}^{n} TBL_j}\,.$$	United Nations (2018)
Growth-equalized output multipliers	"Growth equalization" of output multipliers indicate the sectoral impacts of a general expansion in final demand in all sectors. These multipliers show the increase (or decrease) in sector-specific output due to a unit increase (or decrease) in all final products weighted by its relative importance to the total final demand basket.	In matrix terms, $\mathbf{L}\,\langle \mathbf{f}\,\langle \mathbf{i'f}\rangle^{-1}\rangle \mathbf{i}$. See description of notations above.	Miller and Blair (2009)
Output-to-final demand elasticity	Measures the sensitivity of the economy to a percentage change in final demand in a given sector.	In matrix terms, $oe_j^f = 100 \times (\mathbf{i'}\Delta\mathbf{x}/\mathbf{i'x})$ where $\Delta\mathbf{x} = \mathbf{Lf}(0.01)$.	Miller and Blair (2009)

Indicators	Description	Formula and Notations	Reference
Index of Power of Dispersion	This index measures the relative extent to which an increase in final demand for the products of a given industry is dispersed throughout the total system of industries.	This index is expressed mathematically as ni**L**/i'**Li**.	Rasmussen (1957)
Supply-side			
Direct forward linkage	Direct forward linkage is defined as the first round of economy-wide impacts induced by a change in primary inputs availability in sector j.	Direct forward linkages are measured as the row sums of output coefficients matrix **B**, formulaically expressed as $DFL_i = \sum_{j=1}^{n} b_{ij}$ where b_{ij} is ratio of an intermediate transaction from sector i to j to the gross output of sector i.	United Nations (2018)
Total forward linkage	Total forward linkage is defined as the total economy-wide impacts induced by a change in primary inputs in sector j.	Total forward linkages are measured as the row sums of Ghosh inverse matrix, formulaically expressed as $TFLi = \sum_{j=1}^{n} g_{ij}$ where g_{ij} are elements of the Ghosh inverse matrix, **G**.	United Nations (2018)
Normalized forward linkage	Normalized forward linkage is a measure of an industry's total forward linkage relative to the average of the economy. Values above one (1) indicate a stronger-than-average supply-inducing effects of a primary input change in sector j to the economy.	Normalized backward linkages are formulaically expressed as $$FL_i = \frac{TFL_i}{\frac{1}{n}\sum_{i=1}^{n} TFL_i}.$$	United Nations (2018)
Growth-equalized input multipliers	"Growth equalization" of input multipliers indicate the sectoral impacts of a general expansion in primary input availability in all sectors. These multipliers show the increase (or decrease) in sector-specific output due to a unit increase (or decrease) in the availability of all primary inputs weighted by its relative importance to the total economy.	In matrix terms, **i**'⟨**v** ⟨**i**'**v** ⟩$^{-1}$⟩**G**. See description of notations above.	Gray et al (1979)
Output-to-value added elasticity	Measures the sensitivity of the economy to a percentage change in value-added in each sector.	In matrix terms, oe_i^v = 100 × (**i**'Δ**x**'/**i**'**x**) where Δ**x**' = (0.01)**vG**.	Miller and Blair (2009)

Indicators	Description	Formula and Notations	Reference
Index of Sensitivity of Dispersion	A supplementary index to power of dispersion, sensitivity of dispersion index measures the increase in production of industry *i* driven by a unit increase in the final demand for all industries in the system.	This index is expressed mathematically as $n\mathbf{L}i/\mathbf{i}'\mathbf{L}i$.	Rasmussen (1957)
Multipliers and Other Variants			
Simple output multiplier	Simple output multipliers are defined as the total amount of economy-wide production that is induced by a unit of final demand in a given sector.	Output multipliers are derived as the column sums of the Leontief inverse, mathematically $\sum_{i=1}^{n} l_{ij}$ where l_{ij} refers to the elements in the Leontief inverse. Two further variants are introduced—a competitive and a non-competitive model. In a competitive model, the Leontief inverse was computed with no distinction between foreign- and domestically sourced inputs such that $\mathbf{L} = \mathbf{L}^r$. In a non-competitive model, the output multipliers refer to impacts to domestic output only such that, $\mathbf{L} = \mathbf{L}^{rr}$.	Miller and Blair (2009)
Type I output multiplier	The type I output multiplier is the ratio of the total output effects to the initial effect of an exogenous demand. With output multipliers, sector *j* production must increase by one dollar because of a new dollar's worth of final demand for the same sector *j*. Since the initial effect is also the same as the new final demand levels with output multipliers, type I output multipliers are the same as simple output multipliers.	Type I output multipliers are calculated using $\sum_{i=1}^{n} l_{ij}/(\Delta f_j)$ where f_j refers to the exogenous final demand (i.e. considered as initial effects in output multipliers).	Miller and Blair (2009)
Simple value-added multiplier	Simple value-added multipliers are defined as the total amount of economy-wide gross value-added that is induced by a unit of final demand in a given sector.	Value-added multipliers are derived as the column sums of the Leontief inverse, that was pre-multiplied by the diagonalized value-added coefficients $\hat{v}_c^t$. The vector of simple value-added multipliers is calculated using $\mathbf{i}'\hat{v}_c^t\mathbf{L}$ where $\mathbf{i}'$ is the unit summation vector for the matrix $\hat{v}_c^t\mathbf{L}$.	Miller and Blair (2009)

Indicators	Description	Formula and Notations	Reference
Type I value-added multiplier	Type I value-added multiplier is the ratio of the total value-added effects to the initial value-added effect of an exogenous demand.	The initial value-added effects are simply equal to the value-added per unit of output $\hat{\mathbf{v}}_c^t$. Therefore, type I value-added multipliers are calculated as the ratio between simple value-added multiplier of sector j and the value added (GVAR) coefficient of the same sector j.	Miller and Blair (2009)
Intersectoral output multiplier	Intersectoral output multipliers are defined as the total economy-wide effects of an exogenous demand excluding the intra-sector transactions effects. These multipliers generally measure the demand-pulling effects of the sector to *other* sectors in the economy.	This is simply derived using $\mathbf{i'\check{L}} = \mathbf{i'(I-\check{A})^{-1}}$ where $\mathbf{\check{A}}$ is the input coefficients matrix with zeroes if $i = j$.	Miller and Blair (2009)
Intersectoral value-added multiplier	Intersectoral value-added multipliers are defined as the total economy-wide value-added effects of an exogenous demand excluding intra-sector effects. These multipliers generally measure the demand-pulling effects of the sector to *other* sectors in the economy in value-added terms (as opposed to gross output terms).	The vector of intersectoral value-added multipliers is derived using $\mathbf{i'\,\hat{v}_c^t\,\check{L}}$. See description of notations above.	Miller and Blair (2009)
Backward import multiplier	Backward import multipliers (or backward "leakage" effects) indicates the total amount of production that accrues outside the economy as a result of an exogenous change in final demand of sector i. This is a measure of the total imported inputs required per unit of final demand in a given sector.	The vector of backward (or demand-side) import multipliers is represented as the column sums of the matrix $\mathbf{A}^m(\mathbf{I}-\mathbf{A}^d)^{-1}$, where $\mathbf{A}^m$ is the input coefficients matrix of imported intermediates and $\mathbf{A}^d$ is the input coefficients matrix of domestically produced intermediates.	Dietzenbacher, Luna, and Bosma (2005); Reis and Rua (2006)
Forward import multiplier	Forward import multipliers (or forward "leakage" effects) indicates the total amount of production that accrues outside the economy because of exogenous changes in the availability of primary inputs in sector j. This is a measure of the total imported inputs that are available to the economy due to changes in primary inputs.	The vector of forward (or supply-side) import multipliers is represented as the row sums of the matrix $(\mathbf{I}-\mathbf{B}^d)^{-1}\mathbf{A}^m$, where $\mathbf{A}^m$ is the input coefficients matrix of imported intermediates and $\mathbf{B}^d$ is the output coefficients matrix of domestically produced intermediates.	Reis and Rua (2006)

Indicators	Description	Formula and Notations	Reference
Intraregional transfer multiplier	Intraregional transfer effects refer to the amount of indirect production required from domestic producers to satisfy a unit of an exogenous final demand of a given sector in the economy.	Intraregional transfer effects or multipliers ($\mathbf{M}1$) are calculated as the column sums of the matrix $\begin{bmatrix} (I - A^{rr})^{-1} & 0 \\ 0 & (I - A^{ss})^{-1} \end{bmatrix}$ where $\mathbf{A}^{rr}$ refers to the domestic input coefficients for economy r, and $\mathbf{A}^{ss}$ refers to domestic input coefficients for another economy s.	Miller and Blair (2009)
Interregional spillover multiplier	Interregional spillover effects refer to the amount of indirect production required from foreign producers to satisfy a unit of final demand of a given sector in the economy.	Interregional spillover effects or multipliers ($\mathbf{M}2$) are calculated as the column sums of the matrix $\begin{bmatrix} I & (I - A^{rr})^{-1} A^{rs} \\ (I - A^{ss})^{-1} A^{sr} & I \end{bmatrix}$ where $\mathbf{A}^{rs}$ refers to the input coefficients of intermediate products produced in economy r and used in economy s, and $\mathbf{A}^{sr}$ refers to input coefficients of intermediate products produced in economy s and used in economy r.	Miller and Blair (2009)
Interregional feedback multiplier	Interregional feedback effects refer to the additional amount of indirect production required from domestic producers as a result of production linkages with foreign producers engaged in the supply chain for final product i.	Interregional feedback effects or multipliers ($\mathbf{M}3$) are calculated as the column sums of the matrix $\begin{bmatrix} [I - (I - A^{rr})^{-1} A^{sr} (I - A^{ss})^{-1} A^{sr}]^{1} \\ 0 \\ 0 \\ [I - (I - A^{ss})^{-1} A^{sr} (I - A^{rr})^{-1} A^{rs}]^{1} \end{bmatrix}$	Miller and Blair (2009)
Factor Content Analysis			
Total domestic factor content of consumption	The dollar measure of gross value added that was attributable to the production process required to satisfy household, NPISH, and government final consumption expenditures.	The economy-wide factor content of consumption is calculated using $\hat{\mathbf{v}}_c \mathbf{L} \mathbf{c}_i$ where $\hat{\mathbf{v}}_c$ is the diagonalized value-added coefficients, $\mathbf{L}$ is the Leontief inverse, and $\mathbf{c}_i$ refers to the vector final demand consumption of sector i.	United Nations (2018); Miller and Blair (2009)

Indicators	Description	Formula and Notations	Reference
Total domestic factor content of investments	The dollar measure of gross value added that was attributable to the production of fixed assets.	The economy-wide factor content of investments is calculated using $\hat{\mathbf{v}}_c \mathbf{L}(\mathbf{GFCF}_i)$ where $\hat{\mathbf{v}}_c$ is the diagonalized value-added coefficients, $\mathbf{L}$ is the Leontief inverse, and $\mathbf{GFCF}_i$ refers to the vector investment demand of sector i.	United Nations (2018); Miller and Blair (2009)
Total domestic factor content of exports	The dollar measure of gross value added that was attributable to the production of exports.	The economy-wide factor content of investments is calculated using $\hat{\mathbf{v}}_c \mathbf{L}\mathbf{E}_i$ where $\hat{\mathbf{v}}_c$ is the diagonalized value-added coefficients, $\mathbf{L}$ is the Leontief inverse, and $\mathbf{E}_i$ refers to the vector export demand of sector i.	United Nations (2018); Miller and Blair (2009)
Total foreign input content of consumption	The dollar measure of foreign intermediate inputs that were attributable to the production process required to satisfy household, NPISH, and government final consumption expenditures.	The economy-wide foreign input content of consumption is calculated using $\mathbf{A}^m \mathbf{L}\mathbf{c}_i$ where $\mathbf{A}^m$ is the matrix of foreign intermediate input coefficients, $\mathbf{L}$ is the Leontief inverse, and $\mathbf{c}_i$ refers to the vector of final demand consumption of sector i.	United Nations (2018); Miller and Blair (2009)
Total foreign input content of investment	The dollar measure of foreign intermediate inputs that were attributable to the production of fixed assets.	The economy-wide foreign input content of investment is calculated using $\mathbf{A}^m \mathbf{L}(\mathbf{GFCF}_i)$ where $\mathbf{A}^m$ is the matrix of foreign intermediate input coefficients, $\mathbf{L}$ is the Leontief inverse, and $\mathbf{GFCF}_i$ refers to the vector of investment demand of sector i.	United Nations (2018); Miller and Blair (2009)
Total foreign input content of exports	The dollar measure of foreign intermediate inputs that were attributable to the production of exports.	The economy-wide foreign input content of exports is calculated using $\mathbf{A}^m \mathbf{L}\mathbf{E}_i$ where $\mathbf{A}^m$ is the matrix of foreign intermediate input coefficients, $\mathbf{L}$ is the Leontief inverse, and $\mathbf{E}_i$ refers to the vector of exports demand of sector i.	United Nations (2018); Miller and Blair (2009)

Indicators	Description	Formula and Notations	Reference
Hypothetical Scenario Analysis			
Gross output of sector j based on the hypothetical extraction of sector i	Quantifies how much the total output of an n-sector economy would decrease if the *j*th sector were removed from the economy, including its mutual interrelationships with other producers in the economy. This measure may be presented in % change terms.	This decrease in the total economic activity is estimated using the usual Leontief equation with elements in sector *j* column and row set to zero, such that $\bar{\mathbf{x}}_{(j)} = \mathbf{I} - \bar{\mathbf{A}}_{(j)})^{-1} \bar{\mathbf{f}}_{(j)})$.	Miller and Blair (2009)
Gross value added of sector j based on the hypothetical extraction of sector i	Quantifies how much the total value-added of an n-sector economy would decrease if the *j*th sector were removed from the economy, including its mutual interrelationships with other producers in the economy. This measure may be presented in % change terms.	This decrease in the total value added is estimated using the central Leontief equation with elements in sector *j* column and row set to zero, such that $\hat{\mathbf{v}}_c \bar{\mathbf{x}}_{(j)} = \hat{\mathbf{v}}_c (\mathbf{I} - \bar{\mathbf{A}}_{(j)})^{-1} \bar{\mathbf{f}}_{(j)}$.	Miller and Blair (2009)
Gross output of sector j based on the hypothetical insertion of sector i	Quantifies how much the total output of an *n*-sector economy would increase if a new firm were to enter the economy. This measure may be presented in % change terms.	In an n-sector economy, $$\Delta x = L \begin{bmatrix} a_{nj} x_j^* \\ \vdots \\ a_{nj} x_j^* \end{bmatrix}$$	Miller and Blair (2009)
Spread of Economic Linkages			
Relative evenness of direct backward linkage	An aggregate measure of the variation of direct demand-side impacts across different sectors. A higher variation indicates that impacts are extremely concentrated in a few sectors, while a lower variation index indicates that dispersion of impacts are evenly distributed.	Rasmussen (1957) supplements the linkage indices with coefficient of variation indices. Sector-specific relative evenness of a given stimulus (direct backward linkage) is given by $$CoV_j^{DBL} = \frac{[(1/n) \sum_{i=1}^{n} [a_{ij} - (\frac{1}{n}) a_{.j}]^2]^{1/2}}{(\frac{1}{n}) a_{.j}}.$$ Similarly, economy-wide relative evenness of direct backward linkage is given by $$CoV_j^{DBL} = \frac{[(1/n) \sum_{i=1}^{n} [\sum_{i=1}^{n} a_{ij} - (\frac{1}{n}) \sum_{j=1}^{n} \sum_{i=1}^{n} a_{ij}]^2]^{1/2}}{(\frac{1}{n}) \sum_{j=1}^{n} \sum_{i=1}^{n} a_{ij}}.$$	Rasmussen (1957); Claus (2002)

Indicators	Description	Formula and Notations	Reference
Relative evenness of total backward linkage	An aggregate measure of the variation of total demand-side impacts across different sectors. A higher variation indicates that impacts are extremely concentrated in a few sectors, while a lower variation index indicates that dispersion of impacts are evenly distributed.	Rasmussen (1957) supplements the linkage indices with coefficient of variation indices. Sector-specific relative evenness of a given stimulus (direct backward linkage) is given by $$CoV_j^{TBL} = \frac{\left[(1/n)\sum_{i=1}^{n}[l_{ij} - \left(\frac{1}{n}\right)l_{.j}]^2\right]^{1/2}}{\left(\frac{1}{n}\right)l_{.j}}.$$ Similarly, economy-wide relative evenness of direct backward linkage is given by $$CoV_j^{TBL} = \frac{\left[(1/n)\sum_{i=1}^{n}[\sum_{i=1}^{n}l_{ij} - \left(\frac{1}{n}\right)\sum_{j=1}^{n}\sum_{i=1}^{n}l_{ij}]^2\right]^{1/2}}{\left(\frac{1}{n}\right)\sum_{j=1}^{n}\sum_{i=1}^{n}l_{ij}}.$$	Rasmussen (1957); Claus (2002)
Relative evenness of direct forward linkage	An aggregate measure of the variation of total supply-side impacts across different sectors. A higher variation indicates that impacts are extremely concentrated in a few sectors, while a lower variation index indicates that dispersion of impacts are evenly distributed.	Sector-specific relative evenness of a given stimulus (direct backward linkage) is given by $$CoV_i^{DFL} = \frac{\left[(1/n)\sum_{j=1}^{n}[b_{ij} - \left(\frac{1}{n}\right)b_{i.}]^2\right]^{1/2}}{\left(\frac{1}{n}\right)b_{i.}}.$$ Similarly, economy-wide relative evenness of direct backward linkage is given by $$CoV^{DFL} = \frac{\left[(1/n)\sum_{j=1}^{n}[\sum_{j=1}^{n}b_{ij} - \left(\frac{1}{n}\right)\sum_{j=1}^{n}[\sum_{j=1}^{n}b_{ij}]^2\right]^{1/2}}{\left(\frac{1}{n}\right)\sum_{j=1}^{n}[\sum_{j=1}^{n}l_{ij}}.$$	Rasmussen (1957); Claus (2002)
Relative evenness of total forward linkage	An aggregate measure of the variation of total supply-side impacts across different sectors. A higher variation indicates that impacts are extremely concentrated in a few sectors, while a lower variation index indicates that dispersion of impacts are evenly distributed.	Sector-specific relative evenness of a given stimulus (direct backward linkage) is given by $$CoV_i^{TFL} = \frac{\left[(1/n)\sum_{i=1}^{n}[g_{ij} - \left(\frac{1}{n}\right)g_{i.}]^2\right]^{1/2}}{\left(\frac{1}{n}\right)g_{i.}}.$$ Similarly, economy-wide relative evenness of direct backward linkage is given by $$CoV^{TFL} = \frac{\left[(1/n)\sum_{j=1}^{n}[\sum_{j=1}^{n}g_{ij} - \left(\frac{1}{n}\right)\sum_{j=1}^{n}\sum_{j=1}^{n}g_{ij}]^2\right]^{1/2}}{\left(\frac{1}{n}\right)\sum_{j=1}^{n}\sum_{j=1}^{n}g_{ij}}.$$	Rasmussen (1957); Claus (2002)

Indicators	Description	Formula and Notations	Reference
Forward measure of concentration based on output coefficients	A measure of distribution of a sector's intermediate sales structure to all other sectors. A sector which sells its output to only one sector will record a concentration index of $(n-1)^{1/2}$; the index equates to one (1) in the case of complete uniformity (or evenness) of output coefficients.	Forward concentration index is defined as $GN_i\,(b_{ij} = [\,n(1 - \sum_{j=1}^{n}(\bar{b}_{i.ij})^2)\,]^{1/2}$ where $\bar{b}_{i.ij} = b_{ij}/b_i$. See description of notations above.	Rasmussen (1957); Claus (2002)
Backward measure of concentration based on input coefficients	A measure of distribution of a sector's intermediate purchases structure from all other sectors. A sector which purchases its inputs to only one sector will record a concentration index of $(n-1)^{1/2}$; the index equates to one (1) in the case of complete uniformity (or evenness) of input coefficients.	Backward concentration index is defined as $GN_j\,(a_{ij} = [\,n(1 - \sum_{i=i}^{n}(\bar{a}_{j.ij})^2)\,]^{1/2}$ where $\bar{a}_{j.ij} = a_{ij}/a_{.j}$. See description of notations above.	Rasmussen (1957); Claus (2002)

Sensitivity of Economic Linkages

Economic Complexity

Indicators	Description	Formula and Notations	Reference
Percentage intermediate transaction	The percentage of the production of industries in the economy which is used to satisfy the needs for intermediate inputs	Mathematically defined as, $$PINT = 100\,\frac{i'Ax}{i'x}$$	Chenery and Watanabe (1958)
Average output multiplier	The average amount of production induced in the economy as a result of exogenous changes in final demand. This amount is used to measure interindustry connection owing to its ability to capture indirect production requirements.	Mathematically defined as, $$AVOM = \left(\tfrac{1}{n}\right) i'\,(I - A)^{-1}i$$	Rasmussen (1957); Hirschman (1958)
Average of Leontief inverse	Similar to average output multiplier but uses n^2 as denominator.	Mathematically defined as, $$ALIV = \frac{1}{n^2}\,i'(I-A)^{-1}i$$	Blin and Murphy (1974)
Average technical coefficient	The average value of elements in the intermediate input coefficients matrix. A higher value indicates higher degree of intersectoral dependency.	Mathematically defined as, $$ATC = \frac{i'Ai}{n}$$	Burford and Katz (1977); Bekhet (2009)
Mean intermediate coefficient	The average of the column sums of the intermediate input coefficients. A higher value indicates higher degree of intersectoral dependency.	Mathematically defined as, $$MIC = \frac{i'Ai}{n^2}$$	Jensen and West (1980); Hamilton (1979); Bekhet (2009)

Indicators	Description	Formula and Notations	Reference
Percentage of above-average coefficients	Measures the degree of economic connectedness between sectors whose transactions coefficients are above the average of the whole economy.	Mathematically defined as, $I^{PAC} = \dfrac{i'Ki}{n^2}$ where **K** is a Boolean matrix of the same dimension as the input coefficients matrix defined by the following $K_{ij} = \begin{cases} 1, & if\ a_{ij} \geq MIC \\ 0, & otherwise \end{cases}$.	Adopted from Peacock and Dosser (1957)
Determinant of non-competitive Leontief inverse	A measure which indicates the potential magnitudes of the elements of the Leontief inverse as a measure of economic interconnectedness. Higher determinants are suggested to be correlated to higher multipliers and therefore interindustrial activity. This measure is particularly calculated using a non-competitive input–output model.	Mathematically defined as $\|I-\mathbf{A}^{rr}\|$	Wong (1954)
Determinant of competitive Leontief inverse	A measure which indicates the potential magnitudes of the elements of the Leontief inverse as a measure of economic interconnectedness. Higher determinants are suggested to be correlated to higher multipliers and therefore interindustrial activity. This measure is particularly calculated using a competitive input–output model.	Mathematically defined as $\|I-\mathbf{A}^{\cdot r}\|$	Wong (1954)
Mean path length	Defined as the total gross output divided by the economy's total final demand flow. This term is also used as the actual gross quota of the economy. Measures the average number of 'flows' that a final product passes through in the input–output system. In ecology, path length is expected to increase with maturity and diversity of systems.	Mathematically defined as $MPLE = \dfrac{i'Xi}{i'f}$	Finn (1976); Ulanovics (1983)
Cycling index	Define as the average fraction of sectors' gross output that is circulated within the intersectoral flows. The numerator describes the portion of total ecosystem output that returns to the same sector one or more times. Higher value of cycling index is associated with higher complexity or maturity	Mathematically defined as $CYCI = \dfrac{cyc}{i'xi}$ where $cyc = \sum_j \left(1- \dfrac{1}{l_{jj}}\right)$ where l_{jj} are the main diagonal elements of the Leontief inverse matrix.	Finn (1976); Ulanovics (1983)

Indicators	Description	Formula and Notations	Reference
Average propagation length	Defined as the average number of steps taken by the final product of one sector to affect the gross output of another sector	Average propagation length is measured using $\frac{1}{n}\sum_i[\frac{1}{n}\sum_j APL_{ij}]$ where $APL_{ij} = \frac{h_{ij}}{l_{ij}}$ $for\ i \neq j$ and $APL_{ii} = \frac{h_{ii}}{(l_{ii}-1)} = APL_{jj} = \frac{h_{jj}}{(l_{jj}-1)}$ $for\ i = j$. Further, $\mathbf{H} = \mathbf{L}(\mathbf{L} - \mathbf{I})$ where is the Leontief inverse.	Dietzenbacher (2005); Dietzenbacher and Romero (2007)
Overall sensitivity of the economy	An index which measures the interrelatedness of sectors in the economy irrespective of the magnitude of these transactions. This function is defined as the reciprocal of the harmonic mean of the elements of an order matrix **Y** (which records the number of input–output rounds which are needed for the first i-j connection to occur). The index ranges from 0 to 1. A value of zero indicates that no interconnection exists if any of the sectors in the economy that may be considered significant. A value of 1 indicates that "significant" direct interconnections occur among all sectors in the economy and may imply complete diversification.	The overall measure of interconnection of the economy is computed as the average of the reciprocals of entries of the **Y** matrix, $I^{YA} = \frac{1}{n}\sum_{i=1}^{n}\frac{1}{y_{ij}}$ where **Y** is the order matrix of the input coefficients matrix **A**.	Yan and Ames (1965)
Index of direct interrelatedness	A sub-index of the overall interrelatedness index which measures the amount of direct intersectoral connections in the economy. The index ranges from 0 to 1. A value of zero indicates that no "significant" intersectoral connection exists during the first cycle of input-output transactions. A value of 1 indicates that significant interconnections occur among all sectors in the economy in the first cycle of input-output transactions, hence implying a degree of diversification in the economy.	Defined as $\frac{n_1}{n_2}$ where n_1 indicates the number of elements of a sub-matrix of the order matrix **Y** whose values are equal to 1 (Yan and Ames 1965).	Yan and Ames (1965)

Indicators	Description	Formula and Notations	Reference
Index of indirect interrelatedness	The index ranges from 0 to 1. A value of zero indicates that no "significant" intersectoral connection exists in all cycles of input-output transactions. A value of 1 indicates that significant interconnections occur among all sectors in the economy in the subsequent rounds of input-output transactions.	Defined residually as the difference of the overall sensitivity of the economy and the direct interrelatedness index of Yan and Ames (1965)	Yan and Ames (1965)
Global intensity index	Simply the sum of all the elements of the Leontief inverse, the global intensity index was used to normalize the economic landscape used by Guo and Planting (2000). This measure gives the explicit magnitude of all elements of the output multiplier matrix.	Mathematically, **i'Li**.	Guo and Planting (2000)
Important Coefficients			
Important cells in transactions table	An evaluation of importance of each element in the intermediate transactions table by comparing each transaction with the average transaction amount.	The criterion φ used was $\mathbf{i'Zi}/n^2$ such that "importance" is evaluated as $Imp_{(Z)} = \begin{cases} z_{ij}, & if\ z_{ij} \geq \varphi \\ 0, & if\ z_{ij} < \varphi \end{cases}$	Okamoto (2005)
Important cells in input coefficients table	An evaluation of importance of each element in the input coefficients table by comparing each coefficient with the average coefficient.	The criterion used was $\mathbf{i'Ai}/n^2$ such that "importance" is evaluated as $Imp_{(A)} = \begin{cases} a_{ij}, & if\ a_{ij} \geq \varphi \\ 0, & if\ a_{ij} < \varphi \end{cases}$	Okamoto (2005)
Important cells in output coefficients table	An evaluation of importance of each element in the input coefficients table by comparing each coefficient with the average coefficient.	The criterion used was $\mathbf{i'Bi}/n^2$ such that "importance" is evaluated as $Imp_{(B)} = \begin{cases} b_{ij}, & if\ b_{ij} \geq \varphi \\ 0, & if\ b_{ij} < \varphi \end{cases}$	Okamoto (2005)
Inverse-important coefficients	Traces the influence of a change in an element of the input coefficients matrix (A) and hence in the Leontief matrix (I-A) on the associated Leontief inverse. An element of the technical input coefficients matrix A is considered important if a 20% change in its value generates a 10% or larger change in one or more elements of the Leontief inverse.	Relative changes in the Leontief inverse elements are calculated as $$\frac{\Delta l_{rs(ij)}}{l_{rs}} = \frac{l_{ri}\,lf_{js}\Delta a_{ij}}{l_{rs}\,(1 - l_{ji}\Delta a_{ij})}.$$ a_{ij} is considered "inverse-important" if the amount of change in an inverse element is greater than or equal to the specified threshold (β = 10%)	Hewings (1981)

Indicators	Description	Formula and Notations	Reference
Important coefficients based on impact to gross output (max %)	Traces the influence of a change in an element of the input coefficients matrix (A) to % changes in gross output. An element of the technical input coefficients matrix A is considered important if a 20% change in its value generates a 10% or larger change in output in at least one sector in the economy	Relative changes in gross output x_r are calculated as $$\frac{\Delta x_{r(ij)}}{x_r} = \frac{l_{ri} x_j \Delta a_{ij}}{x_r (1 - l_{ji} \Delta a_{ij})}.$$ a_{ij} is considered "important" if the at least one sector exhibited a change greater than or equal to the specified threshold ($\gamma = 10\%$).	Miller and Blair (2009); Sekulic (1968); Jilek (1971)
Important coefficients based on upper threshold (% change)	Defined as the allowable error limit or tolerable limit which establishes an upper limit on the relative change in the elements of the A matrix that assures that no gross output will be changed by more than one (1) percent. This measure is derived from the tolerable limits approach which creates a measure of the degree of importance of input coefficients. The smaller the tolerable limit, the more important the coefficient is.	Relative changes in technical coefficients are calculated as $$\frac{\Delta a_{ij}}{a_{ij}} = \frac{\Delta x_{r(ij)}/x_r}{\Delta a_{ij}[(l_{ij}\Delta x_{r(ij)}/x_r) + (l_{ri}x_j/x_r)]}.$$ a_{ij} is considered "important" if sectors in the economy exhibited a change in gross output greater than or equal to the specified threshold ($\gamma = 1\%$).	Miller and Blair (2009); Sekulic (1968); Jilek (1971)
International Trade Coefficients			
Trade openness	The ratio of total exports and imports to total gross domestic product in the economy. Trade openness determines the degree of international trade activity relative to domestic production.	Trade openness is defined as $$\frac{\sum_i^n e_i + \sum_j^n m_j^a}{GDP}$$ where e is the export of sector i, m is the total imported inputs of sector j, and GDP is the gross domestic product of the economy.	World Bank (n.d.)
Self-sufficiency ratio	The ratio of domestic output to the amount of demand in the local economy. If the domestic output exceeds the demand in the local economy, then the sector is self-sufficient, i.e. ratio exceeds 1.	Self-sufficiency ratio of sector i is defined as $$\frac{\sum_{j=1}^n z_{ij}^{.r} + f_j^{.r} - e_i}{x_i}$$ where $z_{ij}^{.r}$ is the intermediate purchase of sector j of sector i inputs irrespective of the country of origin, $f_i^{.r}$ is the final consumption within country r of product i irrespective of the country of origin, and e is the export demand of sector i.	Miller and Blair (2009)

Indicators	Description	Formula and Notations	Reference
Regional supply percentage	The ratio of amount of domestic output of sector i minus exports to the total supply in of product i intended for domestic demand. A ratio of 1 indicates that the domestic sector has the capacity to supply its own requirements internally.	Regional supply percentage is defined as $\dfrac{x_i^r - e_i}{\sum_{j=1}^{n} z_{ij}^{.r} + f_j^{.r} - e_i}$. See description of notations above.	Miller and Blair (2009)
Regional purchase coefficient	Measures sector i's intermediate inputs purchased by domestic sectors relative to the total (domestic and imported) intermediate sales. This indicator is also known as "relative shipments" in multi-regional studies.	Regional purchase coefficient uses the similar approach to regional supply percentage but excluding the final demand. It is defined as, $\dfrac{\sum_{j=1}^{n} z_{ij}^{rr}}{\sum_{j=1}^{n} z_{ij}^{.r}}$.	Miller and Blair (2009)
Sectoral purchase coefficient	This is the ratio of domestic purchases by sector j to its domestic output excluding exports. This measures the relative degree of dependence of each sector on the domestic economy.	Sectoral purchase coefficients are defined as $1 - \dfrac{\sum_{j=1}^{n} z_{ij}^{sr}}{\sum_{i=1}^{n} z_{ij}^{rr} + f_i^{rr} - e_i}$ where z_{ij}^{sr} refers to the imported inputs of country r.	Miller and Blair (2009)
Simple location quotient	This is defined as the ratio of the (a) sector i's share in the total output of the economy to the (b) share of rest of the world's sector i output in the total output of the rest of the world. If the location quotient is greater than 1, it means that the sector is concentrated in the domestic economy as compared to the rest of the world.	A simple location quotient LQ is defined as $LQ_i^r = \left(\dfrac{x_i^r/x_i^W}{x^r/x^W}\right)$ where x^W is the total gross output of the global economy, and x^r is the gross output of economy r.	Miller and Blair (2009)
Cross industry quotient	An extension of simple location quotients, cross industry quotients (CIQ) are defined as the ratio of simple location quotient of sector i to sector j. If the output of domestic sector i relative to the global output of i is larger than the output of domestic sector j relative to the global output of sector j (CIQr > 1), then all of j's needs of input i can be supplied from within the domestic economy. Similarly, if sector i at the domestic level is relatively smaller than sector j at the global level (CIQr < 1), then it is assumed that some of j's needs for i inputs will have to be imported.	A cross industry location quotient CLQ is defined as $CLQ_{ij}^r = \left(\dfrac{x_i^r/x_i^W}{x_j^r/x_j^W}\right)$.	Miller and Blair (2009)

Indicators	Description	Formula and Notations	Reference
Semilogarithmic quotient	Integrating the properties of both SLQ and CIQ, the Semilogarithmic quotients intend to maintain the measure of relative size of the region, selling sector, and purchasing sector in deriving a measure of regional specialization of an economic activity.	A semilogarithmic quotient SLQ is defined as $SQR_{ij}^{r} = LQ_{i}^{r}/log_2 (1 + LQ_{j}^{r})$.	Miller and Blair (2009)
Fabrication effect	Fabrication effects are calculated as a ratio of input dependence ratios between two different regions/economies. The first ratio measures the relative dependence of sector j in the domestic economy on inputs from itself and all other sectors; while the second ratio measures the relative dependence of global sector j on inputs from itself and other sectors. If fabrication effects are greater than 1, it may be considered that the input dependence of the domestic sector is higher than the global average of the same sector.	Fabrication effects ρ are calculated as $\rho = \dfrac{1 - (v_j^r/x_j^r)}{1 - (v_j^W/x_j^W)}$ where v_j^W is the combined value added of sector j of all economies in the world.	Round (1978)
Export-to-output ratio	Defined as sector i's share of exports to its gross output, export-to-output ratios explain the relative levels of exporting activity within sector i.	Mathematically expressed as e_i/x_i.	Miller and Blair (2009)
Import-to-input ratio	Defined as sector j's share of imported inputs to its gross outlays (or output), import-to-input ratio explain the relative dependence on foreign inputs within sector j.	Mathematically expressed as $\sum_{i=1}^{n} z_{ij}^{sr}/x_r$.	Miller and Blair (2009)

Participation in Global Value Chains

Indicators	Description	Formula and Notations	Reference
Backward GVC Participation	The sum of backward measures of simple and complex GVC participation.	The sum of the $\hat{V}B\hat{Y}$ matrix along the columns provides the decomposition of an economy-sector's final goods production, which indicates GVC participation based on backward linkages, *GVCPt_B*. It refers to the sum of value-added in an economy-sector's final goods production that is involved in GVC activities from all upstream sectors. Mathematically, $\hat{V}B\hat{Y} = \underbrace{VL\hat{Y}^D}_{Y\_D} + \underbrace{VL\hat{Y}^F}_{Y\_RT} + \underbrace{VLA^F L\hat{Y}^D}_{Y\_GVC\_S} + \underbrace{VLA^F(B\hat{Y} - L\hat{Y}^D)}_{Y\_GVC\_C}$	Wang et al. (2017b)

Indicators	Description	Formula and Notations	Reference
Backward measure of simple GVC participation	Backward measure of Simple GVC participation is defined as the foreign value-added in an economy-sector that is imported directly from partner countries and are used to produce domestic final goods consumed domestically. This measure is expressed as the ratio to the economy's total final demand.	Equal to $\dfrac{VLA^F L \hat{Y}^D}{Y\_GVC\_S}$ (see above)	Wang et al. (2017b)
Backward measure of complex GVC participation	Backward measure of Simple GVC participation is defined as the returned domestic value-added or foreign value-added embodied in an economy-sector's intermediate imports that are used to produce final goods absorbed at the home economy or exported to other countries. This measure is expressed as the ratio to the economy's total final demand.	Equal to $\dfrac{VLA^F(B\hat{Y} - L\hat{Y}^D)}{Y\_GVC\_C}$ (see above)	Wang et al. (2017b)
Forward GVC participation	The sum of forward measures of simple and complex GVC participation.	The sum of the matrix along the rows provides the decomposition of value-added from an economy-sector from upstream activities, which indicates GVC participation based on forward linkages, *GVCPt_F*. It refers to the sum of each economy-sector's value-added used in all downstream sectors. Mathematically, $\hat{V}B\hat{Y} = \underbrace{\hat{V}LY^D}_{(1)V\_D} + \underbrace{\hat{V}LY^F}_{(2)\hat{V}\_RT} + \underbrace{\hat{V}LA^F LY^D}_{(3a)V\_GVC\_C} +$ $\underbrace{\hat{V}LA^F(BY-LY^D)}_{(3b)V\_GVC\_S}$	Wang et al. (2017b)
Forward measure of simple GVC participation	Forward measure of simple GVC participation is defined as the domestic value-added embodied in an economy-sector's intermediate exports that are used by the direct importer to produce domestic final goods that are absorbed by domestic final demand. This measure is expressed as the ratio to the economy's total value added.	Equal to $\dfrac{\hat{V}LA^F LY^D}{(3a)V\_GVC\_S}$ (see above)	Wang et al. (2017b)

Indicators	Description	Formula and Notations	Reference
Forward measure of complex GVC participation	Forward measure of complex GVC participation is an economy-sector's value-added embodied in its intermediate exports and used by the direct importer to produce intermediate and final exports to other countries. This measure is expressed as the ratio to the economy's total value added.	Equal to $\dfrac{\hat{V}LA^F(BY-LY^D)}{(3b)V\_GVC\_C}$ (see above)	Wang et al. (2017b)
Specialization in Global Value Chains			
Vertical specialization ratio	Measures the extent of production-sharing arrangements in country's gross exports	The ratio $(FVA + PDC)/e_i$ measures the extent of vertical specialization (VS) in a country (or sector's) gross exports.	Wang, Wei, and Zhu (2013)
Traditional revealed comparative advantage	Measures the relative advantage or disadvantage of a country-sector as "revealed" by trade patterns	Traditional revealed comparative advantage (TRCA) of economy r is defined as: $$TRCA_i^r = \dfrac{\dfrac{e_i^{r*}}{\sum_i^n e_i^{r*}}}{\dfrac{\sum_t^G e_i^{t*}}{\sum_i^n \sum_t^G e_i^{t*}}}$$ That is, the TRCA is equal to the export share of an industry to the total exports of an economy, $\dfrac{e_i^{r*}}{\sum_i^n e_i^{r*}}$, divided by the export share of this industry in the world, $\dfrac{\sum_t^G e_i^{t*}}{\sum_i^n \sum_t^G e_i^{t*}}$. An RCA value of less than 1 implies that the economy is not specialized in exports of this industry. Similarly, an RCA value exceeding 1 implies that the economy is specialized in this industry's exports.	Bela Balassa (1965)

Indicators	Description	Formula and Notations	Reference
New revealed comparative advantage	Wang, Wei, and Zhu (2013) proposed a new measure of revealed comparative advantage (NRCA) that excludes foreign value-added and pure double-counted terms in gross exports, but includes indirect exports of an economy-sector's value-added through other sectors of the exporting economy. The authors defined NRCA as the share of an economy-sector's forward-linkage-based measure of domestic value-added in exports, *dvix_f*, in the economy's total domestic value-added in exports relative to the sector's total forward-linkage-based domestic value-added in exports from all economies as a share of global value-added in exports.	The NRCA is defined as: $$NRCA_i^r = \frac{\dfrac{dvix\_f_i^{r*}}{\sum_{i=1}^n dvix\_f_i^{r*}}}{\dfrac{\sum_t^G dvix\_f_i^{t*}}{\sum_i^n \sum_t^G dvix\_f_i^{t*}}}$$ NRCA uses the same interpretation as TRCA, except that, instead of using gross exports, e, NRCA only includes the domestic value-added component of export in each sector.	Wang, Wei, and Zhu (2013)
Position in Global Value Chains			
Upstreamness index	Fally (2012) and Antràs and Chor (2013) have proposed a measure of position in GVCs of an economy-sector through the upstreamness index. The index is the average distance of a sector to its final use. Miller and Temurshoev (2018) described an upstream sector to be that whose outputs goes through multiple stages before being absorbed as final use in the economy. A simpler measure of upstreamness also relates the share of gross output of an economy-sector that is sold to final consumers. In this case, an economy-sector that sells a large amount of its output for intermediate use, i.e. it has a lower ratio between final use and total output, is said to be relatively upstream.	Fally (2012) and Antràs and Chor (2013) developed a measure of distance of a production sector from final demand called *upstreamness*. Succinctly, the *upstreamness* of sector r in economy i, or U_i^r, is the average distance from final use and is given by: $$U_i^r = 1 \times \frac{F_i^r}{X_i^r} + 2 \times \frac{\sum_{s=1}^S \sum_{j=1}^J a_{ij}^{rs} F_j^s}{X_i^r}$$ $$+ 3 \times \frac{\sum_{s=1}^S \sum_{j=1}^J \sum_{t=1}^S \sum_{k=1}^J a_{ij}^{rs} a_{jk}^{st} F_k^t}{X_i^r} + \dots$$ where F is final demand, X is gross output, superscripts refer to sector, and subscripts refer to in economy. Moreover, a_{ij}^{rs} is the dollar amount of sector r's output from economy i needed to produce a dollar's worth of sector s's output in economy j.	Fally (2012); Antràs and Chor (2013); Wang et al. (2017a); Miller and Temurhsoev (2017)

Indicators	Description	Formula and Notations	Reference
	Note that $U_i^r \geq 1$, and that the higher U_i^r is, the higher is the upstreamness of the output from sector r in economy i. A sector that sells a higher proportion of output to final consumers would appear to be relatively downstream (i.e., relative low U_i^r), while a sector that sells a smaller proportion to final consumers would be relatively more upstream (i.e., relatively high U_i^r.	Antràs and Chor (2018) show that given $\sum_{s=1}^{S}\sum_{j=1}^{J} a_{ij}^{rs} < 1$ for all j–s pairs, then the numerator of U_i^r is just the $((i-1) \times S+r)$-th element of the $J \times S$ by 1 column matrix $[I-\mathbf{A}]^{-2}\mathbf{F}$, where $\mathbf{A}$ is a $J \times S$ by $J \times S$ matrix whose $((i-1)\times S+r)$-th element is a_{ij}^{rs}, while $\mathbf{F}$ is a column matrix whose $((i-1) \times S+r)$-th row is $F_{i.}^r$. Furthermore, given that the gross output column matrix satisfies, $\mathbf{X} = [I-\mathbf{A}]^{-1}\mathbf{F}$, the numerator of U_i^r is also equal to the $((i-1) \times S+r)$-th element of the $J \times S$ by 1 matrix $[I-\mathbf{A}]^{-1}\mathbf{X}$, where $\mathbf{X}$ is a $J \times S$ by 1 column matrix whose $((i-1) \times S+r)$-th row is $X_{i.}^r$.	
	Production Length of Global Value Chains		
Backward measures of average production length	Average production length of a given sector i in economy s based on backward industrial linkage is the ratio of the induced total intermediate inputs in sector j of country r to value of final goods and services produced in the given sector i in economy s which induced these inputs. Average production length indicates the number of upstream processes before the final product is realized in the economy, i.e., the relative *downstreamness* of an economy or economy-sector.	Taking all economy-sector pairs (s,i) where final goods and services which induced the intermediate inputs in economy-sector (r,j), the average production length in the economy based on backward industrial linkage is given by: $PLy = 1 \frac{VBB\hat{Y}}{VB\hat{Y}}$ where V is the value-added coefficient matrix vector, B is the Leontief inverse matrix, and $\hat{Y}$ is the diagonal matrix of final demands.	Wang et al. (2017a)
Forward measures of average production length	The average production length of a given sector i in economy s based on forward industrial linkage is defined as the ratio of total gross outputs in all product j of economy r to the value added of given sector i in economy s that induced these gross outputs. Average production length based on forward industrial linkage measures the number of downstream processes that the value added of an economy-sector is counted as gross output. Hence, this measure also gives the relative *upstreamness* of an economy or economy-sector.	Taking all economy-sector pairs (s,i) where the value added originated and all economy-sector pairs (r,j) where the value-added is counted as gross output, the average production length in the economy based on forward industrial linkage is given: $PL_v = 1 \frac{\hat{V}BBY}{\hat{V}BY}$ where $\hat{V}$ is the diagonal matrix of value-added coefficient vector V, B is the Leontief inverse matrix, Y is the final demand vector, and X is the output vector.	Wang et al. (2017a)

REFERENCES

J. Amaral and J. Lopes. 2007. Complexity and Interdependence: A New Measure of Connectedness of Input–Output Systems. *Environment and Planning.* A39. pp. 1170–1182.

P. Antràs and D. Chor. 2017. On the Measurement of Upstreamness and Downstreamness in Global Value Chains. *National Bureau of Economic Research Working Papers 24185.* https://www.nber.org/papers/w24185.pdf

P. Antràs, D. Chor, T. Fally, and R. Hillberry. 2012. Measuring the Upstreamness of Production and Trade Flows. *American Economic Review. 102 (3).* pp. 412–416.

Asian Development Bank. 2020. *Asia's Journey to Prosperity: Policy, Market, and Technology over 50 Years.* Mandaluyong City, Metro Manila: Asian Development Bank.

_____. 2017. Compendium of Supply and Use Tables for Selected Economies in Asia and the Pacific. Mandaluyong City, Metro Manila: Asian Development Bank.

B. Balassa. 1965. Trade Liberalisation and "Revealed" Comparative Advantage. *The Manchester School.* 33 (2). pp. 99–204.

H. Bekhet. 2009. Assessing Economic Connectedness Degree of the Malaysian Economy: Input–Output Model Approach. *International Journal of Economics and Finance.* 1 (2). pp. 134–143.

J. Blin and F. Murphy. 1974. On Measuring Economic Interrelatedness. *Review of Economics and Statistics.* 41. pp. 437–440.

R.L. Burford and J.L. Katz. 1981. A Method for Estimation of Input–Output Type Output Multipliers When No I–O Model Exists. *Journal of Regional Science.* 21. pp. 151–163.

H. Chenery and T. Watanabe. 1958. International Comparisons of the Structure of Production. *Econometrica.* 26. pp. 487–521.

I. Claus. 2002. Interindustry Linkages in New Zealand. *Australasian Macroeconomics Workshop.* Wellington: New Zealand Treasury.

I. Claus, R. Lattimore, T. Le, and A. Stroombergen. 2011. 50 Years of Structural Change: An Analysis of Input–Output Tables Since 1953. New Zealand Association of Economists. https://www.nzae.org.nz/wp-content/uploads/2011/08/50_Years_of_ Structural_Change_An_Analysis_of_Input-Output_Tables_since_1953.pdf.

K. Dervis, J. de Melo, and S. Robinson. 1982. *General Equilibrium Models for Development Policy.* Washington, DC: World Bank.

E. Dietzenbacher. 2005. More on Multipliers. *Journal of Regional Science. 45 (2). pp.* 421–426.

E. Dietzenbacher and I. Romero. 2007. Production Chains in an Interregional Framework: Identification by Means of Average Propagation Lengths. *International Regional Science Review. 30 (4).* pp. 362–383.

E. Dietzenbacher, I.R. Luna, and N. Bosma. 2005. Using Average Propagation Lengths to Identify Production Chains in the Andalusian Economy. *Estudios Economia Aplicada.* 23 (2). pp. 405–422.

Eurostat. 2008. *Eurostat Manual of Supply, Use and Input–Output Tables.* Luxembourg: European Commission. https://ec.europa.eu/eurostat/documents/3859598/5902113/KS-RA-07-013-EN.PDF/

J. Finn. 1976. Measures of Ecosystem Structure and Function Derived from Analysis of Flows. *Journal of Theoretical Biology. 56 (2).* pp. 363–380.

L. Gray, J. McKean, E. Sparling, and J. Weber. 1979. Measurement of Growth Equalized Employment Multiplier Effects: An Empirical Example. *Annals of Regional Science. 13.* pp. 68–77.

J. Guo and M.A. Planting. 2000. Using Input–Output Analysis to Measure US Economic Structural Change Over a 24-Year Period. *13th International Conference on Input-Output Techniques.* Macerata, Italy. https://www.bea.gov/system/files/papers/WP2000-1.pdf.

J. Hamilton and R. Jensen. 1983. Summary Measures of Interconnectedness for Input-Output Models. *Environment and Planning.15 (1).* pp. 55–65.

A. Hirschman. 1958. *The Strategy of Economic Development.* New Haven: Yale University Press.

R. Jensen and G. West. 1980. The Effect of Relative Coefficient on Input–Output Multipliers. *Environment and Planning.* 12 (6). pp. 659–670.

T. Jian. 1996. Input–Output Analysis of Economic Growth and Structural Changes in China. *Journal of Applied Input–Output Analysis (Pan Pacific Association of Input–Output studies). 3.* pp. 18–53.

J. Jilek. 1971. The Selection of the Most Important Coefficient. *Economic Bulletin for Europe.* 23. pp. 86–105.

W.W. Leontief. 1936. Quantitative Input and Output Relations in the Economic Systems of the United States. *Review of Economics and Statistics.* 18 (3). pp. 105–125. https://www.jstor.org/stable/1927837?seq=1

W.W. Leontief. 1985. Why Economics Needs Input–Output Analysis. *Challenge.* 28 (1). pp. 27–35. https://www.jstor.org/stable/40720309.

J. Lopes, J. Carlos, J. Dias, and F. Amaral. 2007. Economic Complexity as Input–Output Interdependence: A Comparison of Different Measurement Methods. *Proceedings of the 16th International Input–Output Conference.* Istanbul, Turkey.

J. Lopes, J. Dias, and F. Amaral. 2008. Assessing Economic Complexity with Input–Output Based Measures. *Technical University of Lisbon Working Papers.* https://ideas.repec.org/p/ise/isegwp/wp492008.html.

R. Miller and U. Temurshoev. 2017. Output Upstreamness and Input Downstreamness. *International Regional Science Review.* 40 (5). pp. 443–475.

R.E. Miller and P.D. Blair. 2009. *Input–Output Analysis: Foundations and Extensions.* Second edition. Cambridge, UK: Cambridge University Press.

N. Okamoto and T. Ihara. 2005. *Spatial Structure and Regional Development in China: An Interregional Input–Output Approach.* Basingstoke, UK: Palgrave Macmillan.

A. Okuyama. 2007. Economic Modeling for Disaster Impact Analysis. *Economic Systems Research.* 19. pp. 115–124.

Y. Okuyama and K. D. Yu. 2018. Return of the Inoperability. *Economic Systems Research.* 31 (4). pp. 1–14.

A. Peacock and D.G. Dosser. 1957. Input–Output Analysis in an Underdeveloped Economy: A Case Study. *Review of Economic Studies.* 25. pp. 21–24.

N. Rasmussen. 1956. *Studies in Inter-Sectoral Relations.* Copenhagen: E. Harck: North Holland, Amsterdam.

H. Reis and A. Rua. 2006. An Input–Output Analysis: Linkages vs Leakages. *Estudos e Documentos de Trabalho Working Papers.* 17. https://www.bportugal.pt/sites/default/files/anexos/papers/wp200617.pdf

J. Round. 1978. An Interregional Input–Output Approach to the Evaluation of Nonsurvey Methods. *Journal of Regional Science.* 18 (2). pp. 179–194.

M. Sekulic. 1968. Application of Input–Output Models to the Structural Analysis of the Yugoslav Economy. *Ekonomska Analiza.* 2 (1-2). pp. 50–61.

M. Sonis and G.J. Hewings. 1998. Economic Complexity as Network Complication: Multiregional Input-Output Structural Path Analysis. *Annals of Regional Science.* 32. pp. 407–436.

M. Syrquin. 1988. Patterns of Structural Change. *Handbook of Development Economics.* 1. pp. 203–273.

E. Timmer, E. Dietzenbacher, B. Los, R. Stehrer, and G. de Vries. 2015. An Illustrated User Guide to the World Input–Output Database: the Case of Global Automotive Production. *Review of International Economics.* 23 (3). pp. 575–605.

C. Ugarte. 2014. Weak Links and Diversification: Policy Issues in International Trade and Commodities. *Research Study Series No. 67.* https://unctad.org/en/PublicationsLibrary/itcdtab69_en.pdf

R.E. Ulanowicz. 1983. Identifying the Structure of Cycling in Ecosystems. *Mathematical Biosciences.* 65 (2). pp. 219–237.

United Nations. 2018. *Handbook on Supply, Use and Input–Output Tables with Extensions and Applications.* Studies in Methods. New York: United Nations. https://unstats.un.org/unsd/nationalaccount/docs/SUT_IOT_HB_wc.pdf.

Z. Wang, S.J. Wei, and K. Zhu. 2013. Quantifying International Production Sharing at the Bilateral and Sector Levels. *National Bureau of Economic Research Working Paper No. 19667.* https://www.nber.org/papers/w19677.pdf

Z. Wang, S.J. Wei, X. Yu, and K. Zhu. 2017. Characterizing Global Value Chains: Production Length and Upstreamness. *National Bureau of Economic Research Working Paper No. 23261.* https://www.nber.org/papers/w23261.pdf

Z. Wang, S.J. Wei, X. Yu, and K. Zhu. 2017. Measures of Participation in Global Value Chains and Global Business Cycles. *National Bureau of Economic Research Working Paper No. 23222.* https://www.nber.org/papers/w23222.pdf

B. Wixted, N. Yamano, and C. Webb. 2006. Input–Output Analysis in an Increasingly Globalised World. *OECD Science, Technology and Industry Working Papers* 2006/07. OECD Publishing. https://doi.org/10.1787/18151965.

Y. Wong. 1957. Some Mathematical Concepts for Linear Economic Models. In *Economic Activity Analysis* by O. Morgenstern. pp. 283–341. New York: Wiley.

World Bank. (n.d.). World Bank Open Data. https://data.worldbank.org/indicator/NE.TRD.GNFS.ZS (accessed January 2020).

World Bank. 2020. Trading for Development in the Age of Global Value Chains. *World Development Report.* Washington, DC: World Bank.

C. Yan and E. Ames. 1965. Economic Interrelatedness. *Review of Economic Studies.* 32 (4). pp. 299–310.

www.ingramcontent.com/pod-product-compliance
Lightning Source LLC
Chambersburg PA
CBHW050041220326
41599CB00045B/7242